BEYOND TRADEOFFS

Market Reforms and Equitable Growth in Latin America

Nancy Birdsall, Carol Graham, and Richard H. Sabot

Editors

Inter-American Development Bank
Brookings Institution Press

1998

BMH 1849-7/1

To order this book, contact:
Brookings Institution Press
1775 Massachusetts Avenue N.W.
Washington, D.C. 20036
Tel: 1-800-275-1447 / (202) 797-6258
Fax: (202) 797-6004

**Cataloging-in-Publication data provided by the
Inter-American Development Bank
Felipe Herrera Library**

Beyond tradeoffs : market reforms and equitable growth in Latin America
Nancy Birdsall, Carol Graham and Richard Sabot, editors.
p. cm.
Includes bibliographical references.
ISBN: 0815709218

1. Latin America—Economic policy. 2. Economic development. 3. Income distribution—
Latin America. 4. Equality—Latin America. I. Birdsall, Nancy. II. Graham, Carol, 1962-
III. Sabot, R.H. IV. Inter-American Development Bank. V. The Brookings Institution.
VI. Conference Inequality-Reducing Growth in Latin America (1997 : Washington, DC)
338.98 B39—dc20   98-072692

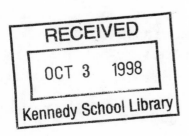

Table of Contents

Acknowledgements

The editors of this volume wish to thank Karla Hoff, Hernando de Soto, and Richard Webb for their valuable contributions at the 1997 conference. Marcela Etcheverry, Beth Lundquist, Kris McDevitt, and Soledad Rothschild provided invaluable logistical support for the conference and the project, and Julie Clugage and Leslie O'Connell gave excellent research assistance. The editors also would like to acknowledge the support for this project from the John D. and Catherine T. MacArthur Foundation.

Foreword

Latin American income distribution is among the most unequal in the world. Both the poor and the wealthy have paid a price for this inequality, which is in part responsible for the region's low growth rates. The essays in this book propose new ways of reducing inequality, not by growth-inhibiting transfers and regulations, but by enhancing efficiency—eliminating consumption subsidies for the wealthy, increasing the productivity of the poor, and shifting to a more labor-and skill-demanding growth path.

In *Beyond Tradeoffs*, a score of Latin American experts demonstrate how market-friendly measures in key policy areas can simultaneously promote greater equity and greater efficiency. By identifying win-win strategies, the authors challenge the conventional wisdom that there is always a tradeoff between these two objectives. Extensive macroeconomic reforms in the region have provided opportunities to implement such strategies across many sectors. At the 1998 Santiago Summit, the heads of state of the Americas endorsed a second round of reforms—to strengthen education, financial, and judicial institutions, for example. This volume shows how these and other second round reforms can address the urgent issue of inequality without undermining efficient growth.

The chapters draw on discussions at a conference sponsored by the IDB and the MacArthur Foundation, titled "Inequality-Reducing Growth in Latin America," held in Washington, D.C. in January 1997. Valuable contributions and comments came from many participants, including government officials from Latin American countries and staff of the Brookings Institution, the Inter-American Development Bank, and the World Bank.

Michael Armacost
President
The Brookings Institution

Enrique V. Iglesias
President
Inter-American Development Bank

CHAPTER ONE

Virtuous Circles
in Latin America's Second
Stage of Reforms

Nancy Birdsall, Carol Graham, and Richard H. Sabot

Latin America stands out as a region that has made remarkable progress in implementing macroeconomic and structural reforms while under democratic auspices. Fiscal and monetary discipline have reduced annual inflation rates to single digits in most countries. Once largely state-run economies have been transformed; the region accounted for over half the total worldwide value of divestitures in 1988–93, far outpacing Asia and Eastern Europe. Markets have opened to global competition; tariff rates in the region declined from an average of over 50 percent in 1985, to about 10 percent in 1996. New institutions have been created: for example, Latin America is unique in the number of countries that have implemented sweeping social security reforms, spurred by Chile's successful adoption of a fully funded, contribution-based system.

Yet economic growth rates, though positive once again in the 1990s, remain modest at about 4 percent a year—compared to the 8 percent annual growth enjoyed by the Asian tigers and their East Asian neighbors for more than two decades. Latin America's low- and middle-income workers have shared only to a limited extent in the benefits of growth. Unemployment rates have been rising inexorably throughout the reform years of the 1990s. In responses to surveys, the citizens of Latin America see their countries as failing to address problems of poverty, joblessness, and injustice. There are increasing political pressures to ensure that growth in the region is inclusive, and increasing fears about a political backlash against reform.[1]

In reality, Latin American income distribution is among the most unequal in the world.[2] Both the poor and the wealthy have paid a price for this inequality, which has contributed to the region's low growth rates. By way of contrast, in East Asia, low inequality fostered growth over more than two decades—by stimulating the savings and investment of the poor, and by minimizing pressures for the kinds of populist policies that contributed to high inflation in Latin America.[3] (In recent years, East Asia experienced a growing concentration of wealth and of economic privileges. This, coupled with lack of transparency and inadequate regulation—so-called "crony capitalism"—may have triggered the 1997–98 financial crisis.)

Latin America has a long history of income redistribution through populist transfer programs and policies that have proven both economically and politically unsustainable.[4] The essays in this book take a new approach to the distribution issue. The challenge is to find new ways of reducing inequality, not by growth-inhibiting transfers and regulations, but by enhancing efficiency—by eliminating consumption subsidies for the rich, increasing the productivity of the poor, and shifting to a more labor and skill-demanding growth path. An emphasis on these efficiency measures would ensure that the poor contribute to growth, making growth more sustained and rapid, and obviously more equitable.

Many of these measures can do much to reduce absolute poverty, and that should be paramount among the concerns of reformers. Reducing *inequality* is a separate objective, but just as important in the Latin American context. Some inequality is necessary for markets to function, and encourages productivity and innovation. Yet high levels of inequality, such as those that characterize the region, are often destructive and block the productive potential of the poor. High inequality is often accompanied by a concentration of economic and political power, which encourages rent-seeking behavior rather than rewarding productivity. A small number of economic agents may hold the political power to maintain distortions that benefit them, such as monopolies in the provision of public goods and services, or captive regulatory systems. Contrary to the common perception that market-oriented reforms increase inequality, in this volume we demonstrate that they can reduce inequality by eliminating such distortions in a number of economic sectors.

The Washington consensus on macroeconomic reforms has proven to be remarkably successful in Latin America. Most countries in the region are on a much sounder economic footing than they were a decade ago. Reducing inequality has now taken on increasing urgency and importance, and despite many obstacles, there are numerous opportunities for implementing win-win policies. This volume aims at building a "Latin consensus" on a second round of reforms—reforms that would address the inequality issue without undermining efficient growth.

It is one thing to advocate more inclusive growth; the real question is how to achieve it. The essays in this volume explore how market-friendly measures in a number of key policy areas can simultaneously promote greater equity and greater efficiency. The channels of such strategies could work in two directions. In some circumstances, greater efficiency can lead to greater equity, while in others, the achievement of greater equity can increase efficiency.[5]

It has long been the conventional wisdom that there is a tradeoff between reducing inequality and stimulating economic growth. By identifying win-win strategies, the authors challenge the conventional wisdom. Yet they also identify circumstances in which a tradeoff must be confronted and difficult choices made. What runs through all the chapters is a sense that the need to reduce inequality has taken on increasing urgency and importance, and that, despite many obstacles, there are numerous opportunities for implementing win-win policies.

Vicious Circles: Inequality, Market Failures, and Government Failures[6]

In describing the kinds and causes of inequality in Latin America, John Sheahan and Enrique Iglesias make a distinction between constructive and destructive kinds of inequality (Chapter 2). The first rewards productivity and innovation. The second blocks the productive potential of the poor. A great deal of evidence suggests that high inequality and low growth in Latin America reflect and reinforce the lack of productive opportunities for the poor, the second kind of inequality.[7]

One kind of vicious circle is created by the reality of persistent income and asset inequality. With low income and few assets, in economies where opportunities are limited to those with privileged access, the poor have neither the capacity nor the incentive to make human capital investments.[8] This lack of capacity stems partly from sheer inadequacy of income and assets. It is further reinforced by negative incentives and low expectations. Without the critical asset of human capital (*per se* a productive asset), the poor remain impoverished, and as their productive potential is squandered, overall economic growth suffers. Thus with the elimination of fiscal problems and trade barriers, a newly visible constraint on growth in Latin America emerges: unequal distribution of income and assets.[9]

For a variety of reasons, initial inequality of income and assets was perpetuated in Latin America. The first of these was the distribution of political power. Political systems, designed by elite, colonial minorities were able to maintain social and political control of government, and thus of land, mining, and other natural resources. The result was a poor majority with unequal access to social and political rights and to economic opportunities.

Income inequality was also perpetuated by factor endowments and by the concentration of ownership of assets. The rapid growth of the population and labor force in the first half of the twentieth century in the region was not met with comparable growth of opportunities for education. This made unskilled labor much more abundant relative to land, capital, and skilled labor.

The absence of opportunities for productive employment outside agriculture was further complicated by highly concentrated ownership of land. In the postwar period, the growth of employment opportunities in the region was constrained by industrialization strategies based on import substitution. Incentives structures worked against labor-intensive production and exports, and repeated macroeconomic downturns resulted from both bad luck and poor economic policies.

Social policies in many countries exacerbated these tendencies towards inequality. In Latin America, partly due to unequal political representation, social policies disproportionately favored tertiary education and higher-level health services, benefiting privileged urban groups at the expense of the poor. By contrast, in the fast-growing economies of East Asia, public investments were directed toward achieving broad access to basic education and health care.

Path dependence also contributed to Latin America's dramatically high inequality. Nowhere is this more obvious than in tracing the contribution of natural resource endowments to the nature and pace of growth and the degree of inequality. It is ironic, but the record shows that in Latin America and elsewhere, countries well-endowed with natural resources do not have better growth performance than do resource-poor ones. Indeed, in many cases they perform less well.

Not surprisingly, the negative effect of natural resource intensity on growth is positively correlated with land inequality.[10] Countries rich in natural resources tend to have unequal distributions of land. They tend to rely on resource-intensive exports rather than on labor-intensive products, and they tend to have low investments in human capital. The availability of easily exploited natural resource wealth also tends to encourage rent-seeking in the public sector, as the experiences of such oil-rich countries as Venezuela and Nigeria demonstrate. An historical reliance on natural resource exploitation often results in nonencompassing elites, who are far less likely to invest in the human capital of the poor. The poor in these very unequal societies face substantial disincentives to making those investments themselves.

Both market failures and government failures perpetuate the negative effects of inequality on investment in human capital and, more generally, on growth. Because of imperfect capital markets, access to capital depends on collateralizable wealth. Thus an individual's initial assets may be an important determinant of his or her ability to finance high-return investments. This poses a particular problem for human capital investments, because future earnings cannot be used as collateral. Insofar as initial assets determine productive potential, high initial inequality results in both high subsequent inequality and slower growth. In a cross-country analysis, Birdsall and Londoño find that the greater the initial inequality in land and education, the lower are growth rates across countries.[11]

Financial market failures, meanwhile, usually have regressive, vicious circle effects. While businesses in the region use banks primarily for payment transactions, banks are the primary vehicle that low- and middle-income consumers have to accumulate assets. When capital markets are repressed, as they have been in the region, controls on interest rates result in negative real rates of interest. And while large businesses and wealthy consumers can usually transfer assets abroad, small consumers and businesses either absorb the costs or exit the banking system. Both efficiency and equity are negatively affected.

A failure that occurs in *insurance markets* results in another vicious circle. In the absence of adequate mechanisms to insure against risk, particularly in Latin America's highly volatile context, workers seek to "legislate" job security through labor laws. Yet rigid labor laws discourage job creation and limit the incomes and opportunities of the poor. And the tendency of the poor to rely on informal insurance arrangements, which emphasize family or community ties and shared incomes and responsibilities, can be a poverty trap. Participation in the risk-sharing arrangements may reduce their aggregate income, savings and investment, but the poor cannot risk removing themselves from the collective help of the group.[12]

A principal/agent problem common in *rural labor markets* also perpetuates high inequality and constrains growth: owners cannot monitor workers free of cost, which gives rise to a divergence of interests between landowners and workers. The problem occurs on large farms that are cultivated by hired workers rather than on small, family-run farms. The high relative costs of monitoring labor leads large farms to adopt more capital-intensive techniques than do small farms, even in economies where labor is abundant. High inequality of landholding in Latin America thus leads to "exclusionary" agricultural growth, limiting the productive potential of the rural poor, whose principal asset is their own labor.

Over time, demographic effects tend to exacerbate the effects on inequality and growth of these market imperfections. For example, women with less education have higher fertility rates, which in turn contributes to lower public expenditures per eligible child. Public expenditure on education absorbs about the same proportion of GDP in Latin America as in East Asia; but in Latin America, where fertility is much higher, those expenditures have been divided among increasing numbers of children. The results are declining quality of education for the poor, diminished access to education, and higher dropout rates, which ultimately have negative effects on growth.[13]

Government failures also contribute to the perpetuation of inequality and to the negative effects that inequality can have on growth. In classic welfare theory, the role of government is to correct for market failure by funding public goods, subsidizing goods that generate externalities, and compensating for market or insurance failures. Yet the behavior of governments in most countries—and the allocation of public goods—reflects the distribution of political power and the organizational capacity of different societal groups.[14] Unequal distribution of political power can lead to a perpetuation or concentration of asset inequality.

The so-called "median voter" approach does not withstand critical scrutiny. The distribution of political voice as well as that of income is skewed towards the wealthy in highly unequal societies. Unequal access to political rights increases the likelihood of "steady states" of inequality that hinder economic growth. Alternatively, high levels of inequality at times encourage voters to opt for redistributive or populist economic policies, which can also hinder growth.[15]

High levels of inequality can also obstruct the development of government structures that enhance productivity.[16] In countries ranging from the United States to East Asia, governments have fostered economic development by promoting education and technology, supporting the financial sector, investing in infrastructure, preventing environmental degradation, and creating and maintaining social safety nets.[17] Yet high levels of inequality tend to result in misallocation of public investments and to ineffective public services, as the benefits of key services are captured by "nonencompassing elites" (Chapter 7). In the agricultural sector, for example, a small number of large-scale producers are often able to form effective political coalitions that allow them to "capture" government agricultural subsidies. These subsidies make it more difficult for small farmers to remain competitive. Likewise in the education sector, the elite, who benefit the most from public expenditures on university education, influence decisions about how education expenditures are allocated and skew expenditures toward tertiary education.

Government monopolies that provide universally subsidized public services, such as water, become targets for rent-seekers or influence-peddlers, as they are often free from the discipline of competition and have no clear standards or performance-based incentive systems (Chapter 10). Because these enterprises are loss-making, they find it impossible to keep up with demand. Supply is rationed and it is the politically influential (and wealthier) groups who maintain access to services and subsidies. The poor have to rely on informal services, such as buying water from trucks, for which they pay above-market costs. Introducing competition (and regulation) thus can have the unexpected outcome of providing the poor with both more accessible and better-priced services. Of course, eliminating subsidies that benefit the wealthier groups is likely to pose a political challenge. This highlights the importance of political as well as economic factors in breaking out of vicious circles that perpetuate inequality.

Virtuous Circles: Efficiency and Equity-Enhancing Reforms

Yet vicious circles can be converted into virtuous circles, and Latin America appears to be at a watershed. A common assumption is that macroeconomic reforms have exacerbated inequality in the region. In some countries that implemented structural reforms, inequality did worsen in the 1980s, but that was due primarily to a decline of investments in physical and human capital associated with the debt crisis, and with the deflationary policies necessary to curb high levels of inflation. The structural reforms themselves, along with the reduction of inflation, *offset* trends towards greater inequality by stimulating income recovery, productivity, and capital investment.[18] And the implementation of macroeconomic reforms has set the stage for a new round of reforms, which, if effective, could break the vicious circles that perpetuate inequality, and perhaps even convert them into virtuous ones.

These reforms address the root causes of inequality. They promise to enhance the productive potential of the poor, rather than merely mitigate the effects of poverty. In the past, interventions designed to help the poor through redistributive transfers often had perverse outcomes, such as the capture of subsidies by the nonpoor. The new reforms emphasize productivity-enhancing measures that are sustainable in fiscal terms. The new reforms avoid the kinds of disincentives at the microlevel that create dependence or disrupt the autonomous efforts and coping strategies of the poor.[19] The emphasis is rather on introducing incentives that encourage the poor to make investments in human capital and to contribute to, as well as benefit from, the growth process.

We are optimistic about the potential for simultaneously increasing equity and efficiency in Latin America for several reasons. First, the successful implementation of macroeconomic reforms has generated powerful incentives for policymakers to sustain market-oriented policies, providing an historic opportunity for "win-win" strategies. Maintaining an open economy and remaining attractive to foreign investment require consistent and prudent fiscal and monetary policies.

And, in addition to increasing efficiency, many of the macroeconomic reforms have already benefited the poor. The reforms reversed a trend towards greater inequality by halting inflation and by rewarding increases in investment and productivity.[20] The economic volatility and high or hyper levels of inflation that preceded macroeconomic reforms imposed high costs on all social groups, but particularly on the poor. During the debt crisis of the 1980s, for example, the wealthy were able to protect their assets by transferring resources abroad, while the costs of servicing the debt fell disproportionately on those who could not seek foreign havens for their assets. And a volatile economy and distorted policy framework make it more difficult for governments to identify vulnerable groups and implement measures to protect them from negative shocks.[21]

The 1980s have been called a lost decade. We disagree. We see the 1980s as a decade of reckoning. The discussion has changed and policies are in flux, due to the introduction of far-reaching economic reforms. Indeed, as a result of the debt and inflation crises in the 1980s, Latin America is much more open to systemic reforms and the debate about inequality has changed. In the 1970s, when inequality was introduced into the policy discussion, there was skepticism among economic elites. Those sectors that were receptive were suspicious of markets and advocated income transfers. Today, both sides recognize the need to reduce inequality and for market-friendly reforms.[22]

Second, the fiscal logic of macroeconomic reform makes second round reforms more compelling. The need to maintain fiscal balance, for example, gives an additional impetus to privatizing inefficient public sector monopolies and reforming social security systems. At the same time, investment and growth spur reform in the labor market, as the private sector demands a flexible and skilled labor force to remain competitive. Financial and education sector reforms are equally critical to sustaining the first round of reforms and the economic growth they have generated. And the second round of reforms has already gained momentum. Social security reforms, and now in a few countries, labor and social sector reforms are under way.

Third, there are unprecedented political opportunities for implementing institutional reforms. The combination of severe economic crises and major fiscal adjustments in Latin America has reduced the capacity of states to deliver. There is far less reliance upon the state, even for the provision of education and protection from crime. Now is the time to implement reforms, as institutional malfunction makes the public more receptive to change. For example, rapid reforms in some of the region's financially troubled social security systems stand in sharp contrast to prolonged debates about reform in OECD countries, where problems with social security are unlikely to be critical and evident to the public for some time.

At the same time, it is widely recognized that effective institutions are important in achieving sustainable and broadly shared economic growth, and the need to rebuild a new, effective state means building institutional capacity in the region. And, as Birdsall and Londoño emphasize, the effectiveness and sustainability of public services such as health, education, and social security can be enhanced by increasing the voice of new actors, particularly the poor—which democracy and political decentralization are currently encouraging in the region. The region is poised to shift from an era of institutional destruction or erosion to one of institutional construction.

A fourth and major reason for optimism is that virtually all of the region's countries, with the exception of Cuba, have adopted democratic governance. While institutions such as judiciaries and legislatures are sounder in some countries than in others, regular elections are held and progress has been made in protecting civil liberties. At the local political level, far-reaching changes have occurred, and are being reinforced by fiscal decentralization. A decade ago, this would have been difficult to imagine. Now Latin America is charting new territory as a region in which almost all countries are implementing extensive economic reform under democratic auspices.

The spread of democracy has positive implications for economic reform; at the same time, the implementation of reforms can also contribute to democracy.[23] The poor are in the majority in the region, and they vote. Evidence to date suggests that the poor reward reforming governments that deliver positive growth results. They also reward public expenditure shifts in their direction during reform. Pressure on governments to make human capital investments that benefit the poor will increase. At the same time, a principal objective of macroeconomic reform is to eliminate distortions and introduce more efficient public institutions and more predictable and enforceable rules of the economic game. This reduces opportunities for rent-seeking, which the poor are least able to take advantage of. The reduction of rent-seeking has positive effects for governance in general, as well as for economic performance.[24]

A fifth reason for optimism is that the region's reform experience is part of a global process, and may have positive demonstration effects for other countries and regions. While a common criticism of globalization is that it exacerbates inequality, recent experience in Latin America suggests that the combined effects of democratization and economic reforms that promote openness may level the playing field for the poor. And by encouraging more open and competitive economies, globalization also creates new incentives for elites to invest in the productivity of the labor force, and therefore the education and skills of the poor.

This book's objective is to identify the areas where there are no tradeoffs between equity and growth. Nevertheless, policymakers must face difficult choices. Social security reforms, for example, may increase efficiency, but they may also confront reformers with a choice between pensions for the lowest income workers or better pensions for those with average incomes. Reforms that stimulate the introduction of export crops may favor small-scale farmers in some countries, but in others result in a greater concentration of landholding.

There will also be intertemporal tradeoffs. Even where efficiency and equity are compatible in the long run, some groups may lose, especially in the short term. Middle- and upper-income households who lose access to subsidized commodities may oppose reforms, requiring governments to expend political capital to build sufficient consensus in favor of proceeding. At times, to make reforms politically viable, compensation may have to be offered to groups who are far less needy than the poor.[25] This makes intertemporal political tradeoffs far more difficult.

Ultimately, "the devil is in the details." Similar reforms can have different outcomes, depending on the details of their implementation, and on the political economy of the country. Peru's social security reform, for example, though modeled on Chile's, was implemented with one key difference: no minimum pension (Chapter 9). One could argue that it is inequitable to use public resources to subsidize low-income pensioners where the majority of workers—and the poorest ones—remain outside the social security system, as in Peru. Yet the effect was to deter lower-income workers from switching from the failing public scheme to the new private scheme, which is likely to pay much better pensions. In Argentina, meanwhile, a reform similar to Chile's was implemented, but the system is designed to provide better pensions for middle-income workers, rather than a more effective safety-net pension for workers at the lower end of the scale.

While these different outcomes result from subtle differences in the design of reforms, they primarily reflect political economy dynamics. The design of second round reforms is affected by how political power is distributed. Unlike macroeconomic reforms, which to a large extent have standard recipes that cannot be easily altered by particular interest groups, second stage reforms affect the allocation of critical public goods and services to which one societal group or another may have privileged access. This is typical in the social services, where certain groups—such as university students and the users of urban hospitals—often claim a disproportionate share of public resources at the expense of more basic service provision for the poor (Chapter 5).

Changing these political economy dynamics is far from easy. In most democratic settings, it is difficult to sustain political support for narrowly targeted social welfare expenditures.[26] Yet the new wave of demand-based social programs in the region, which usually benefit the poor in a manner that relies on their participation and contribution, has heightened the expectations and enhanced the organizational potential of previously marginalized groups. This may alter the political debate over public expenditures, and has at least eroded the influence of clientelist political parties over such expenditures in many countries.[27]

In addition, there is recent experience with strategies that alter the political dynamics of that debate in favor of less privileged groups. Such strategies have been effective in many contexts, even some in which income and political power are highly concentrated. Efforts to increase the voice and choice of users of public services play a positive role in creating new stakeholders in the process of reform (Chapter 12). Once new actors perceive that they have a stake in reforms, the process often takes on its own political momentum. And in contrast to targeted policies, there are potential benefits for fairly broad sectors of society from many of these win-win reforms. Improving the performance of public utilities distributors or of the banking system, for example, has benefits for middle-income consumers as well as for lower-income groups.

Finally, in discussing inequality, a distinction should be made between income and asset distribution. It is politically more feasible to ensure better distribution of a flow of new assets, such as education, than to redistribute existing assets. Similarly, it is easier to affect the incidence of taxes and public expenditures—thus redistributing real income—than to redistribute assets. Yet changes in the distribution of assets such as land and human capital are essential to a sustainable improvement in the distribution of income.[28] Put another way, the distribution of economic opportunity is an essential part of the equation. And reforms of education, of labor markets, of regulatory agencies and the judiciary can substantially improve the economic opportunities available to the poor.

Contents of the Volume

This volume explores a broad range of topics. Some authors cover issues that span economic sectors, such as the political economy of institutional reform, macroeconomic policy, the implications of volatility for inequality, and labor market policy.

Others discuss areas that are critical to achieving inequality-reducing growth: social policies, agriculture, and the financial sector. To the extent possible, the authors also consider how policies might differ according to particular country contexts.

In the second chapter, **John Sheahan and Enrique Iglesias** discuss Latin America's development experience in a comparative context, showing how traits particular to the region resulted in very unequal distributions of income and opportunity. They distinguish between constructive and destructive inequality: the former rewards productivity and innovation, and the latter blocks the productive potential of the poor.

Sheahan and Iglesias emphasize the interactions of multiple channels of causation. These include persistent inequalities of access to education; concentrated ownership of land and mines; the failure to participate in the kind of decentralized innovation and structural change that broadened opportunities in northern countries in the course of the nineteenth and early twentieth centuries. This left the region unable to compete in new industries and dependent on primary exports that reinforced inequality. Through most of the twentieth century, Latin America was unable to generate new openings for productive employment at rates sufficient to keep up with rapid growth of the population and labor force, with the result that market forces have worked against an increase in real wages in most countries. All of these factors are subject to change; some of them have been changing in favorable ways in recent decades. Still, continuing low quality of mass education, high concentrations of asset ownership, and great resistance to progressive taxation, remain among the major factors that make it difficult to do better. Inequality has self-sustaining characteristics all over the world, perhaps more tenaciously so in Latin America than in most other areas, but economic and social policy can still have a positive impact. Differences among countries, some of which have done relatively well, help illuminate possibilities for stimulating inequality-reducing growth throughout the region.

In examining the impact of structural reforms on equity, **Eduardo Lora and Juan Luis Londoño** provide an assessment of the magnitude and significance of the policy changes in the region in the past decade. They note that despite remarkable progress with reforms, results have been disappointing. Growth has recovered, but is far short of the rates of over 7 percent that have been typical in Southeast Asia. Income distribution remains highly unequal, and the absolute number of people in poverty has only declined slightly since reaching a peak of approximately 150 million people in 1990.[29] A number of factors have limited the potential of structural reforms: a volatile macroeconomic environment, poor performance of government institutions, and an unequal distribution of productive assets—in particular ownership of natural resources and access to education. Still, the structural reforms have halted the 1980s decline in distribution by spurring economic growth and productivity. And there are a number of microeconomic channels, described briefly in the chapter and in detail in the rest of the volume, through which the reforms can enhance equity.

Lora and Londoño place a particular focus on trade reform, an area where there is a great deal of debate about the distributional effects. They report the surprising statistical result that the adoption of trade reforms in Latin America is positively associated with faster growth of the real incomes of the poorest 60 percent of the population, and with a decline of the real revenues of the wealthiest 20 percent.[30] Numerous studies, both in and outside Latin America, find that trade liberalization increases the returns to skilled labor relative to unskilled labor.[31] However, the effect on wage inequality is not the whole story. Income distribution is also affected by changes in relative prices that may benefit the poor disproportionately. And the opening of markets reduces opportunities for rent-seeking and other vehicles for capitalizing on distortions that tend to benefit the rich. The authors note the difficulties of measuring the effects of all these trends, and categorically reject a simple relationship between liberalization and negative distributive trends.

Michael Gavin and Ricardo Hausmann analyze how volatility has affected inequality of income distribution in the region. They note that volatility is bad for both growth and distribution. Latin America has traditionally lacked the language and the institutions to plan adequately for economic cycles. Thus in contrast to most OECD countries, in Latin America adjustments are always pro-cyclical, with strong fiscal adjustments at times of recession, and expenditure booms coinciding with economic booms. The poor, meanwhile, have the least protective mechanisms at times of volatility, such as the ability to transfer assets abroad. Recessions coupled with fiscal adjustments tend to exacerbate inequality, and this is coupled with a certain element of hysteresis: equity losses during recessions are not fully recovered during periods of growth. In order to reduce volatility, the region needs to develop institutions that can accommodate booms and busts—such as Chile's copper stabilization facility. Another important part of this equation is international investor confidence: fiscal adjustments during downturns are often intended to restore investor confidence that governments are determined to keep fiscal deficits low. Multilateral institutions have an important role to play here, as they can help restore investor confidence, thereby avoiding excessive recessionary measures, whose costs tend to be worst for the poor.[32]

Nancy Birdsall and Juan Luis Londoño explore the role of human capital investments in determining growth and distribution outcomes. New economic growth models have emphasized human capital as key to growth, but they do not address some of Latin America's chronic problems. Those problems include low *demand* for education among the poor (who in Latin America usually have access only to low-quality schools); inadequate *distribution* of education between rich and poor; and the political obstacles to adequate *delivery* of education, especially to the impoverished, in unequal societies. The authors show that, in a vicious circle, Latin America's unsatisfactory record of human capital accumulation and unequal distribution of human capital both reflect and reinforce the region's low economic growth rates and its high levels of income and asset inequality.

Birdsall and Londoño's analysis indicates that countries with greater asset inequality (in land and education) have consistently shown lower growth and higher wage inequality. They conclude that education and other human capital programs in the region must emphasize equity if they are to be efficient. The authors provide examples of how a more competitive and school-based model of education delivery, with public financing and coordination, is now beginning to reach the poor in Latin America, and increasing both equity and efficiency in education.

Michael Carter and Jonathan Coles explore the roots of inequities in Latin American agriculture, a sector that is critical to the fate of the poor in most countries. One of the most easily perceptible structural differences between Latin America and East Asia is the contrast in the degree of inequality in the distribution of land. Two dimensions must be addressed to achieve broad-based agrarian growth in Latin America: securing the participation of existing small-scale producers in growing technologies and markets, and enhancing the direct access of landless and land-poor households to land.

Despite the latent competitive advantage of small-scale producers, they are subject to countervailing disadvantages in accessing capital and other markets in which the fixed costs of information are important. These disadvantages are magnified by new technologies and markets that put a premium on capital access and risk-bearing capacity. And an initially inegalitarian distribution of land—as exists in Latin America—is likely, via endogenous economic and political mechanisms, to generate prices, policies, and institutions that dampen small farm competitiveness.

The reforms that Carter and Coles propose center first on getting the prices and institutions "right": eliminating price distortions and securing the property rights of small farmers. Yet they caution against assuming that agrarian growth free of capital subsidies and policy distortions will be broadly based. Initial asset

inequality in agrarian structures creates pressures that tend to reproduce themselves, both in terms of the competitive advantage of large farms, as well as in
political economy terms: access to information and political influence, for example.
"New-style" market-assisted market land reform policies, which concentrate on
reducing transaction costs, may not be a substitute for "old-style" land redistribution strategies. In some contexts, however, where crop structure and country context give a competitive advantage to small farmers, the former policies can indeed
be very effective. In others, changes of a more structural nature may be necessary
to attain growth with equity, and here there may indeed be real tradeoffs between
the two objectives.

René Cortázar, Nora Lustig, and Richard Sabot examine the critical issue of
labor market reform. First, they compare how labor fared in the fast-growing East
Asian economies versus those in Latin America. Fast-growing, export-led demand
for manufactured goods in East Asia, coupled with government policies that stimulate accumulation of human capital, contributed to efficient labor markets and to
rapid increases in the returns to labor. In Latin America, by contrast, capital-intensive manufacturing growth—and therefore weak labor demand—high fertility rates,
and weak investments in basic education resulted in a large pool of poorly paid
unskilled labor, and a small and segmented market for skilled labor.

In East Asia, more equitable income distribution, adequate social protection
(primarily due to high levels of growth and macroeconomic stability), and an "encompassing" attitude on the part of elites led to relatively harmonious relations
between workers and employers. In Latin America, by contrast, the absence of
macrostability, high levels of inequality, inadequate social insurance mechanisms,
and a "nonencompassing" attitude on the part of elites led to a much more confrontational and short-term profit-maximizing strategy on the part of labor. Labor
codes, for example, were extremely rigid and emphasized job protection, as workers sought to ensure themselves against an uncertain future. Payroll taxes remain
very high in the region, which also discourages employment. Finally, unions often
have influence far beyond the enterprise level, which leads to wage and employment agreements that yield them high rents.

The obstacles to labor market reform in Latin America include mutual mistrust between workers and employers. This mistrust leads to short-term, confrontational bargaining behavior; legitimate fear of job loss; and hysteresis: "insiders"
may believe their interests in protecting their rents exceed the perceived gains from
reform. Still, some progress has been made in making labor regimes more flexible
in the region, and many countries have implemented partial if not complete re-

forms. Unions are neither as powerful nor as confrontational as they once were, due in part to prolonged economic crisis. While obstacles exist, progress in reforming labor markets is certainly critical, and to some extent inevitable, with large potential gains in efficiency and equity.

In analyzing financial sector reform, **Liliana Rojas-Suárez and Steven Weisbrod** explore the equity effects of a reform usually evaluated in terms of efficiency. They examine the extent to which financial sector reforms in the region have improved the availability of banking services. Their focus extends to large corporate consumers, small and medium businesses, and wealthy and low- and middle-income consumers. While businesses primarily use banks for transactions, banks are an important vehicle for accumulating financial assets for low- and middle-income consumers. Small businesses and small consumers are much more dependent on the local banking system than are larger, wealthier actors, who can usually transfer assets abroad. In prereform, repressed systems, controls on interest rates and credit resulted in negative real rates of interest, at a high cost to less wealthy consumers.

Liberalization of financial markets encourages consumers and large businesses to return to the banking system, by providing some assurance that the real value of bank deposits will not be eroded, although adequate public safeguards are also necessary. The demand of small and medium businesses for the kinds of transactions that banks can provide is relatively inelastic, regardless of the rate of return. Thus they stand to benefit a great deal from reform of the system. Middle-income consumers who can exit during crises still face losses, as the real value of their deposits usually erodes before they exit, and cash holdings are eroded by inflation.

Since the liberalization of financial systems in the early 1990s in much of the region, many consumers have returned to the banking system. In addition, there is some evidence that the availability of credit to small and medium businesses has increased with reform. In contrast, the previously state-owned dominated systems tended to concentrate loans in the hands of large enterprises. Still, further reforms remain necessary to establish greater confidence in—and broader access to—financial systems in the region. These include better accounting methods and supervision, and increased competition and diversity of ownership. Even then, these reforms would still not resolve the problem of access for the poorest groups to credit, which requires more proactive policies ranging from microcredit schemes to reform of property rights systems.[33]

Estelle James, in the chapter on pension reform, explores the efficiency and equity implications of traditional pay-as-you-go defined-benefit (PAYG DB) and reformed social security systems that are funded by defined contributions. While these reforms produce clear efficiency gains, their impact on equity is more ambiguous. PAYG DB schemes, contrary to popular misconception, often have negative equity effects, and this has particularly been the case in Latin America. First of all, poor people live shorter lives and therefore receive benefits for fewer years than do rich people. In addition, people often get credit for their university years in PAYG schemes, which tends to benefit wealthier groups, as does the indexation of pensions to wages in the final years. Powerful interest groups and unions often manage to claim special benefits for their members. Typically only wages are taxed for social security, with a ceiling on taxable earnings, making the financing system regressive. And, James notes, PAYG schemes are, in effect, an intergenerational contract that is constructed by the generations who establish the system and benefit most from it.

Funded defined-contribution systems correct many of the above inequities, by connecting lifetime benefits more closely to lifetime contributions. Yet they raise new equity issues and tradeoffs. In some cases, a flat fee—the same amount for high- and low-income workers—is charged for managing the funds, which obviously produces a lower net return for low earners who have smaller funds. Secondly, these systems typically introduce choice among pension fund managers, and lower income workers are likely to make less educated choices. Empirical evidence suggests that low earners are more risk-averse and tend to opt for the lowest risk investments, which yield the lowest return. Moreover, in a system of choice, the variance in returns is likely to increase, thereby increasing inequality even if it also increases the average return.

Most reformed systems have introduced a redistributive public pillar to accompany the private-funded pillar and to offset these inequities—but the degree and kind of redistribution varies among the Latin countries. In Chile, the public pillar takes the form of a minimum pension guarantee, which provides a redistribution to the poorest workers in the system, while the middle-income workers who contribute for a long time do not benefit at all. In Argentina, which pays a flat benefit, middle-class workers who contribute for a long time fare well, while even the poorest workers who participate for less than 30 years get nothing. Peru offers no public pillar, which has discouraged lower-income workers from leaving the old PAYG scheme. James concludes that the details of reform design are critical. Designing social security reforms to achieve equity as well as efficiency objectives can be difficult because the structure of the reform is itself endogenous, tending to reflect the underlying political economy dynamics, which ultimately determine the equity outcomes.

Raquel Alfaro, Ralph Bradburd, and John Briscoe examine the issue of re-forming public monopolies, with a case study of the water sector. For years Latin American governments considered government provision of water and sanitation services as a necessity, with consumption tariffs set at the lowest level possible. But because utilities did not have a commercial orientation, they typically were highly inefficient and had high operating costs. Subsidies were universal, increasing the gap between costs and revenues, and decreasing the quality of services. Public companies could not cope with urban growth or with the actual costs of provision, and increasingly relied on government transfers. Lack of separation between the regulating and regulated entities contributed to poor performance. The outcome was one where wealthier groups consumed unlimited quantities of subsidized services, while the poor's primary problem was access, resulting in their having to pay well above market costs to purchase services informally, such as water from trucks.

The adoption of "market-friendly" approaches to the delivery of public utilities introduced the concepts of subsidies targeted towards the poor, and decentralization and co-production of services. This introduced several options ranging from commercially oriented public providers, to subcontracts, to full privatization. The efficiency benefits from shifting to new providers are so great that in many cases it has been possible to have water tariffs cover full costs with only minimal rises, and even reductions, in rates. The introduction of competition, meanwhile, even where imperfect, has tended to increase access. And competition itself introduces a form of self-regulation into the process. An issue that remains outstanding, however, is how to introduce efficient regulation in an institutional framework that is rife with inefficiencies, and with mutual suspicions between business entities and government regulatory bodies. And while the shift from public provision may entail a reduction in employment in the previously overstaffed utility, experience shows that there are large gains in employment as a result of the higher levels of investment that private sector participation brings.

Some underlying conditions are necessary for a market-friendly approach, such as macroeconomic stability and developed financial markets. And the public companies that remain involved may face some of the same problems that they did prior to reforms, such as contentious relations with powerful public sector unions. Finally, as users of services shift from being consumers to being clients, low-income groups will need assistance in overcoming information constraints.

Joseph Stiglitz discusses the implications of efficiency and equity tradeoffs in the realm of public finance. His discussion is based on the recent experience of the United States, but has many relevant lessons for Latin America: The region's political economy has become more similar to that of the United States since its adoption of democracy and market reforms. Stiglitz identifies public investments in education as an area where the United States can implement win-win policies. The returns to investments in education in the U.S. labor market have been increasing. Yet as the mean incomes of families at the bottom quintile of the distribution has decreased in real terms in the last 20 years, and the cost of going to college has increased, the children of low-income families have not increased their college enrollments in response to higher returns to investments in education, in contrast to wealthier groups, and there is a growing disparity. Increasing the availability of loans and tax credits for low-income families that invest in higher education would reach both the efficiency and equity objectives of fiscal policy. A related and equally important investment is in preschool education for children in poverty.

Stiglitz identifies trade policy as another area where equity and efficiency gains can be made, but where tradeoffs exist. Trade has been one of the real engines of growth for the U.S. economy in recent years. But the net gain has come with concerns about the negative distribution effects for the bottom end of the distribution—precisely where people have seen their real incomes fall. While these drops are not due solely to trade—indeed factors such as technology have played a more dominant role—the overall trends have led to staunch opposition to free trade by a number of strong, well-organized groups. Stiglitz argues that the government has a direct role to play in investing in assisting individuals who are adversely affected by trade in the transition, through training or loans. These investments in a transition safety net can have efficiency as well as equity returns, as they reduce the time individuals spend being unproductive between jobs. Such investments are also critical to building stronger political constituencies for trade reform. Stiglitz concludes by noting that while there are many opportunities for improving equity and efficiency, most societies still face difficult tradeoffs in the area of public finance, such as between expenditures on entitlements for the elderly versus on growth-enhancing investments such as education or in science and technology. Because most governments make decisions about such investments in a piecemeal manner, the full implications of these tradeoffs are rarely evident in public debates.

In the final chapter, **Carol Graham and Moisés Naím** highlight the regionwide recognition of the need for stronger institutions in order to make growth sustainable and more broadly shared. Yet they note that while the diagnosis is correct, there is an absence of prescriptions for policymakers to follow. They attempt to unbundle the concept of institutions by providing a taxonomy of four kinds: rule-making institutions, rule enforcement institutions, the providers of public services such as road maintenance and water, and the providers of public goods such as defense and education. They then identify ten of the most common types of institutional failure, with a focus on how these failures exacerbate inequality. Judicial systems that suffer from chronic overcongestion, for example, are the least accessible to those without financial means or political influence.

Graham and Naím identify some general political conditions that are necessary, if not sufficient, for institutional reform. These include a coherent macropolicy framework and preferably fast-paced economic reforms; extensive government efforts at communicating and building consensus; and progress in "symbolic" reform areas that lock in prudent macroeconomic management and set the stage for further institutional reform, such as tax reform and the establishment of autonomous central banks. They then identify strategies that have succeeded in overcoming some traditional obstacles to institutional reform by creating new stakeholders in reformed systems. The prospects for successful second stage reforms in Latin America are seen as greatly enhanced by the broader context of extensive macroeconomic change, as well as the region's success with certain kinds of institutional reforms and the creation of new stakeholders.

Another important element for sustainable and equity-enhancing growth in Latin America (which is not covered in detail in this volume) is capital accumulation. Countries must enhance the capacity of the institutions and mechanisms that accumulate capital, in order to allow a wider range of social groups to contribute to this process. As in all of the sectors covered in the study, reforms in this area, implemented in sound macroeconomic policy contexts, have strong potential to increase efficiency and equity at the same time, replacing vicious circles with virtuous ones.

Elements such as institutions, culture, political economy, and even design details of specific policies are critical to this process. The same policies that lead to virtuous circles in some contexts may have less success in other ones. Progress in all the sectors we have identified will be needed to break vicious inequality circles. Yet progress is likely to be uneven among the various countries and sectors. There is no established recipe for implementing this set of reforms, or for determining their appropriate timing and sequence. However, there has been sufficient progress in a number of countries to demonstrate the benefits of most reforms and to provide critical examples for other countries to use. Regionwide, the successful implementation of extensive macroeconomic reforms has altered the political economy dynamic in favor of further reforms, providing additional momentum for progress.

Latin America is unique in terms of the number of countries implementing far-reaching economic reforms under democratic auspices. Based on recent experience and the current policy agenda, we strongly believe that the region is now capable of achieving both continued growth and a more equitable distribution of income. Several decades from now, other regions may look to Latin America for lessons about efficient, equitable, and sustainable growth under democratic auspices and in a globalized economy.

Endnotes

[1] For example, surveys conducted in the region in the mid 1990s found that two-thirds of the population surveyed believe the current distribution of wealth is unfair, while half believes that the situation in its country is bad. While this urgency stems as much from public perceptions as it does from reliable information about income trends, perceptions influence voters as much as actual trends do (Latin Barometer surveys, cited in IDB 1996). See also *The Economist* (1996).

[2] Reasonably systematic comparisons only go back to 1960, and are subject to a variety of doubts regarding the reliability and comparability of data. The data are far from complete, particularly in the area that most concerns us: the mobility of low-income groups. In recent years progress has been made in compiling reliable, time-series household survey data for a number of countries, and there are ongoing efforts among the research community to broaden the sample. The available evidence supports the generalization that inequality in the region is exceptionally high, and has been over time. Yet Argentina, Costa Rica, Cuba and Uruguay have much more equal income distributions than their regional counterparts. In Chapter 2, Sheahan and Iglesias examine this in detail.

[3] The relationship between inequality and growth was recently analyzed by Birdsall and Sabot in two papers (1995). The first provides econometric evidence of a negative relationship between growth and inequality. The second demonstrates theoretically how poor households respond to decreased inequality by saving and investing more, thereby generating "growth from below". Several other authors have found a negative relationship between inequality and growth. See, for example, Alesina and Perotti (1994), Benabou (1996), and Bruno, Ravallion, and Squire (1996).

[4] See Sachs (1990) and Dornbusch and Edwards (1990).

[5] The terms equity and equitable, while they have distinct definitions, are used interchangeably throughout this volume. Equitable is a descriptive term that implies a distribution as fair and equal as possible. Equity relates to social justice, and is both a descriptive and a functional term. At one level it implies an amount of equality deemed "optimal" by particular societies, and varies accordingly. At another level, equity norms and standards allow societies to make decisions in certain realms where market criteria are insufficient, such as the distribution of the tax burden. To determine what the "optimal" or equitable distribution of income would be for Latin America is a theoretical exercise we shall not attempt. However, we recognize that the current distribution is extremely unequal by international standards, and has significant efficiency costs. When the terms are used interchangeably, this reflects a fairly general interpretation, which suggests movement in the direction of greater equality. For a discussion of different societies' tolerance for inequality, see Esping-Andersen (1990). For a discussion of the evolution and role of equity norms and standards, see Young (1994). For a philosophical discussion of socially optimal levels of equity, see Rawls (1971). Amartya Sen has written extensively on several aspects of this theme. See, for example, Sen (1995).

[6] We draw here on ideas presented at the January 1997 conference by Karla Hoff, who provided a written summary of her presentation. For more detail, see Hoff (1996), in which she demonstrates that imperfect information undermines the assumption that market equilibria are always efficient and that distributional and efficiency considerations are separable.

[7] See, for example, Birdsall and Sabot (1995); and Birdsall and Sabot, *Virtuous Circles: Human Capital and Growth with Equity in East Asia* (forthcoming).

[8] While much of the literature describing the effects of human capital investments on growth focuses primarily or solely on the effects of education, we define human capital broadly here, to include investments in education, health, and occupational skills.

[9] For a detailed description of how asset inequality has constrained growth in the region, see Birdsall and Londoño (1997).

[10] See Birdsall and Londoño (1997) and Sachs and Warner (1995).

[11] The impact of inequality in these two productive assets on income growth more than doubles when the sample is restricted to the poor (Birdsall and Londoño 1997).

[12] Women who work in communal kitchens in exchange for their children's receiving free meals, for example, may not seek out better-paying jobs because they do not want to risk losing the benefits for their families.

[13] See Birdsall, Bruns, and Sabot, "Education Policy in Brazil: Playing a Bad Hand Badly," in Birdsall and Sabot (1996).

[14] See Birdsall and James, "Efficiency and Equity in Social Spending: How and Why Governments Misbehave," in Lipton and van der Gaag (1990).

[15] For a discussion of how high inequality can lead to "populist" voting patterns, see Alesina and Perotti (1994). For a view that questions median voter theory, in which the poor have equal political voice, see Benabou (1996).

[16] See Samuel Bowles and Herbert Gintis, cited in Hoff (1996).

[17] See Stiglitz (1997).

[18] For empirical evidence, see Londoño and Székely (1997). The earlier work of Samuel Morley (1994) hints at the beginnings of this trend. Others such as Albert Berry (1996) do not agree about these positive trends.

[19] For a review of such strategies, see Graham (1994).

[20] See Londoño and Székely (1997).

[21] For details, see Graham (1996).

[22] In many countries, reaching "rock bottom" seems to provide broadly shared incentives that forge political consensus in favor of far-reaching policy reform. Michael Bruno and William Easterly show that countries with high levels of inflation (over 40 percent annual) grow faster on average after they stabilize than those countries that just muddle along at medium inflation rates. Crises in the high inflation countries were severe enough to generate strong political consensus in favor of far-reaching re-

forms, including those that lock in prudent economic policies, such as the introduction of independent central banks (Bruno and Easterly 1996). For a different description of the same dynamic, see Bradburd and Schulz (1997). For detail on the role of independent central banks, see Cukierman, Webb, and Neyapti (1992).

[23] Empirical studies show that the introduction of elections in the region since 1980 has actually enhanced economic management (Remmer 1993). For voting and adjustment policies, see Joan M. Nelson, "Poverty, Equity, and the Politics of Adjustment" in Haggard and Kaufmann (1992). For empirical evidence of how voting can sway public expenditures in favor of the poor, see Graham and Kane (1998).

[24] See, for example, Kaufmann (1997).

[25] For a discussion of such compensatory strategies, see Graham (1994).

[26] See, for example, Nelson's chapter in Haggard and Kaufmann (1992); Skocpol (1991); and Pritchett and Gelbard (1996).

[27] See, for example, Graham and Kane (1998).

[28] For empirical evidence on the effects of asset distribution on the economic performance of different income cohorts in Latin America, see Birdsall and Londoño (1997).

[29] Recent surveys indicate that the region's poor population has since declined. While an absolute figure is not yet available, it is clear that the fraction of people in poverty has fallen faster than population growth, and that the absolute number has also fallen, possibly by as much as 4 million people. These estimates are from the IDB Poverty and Inequality Advisory Unit.

[30] See Londoño and Székely (1997).

[31] See, for example, Robbins (1996).

[32] For an excellent account of the extent to which poverty in Latin America is countercyclical (increases with recessions and declines with growth), see Morley (1995).

[33] The establishment of property rights is a critical first step towards providing the poor with the collateral that is usually necessary for access to credit. The critical role of property rights in the economic potential of the poor was emphasized throughout the conference by Hernando de Soto, and has been described by him in *El Otro Sendero* (de Soto 1986).

References

Alesina, Alberto, and Roberto Perotti. 1994. The Political Economy of Growth: A Critical Survey of the Recent Literature. *World Bank Economic Review* 8(3).

Benabou, Roland. 1996. Unequal Societies. NBER Working Paper Series No. 5583, Cambridge, May 1996.

Berry, Albert. 1996. Inequality Trends in Latin America. *Latin American Research Review* 32(2).

Birdsall, Nancy, Barbara Bruns, and Richard Sabot. 1996. Education Policy in Brazil: Playing a Bad Hand Badly, in Birdsall and Sabot, eds., *Opportunity Foregone: Education in Brazil.* Washington, D.C.: Inter-American Development Bank.

Birdsall, N., and Estelle James. 1993. Efficiency and Equity in Social Spending: How and Why Governments Misbehave, in Michael Lipton and Jacques van der Gaag (eds.), *Including the Poor.* New York: Oxford University Press for The World Bank.

Birdsall, N., and Juan Luis Londoño. 1997. Asset Inequality Does Matter: Lessons from Latin America. OCE Working Paper Series 344, IDB, Washington, D.C. (Another version of this paper appeared in *American Economic Review,* March 1997).

Birdsall, N., and R. Sabot. 1995. Inequality and Growth Reconsidered. *World Bank Economic Review* (September).

Birdsall, N., D. Ross, and R. Sabot. 1995. Inequality, Savings, and Growth. Mimeo, Williams College and IDB, November.

Bowles, Samuel, and Herbert Gintis. 1996 cited in Karla Hoff, Market Failures and the Distribution of Wealth: A Perspective from the Economics of Information. *Politics and Society* 24(4).

Bradburd, Ralph, and Eric Schulz. 1977. Why Things Have to Get Worse Before They Can Get Better: Institutions, Interest Groups, Decline and Reform. Williams College, Mimeo, May 1977.

Bruno, Michael, and William Easterly. 1996. Inflation's Children: Tales of Crisis That Beget Reforms. Paper presented to the Annual Meeting of the American Economics Association, January.

Bruno, M., Martin Ravallion, and Lyn Squire. 1996. Equity and Growth in Developing Countries: Old and New Perspectives on the Policy Issues. Policy Research Working Paper 1563, The World Bank, Washington, D.C., January.

Cukierman, Alex, Steven B. Webb, and Benjamin Neyapti. 1992. Measuring the Independence of Central Banks and Its Effects on Policy Outcomes. *World Bank Economic Review* 6(3).

de Soto, Hernando. 1986. *El Otro Sendero*. Lima: Editorial El Barranco.

Dornbusch, Rudiger, and Sebastian Edwards. 1990. Macroeconomic Populism. *Journal of Development Economics* 32(2).

Economist, The. 1996. The Backlash in Latin America: Gestures against Reform. *The Economist*, 30 November 1996.

Esping-Andersen, Gosta. 1990. *Three Worlds of Welfare Capitalism*. Princeton: Princeton University Press.

Graham, Carol. 1994. *Safety Nets, Politics, and the Poor: Transitions to Market Economies*. Washington, D.C.: The Brookings Institution.

————. 1996. From Safety Nets to Social Sector Reform: Lessons from the Developing Countries for the Transition Economies. Paper presented to National Academy of Sciences Task Force on Economies in Transition, Washington, D.C., September 1996.

Graham, C., and Cheikh Kane. 1998. Opportunistic Government or Sustaining Reform: Voting Trends and Public Expenditure Patterns in Peru, 1990-95. *Latin American Research Review* 33 (1).

Hoff, Karla. 1996. Market Failures and the Distribution of Wealth: A Perspective from the Economics of Information. *Politics and Society* 24(4): 411-432.

IDB (Inter-American Development Bank). 1996. *Economic and Social Progress in Latin America, 1996 Report*. Washington, D.C.: IDB.

Kaufmann, Daniel. 1997. Corruption: The Facts. *Foreign Policy* 107 (Summer).

Londoño, Juan Luis, and Miguel Székely. 1997. Distributional Surprises after a Decade of Reforms: Latin America in the Nineties. Mimeo, Inter-American Development Bank, March 1997.

Morley, Samuel A. 1995. *Poverty and Inequality in Latin America*. Baltimore: Johns Hopkins University Press.

Nelson, Joan M. 1992. Poverty, Equity, and the Politics of Adjustment, in Stephan Haggard and Robert Kaufmann, eds., *The Politics of Adjustment*. Princeton: Princeton University Press

Pritchett, Lant, and Jonathan Gelbard. 1996. More for the Poor is Less for the Poor: The Politics of Targeting. Discussion Paper, Policy Research Department, The World Bank, Washington, D.C.

Rawls, John. 1971. *A Theory of Justice.* Cambridge: Harvard University Press.

Remmer, Karen. 1993 The Political Economy of Elections in Latin America, *American Political Science Review* 87: 393-407.

Robbins, Donald. 1996. HOS Hits Facts: Facts Win—Evidence on Trade and Wage Inequality in the Developing World. Mimeo, Harvard Institute for International Development, Cambridge, October 1996.

Sachs, Jeffrey. 1990. Social Conflict and Populist Policies in Latin America. Occasional Paper No. 9, International Center for Economic Growth. ICS Press, San Francisco.

Sachs, J., and Andrew Warner. 1995. Economic Reform and the Process of Global Integration. *Brookings Papers on Economic Activity* 1: 1-95.

Sen, Amartya. 1995. *Inequality Re-examined.* Cambridge, MA: Harvard University Press.

Skocpol, Theda. 1991. Universal Appeal: Politically Viable Policies to Combat Poverty. *The Brookings Review 9* (Summer).

Stiglitz, Joseph. 1997. Keynote Address, Annual World Bank Conference on Development Economics. Washington, D.C.: The World Bank.

Young, Peyton. 1994. *Equity: In Principle and in Practice.* Princeton: Princeton University Press.

CHAPTER TWO

Kinds and Causes of Inequality in Latin America

John Sheahan and Enrique V. Iglesias

Rightly or wrongly, Latin America has long been faulted for high degrees of inequality in the distributions of income, assets, health, education, and opportunity. Systematic comparisons go back no further than 1960 and are always subject to an army of doubts, but they support the generalization that inequality was then, and had long been, exceptionally high. That does not mean that high inequality is an inescapable characteristic of all Latin American countries: several have been consistently less unequal than the majority, and in some the degree of inequality has changed considerably in response to changes in economic strategy.

Inequalities of income reflect the results of productive effort to some degree, and they can also provide incentives for initiative. Some part of the inequality in Latin America is surely related to differences in achievement or initiative, but not all of it. The underlying and persistent causes of income concentration in the region relate primarily to blocked opportunities at the low end, to failures of social institutions, to restriction of competition, and to an enormous waste of human potential.

Why should these universal problems be worse in Latin America than elsewhere? Latin Americans have been asking themselves that question for a long time, and have answered in a dazzling variety of ways.[1] Without trying to rule out the world of possible answers, we will focus on four interrelated issues. The first concerns values and institutional structures developed throughout Latin American history, especially those that affect economic flexibility, opportunities to advance, and access to education. The second is the severe imbalance between growth of the labor force and growth of opportunities for productive employment, during much of the twentieth century. Third are adverse patterns of international trade; and fourth, orientations of economic strategy and social policy.

In his path-breaking analysis of growth and inequality, Simon Kuznets describes a movable balance between the dynamics of structural change, working toward equality, and adverse factors that go the other way. The main adverse factor in his picture is that upper-income groups save more than other groups, which favors increasing concentration of earning assets. The positive offset is "the very nature of a dynamic economy with relative freedom of individual opportunity. In such a society technological change is rampant, and property assets that originated in older industries almost inevitably have a diminishing proportional weight in the total because of the more rapid growth of younger industries (Kuznets 1955, 10)." Strong currents of innovation and structural change can undercut privileged positions. If they are weak, any possibility of reducing inequality would be weakened too.

Innovation and the pace of structural change have been relatively weak in Latin America. That fact alone does not explain inequality; it is more of a transmission variable through which underlying factors work out their consequences. Some of the consequences are self-perpetuating; others set up counterforces that limit the damage. The balance has been changing in intriguing ways. Some persistent underlying factors have been evolving favorably, but the most recent trends have still been toward worsening inequality.

To evaluate these changes in inequality across countries, we first review several fundamental indicators of kinds of inequality. Though inequality appears exceptionally high in the region, and thus related to regional factors, particular countries have done well compared to the rest of the world. In the subsequent four sections, we examine the issues concerning causation specified above. The concluding section discusses possibilities for greater equality in the future.

Indicators of Regional and National Differences

Though distribution of income is central to discussions of inequality, it is not the only concern. Unequal access to education and medical care, as well as the inequality of assets and of political voices between genders and across ethnic groups, are all serious questions in themselves. The selective comparisons outlined below will be limited to income shares, infant mortality rates, education, and some clues about gender and ethnic inequalities.

For *inequality of income*, Latin America stands out from all other regions in the earliest systematic comparisons made by the World Bank, for 1960, and again in a more comprehensive review published in 1996. The early study compared inequal-

Table 1. Regional Indexes of Inequality, 1960s–1990s
(Average Gini coefficients by decade)

Region or group	1960s	1970s	1980s	1990s
Latin America and Caribbean	.532	.491	.498	.493
Sub-Saharan Africa	.499	.482	.435	.470
Middle East and North Africa	.414	.419	.405	.380
East Asia and Pacific	.374	.399	.387	.381
South Asia	.362	.340	.350	.319
Industrial countries and high-income developing countries	.350	.348	.332	.338
Eastern Europe	.251	.246	.250	.289

Note: Changes in averages for a given region across decades may be due to differences in the countries included in the averages, not necessarily to any actual changes in inequality (see text).
Source: Deininger and Squire 1996.

ity in terms of percentage of income received by the lowest quintile. Their share in Latin America (3.7 percent) was lower than in any other region in 1960, and even lower in the late 1970s (World Bank 1980, 461). Similarly, in the more recent study, Latin America and the Caribbean had the highest average Gini coefficients of inequality of all regions, from the 1960s through the first half of the 1990s (Table 1).

These comparisons are valuable attempts to generalize from limited information. While many other studies also suggest that Latin American inequality has been exceptionally high, all have some serious flaws, and the newer World Bank study makes them clear. It also introduces distortions of its own. Due to the exclusion of all estimates not based on household surveys covering the whole country, this study rules out any estimates for Argentina and Uruguay. Since estimates of the distribution of urban incomes indicate that these two countries were among the least unequal in Latin America until the 1990s—and Uruguay still is—their exclusion makes the region's average Gini coefficient higher than it otherwise would be.[2]

Another difficulty is that acceptable measures have been so infrequent that the countries included in the averages are not the same across decades. For Latin America and the Caribbean, they include only nine countries for the 1960s, but 15 for the 1970s. Table 1 registers a decrease in the index of inequality from the 1960s to the 1970s, but a good part of that could be accounted for by changed composition: Honduras pulls up the regional average considerably for the 1960s, with a championship Gini coefficient of .619, but is not included in the 1970s average.[3]

The remarkable stability of the Latin American averages from the 1970s into the 1990s is surprising in light of measures, to be discussed below, that show increased inequality in a considerable number of countries in the 1980s and early 1990s. By leaving out Argentina, they exclude one case of deterioration, and by including measures for Ecuador and Panama only for the 1990s (and not the two preceding decades), they miss evidence of deterioration in these cases as well.

Worldwide econometric models testing determinants of income distribution, with dummy variables to bring out regional characteristics, naturally give results that differ with the models and the variables they include. Gustav Papanek and Oldrich Kyn, using data for 80 developing countries, tried out many alternative specifications and concluded that dummy variables for differential inequality in Latin America were not statistically significant (Papanek and Kyn 1987, Tables 2 and 3, 14-19).

A recent analysis by Juan Luis Londoño, using cross-section data for 102 countries, reached a contrary conclusion: the dummy variable for Latin America turned out to be highly significant, indicating average Gini coefficients four percentage points above predicted levels (Londoño 1996, 3-4). Differences in the databases and reference periods could explain some of the contrasting results, but the main factor is that of concepts. Papanek and Kyn included a series of variables other than income levels to explain inequality, most successfully for differences in education, structure of foreign trade, and "dualism" in the sense of ethnic and racial division between ruling urban elites and rural populations. In their specifications, inequality is accounted for mainly by these factors. The Londoño test does not specify such structural characteristics: their influences are caught up by the regional variable. The earlier study has the advantage of directing attention to differential structural characteristics regardless of region. The Londoño study has the advantage of directing attention to questions of how such structural conditions have affected Latin America, and to what extent they could be changed.

Although some adverse structural factors are common to all countries in the region, a few have done relatively well, at least by the standards of this imperfect world. Some of the contrasts are illustrated in a major study that includes Latin American and East Asian economies (Table 2). On one level, it reinforces the picture of high inequality in Latin America. The poorest four deciles had highest shares of total income in two East Asian countries; five Latin American countries were grouped at the bottom. On a second level, the regional weakness looks less pervasive: two Latin American countries, Argentina and Chile, ranked above all except the highest two in East Asia. Moreover, a separate study indicates that Cuba in

Table 2. Estimates of Income Shares of Poorest Quintiles, 1975

Economy	Income share of lowest 40 percent	Economy	Income share of lowest 40 percent
Taiwan	22.3	Malaysia	11.1
Republic of Korea	16.9	Colombia	9.9
Argentina	15.1	Brazil	9.1
Chile	13.1	Venezuela	8.5
Philippines	11.6	Mexico	8.2
Guatemala	11.3	Peru	7.3
Thailand	11.1		

Note: Included are all countries in East Asia and Latin America for which the source gives estimates. Argentina's estimate is for Buenos Aires only, not rural areas.
Source: Ahluwalia, Carter, and Chenery 1979, 312-13.

Table 3. Rural and Urban Income Shares of Poorest Quintiles; Changes in Their Urban Shares from the 1980s

	Income share of lowest 40 percent		Changes in urban shares
	Rural	Urban	(percent)
Uruguay, 1994	—	21.6	+22 from 1981
Costa Rica, 1994	17.1	17.4	- 8 from 1981
Mexico, 1994	20.1	16.8	- 16 from 1984
Venezuela, 1994	18.6	16.7	- 17 from 1981
Paraguay, 1994	—	16.2	- 1 from 1986
Bolivia, 1994	—	15.1	—[b]
Argentina, 1994	—	14.4	- 20 from 1980 [c]
Panama, 1994	15.5	13.8	- 11 from 1979
Chile, 1994	17.1	13.4	+6 from 1987 [a]
Honduras, 1994	12.1	13.3	—[b]
Colombia, 1992	—	12.9	+5 from 1980 [c]
Guatemala, 1989	14.4	12.1	- 3 from 1986
Brazil, 1993	13.4	11.8	+1 from 1979

[a] For Chile, the short period of change covered obscures a worsening trend through most of the 1980s. Estimates for Gran Santiago show a deterioration of 13 percent from 1978 to 1988 (ECLAC 1995, 147).
[b] No estimates are earlier than 1989.
[c] Urban areas covered for initial year were narrower than those for the end year.
Source: ECLAC 1996, 203-205.

1973 could have outranked Argentina and the Republic of Korea as well, with a share of 20 percent for the lowest four deciles (Brundenius 1982, 156).[4] Of course, much the same applies to the omission of China from the East Asian group. The point is not the regional contrast, but that the negative balance for Latin America, especially for the cluster of countries at the bottom, is not applicable to all countries in the region.

Income distributions can change considerably in short periods. Single-year comparisons such as that in Table 2 may show an unrepresentative year: for example, in Brazil the share of the lowest 40 percent was 12.9 percent in 1974, but only 9.6 percent in 1976 (Deininger and Squire 1996, database, 5). Brazil appears to have been somewhat less unequal than Mexico in 1974, as in Table 2, but then more unequal by 1976. For Chile, Deininger and Squire show a Gini coefficient of .46 for 1971, but then a drastic .53 by 1980. By then, Chile had clearly lost the high ranking suggested by Table 2.

Estimates of income inequality are always subject to serious question, for no household survey ever obtains adequate information from the handful of ultra-wealthy at the top. Many available estimates are exasperatingly contradictory, even for the 1990s, despite improved methods. Table 3 provides some help by clearly separating urban and rural distributions (instead of using urban data to stand for the whole country). This study by ECLAC also avoids mixing distributions of expenditures together with distributions of income (a problem with Table 1), and covers 13 countries. Even then, the estimates leave much room for doubt: the figures for Mexico and Venezuela in the first two columns, and the change shown for Chile in the fourth column, are questionable. For Mexico, independent calculations for 1992 indicate an overall share of 12.0 percent for the lowest four deciles, well below both the urban and the rural shares estimated by ECLAC. Similarly for Venezuela, the new World Bank database gives an overall share of 14.3 percent for 1990, much below both the urban and rural estimates in this table.[5] Nevertheless, the range from top to bottom appears striking: the share of the lowest four deciles in the urban sector was 80 percent higher in Uruguay than in Brazil.

For eleven countries, changes in urban inequality are indicated by the last column in Table 3, covering a decade from the early 1980s. In five countries, the shares of the poorest four deciles fell by 8 percent or more. Only one improved by more than 8 percent. Chile stands out for an instructive reversal. The improvement shown by the ECLAC measures for 1987-94 was preceded by sharply worsening inequality: national Gini coefficients increased from .46 in 1968 to .58 by 1989, and then came a small step back down to .565 by 1994 (Deininger and Squire 1996, database, 9). Albert Berry provides details of predominantly negative changes for many countries in the last two decades, which he finds to be closely associated with the timing of economic liberalization (Berry 1997). A broader cross-section study by Londoño and Székely (1997) adds to the picture of increasing inequality in the 1980s, though it contradicts Berry in concluding that liberalization itself acted as a positive factor, offset by other changes that explain the worsening. (This issue is discussed in the last section.)

Inequalities in living standards depend on many factors other than the distribution of earned incomes. Patterns of access to education and medical care result in major differences, vividly illustrated by contrasts in rates of infant mortality. In Peru, there are exceptionally wide gaps in health care and safe water supplies between urban areas and the rural sierra. For the poorest five rural departments in Peru, infant mortality in 1993 ranged from 3.2 to 4.0 times higher than in Lima (Instituto Cuánto 1994, 270).[6]

Unequal rates of *infant mortality,* among regions or social groups, are not direct indicators of income distribution: they illustrate a distinct kind of inequality, more painful in human terms than other kinds. Infant mortality can be changed significantly by improved access to social services: the Pinochet government in Chile managed to bring it down greatly even while its economic policies were worsening inequality of incomes. Still, differences among national rates of infant mortality are partly explicable by differences in per capita incomes. Table 4 gives measures of infant mortality for twenty Latin American countries for 1992, and levels of GDP per capita for all of them except Cuba. Column three of Table 4 gives computed norms for each country, based on its GDP per capita. Column four gives the differences between actual and computed rates. Simple regression between the two variables for 1992 indicates that levels of GDP per capita accounted for slightly over half of the variance of mortality rates.

The two countries with the lowest inequality of incomes (see Table 3), Costa Rica and Uruguay, both stand out for low rates of infant mortality relative to their computed norms in Table 4. Cuba had the lowest infant mortality rate in the region, but cannot be so directly compared because of the lack of GDP data. Since a careful estimate for 1977 placed Cuba's per capita GDP directly between those of Chile and Costa Rica (Mesa-Lago and Pérez-López 1986), its infant mortality rate was also apparently below any comparable norm for its level of income.

Comparing the distributions of infant mortality rates in Latin America and in East Asia, the 1992 median in East Asia was slightly lower: 37 infant deaths per thousand births, compared to 40 in Latin America. That difference closely paral-

Table 4. Infant Mortality Rates and GDP per Capita in 1992, Compared to Computed Norm at Country's GDP Level

	GDP per capita, dollars at PPP[a]	Infant mortality per thousand births		
		Actual	Norm[b]	Deviation
Argentina	8,860	24	16	8
Bolivia	2,410	75	57	18
Brazil	5,240	58	39	19
Chile	8,410	16	19	- 3
Colombia	5,480	37	37	0
Costa Rica	5,480	14	37	- 23
Cuba	—	12	—	—
Dominican Republic	3,280	42	51	- 9
Ecuador	4,350	50	45	5
El Salvador	2,250	46	58	- 12
Guatemala	3,350	48	51	- 3
Haiti	1,046	86	65	21
Honduras	2,000	43	59	- 16
Mexico	7,300	36	26	10
Nicaragua	2,790	52	54	- 2
Panama	5,600	25	37	- 12
Paraguay	3,390	38	51	- 13
Peru	3,300	64	51	13
Uruguay	6,070	20	34	- 14
Venezuela	8,520	23	18	5

[a] GDP measures are adjusted for purchasing power parity.
[b] Norms are computed for corresponding income levels from OLS regression:
mortality rate = 72 - 0.0063 GDP; adj. r2 = 0.52 (t = 4.55).
Source: UNDP 1995, 162-63.

leled the income levels of the median countries in the two regions: Thailand's GDP per capita was nine percent higher than Colombia's (UNDP 1995, 162-63). Hong Kong and Singapore, with per capita incomes more than double the highest in Latin America, had the lowest mortality rates of all. Otherwise, the two distributions are closely matched. Both regional averages remain painfully high, compared to what should be possible, but at least Latin America's progress has been on a par with East Asia.

Inequality of *educational opportunities* and achievement has aggravated the inequality of incomes, and probably that of health as well. In most of Latin America, the human potential of nearly all people in rural areas, and much of the urban poor, was blocked by lack of primary education until the latter half of this century. Regional averages for measures of education are rendered almost meaningless by the stark contrast between effective concern with education in the Southern Cone countries, along with Costa Rica and Cuba, and its absence in most of the others. As of 1960, adult literacy rates in the Southern Cone ranged from 84 to 91 percent, and as of 1970 were 88 percent in Costa Rica and 87 in Cuba. But in twelve other countries less than two-thirds of the adult population was literate in 1960 (World Bank 1983, individual country pages). That record changed markedly for the better in the following decades. By 1992, the median illiteracy rate came down from 39 percent to 12 (UNDP 1995, 162-63). Peruvian data by age groups underline both the earlier failure and the later improvement: as of 1993, the illiteracy rate for people over the age of 65 was 38 percent; for people in their twenties it was down to 6 percent (Instituto Cuánto 1995, 264).

Neglect of mass education prior to the 1960s was so severe that even the marked improvements since have not brought education for the poor anywhere close to that of upper-income families. Londoño calculates that the average worker still has two years less education than would be expected for the region's level of income, that decreases in illiteracy and increases in secondary school enrollment have been slower than in either East or South Asia, and that differences in human capital have increased in importance as determinants of inequalities of income (Londoño 1996, 10-17).

Beyond such differences in enrollment ratios and years of schooling, the even more tenacious problems concern motivation by parents and students and differences in educational quality (Behrman and Birdsall 1983). Studies of educational reform in Latin America frequently underline weakness of teacher training and classroom methods, deficiencies of books and other materials, and problems of motivation as indicated by high rates of repeated classes and dropouts. Attempts to make international comparisons of educational achievement usually confirm a picture of relative weakness (Hanushek and Kim 1995). That weakness is largely due to the main characteristic of inequality within Latin American educational systems. The children of upper-class Colombians in Bogotá normally go to French or North American *liceos*, or the outstanding *Gimnasio Moderno*, with motivation favored by both the quality of the schools and confidence of students (and parents), in their economic and social opportunities. The children of lower-income groups, even in Bogotá but especially in rural areas, attend underfinanced and underequipped public schools, with motivation undermined by realistic doubts about the economic and social opportunities open to them.

Private schools in general perform more effectively than public schools, in and out of Latin America, and the more expensive and exclusive private schools better than others. Tests of relative effectiveness of schools in the Dominican Republic, adjusted for the higher family incomes and greater parental education of children in private schools, concluded that "ordinary" private schools scored 31 percent higher than public schools and "prestigious" private schools scored 47 percent higher (Jiménez, Lockheed, and Paqueo 1991, 211).[7] Inequality of current incomes is perpetuated with compelling force through inequality in the schooling available to children of upper-income groups and of the poor.

Inequalities between *female and male education* were historically very high in Latin America, and still are in some countries, but by 1992 combined enrollment ratios (for primary, secondary and tertiary education), were higher for women than for men in eight countries. That does not mean that discrimination has become irrelevant for inequality of incomes. The probability of belonging to the bottom 20 percent of the income distribution in 1989 was more than twice as high for females as for males (Psacharopoulos et al. 1997, 49). Relative earnings of women are held down by discrimination even for equal levels of education: differences in human capital explain only 20 percent of the gender gap for wages (Psacharopoulos and Tzannatos 1992, 23; Helwege 1996, 23-25). The United Nations Development Programme has combined enrollment ratios, relative earnings, and life expectancy in a "gender-related development index" (GDI). The index as based on data for 1990 and 1992 indicated closer approaches to equality in Hong Kong and Singapore than in any Latin American country (UNDP 1995, 76). But then a large cluster of Latin American countries ranks up with or above the highest of the other East Asian cases. For the region as a whole, the GDI index indicates lower gender inequality than in any other developing area, though far more than in the industrialized countries (UNDP 1995, 5). We all have a long way to go.

Ethnic and racial inequalities are difficult to measure in countries with so many people of mixed race, but estimates of poverty rates among descendants of indigenous people in four countries indicate that they range from 1.3 times as high as for non-indigenous families in Bolivia to 4.5 times as high in Mexico (Psacharopoulos and Patrinos 1994, 41). These differences reflect the near-universal gaps between rural and urban incomes: the indigenous people have long been concentrated in rural areas. That concentration might be seen as a matter of tradition and preferences on their part, but the more fundamental factor has been persistent discrimination against them in educational systems and opportunities for urban employment. As Dudley Seers emphasized many years ago, neglect of rural areas is greater in countries in which the rural poor are ethnically or racially distinct from the predominant urban population than it is in countries, like Costa Rica and Uruguay, where such differences are not pronounced (Seers 1977).

In addition to social and economic barriers against people of indigenous descent, discrimination against black people has contributed to high rates of inequality in Brazil and the Caribbean basin countries, including Colombia and Venezuela. Comparisons of child malnutrition, life expectancy, education and earnings, show marked differences in incomes and life chances for black groups, and for particular geographical areas in which they are concentrated (Helwege 1996, 20-23).

These diverse comparisons of inequality, subject to doubts as they are, suggest two contrasting kinds of questions. First, why should the region have higher average inequality than the rest of the world? Second, why have a minority of Latin American countries done distinctly better in sustained (nonrandom) ways, and what factors account for the individual cases of both substantial improvement and of weakening in recent decades?

Long-term Evolution of Institutional and Economic Structures

Two different lines of interpretation combine to explain the evolution of the region's institutions and economic structures. One centers on Iberian or South European cultural and political traditions, and institutional systems designed by elite minorities to maintain social and political control. The second centers on economic variables with emphasis on labor, land, and human capital.

The first approach often draws Latin American social scientists (except perhaps Brazilians) back to the Spanish conquest to explain tenacious inequalities (Cotler 1978; Ramos 1996). In several ways that tendency is understandable and illuminating. The conquest created a long-lasting division between a minority with control of government, land, and mining resources, dominant over a majority treated as inferior and often subject to forced labor (Flores Galindo 1987; Tandeter 1993; Bulmer-Thomas 1994, 85-92). When high death rates for indigenous labor made it scarce, the region's economic systems were shaped to override market forces in order to restrain labor mobility and hold down wage costs (Ramos 1996, 146-47). Markets were regarded with suspicion, as problems undermining systems of control.

Spanish and Portuguese rule transmitted a structure of thought and values directly opposed to the forces of individualism, materialism, and scientific inquiry that so strongly characterized northern Europe in the colonial period. Under the tensions of the Reformation and the prolonged religious wars of the sixteenth and seventeenth centuries, the Spanish state and church did their best to defend values of tradition, order, and spiritual concerns.[8]

That emphasis has clearly lost much of its hold in this more secular age; one might well wish that both Latin America and North America had kept a better balance between material and spiritual values. But in the seventeenth and eighteenth centuries it helped turn Spain, and Italy under its domination, from world leaders in economic power and scientific inquiry into economic and intellectual backwaters (Trevor-Roper 1967, 1-45 and 193-236; Vicens Vives 1965, 301-427). For Latin America in the eighteenth and nineteenth centuries, opposition to changing values may well have restrained the kind of independent, decentralized forces that played important roles in favor of economic innovation and social change in northern Europe and the United States (Véliz 1980).

The distinctive set of values transmitted to Latin America from southern Europe may also have worked against equality by fostering acceptance of poverty as something beyond society's control. Although such attitudes have surely been changing, an opinion survey in three Central American countries in 1989 suggests that they have not disappeared. Asked to respond to the interview statement that "The misery of the poor is a test by God," 35 percent of the people interviewed in Nicaragua, and 42 percent in El Salvador, registered their agreement (Interamerican Public Opinion Report 1990). (As one might expect, only 21 percent of Costa Ricans agreed.)

Economic history tends to downplay such factors, emphasizing instead conditions of demand and supply. Stanley Engerman and Kenneth Sokoloff (1997) focus on the late eighteenth and nineteenth centuries, in which many Latin American colonies—and then independent countries—dealt with labor scarcities in the same way as the South in the United States: by importing slaves. They contrast the kinds of large-scale plantation production relying on slave labor, particularly in sugar, with the diversified small-farm production dominant in Canada and the northern United States. Slavery gave Brazil and the Caribbean countries much the same pattern of large-scale land ownership relying on subjugated labor as in the Andean countries, where indigenous people were compelled to do the work for a small minority of landowners.[9] In both areas, the system meant that the mass of the labor force gained practically no access to education, to political voice, or to income above subsistence levels.

Engerman and Sokoloff carry through this interpretation of the earlier period to the modern by a compelling hypothesis. Where immigration and access to land and to education were relatively open, as in Canada and the northern United States, independent small farmers thrived and soon began to participate actively in commercial and early industrial activities: relative equality of incomes favored development of broad markets, inventive activity, and broad political participation.[10] In Latin America, immigration of free labor was often restricted in order to hold down competition for the existing elite, access to land was controlled by political decisions, and access to education extremely limited. Participation in new commercial activities was correspondingly restricted, domestic markets could not grow as readily, industrial activities and new inventions developed more slowly, and political participation remained narrowly restricted. Radical inequality in the early years favored institutional structures that perpetuated it.

With all its suggestive power, this thesis does not apply equally well to all Latin American countries. Engerman and Sokoloff note that Argentina is an "ambiguous" case, without plantation agriculture or significant recourse to either indigenous or slave labor (1997, 275). They might have extended the exceptions to Chile and Uruguay as well. The grain-producing and cattle-raising countries in the temperate zone developed differently. So did Costa Rica: it did not have much of an indigenous population, and it had land available for independent small farmers well into the twentieth century (Seligson 1980; Sheahan 1987, 272-75 and 288-96). It never imported slaves on any significant scale, though after 1870 the United Fruit Company brought in large numbers of West Indian workers to develop banana plantations on the Atlantic Coast, initially under conditions little better than slavery (Chomsky 1996).

Outside of the relatively isolated Atlantic Coast, small-scale farming thrived in Costa Rica, independent farmers gained and held effective political voice, and inequality probably never approached the degrees common in the majority of Latin American countries. Even when agricultural production turned toward large-scale coffee plantations in the late nineteenth century, the country's particular structural conditions gave distinctive results. As Central America became caught up in the worldwide coffee boom of that period, exporters in all the countries sought additional land to increase production. In El Salvador, Guatemala, and Nicaragua, this brought them into direct conflict with indigenous communities. In these countries, coffee growers turned to the power of the state to take land away from indigenous communities. These three states became more entrenched instruments of subjugation of the rural poor. In Costa Rica, where coffee exporters had to deal with independent small farmers who had both political voice and feasible economic alternatives, the resolution took the form of market negotiations that raised everyone's incomes (Williams 1994).

By being exceptions, Costa Rica and the three Southern Cone countries strengthen rather than weaken the Engerman and Sokoloff thesis. They did not follow the paths of dependence on subjugation of indigenous or slave labor, and they achieved a more equal distribution of wealth than most of the region's economies.

The fifth country outstanding for relatively low inequality is Cuba. Given its history of dependence on slave labor and sugar, high inequality would have been the natural result, and certainly was prior to its revolution. Cuba's experience is evidence that socialism can in some ways triumph over history. As demonstrated by Londoño's test for differences in inequality, two groups of countries stand out for significant differences from worldwide norms: Latin America for high degrees, and socialist countries for low (Londoño 1996, note 2). The latter must be due in part, but not entirely, to near-elimination of income from property. Also important in Cuba's case has been its success in providing equal access to education for all children, as well as universally available medical care (Mesa-Lago 1981; Eckstein 1994, 128-48).

Factor Proportions and Concentration of Ownership

Factor proportions changed fundamentally in the early twentieth century because rapid growth of population and the labor force—without comparable growth of opportunities for education—made unskilled labor much more abundant relative to land, capital, and skilled labor. The resulting imbalance would have been difficult to offset even without complicating factors. Complicating factors were fairly abundant, and remain so. In particular, highly concentrated ownership of land, and few opportunities for productive employment outside of agriculture, worsened the consequences.

Population growth speeded up greatly in the twentieth century, as death rates fell without corresponding decreases in birth rates. Population growth in Brazil rose from 1.8 percent a year in the latter nineteenth century to 2.9 percent in the 1960s; in Colombia from 1.1 to 2.2 percent between the same periods; and in Guatemala from 1.0 to 2.8 percent (Sánchez-Albornoz 1974, 169). Fortunately for the future, fertility rates began to fall persistently from 1960. The regional average rate was 6.0 in that year but fell nearly in half, to 3.1, by 1992 (World Bank 1983, 217; UNDP 1995, 216). The rate of population growth slowed down to 2.0 percent a year for the 1980s and 1.7 for 1990-95 (World Bank 1997, 221).

With predominantly rural populations in the early years of the century, growth of the agricultural labor force outran additions to arable land, making it difficult to

achieve rising labor productivity and incomes. As growing urban activities provided new employment openings, agriculture's share of the labor force headed
steadily downward. But in most countries population growth continued to raise
the absolute size of the agricultural labor force. Between 1960 and 1984 it increased
by more than a fifth in the poorest countries, as well as in Brazil and Mexico at
higher income levels (FAO 1972, 19-20 and FAO 1984, 66-68). In contrast, it fell in
the Southern Cone countries and in Colombia, which helped hold down inequality
in the Southern Cone and contributed to Colombia's rare example of decreasing
inequality during this period (Sheahan 1987, 56-57).

   An increasing agricultural labor force does not necessarily depress incomes
for the rural poor, either absolutely or relatively. Rising productivity, or higher agricultural prices, or opportunities for nonfarm employment in rural areas, could all
come to the rescue. Albert Berry concluded that incomes of rural labor in Mexico
rose relatively well in the period 1950-70, as increasing productivity following land
reform offset falling agricultural prices (Berry 1983, 187-89). For rural workers in
Colombia, however, real wages did not rise at all from the mid 1930s to the mid
1960s, while urban incomes were increasing fairly rapidly (Urrutia and Berry 1975,
82-89; Londoño 1995, 41-66). Similarly in Peru, Richard Webb estimated that incomes in the modern sector increased 4.1 percent a year in the decade of the 1950s,
but incomes of small farmers rose barely 0.8 percent a year (Webb 1977, 39).

   In some East Asian countries, an important saving factor for rural incomes
was that nonagricultural activity moved strongly into rural areas, providing good
alternative earnings. Ranis and Orrock (1985, 61), point out that in Taiwan the share
of rural family income from nonfarming activities increased from 30 to 50 percent
in the course of three decades, while in Colombia it fell from an originally low 15
percent, to 10 percent.[11] That difference reflects the presence of tight urban labor
markets in Taiwan contrasted to weakness in Colombia, and the weakness of rural
education for the latter. Uneducated rural workers do not offer promising possibilities for new industrial production.

   The negative consequences of rising population pressure on the land have
long been aggravated by high ownership concentration. As of 1950, the largest 9.5
percent of land holdings included 90 percent of the region's agricultural land (Carroll
1961, 165). Degrees of concentration varied greatly by country but stood out as
high relative to other regions of the world, and particularly so as compared to the
East Asian countries after their land reforms (Barraclough 1973; Eckstein 1978).
Mexico's Gini coefficient for land ownership concentration was an amazing .96 as
of 1930 (Eckstein 1978, 2). The land reforms of the Cárdenas government in the
1930s did a good deal to lessen that concentration: the share of total crop land held

by large farms fell from 70 percent prereform to 29 percent as of 1960, and the share of landless labor in the rural labor force fell as well (Eckstein 1978, 13 and 17). Following the reforms, Mexico achieved two decades of exceptional agricultural growth and rising rural incomes (Berry 1983), before population growth and adverse national policies eroded these gains. A good many other Latin American countries also tried, and some succeeded, in carrying out major and minor land reforms from the 1950s into the 1970s (Thiesenhusen 1989). But Brazil, Colombia, Ecuador, Guatemala, Haiti, and Honduras either made little serious effort in this direction, or quickly abandoned it because of adverse political reactions.[12]

Karla Hoff makes the important point that the productive potential of the great majority of small landowners can be blocked by highly concentrated land ownership. Their inability to provide the collateral needed to assure lenders can shut them out of credit markets: "a highly concentrated wealth distribution may restrict individuals' opportunities to be productive" (Hoff 1996, 412). The question may have lost some of its relevance as agriculture's share of the labor force and national income have fallen, but in many countries large numbers of the rural poor are still trying to survive on infinitesimal land holdings, or are completely landless, in contexts of continuing high ownership concentration.

Concentration of ownership of assets other than land has yet to be measured in any dependable way. The massive increase of Latin American accounts in U.S. banks preceding and during the debt crisis of the 1980s, and the rise of Mexican billionaires on *Forbes'* list of the world's richest, suggest that it must be fairly high. Richard Webb provided an interesting clue for Peru at the beginning of the 1960s: the households in the top one percent of the distribution of income received one-fourth of all personal income, but if the undistributed earnings of their firms were taken into account that share would rise to 31 percent (Webb 1977, 6-7).

Urban labor markets have been under downward pressure through the postwar decades from the joint effects of rapid population growth and heavy migration to the cities. Table 5 gives estimates of long-run trends for real wages in manufacturing for six countries. Three show long downtrends; in two others, wage increases were much below those of GDP per capita. The sixth country, Chile, would have shown a similar picture if the comparison had stopped in the mid 1980s. Since then, Chile's context has changed: it has become a rare example of an economy able to reach nearly full employment.

Increasing opportunities for productive employment can outrun the growth of the labor force at times, as they did in Chile from the mid 1980s on, but the postwar trend has been the opposite for most Latin American countries. That was

Table 5. Long-term Trends of Real Wages in Manufacturing for Six Countries, Compared to Growth of GDP Per Capita

		Annual rates of change (percent)	
		Manufacturing wages	GDP per capita
Argentina	1956-72	0.5	2.6
	1970-80	- 5.5	0.8
	1980-90	- 2.3	- 1.7
Brazil	1963-91	1.6	3.2
Chile	1963-92	2.1	1.2
Colombia	1968-92	0.4	2.5
Mexico	1970-91	- 1.2	1.6
Peru	1963-86	- 1.0	0.7

Sources: World Bank 1995, 149, for all except Argentina. For Argentina: Sheahan 1987, 69, for 1956-72 and 1970-80; OIT 1995, 11, for wages 1980-90; World Bank 1992, 221 and 269, for GDP per capita 1980-90.

not an inevitable consequence of rapid population growth: employment opportunities were held down by structures of incentives that worked against labor-intensive production and exports, and by repeated macroeconomic downturns due to both bad luck and poor economic policies. These problems are closely connected to issues of international trade and finance, discussed in the following two sections.

Interactions with World Markets

International trade and factor movements clearly played significant roles after Latin America entered world markets on a large scale in the latter nineteenth century. They were probably among the most important forces in worsening inequality. Consistent with basic Heckscher-Ohlin analysis, a region with abundant land and natural resources (relative to labor) exported land-intensive products and imported labor-intensive. In some countries, the impact of trade was heavily reinforced by immigration. Jeffrey Williamson estimates that the ratio of wages to the value of land in Argentina fell approximately five-sixths between 1870 and 1910. Although the effect of immigration on wages probably outweighed that of trade, comparative advantage in the Heckscher-Ohlin sense accounted for about one-third of the increase in inequality (as measured by ratios of wages to land values), for the group of countries he studied (Williamson 1996, 15-19 and Table 2).

Explanations in terms of factor proportions are usually relevant, but they can obscure key questions. Relative scarcity of labor in the northern United States helped stimulate a great deal of nineteenth-century innovation, both in labor-saving technology and in new industrial products that gradually entered the structure of exports. Meanwhile, trade reduced the relative earnings of labor in both the United States and Latin America, but one answered by innovation leading to new exports, and the latter did not. Latin America's industrial exports did not begin to be significant until the 1960s. To explain the delay as a consequence of factor proportions would leave out a fundamental difference in economic and social response.

As late as 1962, manufactured products were barely five percent of total Latin American exports, compared to 26 percent for East Asian countries (World Bank 1983, 519 and 521). The leading sectors in East Asian growth were focused on activities that required close attention to standards of quality and to never-ceasing changes in technology—while the leading sectors in Latin America were not.

Two econometric studies of worldwide patterns have indicated why a structure of exports dominated by primary products is systematically adverse for equality (Papanek and Kyn 1987; Bourguignon and Morrisson 1989). Bourguignon and Morrisson emphasize that the negative effects for equality of reliance on primary exports could be counteracted by high levels of education for workers (measured in their study by secondary school enrollments), and by predominance of small farmers in production of export crops. Relative weakness on both counts has made international trade more adverse for equality in Latin America than it need have been.

In postwar Latin America, key factors underlying the close association of primary exports with inequality have been the concentrated ownership of land and mines and—contrary to the situation at the beginning of the century—relatively elastic supplies of unskilled rural workers without alternative opportunities for productive employment. Under these conditions, favorable external markets for primary exports raise profits and rents, but do little to raise earnings of rural workers. In some countries they may even have the perverse effect of financing further concentration of land ownership (Carter, Barham, and Mesbah 1996).

Increasingly abundant labor in the course of the twentieth century should have favored the development of labor-intensive exports, and thereby the growth of employment and possible reduction of inequality. That process was held back for a time by high levels of protection for the sake of import substitution, undermining incentives to export. Latin American exports fell from 13.5 percent of world exports in 1946 to 4.4 percent by 1975 (Bulmer-Thomas 1994, 270-71). But as more countries have moved away from protection, both traditional and new exports have been growing. Nontraditional agricultural products that are relatively labor-intensive have gained increasing importance, and the share of manufactured goods in the region's total exports rose from 11 to 33 percent between 1970 and 1990 (IDB 1992, 192). If this trend can be sustained, international trade could become more helpful for employment and for equality than it has ever been in the past.

Economic Strategy and Social Policy

Economic strategies and social policies can interact with each other in powerful ways. If social policies successfully develop human capital on a decently egalitarian basis, then open-market competitive economies could favor more equal income distribution. If they do not, dependence on market forces is bound to favor inequality. That latter combination gave Latin America much of its deserved reputation for inequality in the long period of open markets up to the 1930s. With greatly widened access to education, the return to economic liberalization now could give less unequal results. But that is an open question: it depends on the course of social policies and institutional reform, and also on exactly what form liberalization takes.

For any general economic strategy, the particulars are what matter most: institutional structures, access to education, questions of discrimination, whether there is a unifying social consensus, management of monetary and fiscal policy, and all the other familiar battlefronts. Social policy could play a fundamental role. Latin Americans as individuals have traditionally shown concern for helping the poor, but that has done little to reduce conditions of inequality. Such help mainly takes the form of support for survival, rather than systematic effort to increase their human capital.

Carol Graham and Dagmar Raczynski bring out the contrast between these two orientations of social policy in their discussions of Chile during the last two decades. The military government in power from 1973 to 1990 had maintained selective social programs, including support for nutrition of the poor, emergency public employment, and a strikingly successful effort to reduce infant mortality. But it did almost nothing to promote improvement of the human capital and earnings potential of the poor (Graham 1994, 38-42; Raczynski 1995, 207-54). When democracy returned in 1990, Chile's new government greatly increased both welfare assistance and the minimum wage, but the more important change it made was to redirect resources toward improving the quality of education, the productive potential, and the economic mobility of the poor. These programs have run into many complications, but the society continues to explore new methods to address the crucial factors underlying inequality of incomes: unequal quality of education, restricted access to acquisition of skills, and handicaps that reduce personal capacity to respond to opportunities.

Many other countries have adopted their own versions of programs to build up the human capital of the poor in recent years. If these attempts can be financed and maintained, either economic liberalization or protection and controls would give better results for equality than they have in the past. Liberalization, clearly the dominant choice for the time being, might well turn out to be more equitable than it was prior to the 1930s. Whether it has actually lessened or worsened inequality in recent years is a much-debated question: the logical implications could go in either direction, and serious empirical investigations have given contrary answers. Albert Berry and the group associated with Victor Bulmer-Thomas in his recent book give good reasons to believe that it has increased inequality; Juan Luis Londoño and Miguel Székely argue with econometric evidence that its effects have been the opposite (Berry 1997; Bulmer-Thomas 1996; Londoño and Székely 1997.)

On the favorable side, trade liberalization opens up competition for previously protected domestic monopolies, reduces prior biases against agriculture and against exports, and exerts greater pressure on firms for efficiency and technological change. It is also associated with intensified and generally successful efforts to reduce inflation, which has been one of the factors contributing to inequality. But that is only one side of the coin. Trade liberalization implies greater pressures to hold down employment and wages, and could block industrialization for those countries—the majority—in which comparative advantage is still on the side of primary products. Even if the structure of exports can be redirected away from capital-intensive sectors like mining toward more labor-intensive manufacturing, the gains are likely to be stronger for workers with the basic skills necessary for industrial production than for the lowest-income workers who may still be functionally non-literate (Wood 1994, 213-46; Robbins 1996a). On that score as so many others, past inequalities in access to education feed current inequalities of income.

Liberalization of international finance similarly offers mixed possibilities. On the positive side, it can release constraints on investment financing and bring in firms and people with new methods. On the negative side, it raises several problems. Open access to external capital has in recent years encouraged exchange rate appreciation adverse to the competitive position of newly open economies, and thereby adverse to employment and equality (Calvo, Leiderman and Reinhart 1993; Griffith Jones 1996). The possibility of bringing in external capital to provide the foreign exchange needed to finance current account deficits, and the fear of crisis if it were to stop coming in, can encourage policies to keep interest rates high even when this policy orientation dampens investment (Morley 1995, 179).

Financial liberalization can also feed inequality by inhibiting progressive taxation. Latin American countries have made serious efforts to restrain fiscal deficits in recent years, and many have introduced major tax reforms. In the new context of open capital movement, the reforms have had to pay particular attention to any negative effects on earnings of capital, without any corresponding increase of concern for taxation of wages or of basic consumer goods. Revisions of tax structures in the process of liberalization for financial markets have consistently made them more regressive (Bird 1992; Bird and Perry 1994).

Reflecting the conflicts among logical probabilities, empirical examinations of the effects of liberalization on inequality have gone in contrary directions. Berry's review of the data for eight countries brings out deterioration associated with liberalization in seven of them (Berry 1997). Some of this evidence applies to very short time periods. Given that liberalization has often been combined with severe monetary and fiscal contraction to stop inflation, and that external conditions can have greatly different effects, it is difficult to sort out the effects of liberalization itself. A different approach (Londoño and Székely 1997), uses cross-section data for 13 countries, with constructed indicators to take separate account of different aspects of liberalization, as well as of changes in human capital, investment, and growth rates. They conclude that inequality increased in the course of the 1980s, then stabilized but failed to come back down in the first half of the 1990s. But they explain the worsening in the 1980s by falling investment and lack of growth as a result of the debt crisis, and for the 1990s they blame increasing inequality of education as the main negative factor offsetting what they consider to be positive consequences of liberalization.

It will take evidence from longer time periods, and more in-depth empirical studies, to resolve these conflicts of interpretation. But these studies include valuable clues that suggest a basic reason for conflicting evidence: liberalization programs are not all alike and country conditions can differ greatly. Empirical studies can give different answers according to which countries they cover for what periods, and exactly what factors other than liberalization they take into account. Two examples of notable changes in degrees of inequality, in Colombia and in Chile, may help bring out some of the contrasting possibilities.

In Colombia, income inequality had increased greatly from the 1930s to the mid-1960s, as the rural poor and uneducated urban workers were left behind in a process of industrialization behind protection (Urrutia and Berry 1975; Londoño

1995). In 1967, a new government revised national economic strategy to promote industrial exports by introducing a controlled moving peg exchange rate, accompanied by a gradual movement toward lower protection, by tax reform, and by encouraging the growth of small business (Urrutia 1981 and 1985; Sheahan 1987, 271-88). Rising investment in education widened the share of the labor force able to respond to new employment opportunities. That experience could be considered an experiment with moderate liberalization, combined with promotion of more diversified exports and with improved social programs. Regarding how much income distribution changed in response to this combination, estimates vary—Londoño reports 67 different estimates at the national level—but most indicate considerable improvement. He concludes that the Gini coefficient came down from .56 in 1964 to .48 by 1978 (Londoño 1995, 3-11).

Colombia's more recent and more thorough liberalization program from 1990 has apparently had the opposite effect: inequality increased markedly (Berry 1997, 23-26; ECLAC 1996, 203). Wage differentials widened, in contrast to their narrowing in the earlier experience (Robbins 1996b). This may be because the earlier liberalization featured promotion of new exports, while the more recent experience has been accompanied by appreciation of the real exchange rate, encouraging imports rather than exports. That tends to slow the growth of employment and, as Donald Robbins suggests, by favoring increased imports of capital equipment, it raises relative demand for skilled workers and increases their wages relative to those of the less skilled (Robbins 1996a and 1996b).

Chile had a more egalitarian economic system than Colombia in the early postwar years and maintained it until the military government took power in 1973. An all-out version of economic liberalization, compounded by reliance on a fixed exchange rate to hold down prices, resulted in greatly higher unemployment, poverty, and inequality. But after that approach led to a deep depression in 1982-83, the government switched over to a more activist program. This second model of liberalization promoted export-led growth by using the exchange rate to strengthen the competitive position of producers rather than fixing it to restrain inflation, and by selective tax advantages for exporters, combined with lower interest rates. That new version of liberalization succeeded in bringing the economy close to full employment by 1988. When the restored democratic government added major social programs from 1990, the combination of strong employment conditions and the social programs began at last to bring the degree of inequality at least part-way back down (Table 3; Ffrench-Davis and Labán 1995; Labán and Larraín 1995; Sheahan 1997; Weyland 1997).

Both of these experiences, like those of the East Asian countries, underline the potential advantages of combining a basically open-economy strategy with active policies to promote competitive industrial sectors. But Chile's experience also has a seriously troubling side. The country's relatively good educational progress and social programs did not prevent inequality from worsening in the 1970s and 1980s, and even Chile's success in combining good employment conditions with greatly improved social programs in the 1990s has not yet reduced inequality to the earlier levels. This suggests that increased inequality of assets, built up under the military government's first model of liberalization, combined with the pressures of international financial liberalization against more progressive tax structures, may be too much to overcome even by more equal investment in human capital.

In other countries as well, evidence of heightened inequality in the initial stages of liberalization underlines the danger that the most common version of liberalization could worsen inequality even under improved structural conditions. The balance is uncertain. The possibilities of more favorable outcomes could be improved by doing what Chile did, only sooner: repudiate the common model of liberalization and adopt alternatives more like its later versions, directed toward strengthened competitive positions and more sustained growth of employment (Sheahan 1997).

Possibilities for Significant Change

In a world oversupplied with forces working against equality, Latin America has had more than its share. That does not mean that the region is condemned to eternally higher degrees of inequality than the rest of the world. Adverse structural factors remain important, but some of them have been changing in favorable directions, opening up new scope for corrective action. Degrees of income inequality can change considerably, both in response to current economic conditions and to changes in economic and social policies. The disquieting consideration is that, despite favorable trends in structural conditions, recent changes have been more toward increased than toward decreased inequality of incomes.

The historical resistances to innovation and structural change discussed in section two, associated with relatively closed social structures, distrust of individualism and competition, and elite reliance on political privilege and ownership of resources rather than leadership toward economic change, have surely not gone away. But attitudes and behavior can change when objective conditions do. Perhaps the clearest changes have been movement away from narrowly based political control to democracies that, with all their remaining weaknesses, have opened up a wider range of political voice; from societies in which majorities or near-majorities were illiterate and unaware of the ways in which social choices damaged their interests to conditions of much greater literacy, organization, and awareness; and from highly protected economic systems that did not force business to seek dynamic change to more open systems in which such effort comes closer to being necessary for survival.

The most costly problem in the past, in countries with the highest degrees of inequality, has been disregard of fundamental inequalities of access to education, skills, and opportunity. That held back people of indigenous descent and blacks, and by extension practically the whole rural population. It wasted many generations of human potential. It built up inequality by hurting the weak, and has left high concentrations of assets that now make it difficult to reduce inequality.

High incomes have so long been associated with special privilege and protection that public opinion, and popularly elected governments, seem prone to identify them with either gross unfairness or outright exploitation. In the light of Latin American economic history, the presumption is hardly surprising. But it can be costly to all sides. Populist governments, responding in unhelpful ways to genuine problems, are renowned for refusing to correct overvalued exchange rates that cripple the economy, or negative real interest rates that work against efficiency and employment, in the belief that such policies mainly benefit the wealthy. Just possibly, if profits can be made to depend more on effective economic performance, in societies that provide more nearly equal opportunities, the pressures to use dysfunctional forms of intervention could lessen.

The change toward broader access to education that gathered regionwide momentum in the postwar period must be testimony to greater awareness and acceptance of the people previously left out, and should help considerably to lessen inequality of opportunity. Still, a good deal of bias remains: the quality of education available for the poor and near-poor is much weaker than that available for upper-income groups, and the constraints of pervasive poverty work against both the efforts of poor families to seek education for their children, and the children's efforts to stay in school and succeed. All this is painfully similar to problems of inner cities in the United States, and certainly not easy to correct.

While progress on the side of human capital is fundamental, it is bound to be slow. It needs the counterpart of institutional reforms combined with economic strategies aimed at generating opportunities for productive employment. The objectives seem clear: to raise skills and productive potential, with special programs directed to the lower income groups for whom it is most difficult, and to make labor so scarce that market forces will come to favor increasing real wages. The chances of success on the latter side should be improving, because the region's labor force is not growing nearly as rapidly as it did in the first two-thirds of the twentieth century. The necessary condition is that economic strategy focus on sustained increases in demand for workers. The standard model of liberalization currently common in the region is a serious handicap in this respect; the alternative model developed in Chile in the 1980s and 1990s is far more promising.

With improved access to education, a gradual slowing of birth rates and population growth, greater openness to competition, considerable growth in nontraditional exports, and just possibly some decrease in the rigidity of ethnic and racial discrimination, the basic economic and social conditions of Latin America have become more favorable. Still, the heavy weight of institutional structures designed to protect special privilege has not disappeared. Tax structures have been evolving in regressive directions; the particular kinds of liberalization programs now common are working against structural transformation; and a wave of reaction against state intervention has weakened many of its potentially helpful forms. Who knows where the balance will go?

Endnotes

[1] Albert Hirschman introduced one of his analyses with a wonderful quotation from Daniel Cosío Villegas (Hirschman 1961, 3). "Why is there so much wretchedness in this fabulous land...? Ah, says one—it is the priests' fault; another blames it on the military; still others on the Indian; on the foreigner; on democracy; on dictatorship; on bookishness; on ignorance; or finally on divine punishment."

[2] An offsetting factor is that the averages for Latin America and the Caribbean include four English language countries in the Caribbean, and Puerto Rico, for which the average Gini coefficient is slightly below that for Latin language countries considered separately, as intended in this discussion (Deininger and Squire 1996, database file). If these five cases were excluded, the index of inequality for the Latin language countries would average 2 percent higher than that for the two groups combined.

[3] An additional problem is that these estimates mix together measures of the distribution of income and the distribution of consumer spending. The distribution of spending is normally less unequal than that of income, in part because higher income groups save higher shares of their incomes. Deininger and Squire calculate that Gini coefficients for expenditures average .06 points lower than the corresponding coefficients for income distribution (1996, 581). This mixture of the two kinds of distributions could cause some bias for regional comparisons: expenditures are used for more African countries than for Latin American, and for more Latin American countries than East or South Asian.

[4] Carmelo Mesa-Lago reviewed this estimate and explained some doubts about it but agreed that "Cuba's distribution is probably the most egalitarian in Latin America" (Mesa-Lago 1981, 144).

[5] The alternative estimate for Mexico is from Pánuco-Laguette and Székely (1996, 191). See also the questions raised about the ECLAC measures for Mexico by Wise and Pastor (1995). The alternative estimate for Venezuela is from Deininger and Squire (1996, database, 58). For other recent estimates of income distribution in Latin America see Altimir 1994 and 1996; Morley 1995, 30-31; Psacharopoulos et al. 1997; and Berry 1997.

[6] The share of the rural population with access to safe water was only 24 percent of the corresponding share for the urban population. The share of rural families with sanitary facilities was 45 percent of that for urban families. As a measure of what might be possible, the same rural/urban ratios for Costa Rica were 86 and 94 percent (UNDP 1995, 166).

[7] The original article refers to the two groups of private schools as "O-type" and "F-type." The terms "ordinary" and "prestigious" are from the summary of this study published in the World Bank *Policy and Research Bulletin* (World Bank 1992, 4).

[8] Driving from France into Spain in the 1950s, with General Franco still in charge, one could meet large signs placed to greet people coming in. Instead of the *Bienvenido* that might be expected, they informed the world that *No hay progreso sin orden*.

[9] The focus of Engerman and Sokoloff on large landholdings and dominated labor may give too bleak a picture, by leaving out the roles of indigenous communities and independent small landholders. Many

of the indigenous people living outside the haciendas maintained a considerable degree of communal cooperation and some entrepreneurial individuals were able to take on active commercial roles (Flores Galindo 1987; Stern 1987).

[10] Consistent with this interpretation, industrialization in the United States became firmly established in the North, and remained almost nonexistent in the South, from the mid-nineteenth century well into the twentieth (Krugman 1991, 10-22).

[11] Taiwan was perhaps exceptional even for East Asia in this respect; South Korea's employment growth was more concentrated in large cities. On the Latin American side, it could be illuminating to examine the relationships among countries between differences in rural education and in nonagricultural employment opportunities.

[12] In Colombia, a conservative government stopped a promising land reform process in 1973, in a style that well illustrated Engerman and Sokoloff's thesis of the self-sustaining momentum of inequality. An additional factor in other countries has been the role of the United States in supporting the overturn of governments trying to implement land reforms, from Guatemala in 1954 to a series of subsequent cases (Sheahan 1987, 340-52).

References

Ahluwalia, Montek S., Nicholas G. Carter, and Hollis B. Chenery. 1979. Growth and Poverty in Developing Countries. *Journal of Development Economics* 6: 299-341.

Altimir, Oscar. 1994. Cambios de la desigualdad y la pobreza en América Latina. *El Trimestre Económico* 61(1).

———. 1996. Economic Development and Social Equity: A Latin American Perspective. *Journal of Inter-American Studies and World Affairs* 38 (2/3): 47-71.

Barraclough, Solon. 1973. *Agrarian Structures in Latin America*. Lexington: Lexington Books.

Behrman, Jere, and Nancy Birdsall. 1983. The Quality of Schooling: Quantity Alone is Not Enough. *American Economic Review* 73(5): 928-45.

Berry, Albert. 1983. Agrarian Structure, Rural Labour Markets and Trends in Rural Incomes in Latin America. In Víctor Urquidi and Saúl Trejo, eds., *Human Resources, Employment and Development in Latin America*. New York: International Economic Association.

———. 1997. The Income Distribution Threat in Latin America. *Latin American Research Review* 32(2): 3-40.

Bird, Richard. 1992. Tax Reform in Latin America: A Review of Some Recent Experiences. *Latin American Research Review* 27 (1): 7-30.

Bird, Richard, and Guillermo Perry R. 1994. Tax Policy in Latin America: In Crisis and After. In Graham Bird and Ann Helwege, eds., *Latin America's Economic Future*, pp. 167-84. London: Academic Press.

Bourguignon, François, and Christian Morrisson. 1989. *External Trade and Income Distribution*. Paris: OECD, Development Centre Studies.

Brundenius, Claes. 1982. Development Strategies and Basic Needs in Revolutionary Cuba. In *Development Strategies and Basic Needs in Latin America*, Claes Brundenius and Mats Lundahl, eds., pp. 143-64. Boulder: Westview Press.

Bulmer-Thomas, Victor. 1994. *The Economic History of Latin America since Independence*. Cambridge: Cambridge University Press.

———. 1996. Conclusions. In Victor Bulmer-Thomas, ed., *The New Economic Model in Latin America and Its Impact on Income Distribution and Poverty*, pp. 271-314. London: St. Martin's Press.

Calvo, Guillermo A., Leonardo Leiderman, and Carmen M. Reinhart. 1993. Capital Inflows and Real Exchange Rate Appreciation in Latin America. International Monetary Fund Staff Papers 40 (1): 108-51.

Carroll, Thomas. 1961. The Land Reform Issue in Latin America. In *Latin American Issues: Essays and Comments*, Albert O. Hirschman, ed., pp. 161-201. New York: Twentieth Century Fund.

Carter, Michael R., Bradford L. Barham, and Dina Mesbah. 1996. Agricultural Export Booms and the Rural Poor in Chile, Guatemala, and Paraguay. *Latin American Research Review* 31(1): 33-65.

Chile, Ministerio de Planificación y Cooperación. 1995. Resultados Encuesta de Caracterización Socioeconómica, Casen 1994. Santiago: Ministerio de Planificación y Cooperación.

Chomsky, Aviva. 1996. *West Indian Workers and the United Fruit Company in Costa Rica, 1870-1940*. Baton Rouge: Louisiana State University Press.

Cotler, Julio. 1978. *Clases, estado, y nación en el Perú*. Lima: Instituto de Estudios Peruanos.

Deininger, Klaus, and Lyn Squire. 1996. A New Data Set Measuring Income Inequality. *World Bank Economic Review* 10-3: 565-91, and database file (internet).

Eckstein, Shlomo, et al. 1978. Land Reform in Latin America: Bolivia, Chile, Mexico, Peru, and Venezuela. World Bank Staff Working Papers no. 275.

Eckstein, Susan Eva. 1994. *Back from the Future: Cuba under Castro*. Princeton: Princeton University Press.

ECLAC (Economic Commission for Latin America and the Caribbean). 1995 and 1996. *Social Panorama of Latin America.* Santiago: ECLAC.

Engerman, Stanley L., and Kenneth L. Sokoloff. 1997. Factor Endowments, Institutions, and Differential Paths of Growth among New World Economies: A View from Economic Historians of the United States. In Stephen Haber, ed., *How Latin America Fell Behind: Essays in the Economic Histories of Brazil and Mexico, 1800-1919*, pp. 260-304. Stanford: Stanford University Press.

FAO (Food and Agriculture Organization of the United Nations). 1972, 1984. *FAO Production Yearbook, 1972, 1984.*

Ffrench-Davis, Ricardo, and Raúl Labán. 1995. Desempeño y logros macroeconómicos en Chile. In Crisóstomo Pizarro, Dagmar Raczynski and Joaquín Vial, eds., *Políticas económicas y sociales en el Chile democrático*. Santiago: CIEPLAN and UNICEF.

Flores Galindo, Alberto. 1987. *Buscando un inca. Identidad y utopía en los Andes.* Lima: Instituto de Apoyo Agrario.

Graham, Carol. 1994. *Safety Nets, Politics, and the Poor: Transitions to Market Economies.* Washington: The Brookings Institution.

Griffith-Jones, Stephany. 1996. International Capital Flows to Latin America. In Victor Bulmer-Thomas, ed., *The New Economic Model in Latin America and Its Impact on Income Distribution and Poverty.* New York: St. Martin's Press.

Hanushek, Eric A., and Dongwook Kim. 1995. Schooling, Labor Force Quality, and Economic Growth. National Bureau of Economic Research Working Paper Series no. 5399.

Helwege, Ann. 1996. Making Sense of Poverty in Latin America. Tufts University, Department of Urban and Environmental Policy (November).

Hirschman, Albert O. 1961. Ideologies of Development in Latin America. In Albert O. Hirschman, ed., *Latin American Issues: Essays and Comments.* New York: Twentieth Century Fund.

Hoff, Karla. 1996. Market Failures and the Distribution of Wealth: A Perspective from the Economics of Information. *Politics and Society* 24(4): 411-32.

IDB (Inter-American Development Bank). 1989 and 1992. *Economic and Social Progress in Latin America. 1989, 1992 Reports.* Washington: IDB.

Instituto Cuánto. 1995. *Perú en números, 1995.* Lima: Instituto Cuánto.

Instituto Cuánto y UNICEF. 1995. *Retrato de la familia peruana: niveles de vida, 1994.* Lima: Instituto Cuánto.

Interamerican Public Opinion Report. 1990. Procadop Study: Political Culture Preview. (Spring) 3.

Jiménez, Emmanuel, Marlaine Lockheed, and Vicente Paqueo. 1991. The Relative Efficiency of Private and Public Schools in Developing Countries. *World Bank Research Observer* 6 (2): 205-18.

Krugman, Paul. 1991. *Geography and Trade.* Cambridge: M.I.T. Press.

Kuznets, Simon. 1955. Economic Growth and Income Inequality. *American Economic Review* 45(1): 1-28.

Labán, Raúl, and Felipe Larraín. 1995. Continuity, Change, and the Political Economy of Transition in Chile. In *Reform, Recovery, and Growth: Latin America and the Middle East,* Rudiger Dornbusch and Sebastian Edwards, eds., pp. 115-48. Chicago: University of Chicago Press.

Londoño de la Cuesta, Juan Luis. 1995. *Distribución del ingreso y desarrollo económico: Colombia en el siglo XX*. Bogotá: Tercer Mundo con el Banco de la República y FEDESARROLLO.

———. 1996. Poverty, Inequality, and Human Capital Development in Latin America, 1950–2025. Washington: World Bank, Latin American and Caribbean Studies.

Londoño, Juan Luis, and Miguel Székely. 1997. Distributional Surprises after a Decade of Reforms: Latin America in the Nineties. Washington: IDB, Office of the Chief Economist.

Mesa-Lago, Carmelo, and Jorge Pérez-López. 1986. A Study of Cuba's Material Product System, Its Conversion to the System of National Accounts, and Estimation of Gross Domestic Product Per Capita and Growth Rates. World Bank Staff Working Paper no. 770.

Morley, Samuel A. 1995. *Poverty and Inequality in Latin America: The Impact of Adjustment in the 1980s*. Baltimore: Johns Hopkins University Press.

OIT (Oficina Regional del Trabajo). 1995. *The Employment Challenge in Latin America and the Caribbean*. Lima: Oficina Regional de la OIT para América Latina y el Caribe.

Pánuco-Laguette, Humberto, and Miguel Székely. 1996. Income Distribution and Poverty in Mexico. In Victor Bulmer-Thomas, ed., *The New Economic Model in Latin America and Its Impact on Income Distribution and Poverty*. New York: St. Martin's Press.

Papanek, Gustav F., and Oldrich Kyn. 1987. Flattening the Kuznets Curve: The Consequences for Income Distribution of Development Strategy, Government Intervention, Income and the Rate of Growth. *Pakistan Development Review* 26 (1): 1-54.

Psacharopoulos, George, et al. 1997. Poverty and Income Distribution in Latin America: The Story of the 1980s. Washington: World Bank, Technical Paper no. 351.

Psacharopoulos, George, and Harry A. Patrinos. 1993. Indigenous People and Poverty in Latin America: An Empirical Analysis. Washington: World Bank, Latin America and Caribbean Technical Department, Report no. 30.

Psacharopoulos, George, and Zafiris Tzannatos, eds. 1992. *Women's Employment and Pay in Latin America*. Washington: World Bank.

Raczynski, Dagmar. 1995. Programs, Institutions and Resources: Chile. In Dagmar Raczynski, ed., *Strategies to Combat Poverty in Latin America*. Washington: Inter-American Development Bank.

Ramos, Joseph. 1996. Poverty and Inequality in Latin America: A Neostructural Perspective. *Journal of Inter-American Studies and World Affairs* 38 (2/3): 141-57.

Ranis, Gustav, and Louise Orrock. 1985. Latin American and East Asian NICs: Development Strategies Compared. In *Latin America and the World Recession*, Esperanza Durán, ed. Cambridge: Cambridge University Press.

Robbins, Donald J. 1996a. HOS Hits Facts: Facts Win. Evidence on Trade and Wages in the Developing World. Harvard Institute for International Development, Discussion Paper 557.

————. 1996b. Stolper-Samuelson (Lost) in the Tropics? Trade Liberalization and Wages in Colombia, 1976-1994. Harvard Institute for International Development, Discussion Paper 563.

Sánchez-Albornoz, Nicolas. 1974. *The Population of Latin America: A History*. Berkeley: University of California Press.

Seers, Dudley. 1977. Urban Bias—Seers versus Lipton. Institute of Development Studies at the University of Sussex, Discussion Paper no. 116.

Seligson, Mitchell A. 1980. *Peasants of Costa Rica and the Rise of Agrarian Capitalism*. Madison: University of Wisconsin Press.

Sheahan, John. 1987. *Patterns of Development in Latin America: Poverty, Repression, and Economic Strategy*. Princeton: Princeton University Press.

————. 1997. Effects of Liberalization Programs on Poverty and Inequality: Chile, Mexico and Peru. *Latin American Research Review* 32(3): 7-37.

Stern, Steve J., ed. 1988. *Resistance, Rebellion, and Consciousness in the Andean Peasant World, 18th to 20th Centuries*. Madison: University of Wisconsin Press.

Tandeter, Enrique. 1993. *Coercion and Market: Silver Mining in Colonial Potosí, 1691-1826*. Albuquerque: New Mexico University Press.

Thiesenhusen, William C. 1989. *Searching for Agrarian Reform in Latin America*. Boston: Unwin and Hyman.

Trevor-Roper, H. R. 1967. *Religion, the Reformation, and Social Change*. London: MacMillan.

UNDP (United Nations Development Programme). 1995. *Human Development Report 1995*. New York: Oxford for the UNDP.

Urrutia, Miguel. 1981. Experience with the Crawling Peg in Colombia. In *Exchange Rate Rules*, John Williamson, ed. New York: St. Martin's Press.

————. 1985. *Winners and Losers in Colombia's Economic Growth in the 1970s*. Oxford: Oxford University Press.

Urrutia, Miguel, and Albert Berry. 1975. *La distribución del ingreso en Colombia.* Bogotá: La Carreta.

Véliz, Claudio. 1980. *The Centralist Tradition in Latin America.* Princeton: Princeton University Press.

Vicens Vives, Jaime. 1965. *Manual de la historia económica de España.* Barcelona: Ediciones Vicens Vives, 4th ed.

Webb, Richard. 1977. *Government Policy and the Distribution of Income in Peru, 1963-73.* Cambridge: Harvard University Press.

Weyland, Kurt. 1997. 'Growth with Equity' in Chile's New Democracy. *Latin American Research Review* 32(1): 37-67.

Williams, Robert. 1994. *States and Social Evolution: Coffee and the Rise of National Governments in Central America.* Chapel Hill: University of North Carolina Press.

Williamson, Jeffrey G. 1991. Inequality, Poverty, and History: The Kuznets Memorial Lectures of Yale University Economic Growth Center. Cambridge, MA: Basil Blackwell.

————. 1996. Globalization and Inequality Then and Now: The Late 19th and Late 20th Centuries Compared. NBER Working Paper Series no. 5491 (March).

Wise, Carol, and Manuel Pastor. 1995. Mexico: The Challenge of Inequality. Paper prepared for Salomon Brothers seminar, Sustainable Growth in Latin America.

Wood, Adrian. 1994. *North-South Trade, Employment, and Inequality: Changing Fortunes in a Skill-Driven World.* Oxford: Clarendon Press.

World Bank. 1980. *World Tables.* Second edition. Washington: World Bank.

————. 1982. *World Bank Policy Review Bulletin* 3(1).

————. 1983. *World Tables* 3(2). Washington: World Bank.

————. 1992 and 1997. *World Development Report 1992 and 1997.* New York: Oxford University Press for the World Bank.

CHAPTER THREE

Structural Reforms and Equity

Eduardo Lora and Juan Luis Londoño

Latin America is the area of the world where income distribution is worst, and that situation has not improved in the nineties. At the start of this decade, the number of impoverished people in the region reached an unprecedented level of nearly 150 million. Moreover, while the region's economic growth has recovered and reached 5.2 percent in 1997, rates this high have not been sustained, as they were in the sixties and seventies.

The insufficient economic and social progress of Latin American countries stands in contrast to the magnitude of the changes that have taken place in their economic policies. During the nineties, the macroeconomic stability lost after the debt crisis has been recovered. Average annual inflation has fallen to around 10 percent, and at the end of 1997, only three countries recorded an inflation rate over 20 percent. The region's fiscal deficit overall is currently around 2 percent of GDP, and only two countries have fiscal imbalances of over 5 percent of GDP.

High inflation and severe fiscal imbalances have become exceptions in the region. In the areas of structural or microeconomic policy, decisive steps have been taken to make markets operate more smoothly and reduce government interference. Restrictions on imports have been virtually eliminated, and tariffs have been cut from 41.6 percent in the prereform years to 13.7 percent at present. Financial liberalization measures have led to lifting controls on interest rates, dismantling systems of targeted credit, and lowering levels of required reserves to under 20 percent in most countries. There have been notable advances, albeit not as deep, in the area of tax simplification and modernization. Moreover, thanks to efforts by a small but important group of countries, Latin America has carried out a substantial proportion of the total amount of privatizations in the world.

This chapter will assess the magnitude of Latin America's structural reforms since the mid-eighties and analyze how they have altered the patterns of income distribution. Clearly, the reforms as a whole halted the decline in distribution apparent during the eighties, because they spurred economic growth and productivity. Although trade reform increased wage differentials, it also generated a redistribution of income from capital to labor, because it lowered the rents derived from protection and brought down the prices of ordinary consumer items. However, the reforms were not able to improve the distribution of income, let alone reduce the number of poor, because of the region's educational gaps.

The remainder of the chapter is organized as follows. The next section describes the most important advances during the past decade in the main areas of market reform. The third section reviews available evidence on the effects of the reforms on economic growth. The fourth discusses the link between macroeconomic performance and income distribution on the basis of existing empirical evidence. The fifth shows how structural reforms may alter patterns of distribution as a result of microeconomic factors, and presents some evidence on the issue. The final section summarizes the results and presents their policy implications.

The Structural Reforms

The focus of structural policies in Latin America has shifted radically since the mid-eighties.[1] The common aim of structural reforms has been to expand the scope of action and to improve the functioning of markets. Behind this aim has been the conviction that freer markets make it possible to use productive resources more efficiently. This has meant eliminating restrictions, reducing and simplifying charges, and encouraging private enterprise.

In the realm of trade, the reforms have consisted of reducing and unifying tariffs, dismantling all kinds of restrictions and permits for imports, and unifying exchange rates. Following trade liberalization programs in the Southern Cone at the end of the seventies, virtually all countries initiated large-scale programs between 1985 and 1991 to open up their trade regimes. Average tariffs dropped from levels of 41.6 percent in the prereform years to 13.7 percent in 1995, and maximum tariffs were cut from an average of 83.7 percent to 41 percent, thereby notably reducing spread (Figure 1). As of 1995, only seven countries (out of a total of 26) had average tariffs of over 15 percent (Figure 2), and only two applied maximum tariffs of over 100 percent to a small number of items. Nontariff restrictions that used to affect 37.6 percent of imports in the prereform period today cover only 6.3 percent (based on information for 11 countries).

By the mid-eighties multiple exchange rate systems had spread to most countries, and absolutely all had established restrictions on capital outflows and re-

FIGURE 1

Trade Opening in Latin America, 1985-96

(In percent)

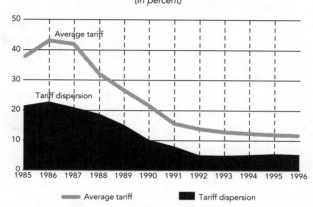

Note: The average tariff is a weighted average of the tariff averages for countries. Tariff dispersion is weighted average of the standard deviations of country tariffs.
Source: IDB, Integration and Trade Division, based on official data.

FIGURE 2

Tariff Reduction in Latin America, 1995 vs. 1986

(Net average of tariffs, in percent)

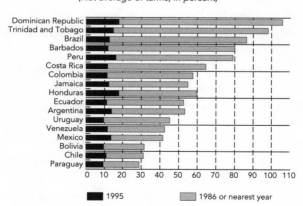

Source: IDB (1997).

quirements for repatriating export revenues. Some countries also imposed surcharges on imports and prepayment deposits. After the wave of recent exchange rate liberalizations, these restrictions have been dismantled. Today multiple exchange rates are the exception; despite the difficulties they experienced in 1995, Argentina and Mexico did not employ that device. Only Venezuela took a step backward in the exchange rate process temporarily in 1994. In 14 countries there is no longer any type of restriction on payment for current transactions, and in most of them conditions for capital transactions have been dismantled or notably softened. In some countries, current restrictions on capital movements are aimed at moderating inflows, especially those of short-term capital, but no longer at preventing capital outflows.

The financial reforms adopted in the countries of the region since the mideighties have focused on lowering or eliminating targeted credit programs, freeing interest rates, reducing reserve rate requirements, and setting up modern banking regulation systems. These reforms represent noteworthy progress toward freeing the operation of financial markets and fashioning adequate regulation systems. The following indicators summarize the stage of financial liberalization policies:

- Eighteen countries (out of 26) have completely eliminated or substantially cut targeted credit programs. Two countries have eliminated such programs and the rest have cut them by at least half.
- Fourteen countries have dismantled administrative controls on some or all deposit rates, and 17 have decontrolled lending interest rates. Currently in 18 countries, all interest rates for deposits and loans are ruled by the market and only one country still has extensive controls on interest rates.
- Required reserve ratios have been cut in 16 countries, and in 7 of them, reductions were of 20 points or more. As a result, a total of 15 countries have reserve rate requirements for cash deposits of no more than 20 percent.
- Modern systems for banking regulation and capital markets have been established in most countries in this wave of financial reforms. Currently 14 countries have regulation and supervision systems that are reasonably appropriate for the level of development of their financial sectors.

Tax policy reforms have been less deep than trade or financial liberalizations, though by no means unimportant. Their most common features have been the pursuit of neutrality, legal and administrative simplification, and greater revenues.

FIGURE 3

Maximum Tax Rate for Companies, 1995 vs. 1986

(In percent)

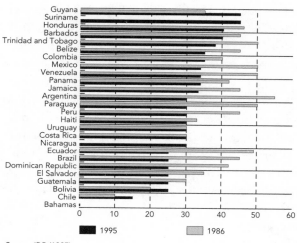

Source: IDB (1997).

Taxes on foreign trade, which in 1980 represented 29.9 percent of the taxes of the average country in the region, were partially replaced by domestic taxes, to the point where they now generate only 16.6 percent of revenue collected. In order to moderate the distorting effects of taxation on production and saving decisions, 23 countries have adopted tax and value-added systems to charge consumption. However, the collection rates on VAT are very much lower than their statutory rates, due to exclusion of many final goods and services from the tax base, and to management and oversight problems, all of which limit the neutrality of this tax. The extreme marginal rates that were formerly applied to company profits have been cut, and in only three countries are they over the highest marginal rate in the United States (39.6 percent, see Figure 3). For reasons of equity, differential rates broader than those over personal income have been maintained, although they are still lower than those in effect in previous decades (see IDB 1996 and 1997).

The scope of privatization has been remarkable, although quite uneven across the region. The 755 sales and transfers to the private sector in Latin America that occurred between 1988 and 1995 represent more than half the total value of privatization operations in developing countries.[2] Mexico and Argentina have carried out the largest privatizations, measured in the sums involved: US$27 billion and $18 billion, respectively. In comparison to the size of their economies, another seven countries have made similar privatization efforts (Figure 4), and a total of 14 countries have carried out privatizations totalling over one percent of GDP in some year. Forty-three percent of the value of privatizations in the region have taken place in utilities (traditionally closed to private participation), where the potential gains from greater productivity and efficiency are high. Another 22 percent have come from the sale of banks and similar entities, thereby bolstering trends toward financial reform.

In short, reforms have been very deep and rapid in the areas of trade and financial policy, and somewhat less complete (although still very significant in some countries) in the area of taxation and privatization. As Dani Rodrik (1996) observes, some countries in Latin America have adopted more trade and finance liberalization policies, and carried out more privatization in a short time period, than the East Asian countries have accomplished in three decades.

By contrast with the foregoing, reforms in labor regulation have been few and of lesser scope. While 23 countries (out of a total of 26) made far-reaching trade reforms, 24 appreciably decontrolled their financial sectors, and 14 carried out privatizations that in some year totaled over one percent of GDP, only six countries made significant labor reforms between the mid-eighties and 1997: Argentina (1991), Colombia (1990), Guatemala (1990), Panama (1995), Peru (1991), and Venezuela (1997).

Reforms in labor have focused on moderating costs of firing and temporary hiring of workers. Given the lack of universal social safeguard systems in most of the countries in the region, the regulations that traditionally have governed labor activity were aimed at assuring job stability and protecting workers from the risks arising from unemployment, illness, and old age, among other things. Those objectives have not always been attained, however, because such restrictions have led to excessive labor turnover, encouraged the use of informal mechanisms, and exacerbated unemployment.

In most countries in the region, dismissing a worker after one year of employment costs more than a month's wages; in six countries, at least three times that amount of compensation is required. With ten years of seniority, the costs of dismissal are even greater: at least six months' pay in most countries, and more than a year's pay in six countries (Figure 5). A common element of recent labor reforms (and some currently under discussion) is amending the regulations governing dismissal costs, with a view to reducing their amounts and/or converting severance pay into predictable annual payments.

In order to promote stable employment, 14 countries have traditionally placed restrictions on temporary hiring, severely limiting or completely forbidding this

FIGURE 4

Privatizations: Accumulated Value, 1988-95
(Percent of GDP)

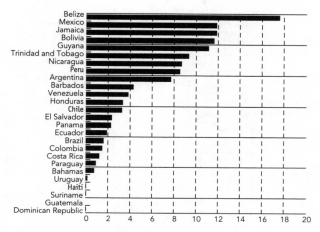

Source: IDB, based on World Bank statistics.

FIGURE 5

Dismissal Costs: Employee with
10 Years of Service, 1995 vs. 1985

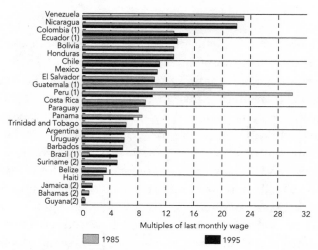

Multiples of last monthly wage

■ 1985   ■ 1995

Note: Includes notification period.
(1) The company deposits an annual sum in an account in the employee's name.
(2) Payment for dismissal negotiated between worker and company; the law does not stipulate any particular arrangement.
Source: IDB, based on information from Ministries of Labor.

FIGURE 6

Contributions to Social Security, 1995 vs. 1986

(As percent of direct wage cost)

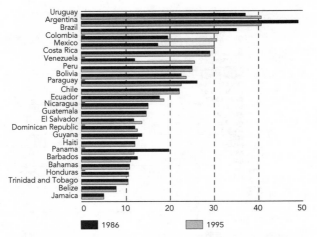

Note: Includes contributions of companies and workers to social security programs for old age, disability, death, illness and maternity, work injuries, family subsidies, and unemployment.
Source: U.S. Department of Health and Social Services, Social Security Programs Throughout the World, various issues.

type of labor relation. They were thereby restricting the labor flexibility that some companies require due to the unstable characteristics of their demand or their production processes. Only four countries (Argentina, Colombia, Ecuador, and Peru) have applied partial correctives to this situation.

In most countries in the region, nonwage costs resulting from contributions by companies and workers to programs for social security, health, family compensation, and unemployment are very high (besides other nonwage costs for contributions to education and training programs or for payments for vacations, bonuses, etc.). In Argentina, Brazil, Colombia, and Uruguay, the cost of contributions to these programs is over 30 percent of direct wage cost; in another eight countries, between 15 percent and 30 percent. Some countries have introduced correctives to this situation, either through reductions in payment rates or by tying individual contributions more closely to benefits from social security systems, thereby reducing their tax character. But in many countries greater correctives are needed to prevent protection programs from being a disincentive to formal employment (Figure 6).

The Effect of Structural Reforms on Growth

A number of studies have analyzed the effect of structural reforms on growth, investment and other economic variables. The main difficulty encountered is how to measure the magnitude of reforms. Available economic statistics deal with *outcomes*, such as growth, inflation, or foreign trade, rather than the *policies* affecting those outcomes. Indeed, variables usually regarded as policy indicators, such as the fiscal deficit or the financial depth of the economy, are actually outcome variables—influenced not only by policy decisions, but also by a variety of other internal and external phenomena, such as the business cycle, the terms of trade, or external interest rates. The lack of precise information on the magnitude of the reforms makes it difficult to assess the relative importance of various reform areas, and to distinguish between the effects of macroeconomic reforms themselves and those deriving from macroeconomic stabilization, although these kinds of reforms tend to be mutually reinforcing.

In order to remedy these lacks, Lora and Barrera (1997) constructed an index of structural policies for 19 countries in Latin America that combines a set of 16 indicators in the five reform areas summarized above (i.e., trade, financial, tax, privatizations and labor). The index only seeks to measure the neutrality of policies—the space that they grant to market decisions. This is based on the assumption that the primary objective of structural economic reforms has been to achieve greater efficiency in allocating productive resources, by eliminating or reducing distortions caused by policies that constrain the operation of markets or that impose costs on transactions or productive activities.

A simple graphic comparison between changes in the structural policy index during the past decade and changes observed in the region's economic growth suggests immediately that the structural reforms have had a decisive impact on growth (Figure 7). Where growth has accelerated most is also where the greatest advances were made in policy reform.[3] Nonetheless, the relation is not totally close (and there are some instances of growth declining despite improvement in structural policies), suggesting that other factors may have altered the pace of growth. Growth depends not only on structural policies, but also on the macroeconomic environment, the international context, and various other factors like per capita income, workforce education level, income distribution, and the quality of government institutions. The influence of these factors has been examined extensively in research covering the performance of a wide range of countries over relatively long time periods.[4]

FIGURE 7

Changes in Growth and Structural Reforms, 1993/95 vs. 1987/89
(Percent change in growth rate)

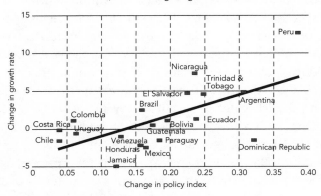

Source: Lora and Barrera (1997).

For Latin American countries as a group in the past decade, Lora and Barrera (1997) found that economic growth has depended very significantly on the macro-economic environment (measured in terms of the level and volatility of inflation) and on the education level of the workforce. Separating the influence of these factors in a sample of 19 countries, they estimated that the region's structural reforms over the last decade increased permanent growth rates by 1.9 points and macro-economic stabilization by 0.3 points, for a combined estimate of 2.2 points. By means of a structural policy index they used containing indicators by reform areas, the authors were able to calculate the contributions to growth from each one of these areas. According to their results, trade reform has been the area with the greatest impact, with a contribution of 1.1 points to the rate of growth of the region. That is so not only because in this area reforms have advanced farthest, but also because trade distortions severely diminish economic efficiency, as has been amply documented.[5] Finance reform has also had a considerable effect on permanent growth, an effect estimated at 0.5 points.

Easterly, Loayza, and Montiel (1997) calculated the combined effect of structural reforms and stabilization at between 1.9 and 2.2 points for 16 countries in the region, included in a worldwide panel of 70 countries. These authors used a variety of policy outcome indicators, and on the basis of the relationship between these outcomes and growth in their world panel, deduced the combined effect that would be expected from stabilization and reforms in Latin American countries. Using a world panel, they also determined whether Latin America's rise in economic growth in 1991–93 (as compared with 1986–90) was above or below what would be expected, given the stabilization and reforms (and other determinants of growth). They concluded that the expansion observed in growth was not different from what would be expected, and that if growth has not been greater, the reason is that the reforms have not been deeper and the external context of the nineties has been unfavorable.

Fernández-Arias and Montiel (1997) extended the work of Easterly, Loayza, and Montiel up to 1995 (for 69 countries, 18 of them Latin American), including as an explanatory variable for Latin America the structural policy index constructed by Lora and Barrera. For the average of countries considered, they found that the effect of stabilization and the reforms was that the growth rate rose by from 1.6 to 1.9 points between 1986–90 and 1991–95. They reaffirmed that Latin America's performance is what would be expected on the basis of international experience, given the depth achieved thus far in the stabilization and reform process.

The three studies calculate the combined effects of stabilization and structural reforms on the individual growth rates of the countries (see Table 1). The estimates of Fernández-Arias and Montiel, and of Lora and Barrera, resemble each other more than those of Easterly, Loayza and Montiel, because the first two use the same structural policy index. The results of the latter study are more influenced by variables connected to macro stabilization, and that may explain the differences in the estimates for Argentina and Brazil.

Therefore, these studies consistently indicate that without the reforms adopted throughout Latin America during the last decade, instead of the mean growth rate of 3.8 percent observed in recent years, average rates of only 1.5 to 2 percent a year would have been attained. The structural reforms thus prevented per capita income, which fell in the first half of the eighties, from continuing to decline.

Macroeconomic Determinants of Income Inequality in Latin America

Latin America is the region of the world where income is distributed most unfairly.[6] The average of the Gini coefficients of the countries of the region is 0.56, more than 15 points higher than that of developed countries or of Southeast Asian countries, and comparable only to the average of African countries. After distribution worsened in the eighties, and despite economic recovery, equity and poverty did not show much progress in the nineties. The poorest 20 percent of the overall population receives only 3 percent of total income, while at the other extreme the

Table 1. Change in Annual Growth Rates due to Stabilization and Reforms
(In percent)

	Easterly, Loayza and Montiel (1997) 1991-93 vs. 1986-90	Fernández-Arias and Montiel (1997) 1991-95 vs. 1986-90	Lora and Barrera (1997) 1993-95 vs. 1987-89
Argentina	6.3	3.1	4.1
Bolivia	3.3	0.9	1.9
Brazil	-0.3	1.4	2.2
Chile	0.9	0.3	0.3
Colombia	0.6	0.7	1.0
Costa Rica	0.7	1.2	0.8
Ecuador	0.3	2.2	3.8
El Salvador	2.9	2.3	2.9
Guatemala	2.1	2.6	2.3
Honduras	1.4	2.1	1.4
Jamaica		1.8	0.0
Mexico	3.4	1.7	1.0
Paraguay	1.7	1.5	2.7
Peru	5.3	4.1	6.6
Trinidad and Tobago		2.8	2.1
Uruguay	1.4	0.8	1.2
Venezuela	1.3	1.5	2.1
Typical country *(simple average)*	2.2	1.6	2.2
Typical country *(weighted average)*	1.7	1.7	2.2

wealthiest 20 percent holds 60 percent, the same proportion as in the early seventies (Figure 8). Something similar has happened with poverty. The percentage of poor people has remained steady at slightly over 35 percent of the total population of the region since the end of the past decade, after a period of deterioration that began with the debt crisis. At that time the number of poor people had fallen below 90 million; since 1990, it has fluctuated at around 150 million people, more than at any time in the two previous decades (Figure 9). Changes in distribution and poverty have also varied widely between countries. Disparities between countries showed some tendency to increase: the most pronounced improvements occurred in countries with better initial distributions, such as Uruguay and Jamaica, while some with poor initial distributions, like Brazil, Guatemala, and Panama, became even worse (Figure 10).

FIGURE 8

Inequality in Latin America, 1970-95

(Gini coefficient)

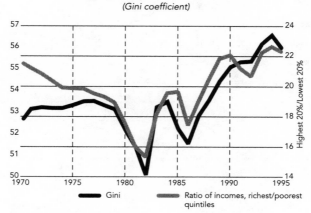

Source: Londoño and Székely (1997).

FIGURE 9

Poverty in Latin America, 1970-95

(Number of persons, in millions)

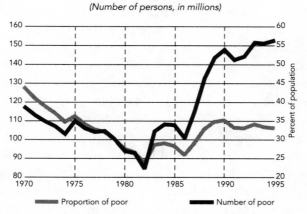

Source: Londoño and Székely (1997).

FIGURE 10

Inequality in Latin America, 1985-95

(Gini coefficient)

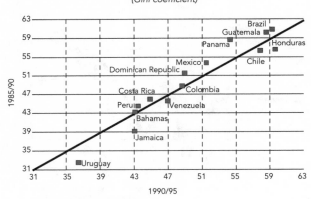

Note: Uruguay data is urban only.
Source: Londoño and Székely (1997).

Work by Londoño and Székely (1997) shows that the high inequality of income in Latin America has its origins in the level and composition of its productive resources and in the way that they are distributed. In comparison with other regions of the world (and taking into account the differences in the level of development of the economies), Latin America has approximately the same relative amounts of physical capital, and is more abundant in natural resources but poorer in human capital. Such conditions are generally associated with greater income concentration. Exploiting natural resources generates rents that go to a few hands, with little employment and as a rule, with few incentives to create new productive activities. Relatively low education levels are an even more important cause of inequality. The relationship between education and inequality is not linear, because at very low education levels the scant income generated is relatively well distributed. Greater concentration of income tends to occur when the average level of education is between 5 and 6 years, precisely the levels that are characteristic of Latin America.

The way the ownership of productive assets is distributed is as important for income distribution as the relationship between the amounts of some assets and others. In this regard as well, Latin America is at a disadvantage. In the countries of the region, ownership of natural resources, and of education in particular, is very concentrated. This means that the economic growth and the new economic opportunities that it brings with it are not spread equally to all population groups, and that in extreme cases they even tend to intensify concentration.

In comparison with Southeast Asian countries, the greater income concentration in Latin America is due especially to the relative abundance of natural resources and poor distribution of land and education. In comparison with Europe, the most important difference is the low accumulation of physical and human capital, although the other factors also have some weight.

Because these structural factors change very slowly over time, the structural reforms should not be expected to have a pronounced effect on income distribution. But that explanation is incomplete, because macroeconomic fluctuations (together with other factors) can produce important changes in income distribution. Sustained growth over time changes the relative remunerations of the productive factors and enables new income and mobility opportunities to appear. In the short run, economic cycles may have more than a proportionate effect on the more vulnerable groups that do not have ways to stabilize their incomes. Londoño and Székely (1997) analyzed these hypotheses for a group of 12 countries in Latin America during the 1970–1995 period. Their results show that income inequality in Latin America has changed according to the pace of the accumulation of physical and human capital. Increased investment of between four and five points of GDP has been associated with a one-point decline in the Gini coefficient; and a one-year increase in average education (above what is expected for the level of development) is associated with a reduction of the Gini coefficient of over two points.

Income distribution has also been associated with the permanent growth rate. Although the statistical relationship is not very strong, greater long-run growth rates are related to lower levels of inequality in Latin America. (This implies that the region is already on the far side of the Kuznets inverted U, which postulates that distribution tends to worsen during earlier states of economic development and to improve later.)

On the other hand, during temporary economic boom cycles the poor have benefited more than the wealthy. An expansion of income 5 percent above their permanent level has tended to improve the Gini coefficient by 2 points. By the same token, recessions have been very inequitable.

High inequality in education, however, has conditioned the impact of accumulation on income distribution. Greater inequality in education has brought with it greater income concentration. But there has also been an indirect effect. Educational inequity has limited the distributive effect of the accumulation of physical capital. In those countries with greater concentration of education, increased in-

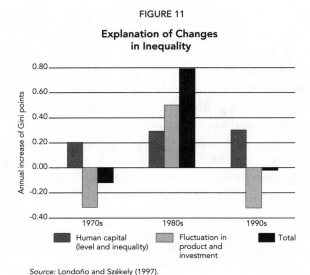

FIGURE 11

**Explanation of Changes
in Inequality**

Source: Londoño and Székely (1997).

vestment has worsened income distribution, possibly because it has increased the benefit of education, which is scarce, and reduced the need for unskilled labor.

The interaction of these factors explains the notable worsening of income distribution in Latin America since the 1970s. Physical investment rates have fallen from a 29 percent average in the seventies to 22 percent since the debt crisis. Education has gone backward, and currently the workforce in Latin America has an average of two years less schooling than it should have for its level of development (and four years less than Southeast Asian countries, discounting the differences attributable to income levels). Moreover, education in Latin America is increasingly concentrated. In the seventies these structural tendencies were combined with a cycle of economic expansion, resulting in slightly improved distribution. The recession of the eighties had the effect of reinforcing all the factors that cause deterioration, producing an abrupt increase in concentration. The recovery of growth and investment in the nineties has compensated for the concentrated effect of the lack of education and its poor distribution, but it has not been enough to produce an improvement (Figure 11).

As we have seen, the structural reforms had a positive effect on growth (and on investment, another source of growth; see Lora and Barrera 1997). They might also be expected to affect income distribution favorably. In fact, during the past decade, changes in income distribution in Latin American countries reflect the influence of the structural and macroeconomic variables in directions that would be expected: greater rates of economic growth or investment have been translated into improvements in income distribution.[7] The direction of these relationships has not been altered by the structural changes.

Microeconomic Distributional Effects of Structural Reforms

Aside from their impact on growth and investment, the structural reforms may also change income distribution as a result of microeconomic factors, or more precisely, through changes in relative prices, remuneration, and chances for employment of some groups as opposed to others. These kinds of redistributions are observed most quickly and may give rise to fears of the distributional effects of the reforms. But the redistributive effects of the reforms are quite diverse and it is difficult to predict their direction. In order to appreciate how complex the matter is, one may consider the following likely consequences of reforms:

Trade Reform. Fears that trade reform worsens income distribution tend to be based on one of the following arguments: (1) increasing imports means displacing national production and employment (at least temporarily), (2) the opening cheapens luxury consumption goods as opposed to mass consumer items, or (3) the opening makes it possible to introduce capital-intensive production technologies that require more trained labor, but lower the demand for unskilled labor. In the opposite direction are the following arguments. First, the opening stimulates export development in those goods that intensively utilize the most abundant resources, especially unskilled labor (nevertheless, if exports are natural resource–intensive, concentration may possibly increase). Second, the opening eliminates the rents that favor importers and protected national producers, who are on the higher income levels. Third, reduction of tariffs and protection on mass consumer goods improve the purchasing capacity of low-income groups. Fourth, the opening broadens investment, production, and employment opportunities to the benefit of groups marginalized from economic activity in the previous situation.

Finance Reform. Financial liberalization may translate into greater income concentration in several ways: (1) liberalization of interest rates may raise the real yield on savings in the financial system which are held by high-income groups, (2) broadening the credit supply and lowering margins of financial services make capital cheaper, facilitating the adoption of capital-intensive technologies to the detriment of labor demand, (3) dismantling targeted credit programs may harm the popular sectors served by such programs, or (4) new financing possibilities may favor those families and businesses that already control the financial groups. Whether or not such effects actually take place will depend on the characteristics of the financial sector and the manner in which the liberalization and regulation process is carried out. Ideally, financial reform can lead to extending the credit supply to sectors formerly excluded, improving competition within the financial sector, moderating the margins between deposit rates and lending rates, and reducing the monopolistic profits of the financial groups.

Tax Reform. Simplification of tax systems can bring about regressive effects in income distribution. This is because: (1) marginal tax rates are lowered for higher-income segments and businesses; (2) value-added taxes are adopted, and they tax less those who save more (higher-income groups); (3) tax exemptions for goods in the basket of basic goods are eliminated, and the rates of the specific tax on luxury consumption are lowered; and (4) special treatments are ended for low-profit or high job-creation businesses or activities, such as agriculture or certain industrial sectors. In the opposite direction, the reforms may be progressive for several reasons. First, simpler systems cut opportunities for evasion (which favor higher-income groups more) and reduce those exemptions and special treatments that favor more influential groups. Second, the adoption of broader bases for taxes on consumption or income avoids imposing greater taxes on certain easier-to-monitor groups, such as wage earners, who are not necessarily the most wealthy. Third, insofar as they encourage investment, more neutral tax systems favor the creation of new job opportunities and stimulate competition.

Privatizations. This may be the reform area that has aroused the greatest resistance for distribution reasons. Although the arguments often presented mistakenly assume that state property is the same as property of the people (and hence redistributive) there are reasons to fear that privatization may worsen income distribution, because: (1) with privatizations, subsidies to public services, which are sometimes truly redistributive, normally disappear; (2) privatization may grant monopoly power to the new companies, who then reap extraordinary profits; (3) privatized companies in utilities may not have incentives to serve the demand from the popular sectors or rural areas; and (4) privatization generally means massive layoffs of employees. As in the case of financial reform, whether or not such things take place depends on factors specific to each country. For other reasons, however, privatization may be redistributive. First, it replaces subsidies on rates, which even if differentiated by income groups, would grant larger total subsidy amounts to those who consume more, namely higher-income groups. Second, privatization tends to introduce competition and efficiency into antiquated companies that previously generated losses at taxpayer expense and provided poor services, especially to popular sectors and to groups unable to exert pressure. Third, privatization stimulates investment in the privatized companies and in other related sectors, compensating for jobs lost as redundant with others that are more productive.

Labor reform. Concern for distribution may have been one of the obstacles to labor reforms in Latin America. Making labor more flexible may reduce real remunerations of permanent workers, may increase their risk of being left unemployed, and may reduce economic protection against illness or old age. However, it is not obvious that any labor reform has to produce such results, and even less that if they do take place they worsen income distribution. Lower unemployment rates are typical of countries with more flexible labor markets, (which depends not only on legislation but on other institutional characteristics proper to each country). More rigid labor legislation provides protection and high incomes only to groups that are not poor while limiting the possibilities for job creation and tending to depress the incomes of temporary workers, the self-employed, and the rural classes. Rigid labor codes may prompt governments to take steps to make labor more flexible on the margins, thereby reducing protection for the more vulnerable groups. For example, making temporary jobs more flexible or an excessive erosion of the minimum wage may help alleviate unemployment but it can have adverse effects on groups of poor workers who lack in bargaining power.

Many of these distributive effects of structural reforms cannot be quantified because the usual indicators of concentration are based on pretax monetary incomes, rather than the incomes received by households. Hence they do not register changes in the incomes that are not received by households, such as earnings withheld by companies. Nor do they register changes in taxation on income (although they do on indirect taxation, which is reflected in prices of consumer goods), nor in nonmonetary subsidies received by households (for example, through free or heavily subsidized education). Because they refer solely to income, the usual indicators of concentration do not take into account the distributive effects of changes in the price of assets (real estate, equipment or financial assets). It is not surprising that there is no conclusive evidence on the distributional impact of the reforms.

In the case of trade reform, where most of the distributional effects do take place through incomes and the relative prices of goods, it is possible to come to more precise conclusions. In 13 countries analyzed by Londoño and Székely (1997) during the 1985–95 period, the adoption of trade liberalization policies was found to be associated significantly with faster growth of the real incomes of the poorest 60 percent of the population and with a *decline* of the real revenues of the wealthiest

20 percent. The effect is highly progressive, since the greatest relative increases have occurred in the lowest income quintile.

The redistributive effect of trade liberalizations found by Londoño and Székely may seem to run contrary to conventional wisdom. Numerous studies of the effects of trade liberalization on wage differentials have concluded that in Latin America since the eighties, increase in international trade has coincided with a rise in demand and returns to skilled labor, relative to unskilled labor, implying unfavorable distribution effects.[8] However, recent international studies indicate that the increase in wage differentials is not limited to Latin America, but has occurred almost everywhere, not only in countries that have opened up to international trade.[9] Most studies credit recent technological change as the most important factor causing changes in the wage structure. The incorporation into international markets of labor-abundant countries, such as China, India and Indonesia, is considered an additional factor.[10]

On the other hand, though empirical evidence on the rise of urban skilled wages is quite solid, this is no proof that trade liberalization increases global income inequality. Wages are only a part of home incomes, and not a majority in the aggregate. Trade liberalization can generate changes in the relative prices of all factors of production, not only of wage labor. It can also induce a resource reallocation in the economy, promote the adoption of different technologies, and modify relative prices of basic consumption goods. The joint effect of all these changes on total income distribution has not yet been clearly established.

Recent research has found that the relationship between trade liberalization and income distribution is far from straightforward. The most complete study is that of Bourguignon and Morrisson (1989 and 1990). Based on a model where income distribution depends on factor endowment and openness, they conclude that the evidence does not support the hypothesis of greater liberalization corresponding to greater inequality. Recently, Edwards (1997) confirms the lack of a systematic relationship between changes in income distribution and openness by utilizing an array of indicators for the latter.

In short, even though trade liberalization seems to have coincided with an increase in the relative wages of skilled urban workers, trade liberalization effects on total income distribution are more complex, and influenced by the countries' relative factor endowments, by global technology changes and by recomposition of world trade patterns. While empirical research continues, the existence of a simple relationship between trade liberalization and worsening income distribution is the only hypothesis that is strongly rejected.

Where Do We Go From Here?

The structural reforms adopted in Latin America during the past decade have helped spur economic growth and halt the trends toward worsening income distribution and increasing poverty. But they have not been sufficient for attaining the levels of growth and social equity that society would regard as acceptable. Part of the reason has been that market reforms have been incomplete. According with Lora and Barrera (1997), a deepening of the reforms would bring the growth rates of those countries that still have low growth rates to levels near or above 5 percent. Even so, in most instances market reforms would not make it possible to reach the sustained growth rates attained by Southeast Asian countries, and in a few countries growth would not even be 5 percent. Nor would the structural reforms suffice to resolve the serious problems of social inequity in Latin America; at best, they can prevent them from becoming worse. The deepest causes of this injustice lie in the slow accumulation of human capital and in the way markets and institutions reproduce the existing patterns of distribution of physical assets and education. Hence, an economic and social policy agenda for Latin America must contain action strategies that tend to deepen market reforms, accelerate the accumulation of human capital and broaden the range of tools for pursuing equity.

Market reforms have not advanced evenly in all areas or among the various countries. Although trade reforms are well advanced, further progress can be achieved by continuing to even out and harmonize tariffs. In the area of finance, liberalization measures have advanced much more quickly than efforts to improve regulatory and supervisory systems. In the tax field, there are large vacuums in administration and collection, especially in income taxes and in broadening the bases of the value-added tax. Privatization has moved along very unevenly from one country to another, and hence there are varying amounts of room in all fields, from the sale of enterprises in the industrial and financial sectors in some countries, to setting up stable systems and institutions for private sector participation in all kinds of infrastructure. Finally, the greatest potential is found in the area of labor legislation, where recent reforms have been meager despite the rigidities that hinder job creation in the region.[11]

But improving the quality of macroeconomic and structural policies would only make it possible to increase the average rate of growth to around 5.5 percent and to maintain approximately the current levels of income inequality in Latin America. The primary further constraint hindering the region's growth rates from rising higher and inequality from declining sharply is the educational level of the

FIGURE 12

Workforce Education, 1970-95
(Average years of schooling)

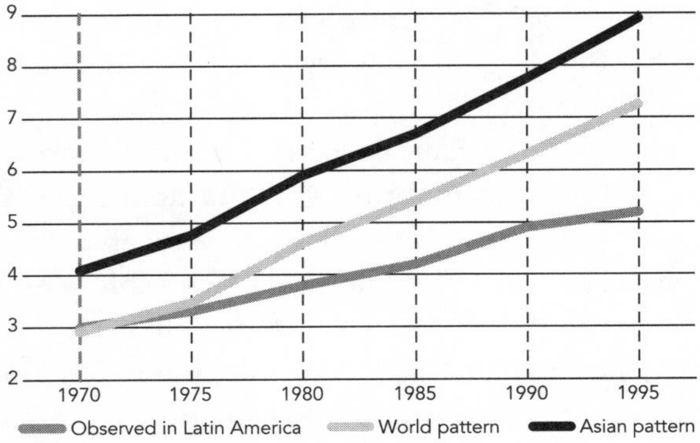

Observed in Latin America   World pattern   Asian pattern

Source: Londoño and Székely (1997).

workforce. The average level of schooling of the workforce in Latin America has risen in the nineties by a 0.9 percent annual rate and is currently at 5.3 years on average. This rate is much lower than it was in the sixties (1.6 percent), and lower than the ongoing rate for the rapidly growing economies. For example, the four Asian tigers (Korea, Taiwan, Singapore, and Hong Kong), have registered education growth rates of around 3 percent in a sustained way for three decades. The result of slow growth of education in Latin America is that its workforce now has two years less schooling than it should have according to world patterns and its own level of development.[12] (Figure 12).

Greater educational levels of the labor force would make it possible to accelerate economic growth and would notably reduce income concentration in Latin America. It is feasible to raise the educational level of the workforce one year every decade above the rate at which it is currently tending to grow. This would mean reaching an average schooling level of 6.8 years by the year 2007 and a level of 8.8 years by the year 2017, instead of the 5.8 and 6.8 years, respectively, that may be expected with current trends. In the next ten years, this additional effort in education would make it possible to raise by one point the rate of income growth and to initiate a declining trend in inequality. The gradual incorporation of the more educated population into the workforce would subsequently bear increasing fruit, until it generated a reduction of the Gini coefficient by approximately five points by the year 2017.

The major obstacle to attaining this objective is not fiscal. In fact, education spending in the region in the nineties (leaving out pension payments for teachers) has risen by 0.5 percent of GDP on average, enough to finance the proposed increases of education.[13] The main challenge is the education system in order to obtain better results in terms of coverage and quality with those resources. Latin America's education systems are typically overcentralized in terms of finance, labor, management, and academic administration. This organization may offer some advantages, but does not guarantee the most efficient or equitable use of resources and does not encourage educational innovation or improvements in school management. Centralized administration of schools also makes it harder to adapt curricula to the students' needs and abilities, and discourages communities and parents from participating in the schools. Although the organization of education is not the only factor that must be taken into account in order to deal with the educational challenge in Latin America, it is indeed an area of immediate priority.[14]

The combination of deeper market reforms and an ambitious education policy would make it possible to eliminate the extra inequality that Latin America currently displays in comparison with worldwide patterns. But such achievements would still be insufficient for reaching the levels of equity of European or Southeast Asian countries. A new generation of public policies is required to change the distribution patterns of physical and social assets much more profoundly. Efforts should be addressed at restructuring factor markets and redesigning public institutions with the aim of improving access of the poor to government services and to decisionmaking bodies.

During the past decade public policies have been intended primarily to remove the distortions preventing markets of goods from functioning. Less attention has been paid to improving the functioning of factor markets, and in particular to broadening and democratizing access to productive resources. Policy actions for restructuring factor markets should include labor and financial reforms. Labor codes should be reformed with the aim of not only improving efficiency but of correcting the inequitable segmentation currently characterizing labor markets, and of offering protection to workers, especially at lower income levels. Financial reforms must include the design and implementation of mechanisms for evaluating and monitoring the credit risks of small borrowers and the strengthening of mortgage financing systems whose foundations were eroded away in some countries by years of inflation and inadequate financial policies.

Not only markets have an impact on inequality of income and opportunity in Latin America. Inequitable access to government services and to the decisionmaking bodies in government and other public institutions also influence the characteristics and persistence of inequality.

Latin America's fiscal volatility has been reduced to levels comparable to those of developed countries. Nevertheless, the fiscal structures that would make social spending an instrument of social protection against business cycles have not been built. In many countries the allocation of resources for social programs is determined on the basis of tax revenues, and their behavior reflects the business cycle. In order to serve as a protective mechanism, social spending ought to be independent of the business cycle, except for items such as unemployment insurance, where it must increase during the downswing, as is the case in developed countries.

Market reforms may have significantly reduced the volatility of the most important macroeconomic variables (IDB 1997, Part Two), but they have not necessarily reduced the ranks of the unemployed or improved the uncertain incomes of specific population groups. Latin America is behind in developing social insurance institutions to protect these groups in the framework of market reforms (Rodrik 1997). Neither the welfare state as found in European countries, nor protection through stable employment (common among Southeast Asian countries), can be appropriate models for Latin American countries. The new institutions should not jeopardize fiscal stability or encourage segmentation of labor markets, for both cause deeper inequities that are difficult to correct, as the region's experience has shown.

Finally, Latin America must develop institutions for handling social conflicts. In the absence of such institutions, economic transformations, such as those wrought by structural reforms or external shocks from prices or technology, are difficult to absorb, and their recessionary and regressive effects tend to be prolonged and to extend unnecessarily. The corporative tradition of some countries of the region has led to the exclusion of many social groups from the negotiating and collective decisionmaking process, where usually only companies that belong to major business associations and formal workers tied to labor federations are represented. Collective bargaining mechanisms in labor are likewise inadequate in many countries, especially when they are industry-wide, because they do not take into account the variety of conditions in companies and the different kinds of workers involved. The weakness and lack of credibility of judicial institutions in some countries of the regions are a further hindrance to resolving individual conflicts.

Endnotes _____

[1] The synthesis of reform that follows is based on IDB (1996 and 1997). Burki and Perry (1997) and Edwards (1995) also provide detailed accounts of the reform process and a wide battery of reform indicators.

[2] Excluding those made by massive distribution of coupons in East European countries.

[3] Not surprisingly, the major reformers, such as Peru or Nicaragua, were the countries whose initial structural policies were more deficient, while countries like Chile and Colombia, which started with better policies, implemented little additional reform.

[4] See Asian Development Bank (1997), Barro (1997), Barro and Sala-i-Martin (1995) and Sachs and Warner (1995).

[5] See, in particular, Dollar (1992) and Sachs and Warner (1995).

[6] Calculations of Londoño and Székely (1997), based on data from Deininger and Squire (1996).

[7] For evidence, see IDB (1997), Part Two, Appendix 4.

[8] For Argentina, see Pessino (1995 and 1997); for Chile, Robbins (1994 and 1995a); for Colombia, Cárdenas and Gutiérrez (1997); for Mexico, Cragg and Epelbaum (1996) and Revenga (1995); and for Peru, Saavedra (1997).

[9] An excellent summary is found in Burtless (1995), and research by Robbins (1996), Wood (1995), Freeman and Katz (1995), Borjas and Ramey (1995), and Slaughter and Swagel (1997).

[10] See, in particular, Wood (1997), who has also sustained this hypothesis for the United States and other developed economies (Wood 1994).

[11] A more detailed policy agenda on structural reforms can be found in IDB (1997), Part Two.

[12] See Londoño (1996).

[13] Londoño (1996) calculated that it would be necessary to raise 1990 education spending by this amount in order to move up one year in education by the year 2000.

[14] A detailed discussion of policy guidelines to the reform of the educational sector can be found in IDB (1996), Part Three.

References

Asian Development Bank. 1997. *Emerging Asia: Changes and Challenges*. Manila.

Atkinson, Anthony. 1997. Bringing Income Distribution in from the Cold. *Economic Journal* (March).

Barro, Robert J. 1997. *Determinants of Economic Growth*. Cambridge, MA: MIT Press.

Barro, Robert J., and Xavier Sala-i-Martin. 1995. *Economic Growth*. New York: McGraw-Hill.

Borjas, G.J., and V.A. Ramey. 1995. Foreign Competition, Market Power and Wage Inequality. *Quarterly Journal of Economics* 110(4).

Bourguignon, François, and Christian Morrisson. 1989. *External Trade and Income Distribution*. Development Center Studies. Paris: OECD.

———. 1990. Income Distribution, Development and Foreign Trade: A Cross-Sectional Analysis. *European Economic Review* 34(6), September.

Burky, Shahid Javed, and Guillermo Perry. 1997. *The Long March: A Reform Agenda for Latin America and the Caribbean in the Next Decade*. Washington, D.C.: The World Bank.

Burtless, Gary. 1995. International Trade and the Rise of Income Inequality. *Journal of Economic Literature* 33(2), June.

Cárdenas, Mauricio. 1997. *Empleo y distribución del ingreso en América Latina: ¿Hemos avanzado?* Bogotá: TM Editores-FEDESARROLLO-CIID-Colciencias.

Cárdenas, Mauricio, and Catalina Gutiérrez. 1997. Impacto de las Reformas Estructurales sobre la Eficiencia y la Equidad, in Cárdenas (1997).

Cragg, Michael Ian, and Mario Epelbaum. 1994. The Premium for Skills: Evidence from Mexico, mimeo, Columbia University.

———. 1996. Why has wage dispersion grown in Mexico? Is it the incidence of reforms or the growing demand for skills? *Journal of Development Economics* 51: 99–116.

Dollar, David. 1992. Outward-Oriented Development Economies Really Do Grow More Rapidly: Evidence from 95 LDCs, 1976–1985. *Economic Development and Cultural Change* 40(3): 523–544.

Easterly, William, Norman Loayza, and Peter Montiel. 1997. Has Latin America's Post-Reform Growth Been Disappointing? Washington, D.C.: World Bank and Williams College. Forthcoming in *Journal of International Economics*.

Edwards, Sebastian. 1995. *Crisis and Reform in Latin America*. Oxford: Oxford University Press.

————. 1997. Trade Policy, Growth and Income Distribution. *American Economic Review Papers and Proceedings* 87(2).

Fernández-Arias, Eduardo, and Peter Montiel. 1997. Reform and Growth in Latin America: All Pain, No Gain? Inter-American Development Bank. Paper presented to the 38th Annual Meeting of the Board of Governors of the IDB, Barcelona, March, 1997.

Freeman, Richard, and Lawrence Katz. 1995. *Differences and Changes in Wage Structures*. NBER/ The University of Chicago Press.

Goldin, Claudia, and Lawrence Katz. 1996. Technology, Skills and the Wage Structure. *American Economic Review* 86(2), May.

Gottschald, Peter, and Timothy Smeeding. 1996. Cross-national Comparisons of Earnings and Income Inequality. *Journal of Economic Literature* 34(2), June.

IDB (Inter-American Development Bank). 1996. *Economic and Social Progress in Latin America, 1996 Report*. Washington, D.C.: IDB.

————. 1997. *Economic and Social Progress in Latin America, 1997 Report*. Washington, D.C. (Part II, Appendix 4).

Londoño, Juan Luis. 1996. Pobreza, desigualdad y formación del capital humano en América Latina, 1950–2025. World Bank, Washington, D.C.

Londoño, Juan Luis, and Miguel Székely. 1997. Distributional Surprises After a Decade of Reforms: Latin America in the Nineties. Inter-American Development Bank. Paper presented to the 38th Annual Meeting of the Board of Governors of the IDB, Barcelona, March, 1997.

Lora, Eduardo, and Felipe Barrera. 1997. A Decade of Structural Reforms in Latin America: Measurement and Growth Effects. Inter-American Development Bank. Mimeo.

Pessino, Carola. 1995. Returns to Education in Greater Buenos Aires 1986–1993: From Hyperinflation to Stabilization. Serie Documentos de Trabajo 104. Buenos Aires: Argentina. CEMA.

————. 1997. Argentina: The Labor Market during the Economic Transition, in Sebastian Edwards and Nora Lustig (eds.), *Labor Markets in Latin America. Combining Social Protection with Market Flexibility*. Washington D.C.: The Brookings Institution.

Revenga, Ana. 1995. Employment and Wage Effects of Trade Liberalization. The Case of Mexican Manufacturing. Policy Research Working Paper 1524, World Bank.

Robbins, Donald. 1994. Relative Wage Structure in Chile, 1957–1992: Changes in the Structure of Demand for Schooling. *Estudios de Economía*, 21: 49–78.

————. 1995a. Earnings Dispersion in Chile after Trade Liberalization. Harvard Institute for International Development, Cambridge, MA. Unpublished mimeo.

————. 1995b. Trade, Trade Liberalization and Inequality in Latin America and East Asia: Synthesis of Seven Country Studies. Harvard Institute for International Development, Cambridge, MA. Unpublished mimeo.

————. 1996. HOS Hits Facts: Facts Win—Evidence on Trade and Wage Inequality in the Developing World. Mimeo, Harvard Institute for International Development.

Rodrik, Dani. 1996. Understanding Economic Policy Reform. *Journal of Economic Literature* 34: 9–41.

————. 1997. *Has Globalization Gone Too Far?* Washington, D.C.: Institute for International Economics.

Saavedra, Jaime. 1997. Calificación, salarios y distribución del ingreso en un contexto de ajuste estructural: El caso del Perú urbano, in Cárdenas (1997).

Sachs, Jeffrey D., and Andrew Warner. 1995. Economic Reform and the Process of Global Integration. *Brookings Papers on Economic Activity* 1: 1–95.

Slaughter, Matthew, and Phillip Swagel. 1997. The Effect of Globalization on Wages in the Advanced Economies. Working Paper, International Monetary Fund, Washington, D.C.

Wood, Adrian. 1994. *North-South Trade, Employment and Inequality: Changing Fortunes in a Skill-Driven World.* Oxford: Clarendon Press.

————. 1995. How Trade Hurt Unskilled Workers. *Journal of Economic Perspectives* 9(3).

————. 1997. Openness and Wage Inequality in Developing Countries: The Latin American Challenge to East Asian Conventional Wisdom. *The World Bank Economic Review* 11(1): 33–57.

CHAPTER FOUR

Growth with Equity: The Volatility Connection

Michael Gavin and Ricardo Hausmann

The measures required to maintain economic stability are generally viewed as separate from, or even conflicting with, the goals of accelerated growth and more equal income distribution.[1] Such compartmentalized thinking may be practical in response to a crisis, when long-term considerations necessarily recede in priority. Even so, advocates of the fiscal and monetary discipline required to promote macroeconomic stability are sometimes faulted for their inattention to the plight of the poor.

Having said that, it is now widely recognized that very high inflation is detrimental to growth, and harms the poor above all.[2] Latin America's inflation stabilization of the 1990s was clearly the prerequisite condition for achieving higher growth rates and a more equitable distribution of income. Inflation stabilization is not the end of the story, however. The region's unstable economic environment not only triggered high rates of inflation, but also led to enormous variability and unpredictability in other dimensions, including output and employment, the real exchange rate, the terms of trade, fiscal balances and monetary aggregates.

Thus despite the approach of low fiscal deficits and single-digit inflation, in many other respects Latin America remains a volatile region. Addressing this unresolved problem of macroeconomic volatility presents an opportunity for a win-win strategy as important as that of the inflation stabilization of the 1990s.

The argument for such a strategy begins with the proposition that macroeconomic volatility, measured as the variability of key macroeconomic policies and outcomes, undercuts economic growth. There is also compelling evidence that volatility worsens the distribution of income. And in terms of both growth and inequality, volatility has taken an enormous toll on Latin America: its more volatile environment accounts for roughly a quarter of the difference in distribution of income between Latin America and the industrial countries, and has reduced the region's long-term rate of growth by a full percentage point per year.

What are the major causes of volatility in Latin America? Although exposure to large external shocks is a significant factor, we argue that the region's macroeconomic policies have also contributed to volatility. They have amplified, rather than offset, the effects of large shocks to the economy, and have sometimes acted as independent sources of macroeconomic disturbance. Fiscal policy has tended to be procyclical, and thus destabilizing, particularly during economic downturns. Boom-and-bust cycles in domestic banking systems, which could have been avoided with appropriate policy management, have amplified booms and deepened economic downturns. Fixed exchange rate regimes have been vulnerable and difficult to sustain, contributing to macroeconomic volatility during crises associated with their collapse.

Could economic policies be used to manage these cycles more effectively? If so, then a more stable macroeconomic environment would positively affect both the distribution of income and prospects for economic growth. The difficulties in doing so are not mainly technical, but political. The "suboptimal" policy responses we mention derive from well-understood pressures, pressures mostly created by the collective nature of democratic decisionmaking. To address this problem, the chapter outlines certain institutional responses that would change the rules of the political game in which macroeconomic policy is determined. These responses, we argue, could promote more effective cyclical management and thus raise growth and reduce inequality in the region.

Macroeconomic Volatility Impairs Economic Growth

Prospects for long-term economic growth are undermined by macroeconomic volatility, as Figure 1 illustrates. Each oval represents average growth and volatility for a quartile of a total sample of 132 countries, ranked by their volatility. There is a strong negative correlation between volatility and growth, visible when the data are grouped by region and also when individual country data are graphed. Latin American economies have been substantially more volatile than the industrial economies, which suggests that volatility has contributed to the region's relatively lackluster economic growth record.

Several recent studies have explored this relationship further, controlling for other determinants of economic growth, and found a strong and statistically robust negative association between macroeconomic volatility and economic growth.[3] This link is economically very significant for Latin American economies. If Latin America had enjoyed the lower macroeconomic volatility typical of the industrial

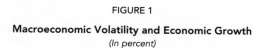

FIGURE 1

Macroeconomic Volatility and Economic Growth
(In percent)

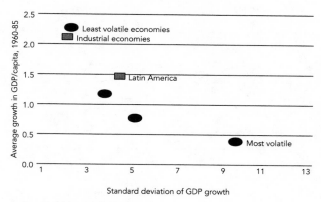

Source: Authors' calculations.

economies, the region's rate of economic growth could have been a full percentage point higher over the 1960-1985 period.[4]

Macroeconomic volatility also discourages investment in physical capital, a conclusion broadly (though not universally) supported by a large body of empirical research. This is primarily because a volatile macroeconomic environment tends to reduce the depth of the domestic financial system. Moreover, some evidence links macroeconomic volatility with low rates of educational investment, with adverse implications for economic growth and the distribution of income.[5]

Macroeconomic Volatility Worsens the Distribution of Income

Macroeconomic volatility is also associated with a more unequal distribution of income. It is easy to understand why: the impoverished are far more vulnerable to fluctuations in the economy. Londoño and Székely (1997) present evidence that short-term fluctuations in income accrue disproportionately to lower-income households, and show that measures of inequality are very negatively correlated with cyclical fluctuations in real GDP. Similarly, Morley (1995) presents evidence that the poor of Latin America suffered disproportionately from the crisis and stagnation of the 1980s.

Severe fluctuations in income and employment have particularly large, long-term effects on the earning capacity of the poor and their families, because they

FIGURE 2

Macroeconomic Volatility and the Distribution of Income
(In percent)

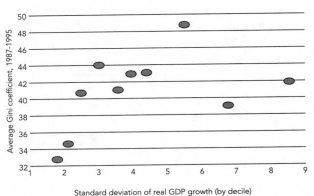

Standard deviation of real GDP growth (by decile)

Source: Authors' calculations.

have fewer resources to cope with economic downturns than do the middle and upper classes. For example, a middle-class family may count on the assistance of a network of relatives and friends, and may also have access to formal financial markets, all of which provide a buffer for the household. Poorer households are unlikely to have access to such buffers. To survive a substantial drop in income or a spell of unemployment, they may be forced into more extreme measures. Some of their children may have to leave school, either because associated costs become unmanageable or because a child's contribution to household income suddenly becomes necessary. When conditions return to normal, the child may still remain out of school. In this way, even a transitory shock can consign poor households to another generation of poverty and perpetuate inequalities in income distribution.

Figure 2 suggests that the relationship of income distribution and macroeconomic volatility is very significant. In that figure we summarize information on the volatility of real GDP growth and the distribution of income, as measured by the Gini coefficient. Each oval in the chart represents averages for a decile of a sample of about 80 countries, ranked by volatility. Though macroeconomic volatility is clearly not the whole story, income inequality is positively associated with macroeconomic volatility. (This association is weaker for the highest volatility countries in our sample, because they include countries from Eastern Europe and the former Soviet Union that maintained very equal income distributions during this period and also experienced high volatility.)

Statistics on income inequality and macroeconomic volatility are closely related, even after taking into account other factors that affect distribution of income, such as the real GDP growth rate, the terms of trade, inflation, and the initial level of per capita income.[6] The positive relationship between volatility and inequality also extends to volatility of the external environment, as measured by the standard deviation of changes in the terms of trade, and in monetary outcomes, as measured by the standard deviation of changes in narrow money.

More to the point, the association between macroeconomic volatility and inequality is highly significant in economic terms. Our estimates imply that, if Latin America had reduced the volatility of its GDP growth to that of the industrial economies, this would have eliminated roughly 25 percent of the very large difference between its Gini coefficient and that of the industrial economies.[7]

Why Is Latin America So Volatile?

In terms of growth and equity, Latin America's volatile macroeconomic environment has exacted a high toll. Whether improved policies can improve the situation is not clear. For example, if volatility in Latin America were entirely attributable to the larger external and other exogenous shocks upon the region's economies, then alternative policies could hardly make a difference. However, while external shocks have been damaging, it appears that suboptimal policy responses to the volatile economic environment have caused further harm. Improvements in the policy response to shocks and economic fluctuations thus offer the promise of securing increased growth and equity.

Sources of Macroeconomic Volatility: External Shocks or Policy?

While it is generally recognized that Latin American and developing economies in other regions are substantially more volatile than industrial economies, there have been few systematic attempts to investigate why. To address this question, we constructed a panel data set on measures of macroeconomic volatility and potential determinants for about 100 countries, and directly measured the correlation between volatility—focusing on the real exchange rate and real GDP growth—and potential determinants, including the volatility of macroeconomic policies, the volatility of the external environment, political instability, and the exchange rate regime. Some of the key results are summarized in Table 1, following.

Table 1. What explains Latin America's macroeconomic volatility? A comparison with the industrial economies

	Real exchange rate	Real GDP growth
Measure of volatility *(standard deviation* *of percentage change)*		
Latin America	13.68	4.31
Industrial countries	4.92	2.00
Difference	8.76	2.31
Estimated effect of:		
Monetary volatility	2.61	0.64
Fiscal volatility	0.72	—
Terms of trade volatility	—	0.14
Capital flow volatility	—	0.2
Revolutions and coups	2.60	0.33
Financial depth	—	0.15
Exchange rate peg	-1.15	0.5
Exchange rate switches	1.83	—
Unexplained	2.15	0.35

Source: Gavin and Hausmann (1996a).
Note: Each row provides an estimate of how much lower the region's real exchange rate volatility would have been, if the indicated explanatory variable had the same value as that recorded in the industrial economies on average.

Each row provides an estimate of how much lower would have been the region's real exchange rate volatility if the indicated explanatory variable had taken on the value recorded in the industrial economies, rather than that actually experienced, on average, in the region in question. Surprisingly, the effects of external volatility on the real exchange rate (measured by the volatility of the terms of trade and volatility of shocks to the capital account) were not marked.[8] Although external volatility had a significant effect on the volatility of real GDP growth, that significance was small in comparison with the estimated impact of monetary and fiscal volatility. Indeed, it would appear that the single most important source of macroeconomic volatility in Latin America is monetary instability.

Volatility in fiscal outcomes, as measured by the standard deviation of shocks to the fiscal deficit, was also positively related to real exchange rate volatility. Political instability (measured by the number of revolutions and coups) was, not surprisingly, related to instability of both real output and the real exchange rate.

These findings do not mean that external shocks are unimportant; other research shows that a key source of fiscal and monetary volatility is the volatility of terms of trade. Shocks to the terms of trade have important fiscal implications that affect monetary outcomes. The highly volatile monetary and fiscal outcomes should thus be understood to reflect a suboptimal response to external and other shocks, as much as an independent source of macroeconomic disturbance.

The exchange rate regime has an important influence on the volatility of macroeconomic outcomes: we found that fixed exchange rates were associated with significantly higher volatility of output and lower volatility in the real exchange rate. However, this is true only if the regime is sustained. Instability in the exchange rate regime, as measured by the number of switches between different regimes, appears to be highly destabilizing. Even if regime switches in themselves are not destabilizing, such switches typically represent forced abandonment of exchange rate pegs that have become unsustainable, in light of the external shocks and policies pursued in a country. The switches from pegged to flexible exchange rate regimes in Latin America tend to be associated with all the signs of a macroeconomic crisis, including a sharp real exchange depreciation, an acceleration of inflation, and a substantial decline in output (Gavin and Perotti 1997).[9] In short, the sustainability of the exchange rate regime is crucial, a point discussed below in more detail.

Fiscal Policy Has Been Procyclical

Fiscal outcomes have been volatile in Latin America, and this volatility has been a source of macroeconomic instability. What is worse, fiscal policy has been not only volatile, but also procyclical: tending toward expansion during macroeconomic booms and contraction during economic downturns. This behavior of course amplifies booms and busts. Gavin, Hausmann, Perotti and Talvi (1996) document this procyclicality, and show that the procyclicality of fiscal policy has been particularly pronounced in bad economic times, just when a countercyclical, stabilizing fiscal response would be most valuable.[10] These patterns differ sharply from those of the industrial economies, where fiscal policy has tended to be countercyclical, and particularly so during bad economic times. This difference is illustrated in Figure 3, taken from Gavin, Hausmann, Perotti and Talvi (1996) which juxtaposes the cumulative decline in real GDP and the change in the fiscal deficit, measured as a share of GDP, during deep recessions in Latin America and the industrial economies.[11]

FIGURE 3

Fiscal Outcomes during Deep Recessions
(In percent)

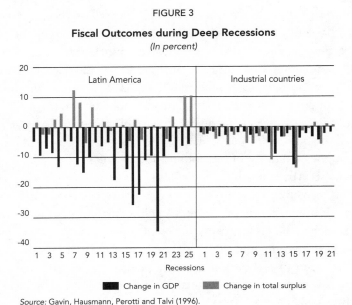

Recessions

■ Change in GDP   ■ Change in total surplus

Source: Gavin, Hausmann, Perotti and Talvi (1996).

In the industrial economies, the fiscal balance moves consistently and significantly into deficit during deep recessions, the mark of a countercyclical fiscal policy. In Latin America, however, this pattern is not observed; in fact, on average over the episodes illustrated in Figure 3, the fiscal balance actually moves into surplus during the recession. This implies that a massive fiscal contraction tends to be engineered during recessions, because if tax rates and spending programs were maintained roughly constant, the fiscal balance would move strongly into deficit during these recessions.

Why this destabilizing response to economic downturns? Consider the fiscal response to the Argentine and Mexican recessions of 1995. As those economies fell into recession, revenue projections declined, and it became apparent that fiscal deficits would be much larger than had been expected. Allowing this deficit to emerge was not a realistic option, because the countries had lost access to noninflationary financing. Indeed, had the authorities announced an intention to permit large deficits to emerge, the financial panic might have intensified, and the financial and economic crisis become deeper. The loss of market access forced authorities in both countries to turn to large tax increases and painful spending cuts. Latin America's precarious access to financial markets, which disappears when it is most needed, has often enforced a destabilizing fiscal response to economic fluctuations.[12] The key to obtaining a more stabilizing fiscal response lies in managing the boom more adequately; then after the boom ends, the country's fiscal position will allow a more stabilizing fiscal response.[13] We elaborate on this point below.

Domestic Banking Systems Amplify Economic Fluctuations

Banking crises have tended to coincide with, and greatly magnify, macroeconomic crises in Latin America. Moreover, banking systems tend to amplify macroeconomic booms by generating bank lending booms, which not only contribute to macroeconomic volatility during the upswing, but also generate the financial vulnerability that sets the stage for financial and macroeconomic crises. The recent Mexican crisis provides a spectacular example. During the early 1990s, inflation stabilization and increased confidence in macroeconomic prospects led to remonetization of the domestic economy, which was associated with large capital inflows. At the same time, the government was using privatization proceeds and increasing its reliance upon domestic and international bond markets to reduce its indebtedness to the banking system. As a result of these developments, the newly privatized banking system suddenly had an enormous capacity to lend to the private sector. And lend it did; from the late 1980s to 1994, bank credit to the private sector rose from less than 10 percent to roughly 40 percent of GDP.

This boom in lending amplified the spending boom that was taking the current account deficit to 8 percent of GDP and driving up the real exchange rate.[14] The lending boom and the existing policy framework were thus more fundamental causes of the crisis than the deficits or real exchange rate appreciation per se. Indeed, the lending boom rendered the banking system highly vulnerable to an adverse shock, or even to a slowdown in the rate of growth in credit and domestic demand.[15] When the shock arrived in Mexico, the vulnerable banking system collapsed, greatly intensifying the economic crisis. While this case was particularly dramatic, it was not unique; bank lending booms have frequently amplified macroeconomic booms in Latin America, and set the stage for subsequent macroeconomic and financial crises. Major bank lending booms have preceded every significant banking crisis of the past two decades, in both Latin America and the industrial economies (Gavin and Hausmann 1996b). The link between lending booms and banking crises is well documented: for example, bank lending booms were a key cause of macroeconomic and financial vulnerability in the 1995 'Tequila' crisis (Kaminsky and Reinhart 1996; Tornell and Velasco 1996) .

What are the possible macroeconomic policy responses to this "boom-bust" behavior in domestic financial markets? Of course, financial intermediation is rife with information and moral hazard problems, partly though not entirely due to official guarantees and safety nets—which imply that individual banks do not bear all the risks they generate during the lending boom. There is thus a need for official intervention to ensure that these information and incentive problems do not induce banks to engage in destabilizing or excessively risky behavior.

Vulnerable Fixed Exchange Rate Regimes Contribute to Instability

The largely inconclusive theoretical literature on the stabilizing properties of alternative exchange rate regimes has demonstrated that almost anything can happen, depending upon the structure of the economy and the nature of the shocks that affect an economy. Since there is no consensus over either, this debate over alternative regimes has only limited relevance. That debate has also neglected a fundamental point about Latin American economies. While there are likely to be tradeoffs between the stabilization of real economic activity and the real exchange rate, there is no doubt about the destabilizing consequences of exchange regime collapses.

The Mexican crisis provides a recent and dramatic example. But the fact, discussed above, that exchange regime "switches" are associated with a significantly more volatile macroeconomic environment indicates a more general association between regime switches and economic crises. In Latin America, the moves from fixed to flexible exchange rates have on average been associated with a decline in GDP growth (reduced by 3.4 percent in the year of the switch and by 1.6 percent the next year), increased inflation (45 percentage points) and a 34 percent depreciation of the real exchange rate (Gavin and Perotti 1997).[16] Thus abandoning a commitment to a fixed exchange rate system is costly, and has been a significant source of macroeconomic volatility in the region.

Thus the sustainability of the exchange rate regime is a fundamental consideration. There is little point in contemplating the relative merits of fixed and flexible exchange rate systems if the fixed regime is going to prove unsustainable, and in its collapse trigger a destabilizing financial crisis.

What causes fixed exchange rate systems to break down? Gavin and Perotti (1997) provided evidence that in Latin America fixed exchange rate systems have tended to break down after a large fiscal expansion, a substantial decline in the terms of trade, and after elections, which they interpret as being associated with heightened uncertainty over the policy environment. Fixed exchange rates are likely to prove unsustainable, and thus over the long term destabilizing, in countries where the ongoing commitment to a cautious fiscal stance is not guaranteed, where terms of trade shocks are large, and where a consensus on fundamental elements of the macroeconomic policy stance has not been achieved. While every country must be evaluated on its own terms, many countries of the region possess some of these characteristics, and should not take lightly a commitment to fixed exchange rates.

Better Cyclical Management Can Raise Growth and Improve Income Distribution

Given that macroeconomic volatility undermines growth prospects and worsens the distribution of income, what are the possible means of reducing it? In Latin America's case, high macroeconomic volatility has to some degree reflected short-comings in the policy environment. The three critical areas appear to be fiscal policy, management of the domestic financial system, and exchange rate policy. What follows is a brief outline of some policy reforms in the areas of fiscal policy and management of domestic banking systems that could reduce macroeconomic volatility, and thereby improve the prospects for economic growth and more equitable income distribution.

Fiscal Policy: Managing the Boom to Stabilize the Response to Downturns

Fiscal volatility is associated with macroeconomic volatility, both directly, and as a major source of destabilizing monetary volatility. There is evidence that it is associated with disruptive exchange regime collapses. And fiscal policy has tended to be procyclical, particularly during bad times.

In bad times, the source of this procyclicality is the precarious access to financial markets, which tends to disappear when most needed, making a procyclical fiscal adjustment the only realistic option. Little can be done about this situation during a downturn, when access to financial markets is threatened or has disappeared. Instead, the need is to institutionalize a management of fiscal policy during good times that leaves the country sufficiently creditworthy to withstand a downturn without losing market access. Some guidelines for this are outlined below:

- Recognize that industrial country standards for fiscal policy management are not adequate benchmarks for Latin American countries, which have to deal with much more volatile macroeconomic environments, in which far larger economic booms and downturns generate more dramatic fiscal fluctuations.

• Budget balance, or a "sustainable" budget deficit, may not be enough during good economic times. Even if the budget is near balance, an economic boom may mask a large underlying deficit that will emerge when the boom ends, leading to a loss of confidence and the need for a wrenching fiscal adjustment just when it is least desirable. More generally, fiscal targets should be set in a cyclical context, taking into account transitory fluctuations in the key determinants of budgetary outcomes.

• Strive to improve the efficiency of tax systems, but leave at least some of the greater fiscal capacity unutilized, so that revenue can be increased if necessary during a fiscal crisis. The knowledge that this spare fiscal capacity exists should reduce the probability of a destabilizing loss of confidence in the sustainability of the public finances.

• Adapt institutions to the Latin American environment. The difficulties involved in carrying out these ideas are not primarily technical, but rather political. While it is easy to say that the authorities should attempt to run fiscal surpluses during economic booms, the "authorities" do not determine fiscal policy in Latin America. As in the industrial economies, fiscal policy is the outcome of a complex, democratic process with many actors, so that it is very difficult to control spending when a fiscal surplus seems to suggest that resources are available to cover pressing legitimate and pressing needs.[17] This problem exists in the industrial countries as well, but the stakes are much higher in Latin America, because fiscal policy needs to cope with much larger economic fluctuations. Latin America therefore requires institutional adaptations that will enable the decisionmaking process to secure sound fiscal outcomes. Examples of such adaptations and evidence of their results are discussed in IDB (1997).

Toward Sound Financial Systems in a Volatile Macroeconomic Environment

Latin America's volatile macroeconomic environment has policy implications for domestic financial markets at least as profound as those for management of fiscal policy. Volatility in production and relative prices means that bank clients are going to be subject to larger shocks to profitability, and thus banks will be subject to larger shocks to their asset quality. Volatile money demand means that Latin American banks need to worry much more about liquidity problems than do banks in industrial countries, where money demand is substantially more stable. And the heightened risk and uncertainty to which Latin American banks are subject implies that, other things (including the regulatory and supervisory framework) being equal, decisions by the region's banks are likely to be more significantly distorted by the information and incentive problems that affect banks everywhere. Thus, while policies toward the banking system are trying to solve the same general problems as policies in the industrial economies and thus are likely to have the same general shape, the Latin American environment requires adaptations. For example, policymakers might consider the following approaches:

- Adopt more conservative regulatory standards. Bank capital is a buffer asgainst the risk of loss which both reduces taxpayer exposure to financial loss and improves incentives for banks to lend prudently. Given the heightened risk and uncertainty implied by the more volatile Latin American environment, a case can be made that capital requirements should be higher than the minimum requirements required for banks operating in industrial economies. Similarly, given the higher volatility in the demand for bank deposits, bank liquidity requirements should be considered as a potentially important element of the prudential regulatory structure.[18]
- Beware of lending booms. There is abundant evidence that very rapid growth in bank lending is dangerous, even if that growth reflects a healthy recovery from repressed levels. This suggests that authorities should "lean against the wind" of major credit booms, with the aim of minimizing the financial vulnerability that may otherwise materialize, and preventing the lending boom from unduly amplifying the macroeconomic boom that it tends to accompany.
- Internationalize the banking system. Allowing domestic banks to expand their international activities carries with it important risks, and should therefore be managed carefully. Nonetheless, it offers the prospect of more diversified financial institutions, which are less exposed to country-specific macroeconomic shocks, and therefore less likely to magnify those shocks. The entry of foreign institutions also offers important benefits: they bring access to the parent institution's reserves of capital and international liquidity, and because they are also supervised by foreign regulators, their entry offers a means of importing scarce regulatory and supervisory services. These benefits suggest that defining financial markets according to economically arbitrary national borders may be counterproductive, and that carefully encouraging the internationalization of financial markets would be conducive to financial and macroeconomic stability.[19]

Conclusion

Macroeconomic volatility is detrimental to growth as well as to equitable income distribution. Much of Latin America's volatility can be attributed to policy frameworks that are ill-equipped to handle the large shocks that affect the region's economies. These policy frameworks have often amplified rather than absorbed such shocks, and have sometimes been independent sources of economic and financial disturbance. This chapter proposes some policy reforms to improve the capacity of Latin American economies to absorb shocks, thus reducing macroeconomic volatility. The proposals are neither definitive nor comprehensive in scope, but point to areas where policy reforms could help to reduce economic and financial vulnerability, without impairing economic efficiency or involving adverse distributional consequences. Such reforms offer the prospect of a win-win solution: reducing volatility, while also securing more rapid growth and increased equity.

Endnotes _____

[1] Until recently, empirical research on the determinants of economic growth typically neglected to study how macroeconomic volatility affects growth. Conversely, when the effects of macroeconomic instability were studied, emphasis was primarily on high inflation and large budget deficits, rather than volatility in rates of economic growth, real exchange rates, or terms of trade.

[2] See, for example, Márquez and Morley (1997).

[3] See, for example, Aizenman and Marion (1993), Hausmann (1995), IDB (1995), Mendoza (1994), and Ramey and Ramey (1995).

[4] The effects of volatility on terms of trade, the real exchange rate, the real growth rate, and indicators of monetary and fiscal policy are discussed further in IDB (1995). The variable showing the strongest negative association with long-term growth was volatility in the terms of trade, but other measures of macroeconomic volatility were also negatively related to growth.

[5] See Flug, Spilimbergo and Wachtenheim (forthcoming).

[6] See IDB (1995).

[7] The estimated impact of lower monetary volatility is even larger, but hardly reliable because Latin America is such an outlier in that category.

[8] For the results of an effort to measure capital flow volatility independent of the fluctuations related to domestic macroeconomic developments, see Gavin and Hausmann (1996a).

[9] Switches from flexible to fixed exchange rates, on the other hand, are not associated with any symptoms of crisis.

[10] Gavin and Perotti (1997) give a more technical presentation of this result.

[11] "Deep recessions" are defined as episodes in which the cumulative decline in a country's real GDP exceeds 1.5 percent (industrial economies) or 4 percent (Latin American economies). The recession episodes were compiled during the period 1970-1994, and refer to individual country experience, not regional aggregates.

[12] Bad economic times are associated with a loss of normal market access in Latin America (though not in the industrial economies). This loss of market access severely affects both the public and private sector response to economic downturns in Latin America (Gavin and Perotti 1996, 1997).

[13] Latin American countries that enter a period with relatively low fiscal deficits tend to have a more countercyclical response to economic fluctuations (Gavin and Perotti 1997).

[14] Copelman and Werner (undated) provide evidence that bank lending, by relaxing the credit constraints that face borrowers, has a powerful impact on private spending in Mexico.

[15] The argument that credit booms reduce the quality of bank portfolios and increase their vulnerability to adverse shocks is developed in more detail in Gavin and Hausmann (1996b). A more complete account of the Mexican case may be found in Birdsall, Gavin and Hausmann (forthcoming).

[16] This evidence does not include the recent Mexican experience, which was not in the sample.

[17] For an extended discussion of the political "distortions" that may affect fiscal policymaking, see Eichengreen, Hausmann and von Hagen (1996).

[18] For more detailed treatments of these and related issues, see Gavin and Hausmann (1996b), Rojas-Suárez and Weisbrod (1996), and de Juan (1996).

[19] See Gavin and Hausmann (1997).

References

Aizenman, Joshua, and Nancy Marion. 1993. Policy Uncertainty, Persistence, and Economic Growth. *Review of International Economics* 1: 145-63.

———. 1996. Volatility and the Investment Response. NBER Working Paper no. 5841.

Birdsall, Nancy, Michael Gavin, and Ricardo Hausmann. Forthcoming. Lessons of the Mexican Crisis. In Shahid J. Burki, Sebastian Edwards, and Moisés Naím (eds.) *Mexico 1994: Anatomy of an Emerging Markets Crisis,* New York: Carnegie Foundation.

Copelman, Martina, and Alejandro Werner. (undated). Credit and Economic Activity in Mexico. Massachusetts Institute of Technology, Cambridge, MA.

Cottani, Joaquín, Domingo Cavallo, and M. Shahbaz Khan. 1990. Real Exchange Rate Behavior and Economic Performance in LDCs. *Economic Development and Cultural Change* 39: 61-76.

de Juan, Aristobulo. 1996. The Roots of Banking Crises: Microeconomic Issues of Supervision and Regulation, in Ricardo Hausmann and Liliana Rojas-Suárez (eds.), *Banking Crises in Latin America.* Washington, D.C.: IDB.

Eichengreen, Barry, Ricardo Hausmann, and Jörgen von Hagen. 1996. Reforming Fiscal Institutions in Latin America: The Case for a National Fiscal Council. Manuscript, IDB.

Flug, Karnit, Antonio Spilimbergo, and Erik Wachtenheim (forthcoming). Investment in Education: Do Economic Volatility and Credit Constraints Matter? *Journal of Development Economics.*

Gavin, Michael, and Ricardo Hausmann. 1996a. Sources of Macroeconomic Volatility in Developing Economies. Manuscript, IDB.

———. 1996b. The Roots of Banking Crises: The Macroeconomic Context, in Ricardo Hausmann and Liliana Rojas-Suárez (eds.), *Banking Crises in Latin America.* Washington, D.C.: IDB.

———. 1997. Make or Buy? Approaches to Financial Integration, in Liliana Rojas-Suárez (ed.), *Safe and Sound Financial Systems: What Works for Latin America.* Washington, D.C.: IDB.

———. (forthcoming). Macroeconomic Volatility and Economic Development: Institutional Dimensions, in Silvio Borner and Martin Paldam (eds.), *Politics and Economic Development.* London: Macmillan.

Gavin, Michael, Ricardo Hausmann, Roberto Perotti, and Ernesto Talvi. 1996. Managing Fiscal Policy in Latin America: Volatility, Procyclicality and Limited Creditworthiness. OCE Working Paper no. 326, IDB.

Gavin, Michael, and Roberto Perotti. 1997. Fiscal Policy and Private Saving in Latin America in Good Times and Bad. In Ricardo Hausmann and Helmut Reisen (eds.), *Promoting Savings in Latin America*. Washington, D.C.: IDB and OECD.

————. 1997. Fiscal Policy in Latin America, in B. Bernanke and J. Rotemberg (eds.), *NBER Macroeconomics Annual 1997*. Cambridge, MA: MIT Press.

Hausmann, Ricardo. 1995. En Camino Hacia Una Mayor Integración con el Norte, in Mónica Aparicio and William Easterly (eds.), *Crecimiento Económico: Teoría, Instituciones y Experiencia Internacional*. Bogotá: Banco de la República and the World Bank.

IDB (Inter-American Development Bank). 1995. Overcoming Volatility in Latin America, in *Economic and Social Progress in Latin America, 1995 Report*. Washington, D.C.: IDB.

————. 1997. Fiscal Stability with Democracy and Decentralization, in *Economic and Social Progress in Latin America, 1997 Report*. Washington, D.C.: IDB.

Kaminsky, Graciela, and Carmen Reinhart. 1996. The Twin Crises: The Causes of Banking and Balance of Payments Problems. International Finance Discussion Paper no. 544. Washington: Board of Governors of the Federal Reserve System.

Leahy, John, and Toni Whited. 1995. The Effect of Uncertainty on Investment, Some Stylized Facts. NBER Working Paper no. 4986. Washington, D.C.: National Bureau of Economic Research.

Londoño, Juan Luis, and Miguel Székely. 1997. Distributional Surprises after a Decade of Reforms: Latin America in the Nineties. OCE Working Paper no. 352, IDB.

Márquez, Gustavo, and Samuel Morley. 1997. Poverty and the Employment Problem in Argentina. Manuscript, IDB.

Mendoza, Enrique. 1994. Terms-of-Trade Uncertainty and Economic Growth: Are Risk Indicators Significant in Growth Regressions? Board of Governors of the Federal Reserve System, International Finance Discussion Paper no. 491, Washington, D.C.

Morley, Samuel. 1995. *Poverty and Inequality in Latin America: The Impact of Adjustment and Recovery in the 1980s*. Baltimore: Johns Hopkins University Press.

Pindyck, Robert, and Andrés Solimano. 1993. Economic Instability and Aggregate Investment, in O. Blanchard and S. Fischer (eds.), *NBER Macroeconomics Annual 1993*. Cambridge, MA: MIT Press.

Ramey, Garey, and Valerie Ramey. 1995. Cross-Country Evidence on the Link between Volatility and Growth. *American Economic Review* 85(5): 1138-1151.

Rojas-Suárez, Liliana, and Steven Weisbrod. 1996. Achieving Financial Stability in Highly Volatile Environments, in Ricardo Hausmann and Helmut Reisen (eds.), *Securing Stability and Growth in a Shock-Prone Region: The Policy Challenge for Latin America.* Washington, D.C.: IDB and OECD.

Tornell, Aaron, and Andrés Velasco. 1996. Financial Crisis in Emerging Markets: The Lessons of 1995. *Brookings Papers on Economic Activity 1.*

Servén, Luis, and Andrés Solimano. 1993. *Striving for Growth after Adjustment: The Role of Capital Formation.* Washington, D.C.: The World Bank.

CHAPTER FIVE

No Tradeoff: Efficient Growth Via More Equal Human Capital Accumulation

Nancy Birdsall and Juan Luis Londoño

The early postwar development model emphasized a strong role for the state. The challenge of coordinating public and private investment in industry, transport, and communications seemed to justify that the state not only assume a leading role as planner, but also take the commanding heights of the economy and manage production. In this early development model, spending on such "nonproductive sectors" as health and education was seen as a drain on the accumulation of productive assets, and thus as a cost in terms of growth. For example, early demographic models emphasized that rapid population growth in developing countries was draining away public resources on schooling and health services, thus reducing the availability of productive physical capital.

The newer growth models introduced the concept of human capital as a productive investment. In new classical growth models, human capital accumulation is as critical to the growth process as the previous narrow concept of physical capital: that is, growth is stimulated by increasing savings and investment in education. The recent endogenous growth models attribute an even stronger role to human capital. Sustainable growth in these models is a result, in part, of positive externalities generated by education, an important form of human capital. New ideas and new technologies are critical to high sustained growth, and in turn rely on high levels of human capital.

The newer growth models provide an elegant and compelling justification for human capital investments as efficient and growth-enhancing. In their simplest form, however (as reflected in the well-known empirical studies of growth of Barro, Sala-i-Martin, Romer, and others), they embody assumptions that are poor guides to policy choices.

First, and most fundamental for our purpose here, the distribution of human capital across individuals is ignored. The implicit assumption is that the accumulation process will "trickle down" and benefit members of all income groups proportionately.

Second, and reinforcing the first shortcoming, demand is ignored. Human capital accumulation is treated as exogenous. The determinants of the accumulation process—household decisions to invest in human capital, and public policy decisions about the size and allocation of such investments—are not modeled. The initial distribution across households of adult education, which is critical to investments in children's education,[1] and the macroeconomic, trade and other economywide policies that also affect household demand of different income groups for education, are not explicitly considered. This ignores the fact that parents who are poorer and less educated are likely to invest less in their children's education.

And third, the problem of delivery—of efficient and equitable production of social services—is ignored. Instead, a major role for the state in providing health and education services is implicitly endorsed. The emphasis on positive externalities of human capital (in new growth models) is based on the logic of a market failure, particularly in capital markets, which inhibits optimal private investment. Because human capital cannot be appropriated, borrowers cannot use future human capital as collateral; even when agents recognize high returns to private investments in health and schooling, they cannot borrow and their investments are therefore liquidity-constrained. Thus in these models the role of the state is critical, reinforcing the traditional view of government as the major financier, producer and provider of all social services.[2]

This lack of emphasis on *demand, distribution, and delivery* of social programs reinforces a longstanding assumption that Latin America's developing societies face an inevitable tradeoff between efficiency and fairness. In the tradition of Kuznets, analysts have tended to view worsening income inequality as an inevitable consequence of economic development. Past efforts to rectify unfairness using populist transfers—with disastrous fiscal results—have reinforced pessimism that Latin America could enjoy growth with equity. Given that pessimism, the recommended policy responses have been comparatively unambitious: a remedial and marginal social policy designed to cushion the impact of increasing poverty, without any emphasis on investment in the poor's human capital.

In challenging the assumptions of the new growth models and the tradeoff pessimists, this chapter will focus on the region's social sectors: education and health. The process of investment in these sectors—of investment in human capital—has not worked well in Latin America. Though governments have committed considerable resources to health and education services, the region has a poor record given its income. Spending on these services, particularly for the poor, has historically been viewed as a transfer, not an investment. Human capital accumulation has been relatively slow, with negative effects on growth, and highly unequal across income groups, exacerbating income inequality. Here we will seek to explain why, and then propose a new approach to help rectify the problem. Our discussion relies on a broader consideration of the three interrelated issues of demand, distribution, and delivery.

First, in Latin America, low accumulation of human capital reflects low household *demand* for education, particularly among the poor. The low household demand for human capital, in turn, reflects the high proportion of poor households in Latin America and the depth of their poverty.

Next, *distribution*: The poor's historically unequal access to income-producing assets (land and human capital) in Latin America helps explain the vicious cycle of low accumulation of human capital and poverty. Moreover, low accumulation of human capital by the poor has been exacerbated by regressive patterns of public spending on social programs—the poor have not benefited much from public spending on education and health services—and by economic policies that have penalized labor and discouraged household investment in education.

In short, we find that the trickle-down approach to human capital accumulation in Latin America has not succeeded. If the region's economies are to exploit the efficiency and growth-enhancing effects of more rapid human capital accumulation, there will need to be more emphasis on equity in the distribution of services that generate human capital.

The third issue is *delivery* of social services. We argue that the centralized bureaucratic model of social service delivery has led to inefficient and inequitable outcomes in Latin America. Public spending on the education and health services necessary for human capital accumulation, particularly by the poor, has been based on a model of industrial organization that reflects historic social and political inequities and does not serve the poor well. Achieving greater equity (and thus faster rates of human capital accumulation, a key to faster as well as more equitable and sustainable growth) calls for a new, "horizontal" approach to the provision of social services. This approach would rely on greater targeting of public spending to the poor, more competitive supply of services, and an emphasis on demand that empowers consumers, including poor consumers.

The first section of this chapter summarizes evidence that, despite adequate public spending, accumulation of human capital in Latin America has been low and inequitable—the distribution of education has hardly improved over time. Low and unequal human capital accumulation in Latin America goes a long way toward explaining not only the region's high level of income disparity and poverty, but also its sluggish capital formation and lack of economic growth. In a vicious circle, the insufficiency of human capital has reflected and also reinforced the high degree of asset and income inequality throughout Latin America.

The second section discusses the underlying reasons for low and unequal human capital accumulation. Among these are weak demand for education among the poor, due to liquidity constraints, and the likelihood of low returns to human capital investment in economies biased against labor. On the one hand, history suggests a discouraging vicious circle, in which initial poverty and income inequality have led to slow and unequal human capital accumulation, which has in turn reduced growth and exacerbated inequality. On the other hand, there is a positive implication: more rapid accumulation, with greater emphasis on equal access to education, can both speed economic growth and reduce income inequality. More and more equal education can enhance both efficiency and equity.

The third section turns to the immediate challenges of how to transform the delivery of social services, including health and education. Latin America's current major systems of service delivery reflect and reinforce underlying economic and social inequities. Neither a centralized bureaucratic approach nor an atomized, market-reliant approach allow optimal access for the poor to opportunities to invest in their human capital. An alternative approach to organizing service delivery would be horizontal—combining centrally determined rules of the game with market-led competitive supply and consumer empowerment. There are promising examples of this approach in the region.

With the new emphasis on productivity-enhancing social investments that will reach the poor, there is reason for optimism. The growing experience with successful horizontal approaches can pave the way for greater internal efficiency in the delivery of social programs. More equitable access to social opportunities will accelerate the accumulation of human capital. That would set in motion a new, virtuous circle that includes fairer distribution of assets and opportunities, faster economic growth, and wider distribution of its benefits.

Low and Unequal Human Capital Accumulation in Latin America

Relative to its per capita income, Latin America's performance in human capital accumulation is weak compared to other regions. This is particularly true for education: average schooling attainment is two years below what would be expected given per capita income, a record barely better than that of sub-Saharan Africa and well below that of South and East Asia. At the beginning of the 1990s, workers had an average of 5.2 years of education, nearly a third less than would be expected for countries with the region's level of development; and more than a third of the children entering primary school were not finishing, over twice the rate of other regions in the world.

The education gap has worsened over the last three decades. At the start of the 1970s, Latin America had a low level of education, lower than the countries of Europe and Southeast Asia with comparable income levels but no different from the rest of the developing world, once adjusted on a per capita basis. Since then, education in Latin America (led by Brazil, Mexico, Venezuela, and Central America) has grown at a slow rate, well below the growth achieved by Asian countries and the rest of the developing world. In 1980, the region's workforce lagged behind the developing world's average by a gap of one year of education. By the mid 1990s, this figure had doubled. Compared to East and Southeast Asia, Latin America's shortfall in education has increased from less than one year in 1970 to about 4 years in 1995 (Figure la).

The shortfall in health is smaller compared to other regions. Average life expectancy is about two years below the expected, given income (Figure lb). This result is perhaps due to a smaller gender gap in education than elsewhere, the positive effect of mothers' education on infant mortality, and relatively more spending and innovation in Latin America's health sector (IDB 1996).

The primary problem is not low public expenditures on health and education; such expenditures are similar to other developing regions, at 6.6 percent of GDP (Table 1).[3] Rather the problem has been the inefficient use of public expenditures (to which we return in the third section below), and the unequal incidence of public spending on these services—that is, the relatively low proportion of public spending that has benefited the poor.[4] Compared to East Asia and the industrialized countries, Latin America has higher inequality of human capital. (Its inequality of land, another critical productive asset, is the highest of any region—see Figure 2.[5]) Thus the low rate of overall accumulation (an average of healthy increases in years of school completed for a small number, and very limited increases for the great majority) is due in part to its unequal nature. Moreover, contrary to what might be expected, the increase in average education in Latin America over the last three decades has not been associated with improvement in the distribution of education. Figure 3 compares the virtually unchanged distribution of education in Latin America to the improvement in East Asia during this period.[6]

FIGURE 1a

The Education Gap

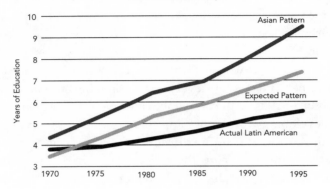

FIGURE 1b

The Life Expectancy Gap

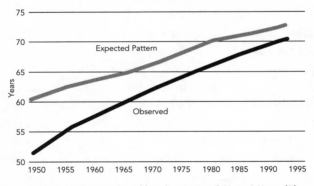

Note: Expected pattern derived from the equation e(ln(y), time). Years of life expectancy and average schooling compared to expected levels based on per capita income.
Source: Inter-American Development Bank (1996).

FIGURE 2

Asset Inequality, c. 1990

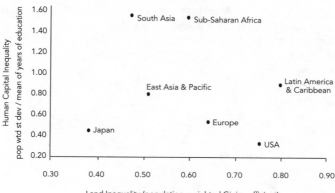

Note: The measure of human capital inequality is the coefficient of variation, i.e., the standard deviation divided by the mean of years of schooling. This measure controls for the effect of any changes in the average level of education on the distribution (see endnotes 5 and 6). Using solely the standard deviation of education (not shown), Latin America has higher levels of human capital inequality than Sub-Saharan Africa; adjusting for its relatively higher mean level of education reduces its measured inequality compared to Sub-Saharan Africa and South Asia. Latin America has high inequality of human capital compared to East Asia and the developed countries.

Sources: Human capital inequality was calculated using Barro-Lee's (1993) education attainment data. Land Ginis are from Deininger and Squire (personal correspondence).

FIGURE 3

Inequality of Human Capital: A Regional Comparison

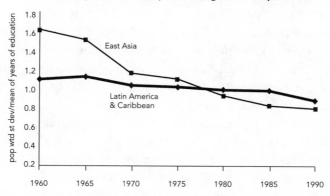

Note: East Asia includes Hong Kong, Indonesia, Rep. of Korea, Malaysia, Singapore, Taiwan and Thailand. Human capital inequality is measured here by the mean-adjusted standard deviation of years of schooling.

Source: Human capital inequality was calculated using Barro-Lee's (1993) education attainment data.

Table 1. Social Expenditure in the 1990s

(As percent of GDP, averaged across each group)

Country group	Public expenditure			Private expenditure
	Total	Education	Health	Health
Latin America	6.6	3.6	3.0	3.1
Other developing countries	6.4	4.2	2.2	1.9
All developing countries	6.5	4.1	2.4	2.2
Worldwide	9.9	5.1	4.8	3.2

Source: Inter-American Development Bank (1996).

Effects on Growth

What have been the effects of low and unequal human capital accumulation on the growth rate in Latin America over the last three decades? Table 2 shows the results of estimating a traditional growth equation across countries, using the best recently available data on the distribution of income (Deininger and Squire 1996). For these estimates, we selected those countries with Lorenz curves available for two periods of time separated by at least five years, with income estimates per capita in international purchasing power prices, and information on physical capital investment, the education of the labor force (which we used to construct our measure of human capital distribution), land distribution, and trade indicators.

Our findings (reported originally in Birdsall and Londoño 1997) are straightforward with respect to the effect on growth of education and of the distribution of education. Education accumulation, along with capital accumulation, is good for growth—a now conventional result (columns 2 and 3). The strong positive effect on growth of human capital accumulation (as reflected in the average years of education of the labor force) is consistent with the theory mentioned in the introduction. That effect also accords with microeconomic evidence that better-educated workers earn higher incomes and are more effective in household production of children's good health and schooling (for women in particular).

That a country's education level, at the beginning of a period, has a positive effect on its subsequent growth is now a commonplace and highly robust result in virtually all cross-country studies of growth (Barro and Sala-i-Martin 1995; Levine

Table 2. Explaining Growth

A. Explaining Aggregate Growth

Independent Variable	(1)	(2)	(3)
Constant	0.01	0.04**	0.03
Aggregate growth			
Capital accumulation	0.53**	0.57**	0.54**
Initial conditions:			
Income level	-0.88	-0.41	-0.42
Education level	0.17	0.28*	0.30*
Income inequality	-0.05*	-0.03	-0.002
Land inequality		-0.02*	-0.01
Educational inequality		-0.09*	-0.09*
Natural resources			-0.01
Changes in:			
Income inequality			
Trade openness			0.02
Manufacturing trade			
Primary trade			
LAC dummy			0.004
R^2	0.61	0.70	0.76

B. Explaining Income Growth of the Poorest

Independent Variable	(4)	(5)	(6)
Constant	0.00	0.05[†]	0.04[†]
Aggregate growth	1.31**		
Capital accumulation		0.72**	0.77**
Initial conditions:			
Income level			
Education level		0.41[†]	0.51[†]
Income inequality		0.05	0.02
Land inequality		-0.07*	-0.02
Educational inequality		-0.20*	-0.18*
Natural resources			
Changes in:			
Income inequality			-0.27**
Trade openness			
Manufacturing trade			0.05[†]
Primary trade			-0.01
LAC dummy			-0.01
R^2	0.51	0.42	0.63

[†] Statistically significant at the 10-percent level.
* Statistically significant at the 5-percent level.
** Statistically significant at the 1-percent level.
Source: Birdsall and Londoño (1997).

and Renelt 1992). Lora and Barrera (1997) estimate that Latin America as a region could increase its growth rate by 2 percentage points a year over the next decade if, in addition to deepening structural reforms, the region were able to increase the pace of human capital accumulation for the labor force as a whole by one year over that which was expected. Viewed from the other side, Birdsall, Ross and Sabot (1995) estimate that Korea, with Brazil's level of primary and secondary education in 1960, would have grown by 0.56 percentage points *less* per year over the next 25 years, and Korea's resulting per capita GDP for 1985 would have been 12 percent lower than it actually was.

In addition, and controlling for the level of education, the degree of inequality in the distribution of education has a strong and robust negative effect on growth (columns 2 and 3). The variable measuring the distribution of education is highly robust;[7] its negative effect operates independently not only of the education level variable, but of the positive effect of trade openness and the negative effect of natural resource endowment.

Note that when we enter the asset distribution variables, the negative effect of income inequality on growth loses statistical significance (columns 2 and 3 versus column 1); the widely reported negative effect (Birdsall, Ross and Sabot 1995; Alesina and Rodrik 1994; Persson and Tabellini 1994) apparently reflects differences in a fundamental element of economic structure, namely the access of different groups to productive assets.

In columns 4 to 6 of Table 2, we assess whether the initial distributions of income and of assets affect the income growth of the poor. The elasticity of income growth of the poor with respect to overall growth is well above one (column 1), confirming the logic of the argument that economic growth is key to poverty reduction. Income growth of the poor also depends heavily upon capital accumulation (columns 2 and 3). Most interesting, initial inequalities in the distribution of land and of human capital have a clear negative effect on the income growth of the poor, at magnitudes twice those of their effects on average income growth (column 2). An unequal distribution of assets, especially of human capital, affects income growth of the poor disproportionately; a better distribution of assets would reduce poverty both directly and indirectly, by enhancing average growth.

Making this point with aggregate economic indicators, Birdsall and Londoño (1997) show that, if the economies of Latin America had maintained the same income distribution throughout the 1980s as in 1970, the increase in poverty over the years 1983 to 1995 would have been smaller by almost half (Figure 4). But the low growth and macroeconomic instability of the 1980s harmed the poor more than others and exacerbated an already poor distribution of assets and income.

FIGURE 4

**The Impact of Inequality on Poverty
in Latin America 1970-1995**

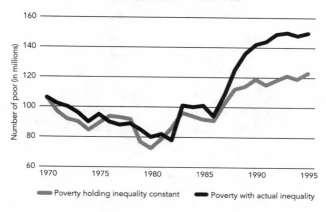

Source: Birdsall and Londoño (1997).

These results are consistent with a view of the world in which opportunities matter. The poor, without assets, cannot take advantage of opportunities to be productive. In economies where a substantial portion of the population is without human capital, and thus without a critical productive asset, only a part of the population can exploit the growth process. The engine of growth is small, and may be periodically stalled by populist roundabouts. Driven by the increasing productivity of the initially poor, East Asian countries, which began the postwar period with relatively low asset inequality, were able to grow at high and sustained rates over more than three decades. In contrast, most countries of Latin America, with greater inequality of assets and presumably fewer opportunities for the poor, grew less (Figure 5). The results of Table 2 and the aggregate indicators summarized above indicate a straightforward if disturbing conclusion: Low and unequal accumulation of human capital in Latin America has slowed aggregate economic growth and has inhibited poverty reduction.

Effects on Income Inequality

Latin America's persistently high income inequality is a second effect of low and unequal accumulation. The Gini coefficient for the region as a whole (about 0.50) is approximately 15 points above the average for the rest of the world. In 1995, the

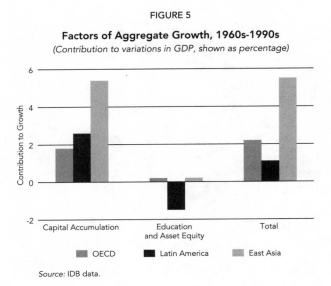

FIGURE 5

Factors of Aggregate Growth, 1960s-1990s
(Contribution to variations in GDP, shown as percentage)

Source: IDB data.

wealthiest quintile of the population was receiving 58 percent of the total income—that is, 12 times the income of the poorest 40 percent and 19 times that of the poorest quintile of the population. The income of the poorest 40 percent of the population is some 20 percent lower than it would be with a typical pattern of income distribution. And the number of impoverished, currently between 140 and 150 million individuals who earn less than US$2 daily, could be a third lower.[8]

Londoño and Székely (1997) show that world income inequality across countries can be reasonably explained by the relative abundance of factors of production such as land and physical and human capital, and by their distribution. As Figure 6 shows, lower physical capital accumulation is not the culprit for Latin America. Rather, the relative abundance of natural resources and the highest concentration of land in the world account for a substantial portion of Latin America's excessive inequality. And the low education levels (human capital) of Latin American workers and the enormous inequality in educational assets play an even larger role in explaining it.

The effect of low and unequal education on income inequality is not surprising. Where a relatively small proportion of the total population completes secondary or higher education, public investment in education has generally been viewed as a mechanism to reduce poverty and inequality, given the strong evidence at the individual level that the educated earn more. At the aggregate level, however, the

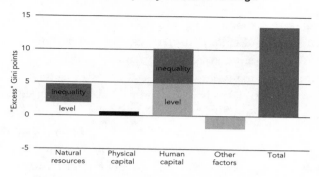

FIGURE 6

**Explaining Latin America's
Excess Inequality vs. World Average**

Note: The columns show 'excess' inequality, distinguishing between the
effect of the level and the inequality of each asset.
Source: Londoño and Székely (1997).

effect of education on poverty and inequality obviously depends on the distribution of education itself, how rapidly it spreads, and how much different groups benefit. In Latin America, only a small proportion of the total population has completed secondary or higher education. These relatively few skilled workers earn a substantial wage premium due to their limited supply, thus contributing to overall high income inequality (Birdsall, Ross and Sabot 1997).

The Latin American experience stands in marked contrast to that of East Asia, where education policy has produced a large supply of skilled workers, eroding any substantial premium they might have earned above the wages of the unskilled. Kuznets' theory (that income distribution will initially worsen as some workers in underdeveloped economies shift to high-productivity sectors) seems to be borne out in Latin America, in part because the limited and slow spread of educational opportunities has created a large productivity gap between a small skilled group and the rest of the population (Birdsall, Stallings and Clugage 1997).

Explaining Latin America's Low and Unequal Accumulation

The above analysis demonstrates that low and unequal accumulation of human capital has limited Latin America's growth, particularly the growth in income of the poor, and has exacerbated the region's high income inequality. We argue now that, in fact, there is a vicious circle: the region's low and unequal accumulation of human capital is not only a cause of current poverty and income inequality, but also an *outcome* of past income inequality. Low and unequal accumulation can be explained by the facts of demand and supply in the market for education.[9]

First, on the demand side, Latin America's large endowment of natural resources historically has limited society's demand for education. The socioeconomic arrangements that accompany large-scale agricultural production and natural resource extraction involve relatively few owners of capital and many unskilled workers (Engerman and Sokoloff 1996). There is little demand for skilled workers, in part because natural resources tend to be complementary to capital, not skilled labor, in production. Perhaps as a result, governments and families in Latin America have invested little in education, seeing relatively higher returns to physical capital. A rich natural resource base in the region also minimized the need to develop competitive nontraditional exports in the early postwar period, thus perpetuating traditional production arrangements.

Second, high income inequality in Latin America has implied that more households are liquidity-constrained, unable to borrow and without the resources necessary to keep their children in school. Flug, Spilimbergo, and Wachtenheim (1996) show that financial depth explains much of the differences in secondary schooling across countries. As shown in Table 3, in 1989 Brazil and Malaysia had similar levels of per capita income. But the poorest quintile in Brazil had only about one-half the absolute income level of the poorest quintile in Malaysia. Given an income elasticity of demand for secondary education of 0.50 (a conservative figure), if the distribution of income had been as equal in Brazil as in Malaysia, secondary enrollments among poor Brazilian children would have been more than 40 percent higher. There is some evidence that, among the poor, the income elasticity of demand for basic schooling exceeds 1.0, in which case secondary enrollments among poor Brazilian children would have been more than 80 percent higher. A quantitative study of how income inequality affects schooling suggests that the huge secondary-school enrollment gap between Brazil and Korea in the 1970s is largely due to Brazil's greater income inequality and resultant lower enrollment of poor children (20 points of a 27 percentage-point gap, according to Williamson 1993).

Third, household demand for education is not only a function of household income and household access to borrowing. It is also a function of expected returns to the family from schooling, in the form of higher future income for educated children. Two different public policies have systematically reduced the demand for basic education among the poor by reducing its expected returns.

First, postwar Latin American governments pursued import-substituting

Table 3. Absolute Income Share of Lowest Quintile of Households, Malaysia and Brazil
(In US dollar terms)

Country	GNP per capita (PPP-adjusted)	Income share of bottom 20% (percent)	Per capita income of bottom 20%
Malaysia, 1989	4,674	4.6	1,075
Brazil, 1989	4,271	2.4	513

Source: Summers and Heston (1995) for GNP; Deininger and Squire (1996) for income share data.

industrialization policies in an attempt to shift away from exporting primary commodities and to promote local manufacturing. These ISI policies resulted in large subsidies and protection for the owners of capital, but did not promote demand for labor (Schiff and Valdes 1992). As increased profits accrued to the owners of capital, real wages declined for the unskilled workforce. Relatively low wage growth among workers, combined with high returns to capital, did nothing to encourage demand for basic education among the poor. Additionally, some Latin American labor markets have discriminated against certain ethnic, linguistic or racial groups that also tend to be poor. This discrimination has reduced the expected returns to education among these groups and further reduced the demand for education among the poor.

The second problem has been educational policy itself. Low and declining quality of basic education in Latin America, an outcome of the inefficient public spending discussed below, has reduced returns to basic schooling in the region, especially for poor households whose children are likely to attend the lowest-quality schools. The high repetition and dropout rates in Latin America, especially among the poor, are sad testimony to parents' initial efforts to enroll children, and their growing discouragement as low quality and low achievement limit their children's learning and the expected economic returns.[10]

In short, expected returns to education are a function of parents' assessment of the future labor market for their children. Where demand for labor is low (and capital subsidized directly or indirectly), schooling is of poor quality, and labor markets discriminate against some groups who also tend to be poor, low expected returns to schooling will reduce household demand for education.

At the same time, the supply of education in Latin America has itself been affected by the region's high income inequality.[11] When the distribution of income is highly unequal, providing subsidized basic education to a large segment of the school-age population implies a relatively large tax burden on the rich. High-income families are likely to resist. One result can be the underfunding of education—and the decline in quality described above. A second result can be the channeling of public subsidies to higher education, where children of the rich are more likely to benefit. In fact, as shown in Table 4, a high share of the region's public spending on education is allocated to higher education—more than 20 percent on average, compared to 15 percent on average in East Asia. Venezuela and Korea are extreme examples. While in the early 1990s Venezuela allocated 35 percent of its public education budget to higher education, Korea allocated just 8 percent of its budget to postsecondary schooling. Public expenditure on education as a percentage of GNP was actually higher in Venezuela (5.1) than in Korea (4.5). However, after subtracting the share going to higher education, public expenditure available for basic education as a percentage of GNP was considerably higher in Korea (3.6) than in Venezuela (1.3) (UNDP 1997).

By expanding the quantity of education and improving quality at the base of the educational pyramid, East Asian governments have stimulated the demand for higher education, while relying to a large extent on the private sector to satisfy that demand. In Latin America, government subsidies have disproportionately benefited high-income families whose children are much more likely to attend university. At the same time, low public funding of secondary education has resulted in poorly qualified children from low-income backgrounds being forced into private universities or excluded from higher-level education. Underfunding of education has meant that the guarantees of universal primary education in Latin America have become false entitlements for the poor: the education available to them has been of such poor quality as to be of little real benefit.

In summary, the relatively poor growth performance of Latin America, the persistence of income inequality, and the difficulties of reducing poverty cannot be separated from the region's troubling record of limited and unequal access to education. In a series of vicious cycles, historically high levels of asset and income inequality have generated an economic and political environment that severely limits the opportunities of the poor. With few opportunities for education despite reasonable government spending, and without other productive assets, the poor are condemned to low-productivity work, low household income, and a new round of limited access to education. The region's societies on the whole also suffer, as educational progress and accumulation of assets are limited to the nonpoor, reducing average growth levels and perpetuating inequality.

Table 4. Budget Allotted to Higher Education, 1990-94
(As percent of overall education budget)

EAST ASIA		LATIN AMERICA	
Malaysia	17	Argentina	17
Thailand	17	Brazil	26
Indonesia	18	Chile	20
Korea, Rep.	8	Colombia	17
Simple avg.	**15**	Costa Rica	31
		Dominican	
		Republic	11
		Ecuador	23
		Honduras	20
		Mexico	14
		Uruguay	25
		Venezuela	35
		Simple avg.	**22**

Source: UNDP (1997).

The Business of Social Services

What is meant by low and unequal accumulation of human capital can be stated more simply: public education has not reached the poor in Latin America. A major culprit in this failure is a model of social service delivery that has reflected and reinforced social, economic and political inequities. To remedy this situation, we propose an alternative model of social service delivery.

With good intentions, but often driven by populist tendencies and patronage, many Latin American countries sought to construct their own versions of the welfare state during the postwar period. Centrally planned public systems were constructed to provide constitutionally guaranteed health and education services for all, and now these systems have acquired their own momentum.

The public systems in effect became state-run pseudo-monopolies,[12] concentrating the functions of financing, purchasing, and production of services in the hands of a central government that allowed providers little autonomy and gave consumers no role in organizing the services. Command and control mechanisms allocated public resources to fund the various inputs (labor, equipment, materials) required for the delivery of social services. In the absence of competition, consumer interests became increasingly irrelevant.

The public state-run pseudo-monopolies in education and health represented a classic case of government or policy failure—in part an outcome of larger failures of accountability in highly centralized and often undemocratic political systems, in which political systems perpetuated and reinforced economic privileges. Birdsall and James (1993) describe how such government "misbehavior" in social programs is likely to be manifested in successful rent-seeking by providers such as teachers, and in successful appropriation of public funding by the wealthy (e.g., by pressure to direct education spending to universities, where they receive the bulk of the public subsidy).

In fact, the early centralization of public systems had three predictable consequences. First, it created bureaucratic incentives for expansion of employment, and in the case of education strengthened the role of centralized (often nationwide) teacher unions. In many countries, extensive hiring depleted budgets, leaving little in the way of additional resources for salary increases. Conflicts between unions and government frequently led to bilateral monopoly compromises in the use of resources. For example, given the constraints on current revenues, union demands were often redirected toward better and earlier retirement conditions as well as toward shorter working hours. Much of the discussion with teachers and other workers in the social sectors focused on consolidating their entitlements or "acquired rights." In health and other public services including education, the system drove up costs while heightening the dissatisfaction of workers and consumers, undermining the quality of public services and weakening community support.

Second, centralized systems precluded feedback from users and made consumer satisfaction irrelevant, thus limiting the public systems' responsiveness and inviting erosion in the quality of services. The lack of autonomy of school directors and teachers contributed to low quality, as they had neither incentives nor power to fully exercise their skills and abilities.

Finally, as demonstrated in the first section, the centralized systems of education failed to reach the poor, even as they gradually forfeited the support of the upper and middle classes. In many countries, growing awareness of the deterioration in school quality prompted the middle classes to begin to use private schools, draining additional resources from the public system and leading to an endless cycle of worsening quality, erosion of political support, and declining resources.

State-run versus Market Systems

During the 1980s, the obvious failure of centralized, state-run systems, the increasing use of private providers by the middle classes, and wider debate about the role of government versus the market, all prompted new discussion about the merits of a market model of social service delivery. The market model leaves the financing, purchase or production, and provision of services to separate and independent entities. The providers (schools, physicians, or hospitals) interact directly with users who seek services and pay for them (sometimes through insurance mechanisms, as in health services). The entire process is coordinated in the deregulated market through the pricing system, whereby resources flow in accordance with ability to pay.

But the market model has its own shortcomings. Without independent assessment and publicly available information, users have limited mechanisms to compare quality across providers—and, in the case of schools, face high costs in switching providers, especially in midyear. And obviously the market model fails to reach the poor, since it relies on ability to pay.

The two systems—state-run centralized and market or private sector—have historically been viewed as polar opposites; indeed, the debate between private versus public provision of services still dominates discussion in a number of Latin American countries. In fact, the two systems actually have much in common. Both are characterized by top-down mechanisms that favor providers and minimize the "voice and choice" options of users.[13] Poor users are in a particularly weak position: they are constrained by lack of choice in the monopolistic public system, by inability to pay in the private system, and by lack of information on the quality of providers' services in both systems. For these reasons, we categorize both the state-run and market systems of social service delivery as top-down "vertical models," where consumer feedback to providers is restricted or irrelevant (Figure 7).

In short, as models for organizing social services, the centralized bureaucracy and market systems are both flawed. Lack of competition severely limits incentives for efficiency and effectiveness in the state-run model. Despite their "public" nature, state systems fail to serve the poor. In the market system, on the other hand, problems of information, opportunistic behavior, and inequitable access raise issues of fairness as well as efficiency. Debating the merits of the two systems may be useful for academic purposes, but the polarization surrounding that debate has postponed the serious policy decisions required to modernize the social sectors.

FIGURE 7

The Vertical Models: State-run and Market Systems

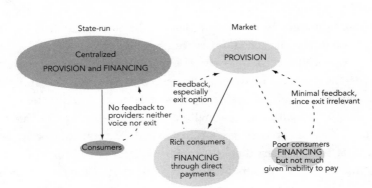

A New Horizontal Model

In response to the failures of the past, a more pragmatic approach is emerging in Latin America.[14] This approach combines the spirit of social responsibility that inspired the old public sector model with efforts to create consumer choice and give voice to ordinary citizens. It also relies upon the power of interaction among free agents that characterizes the new market models. We describe this more pragmatic approach as a horizontal model (Figure 8), in which public and private ownership of the assets involved in social service delivery can complement each other.

The horizontal model relies not on ownership of assets (private or public) as its defining characteristic, but instead on rule-based incentives that strengthen users in their interactions with providers. For education, the horizontal model implies more decentralized public systems with greater parent and community power in local school governance; greater choice for poor parents among public schools and/or subsidies to permit the use of private schools; and much greater government emphasis on assessment, accreditation and provision of information to the public on school quality. Critical characteristics of the model are equitable public financing (i.e., financing that ensures equal access for the poor), greater competition in the delivery of services within and between the public and private sectors, and beneficiaries who are better informed, better represented and more empowered.

These fundamentals can be summarized as consumers, a competitive market, and coordination of the market by government.

FIGURE 8

The Horizontal Model

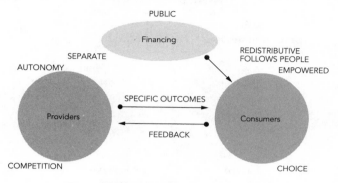

Note: In health, this model also may involve a sponsor or purchasing agent that permits consumers to make purchasing contracts collectively. See the discussion of Colombia in the text and Londoño and Frenk (1997).

• The horizontal model empowers consumers, including poor consumers, through greater voice and choice. Consumers have greater voice in locally managed schools where parents control the hiring of teachers, and poor consumers can be organized into community groups so that they can more effectively assert their views. The poor also have greater choice if they can use publicly financed vouchers to pay for education at the school they choose.[15]

• In order to exercise their powers of voice and choice, consumers need access to a competitive market of service providers. It is unimportant whether these providers are public or private; operational efficiency will decide which suppliers do well in a competitive market.

• Finally, to choose effectively in markets for social services, where the poorest cannot afford to pay and where all consumers may lack information about the quality of services, consumers need a sponsor or a coordinator. This brings us to the role of government in the horizontal model.

A New Role for Government

In the new model of social service delivery, the role of government changes considerably—from focusing primarily on service provision, toward financing and coordination to empower consumers (Table 5). First consider financing. In the bureaucratic model, government provides services directly and finances only the services

Table 5. Models of Social Service Organization

	Vertical		Horizontal
ROLES	**Public pseudo-monopoly**	**Market**	
Functions of financing, provision, coordination	Financing, provision, and coordination integrated and centralized	Diffuse financing and provision No coordination	Government coordinates via information and regulation Government financing, especially for poor Provision decentralized, can be public and/or private
Providers	Centralized	Autonomous Fragmented	Autonomous Pluralistic
Purchasers[1]	Integrated with providers	Diffuse	Purchaser-provider split
Consumers	Limited (some voice)	Segregated (some choice)	Empowered (voice and choice)
RULES			
Finance	Public resources follow inputs	Private resources follow consumers' ability to pay	Public resources subsidize demand
Coordination	Central planning Monopoly	Atomized	Structured competition
DYNAMICS	Controlled by providers and clientelism	Captured by providers and the rich	Enhanced by purchasers and consumers
Focus	Input market	None	Output market
The Poorest	Ignored	Excluded	Empowered

[1] Relevant for health care. See discussion of Colombia health system in text.

it provides. In the horizontal model the government does not monopolize the provision of inputs such as books or even schooling itself. It may finance these inputs—indeed it often should finance inputs—but it shares provision with the private (including nonprofit) sector.

Government finance in the horizontal model is directed toward ensuring that those services with positive externalities for society are adequately financed, independent of who provides them, and that the poor receive subsidies in some form to ensure their adequate access to services as consumers. Mechanisms for financing include vouchers for eligible consumers, and direct payment to private institutions based on their number of users. Tax-financed public spending prevents inability to pay from restricting access to services and ensures that funding constraints do not hamper the functioning of services that have high social benefits. At the same time, public spending is not arbitrary. Resources are allocated on the basis of performance, ideally through demand-oriented subsidies such as vouchers. This implies the use of capitation (adjusted for risk in the case of health services, and for socioeconomic status in the case of education) as a mechanism for allocating public resources.

In the horizontal model, government also takes on the new role of coordination: government channels its energy into promoting public interest, proposing strategic directions and designs, providing comprehensive security, mobilizing resources, setting standards, providing information to consumers—in short, assuring structured markets through the establishment and enforcement of fair and transparent rules. Government as coordinator not only subsidizes the demand of the poor, but may finance the creation of community groups which empower their members with both voice and choice. As coordinator, government also ensures competition (within and between the public and private sectors) in the supply of services, using the private sector and adapting to its methods of operation.

In the vertical models government protects producers; in the horizontal model government empowers people's choices. Enhancing consumer choice—the essence of the horizontal model—requires fair and transparent rules of the game, universally accepted and enforced. Where markets do not exist or when consumers are left unprotected, the case for many health services, governments have a responsibility to develop pluralistic institutional purchasers of services (or consumer sponsors) who can strengthen and simplify the choices available, especially to the poor.

This method of coordinating participants contrasts with the other purely private or public models. Regulatory gaps in the market system allow widely dispersed private suppliers to engage in opportunistic practices, by taking advantage of the power of information and the difficulties of outside monitoring. Command and control rules in the bureaucratic model fail to check natural tendencies toward minimum effort, waste of resources, and corruption.

Because effective coordination requires structured rules and performance incentives, it is greatly eased if there is agreement on specific, standardized outputs.[16] For example, in the health sector the horizontal model seeks to ensure that health care plans are highly specific in determining the responsibilities of producers and the rights of beneficiaries.[17] This regulatory model differs markedly from the purely public model, which is characterized by official and discretionary intervention, and which focuses more on input markets (especially for labor, but also for infrastructure management and supply, medicines and textbooks) or on control of competitors' prices, rather than on setting targets and monitoring performance. The horizontal model also contrasts with the market model where there are no established ground rules governing interactions among agents.

The emphasis in the horizontal model on specific products makes it possible to draw up precise goals for social programs, setting a standard the public can more easily assess. In education, performance standards and periodic and systematic testing make it possible to measure quality. Under the other two models, the absence of such standards leaves the door open for the opportunistic practices of public or private suppliers—escaping detection and avoiding accountability to their consumers as a result of insufficient consumer information.

A Horizontal System Encourages Reform

In the horizontal model, producers of clearly defined services compete to interact with and respond to consumers. Public funds that are allocated by following people—rather than following suppliers—create room for consumers to exercise their decisionmaking ability. The separation of finance and service provision, in combination with service provider autonomy, paves the way for competition in the provision of services. The empowerment of consumers, coupled with measures to support the poorer segments of society through direct subsidies, gives poor consumers the capacity to demand adequate services in a competitive market.

In contrast with the two vertical organization models, the horizontal model encourages change, offering a political advantage from the standpoint of the reform process. The bureaucratic model protects the interests of the internal bureaucracy (the "insiders"). The decentralized market model protects affluent consumers and perpetuates the disadvantages of the lowest-income groups, so that systemic inefficiency goes hand-in-hand with inequity. In the horizontal model, the emergence of a new category of purchasers, coupled with the growing assertiveness of consumers, undermines the power of vested interest groups that could otherwise thwart change.

Latin American Examples of the Horizontal Model

Social Investment Funds. Social investment funds originated in Bolivia, when a Social Emergency Fund was designed and utilized to cushion the impact of the stabilization process in the mid 1980s. This new form of institution, combining public funding with private sector-style competitive contracting, expanded rapidly to now 16 countries, and has succeeded in mobilizing public funding in the amount of approximately US$400 million per year in the 1990s (one-half of 1 percent of total social spending). The establishment of social investment funds in Latin America has made it possible to meet the basic needs of a considerable proportion of the most disadvantaged members of society; even more meaningful for our discussion, it has brought about new roles and rules in the conduct of social policy.

Three major innovations can be observed in the operation of social investment funds: the introduction of a new service-purchaser agency acting on behalf of communities, separate from the ministries (this agency is almost always a special legal entity reporting to the Office of the President of the Republic, with higher pay levels than in the general government); the empowerment of the communities as reflected in their ability to make their voices heard and to demand accountability in project execution; and the competitive and flexible hiring of nongovernmental agencies to execute projects with fixed budgets. These three innovations have made it possible to outline a new horizontal framework for relationships among the state, providers, and consumers. The development of social investment funds has in practice led to demarcation between (i) the finance and the delivery of services, and (ii) purchasing and the production of basic goods and services (see Table 5); it has promoted greater accountability in projects; it has bolstered the ability of the poor consumers to act as consumers by targeting spending to poor communities, enhancing their political access, as well as by providing a focus for community involvement and decisionmaking; and it has strengthened performance-based public funding, which has greatly enhanced flexibility in the procurement of work and inputs, although full supply subsidies have remained in effect.[18]

Competitive decentralization in education. Additional aspects of the horizontal model can be seen in the education reforms which began in Latin America in the 1980s. The reforms are based on the idea that while education policy will remain a function of the center, services should be demand-driven and competitively supplied.

Four examples are particularly noteworthy. First, in rural El Salvador, parents' organizations have considerable authority to hire teachers and to assess their attendance and performance. The system, which also gives school directors un-usual autonomy in day-to-day management, is now being introduced in urban schools.

Second, in the state of Minas Gerais in Brazil, three essential reforms were introduced in the 1990s: school autonomy with community involvement, alloca-tion of resources on the basis of performance, and the development of a system of standardized assessment of students. On the first count, a new form of public school was created, with considerable freedom to prepare and debate five-year develop-ment plans, and with school councils participating in school administration and election of the school principal. Second, the nonwage component of costs is now assigned to the schools through a transparent formula based on capitation per stu-dent enrolled. Finally, a system for the annual assessment of school performance has been introduced.

A third example is the implementation in 1992 of a program of vouchers for secondary education in Colombia. With public funding, an educational scholar-ship system was designed so that lower-income children from the major cities could gain access to precertified private schools on a basis of free individual choice. This reform embodies two profound changes: capitation in allocating resources, and the freedom to choose private schools in the context of the decentralization process.

A fourth example—probably the longest established in Latin America—is the reform of the Chilean public education system. Pursuant to a 1981 law, changes were introduced in the mechanism for allocating public resources so as to favor students' freedom of choice in selecting public and private schools. The resources transferred from the center to municipal governments are allocated to schools on the basis of school attendance. Unfortunately, the reform has not included mea-sures to boost school autonomy or decentralization in the hiring of teachers and wage bargaining. This has prevented public institutions from integrating them-selves more rapidly and responsively into the system, and has created political resistance which has held back the reform process.

New roles and rules in health.[19] The health sector in Latin America has been the setting for the most ambitious efforts to develop entirely new systems of roles and rules. Considerable reform efforts were undertaken in Argentina, Uruguay, and Nicaragua,[20] but the Colombian experience with reform exemplifies the implemen-tation of the new horizontal organization model that is taking hold in Latin America.[21]

In 1993, Colombia began implementing a new modus operandi for its health system, combining a horizontal framework of functionally specialized actors and market-oriented rules to give increasingly free rein to competition and freedom of choice. Mandatory enrollment of the population into a social security system provides centralized funding. The financing is separated from delivery of services by competing providers; and production of services is separated from institutional purchases of services. The state concentrates on mobilizing public funding resources for the system, and on monitoring of the system. The Ministry of Health has withdrawn from the direct management of hospitals, and focuses its efforts on steering the system under the auspices of a national health board in which all participants in the system are represented. A regulatory authority, set up as a specialized public supervisory entity, is responsible for ensuring information flows with a single standard accounting of the system, coordinating the quality assurance system, monitoring the soundness of the various entities, and resolving disputes and grievances within the system. Health agents are in charge of guaranteeing the general public's access to a universal health services plan. Health promotion entities (EPSs), on behalf of their affiliate members, purchase the services included in a universal package of services. The health promotion entities compete among themselves for enrollment by households. Public and private EPSs are governed by the same rules; in the poorer regions the system has developed consumer cooperatives. An EPS may provide services directly, or hire public or private provider entities that operate in accordance with competition-oriented rules and regulations. Public hospitals are being converted into autonomous legal entities. Users must enroll in the system, but they can join any EPS, and can choose to rejoin or switch each year.

The Colombian system overall is self-financed through payroll taxes and user copayments. The system operates a single solidarity and guarantee fund, which collects (on a decentralized basis) all contributions and allocates them to each EPS as a risk-adjusted capitation, in accordance with the estimated costs of the universal health package. The fiscal resources that formerly financed the operation of public hospitals are being gradually converted into demand subsidies to finance freedom of access to the system of the poorest 25 percent of the population. There are neither fiscal incentives nor price controls within the system.

Regulation efforts have focused on devising a health service plan in accordance with criteria of cost-effectiveness and financial security, in addition to establishing a suitable quality assurance system. There is decentralization in wage bargaining and freedom of contract between the EPSs and provider entities, and the drug procurement system is comparatively competitive.

The new system has made remarkable progress in its early years of operation. Enrollment in the social security system has increased by 15 million new individuals, six million of whom come from the poorest segments of society, and who receive a direct demand subsidy. More than 20 new EPSs have been set up, most of them of nongovernmental origin, enrolling five million new members. The 180 consumer cooperatives can claim two million members in rural areas and in the marginal communities in major cities. Although the system has required additional public resources, some of these resources have replaced the out-of-pocket expenses formerly incurred by households, and the average cost per member has declined.

The great majority of public hospitals have gained full autonomy, and as part of the decentralization process, departmental and municipal secretariats have assumed responsibility for 80 percent of the services previously handled by the Ministry of Health. In its role as service provider, the private sector is witnessing a boom in investment and organizational innovation. Colombia's success in structuring competition is a clear indication that the new system of roles and rules has made it possible to combine enhanced fairness and efficiency in the operation of social programs.

Implications and Reflections

The poor growth performance of Latin America, the persistence of high income inequality and the difficulties of reducing poverty cannot be separated from the region's troubled record of limited and unequal access to human capital. Of particular concern are our data suggesting that the distribution of education has seen little if any improvement over the last three decades. This chapter's first section provides evidence that low and unequal accumulation of human capital has done more than delay Latin America's growth: it has also slowed poverty reduction and perpetuated the world's highest levels of income inequality. The implication is straightforward—there is great untapped potential for faster growth in the region. The growth process could benefit from major productivity increases among the poor, if they are provided with access to education. More education, and in particular education that is more equal (i.e., that reaches the poor), could accelerate the growth process and simultaneously reduce inequality.

Second, for Latin America, low accumulation of human capital and its unequal distribution are partly rooted in longstanding inequality, of assets (including human capital itself) and of income. The historic legacy is difficult to alter in the short run. But low and unequal accumulation can also be explained by the economic policies that dominated the region for decades. Closed economies that protected capital and relied heavily on natural resource exports discouraged demand for education in the poor households of Latin America, by discouraging demand for labor, the poor's major asset, and for skilled labor, where lies the poor's greatest potential for income growth. Economic reforms of the last decade in most countries of the region are eliminating the biases against labor typical of protected economies, and they are bringing the macroeconomic stability that is key to private sector investment. This is setting the stage for increased household demand for schooling, and increased interest of the business sector in the skilled labor force necessary to maintain competitiveness in open economies.

Third, the public system of delivery of social programs has been part of the problem in the region. Inequality of access has been embedded in an approach to social service delivery that encourages exclusion, segmentation, and inefficiencies. Traditional vertical, bureaucratic systems for organizing schooling and other services have been inefficient and have failed to serve the poor. The alternative market model has performed no better. The competition it provides in a few countries has left out all those unable to pay. We discuss examples from Latin America of an alternative horizontal model, in which government's role is transformed from provider of services to financier and coordinator, promoting competition in service provision among both private and public suppliers, enhancing consumer voice and choice, and ensuring that the poor, via fair rules of access, vouchers and other demand subsidies, are fully integrated as consumers into the system.

We began this chapter by pointing out the shortcomings, in terms of policy guidance, of those growth models that emphasize education but fail to consider the effects of the *distribution* of education, the relevance of household *demand,* and the institutional problem of *delivering* education, especially to the poor. In the context of Latin America, our discussion highlighted those three factors: (1) the distribution of human capital, with unequal access of the poor to education slowing the accumulation process; (2) the demand of the poor for schooling, inhibited for many decades by economic policies biased against labor; and (3) the delivery system, which has reinforced rather than compensated for prevailing social and economic inequities. Focusing on these normally neglected issues, we have suggested an approach to social policy and its implementation in Latin America that would resolve two apparent tradeoffs:

- Emphasis on more equal education will result in both greater growth and greater equity.
- An approach to service delivery that mimics the market—that is demand-driven with competitive supply—can bring both more equity and more efficiency to the delivery of social services.

We thus challenge tradeoff pessimism. Tradeoffs are not inevitable in the development process; many are the outcome of poor policy decisions and inappropriate institutional arrangements. In fact, the kinds of institutional reforms described here are underway in some Latin American countries, and already demonstrate that efficiency and fairness can be achieved simultaneously.

Ideas about how to achieve equity are undergoing a fundamental change; the focus is now equality of capabilities and opportunities, rather than equality of outcomes. As Latin American countries abandon the public-sector/private-sector dichotomy, they are discarding both populism and paternalism in order to concentrate on broadening access to opportunities.

The globalization of the world economy, the spread of democracy throughout Latin America, and the reforms in fiscal and foreign trade policies have paved the way for a new role for the state in social programs that create human capital—simultaneously using market incentives and guaranteeing equal opportunity. In this way, reorganization of the social sectors can become the centerpiece of more rapid and more inclusive growth.

Endnotes _____

[1] Schultz (1988).

[2] Of course, as we discuss below, the state can play a strong role in the selective financing of social programs, separate from their provision. On this particular issue, the new growth models are silent.

[3] Consistent with performance, spending is relatively greater on health than on education compared to other regions. In the rest of this paper, we concentrate on education as the measure of human capital accumulation. Health and other measures also reflect investment in human capital, but with less linear and thus less easily measured and differentiated effects on productivity and income growth.

[4] Compared to East Asia, low economic growth and later fertility decline also translated into lower per-child spending in Latin America, especially in the 1980s. Now Latin America is beginning to benefit from slower growth of its school-age populations, and the higher per capita spending associated with faster economic growth, even without allotting a higher proportion of GDP to social services. In addition, many countries are increasing that proportion.

[5] In Figure 2, years of schooling are estimated using Barro-Lee's frequency distribution for adults 25 years and over within categories of education, (i.e., no schooling, incomplete primary schooling, completed primary schooling, incomplete secondary schooling, completed secondary schooling, incomplete higher schooling, and completed higher schooling).

[6] As education systems begin to expand, existing disparities in human capital of the population will widen, until average education reaches five to six years (Londoño and Székely 1997). However, the experience of countries like Indonesia shows that even from a low level, rapid accumulation can be associated with improved distribution. There is some evidence that inequality of education is beginning to decline in Latin America: inequality is lower for young adults (aged 20 to 30) than for older groups in 1990 (Elizabeth King, personal correspondence, June 1997).

[7] In these regressions, we use the standard deviation of years of education of adults aged 25 years and older as the measure of the distribution of education.

[8] This and the next paragraph are based on Londoño and Székely (1997).

[9] The discussion in this section and the data referred to are largely from Birdsall, Bruns and Sabot (1996).

[10] The roots of low-quality basic education and its effects on the poor are discussed fully for Brazil in Birdsall, Bruns and Sabot (1996) and for Latin America in Birdsall and Sabot (1996).

[11] Latin America spends as much on education as a percentage of GNP as other developing regions with similar levels of per capita income. But the fact that growth has lagged in Latin America means that education budgets have been smaller in absolute terms. In addition, higher birth rates in Latin America mean that the same percentage of GNP spending translates into lower spending per child (Birdsall and Sabot 1996).

[12] Strictly speaking, the creation of a public monopoly requires explicitly barring the operation of and public access to other providers. In Latin America, this is only the case in Cuba.

[13] The terms voice and exit were suggested by Hirschman (1970). We use choice instead of exit to convey the positive benefit to consumers of competition among suppliers.

[14] This section borrows freely from the ideas of Londoño (1995) and Londoño and Frenk (1997).

[15] The model we describe gives poor consumers the capacity to choose, including through direct demand subsidies. Introducing choice does not solve the problem of the very poorest, most marginalized households, who are least equipped to choose well due to low income and barriers of education, language, or culture. This does not invalidate the more market-oriented approach, but it means that special provisions need to be made for these groups.

[16] The concept of specificity is borrowed from Molina (1997).

[17] In addition, the chosen rules aim to be consistent with the economic behavior of agents, in order to minimize the extent to which the authorities are required to intervene and to minimize the extent to which the supervisory entities are required to exercise discretion.

[18] See Graham (1994) for a thorough discussion of social funds and their characteristics.

[19] In the health sector, noteworthy examples are the household programs for child health care in Colombia, local health action committees [Comités Locales de Acción en Salud (CLAES)] in Peru, and the community-based programs for primary health care in the north of Brazil.

[20] See Medici et al. (1997) for a detailed examination of these reform measures.

[21] Londoño (1996) gives a complete description of this process.

References _____

Alesina, A., and D. Rodrik. 1994. Distributive Politics and Economic Growth: A Critical Survey of the Recent Literature. *World Bank Economic Review* 8(3).

Barro, R.J. 1991. Economic Growth in a Cross Section of Countries. *Quarterly Journal of Economics* 105(2).

Barro, R.J., and J. Lee. February 1993. International Comparisons of Educational Attainment. Paper presented at conference on How Do National Policies Affect Long-Run Growth? World Bank, Washington, D.C.

Barro, R.J., and X. Sala-i-Martin. 1995. *Economic Growth* (New York: McGraw-Hill).

Birdsall, N., B. Bruns and R. Sabot. 1996. Education in Brazil: Playing a Bad Hand Badly. In Nancy Birdsall and Richard H. Sabot (eds.), *Opportunity Foregone: Education in Brazil* (Washington, D.C.: IDB).

Birdsall, N., and E. James. 1993. Efficiency and Equity in Social Spending: How and Why Governments Misbehave. In M. Lipton and J. van der Gaag (eds.), *Including the Poor* (New York: Oxford University Press for the World Bank).

Birdsall, N., and J.L. Londoño. May 1997. Asset Inequality Does Matter: Lessons from Latin America. *American Economic Review* 87(2).

Birdsall, N., D. Ross, and R. Sabot. September 1995. Inequality and Growth Reconsidered: Lessons from East Asia. *World Bank Economic Review* 9(3).

Birdsall, N., D. Ross and R. Sabot. 1997. Education, Growth and Inequality. In N. Birdsall and F. Jaspersen (eds.), *Pathways to Growth: Comparing East Asia and Latin America.* (Washington, D.C.: IDB).

Birdsall, N., and R. Sabot. 1996. *Opportunity Foregone: Education in Brazil*. Washington, D.C.: IDB, distributed by Johns Hopkins University Press.

Birdsall, N., B. Stallings and J. Clugage. Forthcoming. Growth and Inequality: Do Regional Patterns Redeem Kuznets? In A. Solimano (ed.), *Equity, Growth and Social Policy: Issues, Evidence and the Chilean Case.*

Deininger, K., and L. Squire. September 1996. A New Data Base for Income Distribution in the World. *World Bank Economic Review* 10(3).

Engerman, S.L., and K.L. Sokoloff. December 1994. Factor Endowments, Institutions, and Differential Paths of Growth Among New World Economies: A View from Economic Historians of the United States. Washington, D.C.: NBER Working Paper Series on Historical Factors in Long-Run Growth.

Flug, K., A. Spilimbergo, and E. Wachtenheim. 1996. Investment in Education: Do Economic Volatility and Credit Constraints Matter? OCE Working Paper Series 301. Washington, D.C.: IDB.

Graham, Carol. 1994. *Safety Nets, Politics, and the Poor: Transitions to Market Economies*. Washington, D.C.: The Brookings Institution.

Hirschman, Albert O. 1970. Exit, Voice and Loyalty: *Responses to Decline in Firms, Organizations, and States*. Cambridge, MA: Harvard University Press.

IDB (Inter-American Development Bank). 1996. *Economic and Social Progress in Latin America 1996 Report*. Washington, D.C.: IDB.

Levine, R., and D. Renelt. September 1992. A Sensitivity Analysis of Cross-Country Growth Regressions. *American Economic Review* 82(2).

Londoño, J.L. 1996. Restructuring the State and the Role of Social Policy: Developing a Horizontal Model. Technical Department for Latin America Working Paper. Washington, D.C.: World Bank.

Londoño, J.L., and J. Frenk. May 1997. Structured Pluralism: A New Model for Health Reform in Latin America. *Health Policy*.

Londoño, J.L., and M. Székely. 1997. Distributional Surprises After a Decade of Reforms: Latin America in the Nineties. Paper for Seminar, Latin America After a Decade of Reforms: What Comes Next? Washington, D.C.: IDB.

Lora, E., and F. Barrera. 1997. A Decade of Structural Reforms in Latin America: Growth, Productivity and Investments Are Not What They Used to Be. Paper for Seminar, Latin America After a Decade of Reforms: What Comes Next? Washington, D.C.: IDB.

Medici, A.C., J.L. Londoño, O. Coelho, and H. Saxenian. 1997. Managed Care and Managed Competition in Latin America and the Caribbean, Innovations in Health Care Financing.

Molina, C.G. 1997. Options for the Funding and Delivery of Social Services. Teaching notes. Washington, D.C.: IDB.

Persson, T., and G. Tabellini. 1994. Is Inequality Harmful for Growth? *American Economic Review* 84(3).

Schiff, M., and A. Valdés. 1992. *The Political Economy of Agricultural Pricing Policy. Volume 4: A Synthesis of the Economics in Developing Countries*. Baltimore, MD: Johns Hopkins University Press.

Schultz, T.P. 1988. Education Investment and Returns. In H. B. Chenery and T.N. Srinivasan (eds.), *Handbook of Development Economics*. Amsterdam: North Holland.

Summers, R., and A. Heston. 1995. The Penn World Tables, Mark 5.6. University of Pennsylvania, Department of Economics, Philadelphia, PA.

UNDP (United Nations Development Programme). 1997. *Human Development Report.* New York: Oxford University Press.

UNESCO (United Nations Educational, Scientific, and Cultural Organization). Various years. *Statistical Yearbook.* Lanham, MD and New York: Bernan Press and UNESCO Publishing.

Williamson, J. 1993. Human Capital Deepening, Inequality, and Demographic Events along the Asia-Pacific Rim. In Naohiro Ogawa, Gavin W. Jones, and Jeffrey Williamson (eds.), *Human Resources in Development along the Asia-Pacific Rim.* Singapore: Oxford University Press.

World Bank. Various years. *World Development Report.* New York: Oxford University Press.

CHAPTER SIX

Inequality-Reducing Growth in Agriculture: A Market-Friendly Policy Agenda

Michael R. Carter and Jonathan Coles

Does low inequality promote growth? Until recently, the conventional answer was that it does not. However, evidence that East Asian economies experienced rapid growth with low and diminishing inequality has prompted a reexamination of the question. While the precise impact of inequality on growth remains unclear, there is good reason to refocus attention on the more general income dynamics of growth—that is, the impact of inequality on growth, and of growth on inequality. For if initial inequality shapes not only the rate of growth, but also its income distribution consequences, then the East Asian miracle may reflect a virtuous circle in which low initial inequality generates rapid growth and ever-lower inequality (as Birdsall and Sabot 1996 suggest). Conversely, Latin America, with its legacy of steep inequality, may be mired in a vicious circle of self-limiting, inequality-perpetuating growth.

The current rethinking of growth-inequality linkages emphasizes the need to identify inequality-reducing growth strategies. This chapter argues that agriculture and agricultural policy are critical to such strategies in contemporary Latin America. Although agriculture is no longer the predominant sector in many Latin American economies, it continues to house around 50 percent of the region's poor and indigent people. Even this figure understates agriculture's impact on the well-being of the most impoverished people, as intersectoral migration links rural wages and living standards with those of the urban poor (de Janvry, Sadoulet and Wilcox 1979). Agriculture is also a site where initial inequality has reproduced itself over time, making it a key component of the vicious circle linking inequality to growth and growth to inequality. The economywide benefits of a broad-based, agricultural growth strategy that reduces inequality would likely be high.

The contemporary challenge to agricultural policy in Latin America is clear: Can the social base of growth be broadened, such that impoverished people benefit from and actively participate in capital accumulation and growth? Broad-based agrarian growth has two interrelated dimensions. The first is securing the participation of existing small-scale producers in growing technologies and markets. The second is enabling landless and land-poor households to gain access to land.

We approach this challenge of broad-based agricultural growth with some optimism. A similar challenge underlay the land reform period of Latin American policymaking in the 1960s and 1970s. Since that time, however, much has been learned about what markets can and cannot do. First, we understand that policy must be market-friendly. Agricultural policy in the past two decades has undergone significant reform in many countries, and the sorts of price distortions and capital subsidies that unfairly advantaged large-scale farming have been eliminated. Second, we now acknowledge what markets cannot accomplish. Sustaining market-friendly reforms is important, but in dualistic agrarian economies characterized by high levels of inequality, it takes more than unadorned liberalization to level the playing field and secure small farm competitiveness and broad-based growth. Policies must be market-prudent as well as market-friendly, and should pay special attention to financial market failures that undermine the potential for inequality-reducing growth. Third and last, the political-economic prospects for such an approach have improved. The foundations of old antagonistic agrarian coalitions have been shaken, and there is political space within which to make the case for a win-win, inequality-reducing growth strategy.[1]

In light of these circumstances, this chapter will attempt to clarify the policy and research agenda for Latin American agriculture heading into the next century. The remainder of the chapter is organized as follows. We first present some of the two-way linkages between inequality and growth, and explore why agriculture remains a vital component of any inequality-reducing growth strategy in contemporary Latin America. Then the focus shifts to the nature of agricultural growth and income distribution. Using a conceptual framework for the microdynamics of agrarian growth and income distribution, we look at economic and political forces that tend to perpetuate high levels of inequality in Latin America. We then outline the elements of a market-friendly, market-prudent policy agenda on which to base an inequality-reducing growth strategy. Finally, we consider the political and economic challenges of policy implementation, asking whether agricultural policy reform in Latin America can be sustained as market-friendly policies are deepened to become market-prudent.

Agriculture and Vicious Circles of Destructive Inequality

Agriculture as a percentage of GDP has declined modestly since 1970 for most countries in Latin America. Table 1 (on the following pages) displays basic indicators of the place of agriculture within the region's economies. The 1990 agricultural share in GDP ranges from a high of 32 percent (Paraguay) to a low of 5 percent (Venezuela) and averages 11 percent for Latin America as a whole. However, a closer look shows that for almost every country in the region, the agricultural share in GDP increased between 1980 and 1990, after dropping between 1970 and 1980. This increase presumably reflects the combined effects of structural adjustment induced by more open trading regimes and the lingering effects of economic recession, which perhaps hit the industrial sector hardest.

Equally striking here is the evidence that agriculture remains the source of employment and livelihood for a disproportionately large share of the region's economically active population (EAP): a quarter to a third of them work in the agricultural sector. The percentage of poor and indigent households found in rural areas is even higher, with 40 percent to 50 percent of all poor households in rural areas, and 50 to 60 percent of indigent households found in rural locations.

As these figures show, the agricultural sector, and the dynamics of growth within it, are still important in a crude numerical sense. To redress inequality—especially destructively severe inequality that blocks the accumulation capacity of households through income poverty and indigence—ultimately requires changing the way the economy functions for rural people. In a deeper sense, the forces that create a destructive linkage from high inequality to low growth are clearly operative in the agrarian economy. These same forces can also generate a vicious circle of exclusionary growth, in which inequality not only constrains growth, but is itself exacerbated over time by the pattern of growth.

After reviewing mechanisms that link inequality to growth, the next section presents evidence for how agrarian growth has affected inequality in contemporary Latin America. Subsequent sections of this chapter will pursue further the microfoundations beneath these growth-to-inequality linkages, and then discuss the policy options needed to interrupt the vicious circle of inequality and growth.

Linkages between Destructive Inequality and Growth

Evidence from the fast-growing East Asian economies has been central to analyzing the impact of inequality on growth. In particular, statistical evidence that there

Table 1. The Evolving Structure of Production and Poverty in Latin America, 1970-1990

		Share of Agriculture		Households in Poverty		Indigent Households	
		GDP (%)	EAP (%)	Economywide Headcount	Percent in Rural Areas	Economywide Headcount	Percent in Rural Areas
Argentina	1970	6.8	16	8	38	116	
	1980	6.3	13	9	23	2	26
	1990	8.1	—	(16)		(4)	
Bolivia	1970	18	52	—	—	—	—
	1980	18	46	—	—	—	—
	1990	22		(50)	—	(22)	—
Brazil	1970	15	45	49	67	25	75
	1980	11	31	39	49	17	68
	1990	11		43		20	
Chile	1970	7	23	17	34	6	42
	1980	7	17	—	—	—	—
	1990	9		35		12	
Colombia	1970	21	39	45	47	18	49
	1980	19	34	39	39	16	47
	1990	18		(35)		(12)	—
Costa Rica	1970	24	43	24	54	6	50
	1980	18	31	22	39	6	41
	1990	19				24	10
Guatemala	1970	30	61	—	—	—	
	1980	27	57	65	69	33	76
	1990	28		63	37		
Honduras	1970	28	65	65	75	45	56
	1980	21	61	—	—	—	—
	1990	22		75		54	
Mexico	1970	11	44	34	63	12	66
	1980	8	37	32	52	—	—
	1990	8		34		9	

Table 1. *(cont.)*

		Share of Agriculture		Households in Poverty		Indigent Households	
		GDP (%)	EAP (%)	Economywide Headcount	Percent in Rural Areas	Economywide Headcount	Percent in Rural Areas
Panama	1970	15	42	13	—	9	—
	1980	10	32	36	40	19	45
	1990	12		38		18	
Paraguay	1970	35	53	—	—	—	—
	1980	30	49	—	—	—	—
	1990	32		(37)	—	—	—
Peru	1970	16	47	50	64	25	73
	1980	10	40	46	56	21	72
	1990	14		—	—	—	
Uruguay	1970	18	19	(10)	—	—	—
	1980	15	19	11	5	3	44
	1990	14		(12)		(2)	—
Venezuela	1970	4	26	25	37	10	49
	1980	4	16	22	25	7	34
	1990	5		34		12	
Latin America	1970	12	41	40	65	19	73
	1980	10	32	35	49	15	60
	1990	11		39		18	

Note: Poor households are those whose income is less than two times the amount needed to purchase minimum food requirements. Indigent households are those with incomes less than that amount. Calculations of the percent of poor and indigent households in rural areas assume that the percent of households in rural areas is identical to the percent of the economically active population in agriculture. Figures in parentheses are poverty headcounts for urban population only.

Source: ECLAC, *Statistical Yearbook for Latin America.*

is a large residual component to East Asian growth—i.e., growth in excess of what can be explained by these economies' accumulation of factors of production—has encouraged further rethinking about the unconventional, endogenous sources of growth in East Asia.[2] Various attempts are made to explain this large component of unconventional productivity growth in East Asia. But the easily perceptible contrast between the fast-growing, relatively egalitarian Asian economies and the slow-growing, inegalitarian economies of Latin America has led to careful reexamination of how inequality affects growth. Indeed, Rodrik (1994) goes so far as to say there is no residual growth in East Asia to be explained, once the impact of the region's low initial inequality is taken into account. In other words, from the perspective of statistical growth accounting, low inequality promotes growth.

While this broad-brush statistical approach to inequality and growth is informative, Sheahan and Iglesias (Chapter 2) point out that "constructive inequality" reflects the pro-growth working of differential rewards to skill and effort, whereas "destructive inequality" reflects the dysfunctional workings of an economy that slows its own growth by blocking the accumulation and income-generating opportunities of its poorer members.[3] Destructive inequality can result from two sources. One is a narrowly economic linkage between human capital accumulation, growth and inequality (or poverty—see note 2). The other is an endogenous political-economic circuit by which the level of initial inequality shapes constituencies and reduces the likelihood that policies enabling rapid (and broad-based) growth will be chosen.[4]

In a theoretical analysis that brings out the first of these negative linkages between poverty and growth, Lunqvist (1993) explores how the absence of full capital and insurance markets leads poor people to underinvest in human capital. In an empirical study, Birdsall and Sabot (1995) make a similar point when they argue that controlling for the level of per capita GDP, aggregate human capital accumulation has been enhanced by greater income equality (and its implied higher absolute incomes for the poorest members of a society). The rapid, inequality-reducing growth characteristic of the East Asian experience can then be understood as the product of a virtuous circle in which low initial levels of inequality enhance aggregate accumulation and the relative capital accumulation of lower-wealth households, and with them the rate of growth. This interaction is all the more powerful if human capital accumulation is laden with positive externalities that themselves become sources of endogenous growth.

A vision of the political-economic linkage between inequality and growth is offered in a recent study of the East Asian growth experience by Aoki et al. (1995).

Like others writing in this area, these authors note that East Asian governments have engaged in a wide range of policies. Avoiding the pitfall of describing these policies as either market-friendly or *dirigista*, Aoki et al. suggest that they are best seen as "market-enhancing," meaning that the state carefully intervened in those realms where markets work least well (e.g., providing capital and insurance), and by so doing enabled markets to then effectively coordinate fundamental decisions of resource allocation and investment.

While others have noted this disciplined intervention of East Asian states, Aoki et al. provide a material explanation for this behavior, as opposed to a culturally based explanation (e.g., a Confucian ethic). They argue that low levels of initial inequality (and a weak elite) in East Asia implied that the only viable constituency for a government seeking political support was a broad-based one built around shared growth policies. Agricultural policy provides one of the clearest examples of how a broad-based or shared growth strategy is endogenous to low levels of initial inequality. Land reform in much of East Asia not only deeply redistributed land ownership rights, but also imposed land ownership ceilings of only a few hectares. Aoki et al. suggest that the absence of a strong rural elite deprived East Asian governments of a politically influential target group for the sorts of divisible and privately appropriable goods that governments so often provision to develop the rural sector (e.g., subsidized credit, machinery subsidies, investment credits, etc.). Instead, they argue, policy focused on discovering and providing the key indivisible, quasi-public goods that markets were ill-conditioned to offer. What other observers of East Asian agricultural policy have attributed to an (exogenous) strategic objective of shared growth (e.g., Tomich et al. 1995) is, in the argument of Aoki et al., a product of low initial inequality.[5]

Exclusionary Agrarian Growth

While inequality may thus be destructive of growth, how does growth in turn shape inequality? The conventional answer to this question has been deeply shaped by the writings of Simon Kuznets (1955). While empirical and focused on western economies, Kuznets' work called forth a series of theoretical and empirical efforts directed at low-income economies. Various empirical studies (e.g., Ahluwalia 1976) found that cross-sectional data on a broad sample of low- and high-income countries confirmed an inverted U-shaped "Kuznets" relationship between inequality and per capita income. Theoretical explorations of the Kuznets hypothesis—built on the dual economy foundations of the W.A. Lewis (1953) model—demonstrated that a period of increasing inequality (in the factor distribution of income) was entirely consistent with rapid growth and capital accumulation. A wide variety of so-called classical and neoclassical models proved able to account for the Kuznets "U" through the interaction between the distribution and accumulation of productive factors, and the (at least partially) endogenous level of factor prices. While these models differed in many ways, they all similarly portrayed the rural economy as a safe or inclusionary haven for labor.[6]

Yet standing in sharp contrast to the dual economy portrayal of a stable and safe rural sector is the historical experience of Latin America's highly unequal agrarian economies. In these economies, growth has often taken on an exclusionary form—meaning that it displaced peasants and tenants, prematurely mechanized the agrarian economy, and reproduced or even deepened, rural inequality (e.g., see Williams 1986). A number of authors have attributed such exclusionary agrarian growth patterns to a pernicious political economy that subsidized capital for the rich and depressed prices for labor-intensive exportables (see especially de Janvry and Sadoulet 1993; and Binswanger, Feder and Deininger 1995). However, other evidence suggests that more narrowly economic mechanisms and intrinsic market failures have helped create exclusionary growth.

Provocative evidence suggesting the high initial inequality may reproduce or deepen itself through growth comes from a recent time-series econometric study by de Janvry and Sadoulet (1996). They find that agrarian growth in Latin America is associated with sharply increasing rural inequality. While we know of no similar study of East Asian growth, a study by Ravallion and Datt (1995) of growth across Indian states provides an interesting and informative comparison with the de Janvry and Sadoulet results. Ravallion and Datt find that agrarian growth in India is most strongly associated with reduced poverty and inequality. Interestingly, however, they also find that growth in Bihar—the Indian state with the sharp, near Latin American levels of land inequality—appears to contradict this general pattern.

What is worse, de Janvry and Sadoulet find that the association between agrarian growth and increasing rural inequality has been even stronger in recent, post-liberalization growth spells than in earlier periods of growth. The increase in inequality has not been so sharp as to increase rural poverty in the wake of agrarian growth, but it has clearly blunted the potentially positive impact of growth on rural poverty, as de Janvry and Sadoulet analyze in some detail.

While informative, such time-series studies are invariably ambiguous and contestable, because they reflect only indirectly the underlying microeconomic processes of growth and inequality. Several recent microeconomic studies of agrar-

ian growth booms in post-liberalization Latin America provide a more finely tex-
tured picture of agrarian growth and inequality. While largely consistent with the
time-series evidence of de Janvry and Sadoulet, these microstudies add important
nuance and qualification. Carter et al. (1996) summarize the results of coordinated
microstudies of agrarian growth booms in Chile, Guatemala and Paraguay. In two
of the three cases (Chile and Paraguay), rapid growth brought increasing inequality in assets and probably in incomes. In Guatemala, the distributional outcome
appears to have been much more favorable for low-wealth people. While contrasting with the microstudies summarized in Thrupp (1995), which appear to identify
an unambiguously negative impact of growth booms on low-wealth households,
Carter et al. interpret their studies as prima facie evidence that there is space for
policy to reshape the income distribution effects of agrarian growth.

It is interesting to note that in addition to highly equal land distributions,
East Asian governments also undertook a series of measures that bolstered the competitiveness of small farms. Agricultural policy in Japan, Taiwan and Korea shared
a common emphasis on small farm credit, extension and price stabilization.[7] Whatever the political-economic logic behind these shared growth policies, there can be
no doubt that markets were enabled to permit the small farm sector to flourish.

Agriculture and the Inequality-Growth Nexus

For several reasons the agricultural economy is an important part of the inequality-
growth nexus in contemporary Latin America. Not only does the agricultural sector provide a disproportionately large share of employment, it also houses a majority of the region's poor and indigent households. Under these circumstances, both
market and political failures conspire to link inequality to growth and growth to
inequality. Before considering policies to broaden the base of agrarian growth, we
will review what is fundamental to relationships between growth and inequality
in agrarian economies.

Inequality and the Structure of Agrarian Growth

The absence of strong technical-scale economies in agricultural production
processes means that most crops can be, and in fact are, grown at radically different
scales of production. This observation applies equally to basic grains (maize, wheat,
etc.) and to plantation crops (e.g., sugar cane, banana, oil palm) that have also succeeded on a small scale through farming contracts, which can duplicate the coordi-

nation gains of vertical integration.[8] While both large and small-scale production are technically feasible, the scale of production strongly influences patterns of factor allocation and productivity, even within a single economy. Due to this size-sensitivity of factor allocation, the distribution of productive assets between large and small producers tends to shape the overall performance of the agricultural economy. Indeed, the agency costs associated with supervising hired labor have advantaged small-scale, family labor agriculture over large-scale, labor-hiring agriculture (Binswanger et al. 1996 introduce this literature). As a variety of authors have recognized (e.g., Eswaran and Kotwal 1986, Feder 1985), these agency costs can create a destructive linkage between inequality and growth in the agrarian economy.[9]

While this distributional sensitivity of the agricultural economy has been most thoroughly explored at the static level, it has further implications for the nature of agrarian growth and its impact on inequality. In other words, the agrarian economy can experience growth that is highly inclusionary and broad-based, or growth that is highly exclusionary and increases inequality. After outlining a framework for core microeconomic forces that shape the nature of agrarian growth, the next section considers the linkages between initial levels of inequality and the distributional impacts of growth.

Double Development Squeeze of the Peasantry under Exclusionary Agrarian Growth

As an agricultural economy expands and grows in the face of new market demand and new production technologies, sector-level impacts on the well-being of less well-off households occur through three interacting effects:

- Whether small-scale units participate directly in the adoption of new technologies or in the production for new markets—the *small farm adoption effect*;
- Whether growth induces a pattern of structural change that systematically improves or worsens the access of the rural resource poor to land—the *land access effect*;
- Whether production under the new technologies or for new markets—as mediated by the land access effect—absorbs more or less labor of landless and part-time farming households—the *labor absorption effect*.

In the short term, the employment generated by a growing agricultural economy depends on the size distribution, or class, of the farms directly participating in the growth process. Large farms are likely to produce any given crop with less labor per hectare than would a small farm. In combination, the effects of small farm adoption and of labor absorption can have either positive or negative impacts on the rural resource poor. The most virtuous outcome would be one where small farms adopt a labor-absorbing crop on most of their land, resulting in both high direct participation and greater labor opportunities for the rural resource poor. The most negative outcome would be one where small farms find their participation thwarted by resource constraints and the labor intensity associated with larger farms is less than in previous crop choices. In between those two extremes is the ambiguous outcome of relatively low direct participation by small farmers, but increased labor absorption associated with the use of new technologies or production of the new crops on larger farms.

In the medium term, growth may tend to induce a pattern of structural change depending on how the adoption patterns and relative profitability of different classes of producers affect their competitiveness in the land market. If the small farm adoption effect is minimal, and the returns to successful, large-scale adopters are substantial, then the land access effect will tend to generate further changes in net employment by shifting land from small-scale to less labor-absorbing large-scale producers. This effect, in turn, will reduce further labor absorption, unless the labor absorption of new production patterns is greater than that of the traditional small-scale farming it displaces.

The full impact of growth on the rural resource poor thus depends critically on the interacting effects of differential adoption, induced structural change, and labor absorption. The interaction can create a growth dynamic that is broad-based or inclusionary, with structural shifts in land to small-scale producers who thus benefit directly and who also generate more employment per hectare. The interaction can also generate a vicious circle of exclusionary, inequality-producing growth. This happened for example in 17th-century England and postwar Central America, where diminished land access for the rural poor and weak labor absorption surrounded rapid agrarian growth with social controversy and political instability.[10] As mentioned above, evidence on contemporary agrarian growth in Latin America is mixed. As a prelude to considering policy options to encourage broad-based, inequality-reducing growth, the next section examines the forces that shape the inclusionary versus the exclusionary nature of agrarian growth.

Small Farm Competitiveness and the Distributional Impacts of Growth

As the prior discussion makes clear, the competitiveness of small farm producers is critical to the underlying distributional dynamics of growth. When small farms are competitive in the face of a new market or technology, then lower-wealth individuals are able to directly participate in the benefits of growth. Competitive small farms are also unlikely to fall prey to the exclusionary growth dynamics that result when small farms lose access to land. Indeed, to the extent small farms are more competitive than larger-scale producers, a virtuous circle of inclusionary growth is created.

The basic economics of small farm competitiveness can be studied through what might be termed the competitiveness regime. The competitiveness regime is the mapping between farm size and land valuation. A one-dimension measure like land valuation is useful because it captures or summarizes the position of a farming unit in a variety of underlying markets (labor, capital and technology, etc.). A simple net-present value formulation can be used to gain initial analytical purchase on the economics of small farm competitiveness. The full dynamics of accumulation and risk require more complex analysis, as will be discussed below.

For an individual, the capitalized value of the expected production returns from an additional unit of land, ρ_i, can be written as:

$$\rho_i = \sum_{t=1}^{H_i} [\Delta_{it}(T_0)] / (1 + r_i)^t$$

where "t" denotes years, "H_i" is the individual "i's" time horizon, "r_i" is the rate of interest used by "i" to discount the stream of future income, and "$\Delta_{it}(T_0)$" denotes the increment in net income that "i" can earn in year "t" with an additional unit of land. The incremental income an individual can earn from a piece of land will in general be a function of initial landholding, T_0, for the reasons discussed earlier.

The discounted sum given by the equation above is an economic ability to pay, or reservation price for land, in the sense that it represents the maximum amount the individual could pay for the unit of land without losing money.[11] If the market price is below the individual's reservation price, then the individual would be made better off (in terms of expected income) purchasing the land. Symmetrically, if the market price lies above ρ_i, then the individual would be better off selling land and investing the proceeds in an alternative activity that yields the opportunity cost rate of return, r_i.

Using this reservation price concept, it is possible to characterize an agrarian

FIGURE 1

Poverty and Latent Land Market Competitiveness

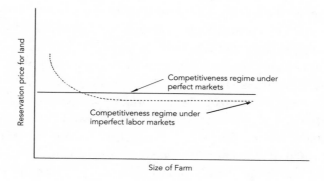

economy's class, or farm size competitiveness regime. This regime can be defined as the function that relates reservation price to initial farm size, as in Figure 1. Systematic (interclass) differences between the reservation price for different-sized farm units would identify potential or pressure for changes in agrarian structure or the size distribution of farms.[12] The shape of this regime, and how it changes as technology and market opportunities evolve, will be key to understanding the income distribution consequences of growth.

The solid line in Figure 1 illustrates the competitiveness regime in the abstract case in which all markets are perfect, technology is scale-neutral so that all farms value land equally, and ρ would be constant across farm sizes. A market economy would in this case present a level playing field to producers of different sizes and wealth.

A number of size-sensitive factors could add shape to the competitiveness regime. How reservation prices change as farm size changes determines the nature of the class competitiveness regime. Those who are tightly constrained in factor markets or otherwise disadvantaged could not adopt remunerative production strategies, and would thus have fairly low Δ's and ρ's. This might apply to large farms that rely on hired labor that is expensive in the sense that relatively little labor effort is received for the wage paid. The labor-cost advantage of family labor farms (where worker-family members are presumably motivated to work hard) versus larger, labor-hiring farms underlies theories of the economic dominance of family farms (e.g., Binswanger et al. 1996).[13]

The labor-cost advantage of small farms creates what Carter and Zegarra (1996) call the latent land market competitiveness of the poor. In this situation, we would observe the varying valuations of land along different land sizes displayed by the downward-sloping dashed line in Figure 1. As can be seen, the labor-cost advantage of family labor farms makes land especially valuable to low-wealth producers, and translates directly into a higher willingness to pay for land. For a given market price of land, say $\underline{P}$, small farmers would outcompete large farmers in the land market (ignoring transaction costs). The landless and small farmers with farms below A_s in size would want to buy land at price $\underline{P}$, whereas the units larger than A_s would want to sell. A well-functioning land market would thus tend to eliminate dualistic agrarian structures, and this change in land distribution structure changes would bring with it unambiguously positive impacts on growth and poverty.

While labor market advantages may tend to make small farms relatively competitive, other factors may cut the other way and disadvantage small-scale producers. Among these factors is the time horizon "H_i" in the formula. A weak legal system that leaves smallholders vulnerable to a taking of their property would tend to shorten the time horizon and reduce land valuation for smallholders, for example. Fixed transaction costs that make land registration relatively expensive for smallholders (on a per hectare basis) could have a similar effect.

Imperfect and incomplete financial markets may also create a countervailing disadvantage for small-scale producers. While there are diverse theoretical perspectives on how rural financial markets operate, most tend to point toward some sort of size-sensitivity or wealth bias that disadvantages low-wealth agents.[14] As the reservation price formula makes clear, weak access to capital has a double-edged impact on the reservation price for land. Individuals with weak access to capital and insurance will realize lower gains from additional land units they cannot use productively ("Δ_{it}" will be low for such individuals). In addition, their high opportunity cost of capital will lead them to discount the future more heavily ("r_i" will be high).

How do these multiple market imperfections interact and influence farm expansion incentives in the land market? If peasant access to cheap family labor creates significant cost advantages, then these differential returns may favor the expansion of small producers in the land market. On the other hand, if larger farms' better access to working capital allows them to earn higher returns than small farmers, then they may be able to outbid smaller farmers for available land.[15]

Figure 2 displays the simulated values of the net present valuation of land $\rho(T_0)$ against land, which reflects the multiple market imperfections. As can be

FIGURE 2

Multiple Market Failures and Small Farm Competitiveness

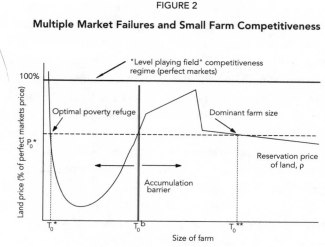

seen, land valuation is very high for the smallest farm units, because their high marginal unemployment in the labor market cheapens the efficiency cost of their own labor. Ability to pay for land, and expansion incentives, fall off quickly for these producers, however, as capital constraints bind their ability to utilize additional area. At some point, ability to pay turns back up for larger farms, as access to rationed capital begins to improve with increasing farm size and tenure status. As the marginal labor cost of supervision increases rapidly for very large holdings, land valuation drops again after some point along the farm-size continuum.

Although the results in Figure 2 are an artifact of a specific numerical model and its assumptions, the figure does give a sense of differential incentives for land transactions in a liberalized market. As discussed above, farm units whose net present valuation of land is higher than the market price P_0^* would do better selling off land. Given the shape of the land valuation curve in 2, operation of a competitive land market creates a sort of "accumulation barrier" depicted as T_0^b. Farms below that size are repelled by the barrier and are better off selling off their land and downsizing to the optimal poverty refuge of T_0^* hectares. At this smaller size, these units become once again competitive in the land market as their marginal valuation of their own labor time becomes quite low, making land valuable as a form of self-employment. However, cheap labor, in the face of capital constraints, is not enough to maintain small farm competitiveness beyond a very modest size. The economically dominant farm size would be T_0^{**} hectares, with units beyond the accumulation barrier expanding or contracting as appropriate to that size over time.

The analysis to this point has relied on the net present value of expected net income streams (including appreciation) as a way to analyze the land-market competitiveness of low-wealth producers. While informative about the core income factors that influence land acquisition, the net-present-value approach disregards both risk and intertemporal considerations that may further shape agents' willingness to pay for land and influence the operation of the land market. Unfortunately, fully dynamic analysis of land markets (i.e., analysis in the face of multiple imperfections and risk) is relatively novel. In their review of recent work in this area, Carter and Zegarra (1996) note that in simplest terms, adding dynamics to the land valuation problem gives more choice, or degrees of freedom, to agents by permitting them to reduce current consumption in order to buy (or capitalize) land in order to realize higher consumption in the future. However, this addition of dynamic choice creates two opposing considerations. One (the strategic value of accumulation as a way to circumvent market failures) favors accumulation by low-wealth agents. The other (risk) may cut the other way, discouraging low-wealth agents from investing in agricultural land with its uncertain returns. Clearly more work, empirical and theoretical, needs to be done to understand the dynamic portfolio considerations that shape small farm competitiveness.

To summarize, the economics of the competitiveness regime cannot be characterized a priori, except that interacting multiple market failures are likely to render it other than horizontal in farm size space. The slope of the class competitiveness regime indicates the degree to which an agrarian market economy departs from a level playing field and tilts in favor of one class or another. Whether the likely labor market advantages of small farms outweigh their financial market disadvantages, and tilt the field in their favor, is an important but difficult question. Moreover, political factors can tilt or distort the competitiveness regime, as the next section discusses.

Small Farm Competitiveness in Inegalitarian Economies

The prior section has identified the way labor, capital and other market and institutional imperfections may influence the competitiveness regime in favor of one farm size class or another. The economic importance of these different biases depends on, inter alia, the characteristics of the relevant crops and production technologies. Carter et al. (1996) identify a series of crop characteristics that shape the economic importance of these imperfections: (1) "interactive-labor" intensity of the crop;[16] (2) working capital intensity; (3) human capital intensity; (4) costliness of determining output quality;[17] (5) product perishability and gains from vertical integration; (6) investment gestation period; and (7) output and price risk.[18]

While the various farm size biases created by these characteristics can be anticipated,[19] the overall bias in a growing, agrarian economy may depend on the underlying distribution of land and other assets. The research on East Asian economies suggests that both economic and political-economic forces may link initial levels of inequality to the patterns of growth.

First, in terms of economic linkages, consider, for example, the capital access advantage of largeholders in a booming fruit orchard sector, where long-term investments are required, and assume this to be the only significant class bias in this boom crop. If both small and largeholders are present, and the holdings of different-sized units are reasonably proximate, then it seems likely that a fruit boom would drive a rapid consolidation of landholdings, with smallholders selling out to nearby largeholders (see note 18). If, however, all existing producers in the locale are small-scale, then competition with larger units that might enjoy advantages in capital market access is in a sense virtual, rather than real. Expansion of existing smallholders (and new entrants) would be limited, in real time, by their ability to capitalize themselves up to the larger, size-advantaged scale of operation. Wealthier new entrants would also face the barrier of having to consolidate many smallholdings, an effort that might confront significant transaction costs. Thus, in an initially egalitarian environment, the overall competitive pressures would be less likely to quickly squeeze out existing smallholders through asset and other prices, than they would be in a context with largeholders as neighbors.

In addition to this distinction between real versus virtual land market competition, there is a second circuit by which initial asset distribution may mediate the importance of farm-size biases. As Carter and Zimmerman (1995) explore in a dynamic simulation model, it is at least theoretically possible that prices in an economy endogenously evolve in a way that reduces the importance of farm-size biases and ratifies the competitive position of the existing distribution of farms. Consider, for example, an initially egalitarian (East Asian–looking) agrarian economy in which all land resources are on small units that are informationally disadvantaged in capital markets. In such a circumstance, agrarian demand for capital would be low, and aggregate production would be highly capital constrained. As long as the land does not instantaneously shift to larger units, there would be downward pressure on interest rates (other things equal) and upward pressure on the prices of agricultural products. Both of these endogenous price movements would tend to make it worthwhile for smallholders to borrow (or for financial institutions to lend to smallholders), thus reducing the importance of the capital market disadvantage of smallholders. By way of contrast, note that such price movements would not tend to occur in a less egalitarian (Latin American–looking) economy in which a large portion of the land stock is already assigned to larger-scale units that are unaffected by the information constraints in capital markets. In this initially inegalitarian environment, smallholders would remain capital constrained with the farm size biases tilted against them. While this argument is best treated as a theoretical conjecture, it does suggest that the importance of intrinsic farm size biases—and their impact on the long-run trajectory of asset accumulation—may be shaped by the initial land distribution.

In addition to these economic mechanisms, the competitiveness regime can also be influenced by policies that favor one class of producers over another, or subsidize prices or inputs more important to one class of producers versus another. De Janvry and Sadoulet (1993), for example, argue that the policy reforms and economic liberalizations of the 1980s deprived large-scale Latin American producers of the subsidies that had artificially enhanced their competitiveness and contributed to the exclusionary nature of prior periods of rapid agrarian growth. Echoing de Janvry's earlier work on biased technological change (and consistent with the argument of Aoki et al. put forward above), de Janvry, Sadoulet and Fafchamps (1989) argue that the presence of a numerically small but economically significant group of large-scale producers is likely to distort the nature of agricultural policy and technological innovation. Coles' (1995) account of Venezuelan efforts to reform agricultural policy and eliminate subsidies largely beneficial to the large farm sector very persuasively reveals the power of political coalitions to tilt the playing field in their favor in inegalitarian economies.

To summarize, this section has made the following points. Securing the economic competitiveness of small farm producers in expanding markets and technologies is vital if a "double development squeeze" of the peasantry (less land, less employment) is to be avoided whereby increasing land concentration fuels diminished labor absorption and push migration. Despite their latent competitiveness advantage—rooted in their access to relatively cheap, hard-working family labor—small-scale producers are subject to countervailing disadvantages in accessing capital and other markets in which the fixed costs of information are important, even when those markets are undistorted by class-biased policies and distorted prices. Moreover, these disadvantages are magnified by new technologies and markets that put a premium on capital access and risk-bearing capacity. Finally, an initially inegalitarian distribution of land is likely, via endogenous economic and political economic mechanisms, to generate prices, policies and institutions that dampen small farm competitiveness.

The daunting task of the next section is to ask what can be done to bolster small farm competitiveness in Latin America's inegalitarian economies in order to underwrite an inequality-reducing form of agrarian growth.

Elements of a Market-Prudent Policy Agenda

To chronicle the microeconomic factors that shape the distributional impacts of agrarian growth in contemporary Latin America, the prior section has laid the basis for an evaluation of the various policy options that are commonly discussed as the basis of an agrarian growth and development strategy. For heuristic purposes, Table 2 arranges those options along a continuum of policy activism from the quietism of laissez faire to the hyperactivity of *dirigista*, centralized planning. The relative ranking of the three interior policy options is somewhat arbitrary and is not central to the argument made here. This section discusses the first four policy groups along that continuum in terms of their direct effects on participation, land access, and employment opportunities of the rural poor. The chief conclusion is that reform of information-constrained and wealth-biased markets must not only be part of a broad-based agro-export growth strategy, but must be pursued first among the policy groups, especially in locales with dualistic agrarian structures.[20]

Getting Prices and Institutions Right

A policy package that (1) eliminated the price distortions and capital subsidies that favor large farmers and discourage labor-intensive production, and (2) legally solidified the property rights of small farmers through land titling, would constitute a minimalist approach to achieving broad-based growth. Historically, price distortions have played an important part in enhancing the relative competitiveness of larger farm units in many parts of the developing world. Indeed, some authors argue that elimination of such distortions can suffice to create poverty-reducing agrarian growth trajectories (de Janvry and Sadoulet 1993, and Binswanger et al., 1996).

While there is no doubt that the elimination of price distortions is important, the contemporary experience of agro-export growth strongly suggests that simply getting prices right is insufficient to generate broad-based growth. Those experiences, buttressed by theoretical advances regarding information constraints and

Table 2. Continuum of Policies for Achieving Broad-based Growth

Laissez faire

Right prices and institutions	Nondistorted price signals
	Secure property rights to enhance investment
Picking winners	Infrastructure investment
	Technical adoption and support services
Land market reform	Land market reform
	Land banks to eliminate transaction costs and land market segmentation
Reform of information-constrained markets	Nontraditional financial intermediation
	Insurance substitutes
	Extension services
	Cooperative marketing arrangement
Asset redistribution	Landholding ceilings
	Land to the tiller and other reforms

Dirigista

wealth biases in key factor markets, suggest that there are intrinsic market imperfections that hamper small farm competitiveness and create exclusionary growth trajectories. This is especially the case for markets in areas characterized by a highly dualistic distribution of land ownership.

Because smallholders often lack well-defined and legally recognized property rights to land, land titling programs appear attractive as a way to provide institutional preconditions for broad-based growth. However, three observations question the necessity for titling all property rights as a precondition for broad-based growth:

(1) Current smallholders may already have localized, but nontransferable, tenure security.[21]
(2) While land titling may make localized tenure security transferable (and thus valuable as a collateral), this may not by itself suffice to improve the

capital access of current smallholders, as Carter and Olinto (1996) find in the case of rural Paraguay;[22] and,

(3) Making tenure security transferable may have its largest impact by enhancing the marketability of smallholder land to other, better capitalized farmers.

Observations (1) and (2) suggest that a careful look be given to the nature of localized tenure security and the nature of the financial system before land titling is pursued as a device to enhance the direct participation of small farmers in a growth process.

Observation (3) indicates that when the existing distribution of land constrains the adoption of high-growth potential crops—as it would if current landholders cannot afford the capital demands of the new crop production—titling and land market activation may actually speed the displacement of current smallholders. While such policies may be very important in activating agrarian growth, they may mitigate against the objective of broad-based growth. This may well be a lesson from the Chilean agro-export boom of the 1980s (see Carter et al. 1996). Once smallholder land titles were made fully secure and transferable, land sales rapidly shifted land to modestly larger and better capitalized units, which have been the most successful in the production of fruit for exports. Based on econometric estimates of the competitiveness gap between producers of different scale operating units, Carter and Zegarra (1995) argue that tenure security reform pursued out of sequence (that is, before efforts are made to mitigate the competitiveness gaps) could have the same effect in Paraguay, indicating that a liberalization-cum-land-titling policy mix would not suffice to resolve the problem of exclusionary growth in that country.

In summary, while a policy of getting prices and institutions right is attractive in the sense that it is relatively straightforward and consistent with the general tenor of market-oriented development strategy, the analysis here suggests that policy must often progress beyond the laissez-faire end of the policy continuum if agricultural growth is to be broad-based at the sectoral level.

Picking Winners

Public investment can play a role in facilitating the growth of the agricultural sector through the creation of infrastructure, identification and development of product markets, and the development of crop varieties suitable to the local environment. Williams (1986), for example, describes the role of such policies in fomenting Central America's agro-export booms in the 1950s and 1960s. Over the 1980s, USAID funded various institutions (e.g., PROEXAG in Central America) devoted to the promotion of agro-exports by developing and sharing information on export markets and by brokering business contacts between local exporters and developed country buyers. A modestly activist approach to creating broad-based growth would try to target such public investment on crops that are most likely to conform to the economic capacity of small farmers, and that are most likely to generate significant employment increases. Thus, agricultural research and infrastructure development related to agro-exports would be undertaken with an eye toward small farmers and their relative competitiveness. In the language of the industrial policy debate, this policy approach would try to pick winners by investing in those activities most likely to generate broad-based growth.

However, two questions confront the effectiveness of a "picking winners" approach to broad-based growth. The first is technical: Do agronomic and commercial realities grant policy any degrees of freedom to choose among alternative crops? The second is economic: Can alternative crops be unconditionally and meaningfully ranked in terms of their potential for generating broad-based growth?

The prior section argued that most crops are technically scale-neutral, but that it is the structure of markets and prices that twists crop characteristics into farm size biases. The conclusion to be drawn from this is not that crop characteristics are unimportant in shaping the distributional impact of growth. Some crops are indeed more labor-intensive than others, and as such they offer advantageous direct and indirect effects. But policy aimed at shaping broad-based growth cannot consider crop characteristics in isolation from initial asset distributions and the factor market structures that affect who eventually grows the crops and how they are grown. There are few crops that cannot be grown on large farms, and most crops are grown with much less labor intensity on large farms than on small farms. The evidence regarding labor absorption in Paraguay's wheat-and-soy-boom region is one example of this phenomenon (see Carter et al. 1996). Even across the narrow size range of Guatemala's export vegetable sample (discussed earlier), labor intensity drops off rapidly as farm size expands, according to regression results reported in Carter and Barham (1996).

In the end, picking winners means careful attention to crops and crop characteristics in the context of existing market and agrarian structures. Crops that seem intrinsically labor-intensive and size-neutral may turn out not to be so, if capital, insurance and output quality factors are skewed against small-scale producers. Thus a policy approach that gives up on direct participation by small-scale producers would probably generate less labor absorption than otherwise. While public investment in agricultural technology and growth implies a responsibility to consider the nature of the growth it will engender, that consideration cannot be isolated from the more activist policies shown in Table 2.

Land Market Reform

Land market reform refers to a set of policies that directly affect either the valuation of land itself (land taxation), costs of transacting in the land market (land banks that bear the transactions costs associated with large farm subdivision), or access to long-term capital (mortgage banks).[23] While a relatively activist policy, land market reform is in practice fairly simple because it does not affect the constellation of factors (access to technology, capital, and labor) that determine productive returns to land. Small farm technology and extension policies can, of course, be implemented as a potential complement to land market reform policies.

Carter and Galeano (1995) identify segmentation in Paraguayan land markets (where smaller units compete in a different land market segment than do large farms), suggesting that at least in some areas of Paraguay, there are barriers preventing the smooth flow of land between larger and smaller farms. But the expectation that land market reform policies can shift land to the rural poor, by facilitating interclass land market transactions, presumes that the rural poor do not suffer a fundamental competitive disadvantage in the sphere of production and marketing that affects their potential to participate in the land market. If such a large competitiveness gap exists, then neither politically feasible progressive land taxation, nor putting the rural poor on an equal transactions cost or mortgage capital basis with the better off, will achieve the desired redistributive effect. They will still be unable to earn sufficient returns to justify paying the market price for the land.

No evidence exists in contemporary Latin America of land market reforms that have fundamentally altered patterns of land ownership, despite recent efforts. Pilot programs such as the Penny Foundation project in Guatemala and the land-purchase financing program of the Honduran Central Bank—in which farms were purchased and subsequently resold under competitive market terms—have had a very limited impact due to the shortage of funds available (see Shearer et al. 1990). Moreover, in Guatemala, case studies of Penny Foundation farms have shown that the typical smallholder beneficiaries may not be able to generate enough income to repay their land purchase loans, forcing them to abandon their parcels (Schweigert

1994). Studies on both the Guatemalan and Honduran land-purchase financing programs have also shown that the households most likely to survive the first years on the farms had savings to support their subsistence or other adults in the household who could contribute to family income with off-farm employment (Shearer et al. 1990). More pointedly, this chapter's identification of capital access problems that have fundamentally constrained and shaped small farm participation in export booms in Paraguay, Chile and Guatemala suggests strong reasons why such programs are likely to be limited in their impact if they are pursued in isolation from more fundamental factor market reform.

In sum, relatively little evidence can be marshaled to show that the nature of the land market per se has inhibited the realization of broad-based growth patterns. Land market reform appears as part of a policy package that could be used to break up the dualistic agrarian structures that are so pervasive in Latin America. However, it is unlikely to be sufficient unless it is part of a broader package that also addresses the concerns regarding size-biased markets raised above.

Factor Market Reform: The Capital-Insurance Nexus

Among the various factors that create farm-size competitiveness gaps, the only one that unambiguously favors small farms is their access to relatively cheap labor. This observation does not denigrate the potential importance of low labor costs: a broad historical pattern of family-labor agriculture has characterized the economic development of now-wealthier countries. However, in the context of the capital, risk and quality requirements of export agriculture, one should acknowledge the sharp difference in absolute size between, say, a North American family farm and a peasant producer in a low-wage economy.[24]

For example, the squeeze on peasant land access in the Paraguayan and Chilean booms appears to be rooted in financial market problems of the small farm sector (Carter and Barham 1996). These capital market disadvantages of the small farm sector are highlighted by the agro-export boom in highland Guatemala, which successfully incorporated small farms (many less than one hectare) as direct producers, despite their weak access to capital. Yet, as Barham et al. (1995) show, small farms that adopt the remunerative export crops devote only a modest fraction of their meager land resources to those crops. This conservative adoption pattern stands in marked contrast to the large farm adopters, who devote nearly their entire farm area to the crops. Barham et al. identify capital and risk constraints as the key factors that discourage small farms from doing the same. Similarly, von Braun et al.

(1989) show that small farmers in this sector pursue costly self-insurance strategies by allocating scarce land resources to basic foodstuffs whose expected economic returns are only a small fraction of the returns obtainable from export crops. At this level, it seems surprising that smallholders remained competitive in the boom sector in spite of these capital and insurance constraints.

Undoubtedly, part of the explanation lies in the labor intensity of the export vegetable crops that put a countervailing premium on small farm access to economically inexpensive family labor. But, while this labor-cost advantage may have given the small farm sector an advantage in the production of vegetables, it would be misleading to read the Guatemalan experience as evidence that labor-cost advantages dominate capital market disadvantages, even for labor-intensive crops. For another component to the Guatemalan story is the nature of the competition in the highland land market in which the boom took place. Unlike the small farm sector in Chile's central valley—which was quickly displaced and excluded from that country's (labor-intensive) fruit export boom by larger and better capitalized producers—the highland Guatemalan smallholder sector seems to have been strongly sheltered from direct competition by a highly fragmented, legally tenuous, and relatively egalitarian pre-boom local land tenure structure.[25] As suggested earlier, the initial distribution of land and wealth may be critical to shaping the dynamic trajectory of growth. In initially dualistic environments, the capital-insurance nexus that disadvantages small-scale agriculture may indeed be enough to swamp any labor cost advantage and underwrite an exclusionary growth path, to say nothing of the human capital intensity, product quality, and marketing disadvantages that small-scale producers may confront.

Unfortunately, rectifying the capital and insurance market disadvantages of small-scale producers is not simple, as the dismal experiences with targeted credit and crop insurance programs demonstrate (Von Pischke et al. 1983). The transactions costs, informational asymmetries and weak collateral base that disadvantage smallholders in financial markets represent real economic problems. While programs like credit cooperatives (which reduce transactions costs and exploit informal, local information) and Grameen Bank-like group lending schemes (which reduce lender risk and substitute peer monitoring for collateral) are promising efforts to address the underlying problems, their generalized effectiveness has yet to be demonstrated, especially in agricultural settings where covariate risk is high.[26] Analysis of credit cooperatives in Guatemala by Barham et al. (1996) and Mushinski (1996) suggests that this institutional form at least improves the credit access of middle-wealth quintiles, but has little impact on the poorest. While these results apply only to one specific institutional experiment, they do raise the question of whether credit market reforms can extend to low-income sectors.

Sustaining and Deepening Reform

East Asia's impressive record of rapid growth and low inequality has rekindled optimism that a broad-based pattern of growth can be realized. We have argued in this chapter that market-prudent agricultural policies have vital roles to play in the creation of win-win, inequality-reducing growth strategies. While agriculture no longer dominates most Latin American economies, rural areas continue to house a majority of the region's poor and indigent households. It is precisely such households—with their absolutely low and insecure levels of income—that bear the brunt of the destructive inequality that underlies the observed macro relationship between inequality and growth. In addition, there is ample evidence that the nature of agricultural growth and transformation has an important impact on the levels and stability of income of these households. While a broad-based agricultural growth strategy to break patterns of exclusionary growth is not the only possible source of income growth for poor households, it is an important one and one that can be pursued on a win-win basis. Trade liberalization of the 1980s raised the relative prices of (tradable) agricultural commodities, and the renewed growth of agriculture throughout the region offers an important chance to make that growth broad-based and inequality-reducing.

The need to stimulate broad-based growth is urgent, because liberalization by itself is not sufficient to assure that the new round of growth is inclusionary and broad-based. Fortunately, the present advances in economic knowledge and political possibilities create the space and the opportunity for broad-based growth strategies.

One of the most significant changes in the Latin American region over the last decade has been the shift toward more open economies. Earlier efforts to develop (through import-substituting industrialization) contaminated agriculture and established a bias toward temperate zone crops for which industrial processes were designed in industrialized countries. The most obvious example of this sort of change is visible in the growth of the animal feed business throughout the developing world, leading to a dependence on the U.S. soybeans-and-corn formula. Another example would be the bias toward powdered milk consumption that has been so controversial. The growth of wheat product consumption (pastas and breads), in tropical countries that can produce rice very competitively, is another example.

These import-substitution policies placed developing agricultural economies in competition with vastly richer exporters who were able to subsidize their exports. Developing countries defended their agricultural sectors by reserving imports to the state-owned enterprises, and later by all types of quota mechanisms. When exchange rate adjustments were necessary, they often established two-tiered exchange systems to benefit imports and maintain food cheap, all of which made it very difficult for the local farmer, and constituted what Krueger, Schiff and Valdes (1989) call the bias against agriculture.

Since these schemes were rectified by trade, fiscal and monetary reform, the immediate negative impacts on urban consumers have been enormous, and the benefits have not appeared in the rural sector, because much of the benefit of the protection systems was capitalized by wealthy traders and financiers concentrated in the cities, and because small farmers are not as prepared or willing to change as their more informed and wealthy counterparts in cities. More generally, we have argued that it often takes more than unadorned liberalization to get agriculture moving (see Barrett and Carter 1998), and moving in the right direction.

The contemporary experience of agricultural liberalization and growth is heterogeneous, and cautions against the presumption that agrarian growth free of capital subsidies and policy distortions will be broad-based. Information constraints and wealth biases often make effective or shadow prices in these markets "size-sensitive," meaning that real economic costs and returns are systematically different for farm units of different sizes. When shadow prices are size-sensitive and render small-scale farms noncompetitive in land markets, there is a danger that growth will be spread thinly across the agrarian structure, and result in a growth trajectory that is not broad-based and that potentially induces a socially destructive structural dynamic in the longer run. The standard liberalization package of right prices, right institutions and macro stability may not suffice to include the poor in agrarian growth. Indeed, a "right-institutions" policy of providing formal land titling may only serve to generalize and make marketable to outsiders what had been locally secure, smallholder tenure. Perhaps useful to get growth moving, such efforts are as likely to work by moving smallholders out, as by including them in the boom.

So our efforts must also be market-prudent, in recognizing that additional policies and innovations are needed to develop the competitiveness of the small farm sector. This chapter argues for matching reforms aimed at getting prices right with efforts aimed at overcoming the financial and other market impediments that specifically thwart the competitiveness of smaller-scale producers. Such an intermediate policy strategy would seek to avoid centralized state intervention, but enlist investment by states, nongovernmental organizations, and international institutions to develop markets and local institutions that improve access to resources for the rural poor and hence improve their competitiveness.

But achieving broad-based agrarian growth requires more than microeconomically coherent policy reform. It requires better institutions, and investments in education, justice and political reform. For how can markets function when contracts are not enforceable, because the justice system takes too long and is dominated by those who can pay more? How can they function if storage facilities are not trustworthy, or if there are no standards to classify different qualities of products? How can smallholder financing be supported by the government when the officials named by the party can control their constituencies by giving loans? How can it be financed by private banks if the government intervenes now and then to pardon all past debts, and then is delinquent in paying off banks who lost their loans?

The difficulty of implementing and sustaining agricultural policy reform in the face of entrenched large farm interests testifies to the power of these political-economic forces (see Coles 1995). Ultimately, realizing agriculture's role in underwriting inequality-reducing growth will require more than sequencing economic policies. It will require a family of policies and actions that different actors can put in place as the windows of opportunity arise. These policies must of course be communicated effectively to policymakers and the politicians behind them, to raise the political discourse and management skill to implement policy transitions to a higher level. Unfortunately, the debate on agricultural policy among practitioners remains theoretical, with little support from new research. And it tends to occur in the separate and fatalistic world of oppositional agrarian politics.

The debate around agriculture and agricultural policy desperately needs new win-win strategies to address both growth and distributional concerns. At the same time, the agricultural sector needs to move beyond its conflict with the newer players in the so-called agrarian transformation. In light of several new factors, such as grassroots political movements and decentralized organization, there are grounds for hope. In recent work, Tendler (1997) notes that Brazil's land reform policies have gained tremendous urban support, based on a recognition that better land access for the rural poor will make for a less dysfunctional rural economy and stem the tide of rural-to-urban migration.

In short, the new political picture that emerges in Latin America promises to address the grassroots problems at the heart of the market biases against the small impoverished farmer. Now stronger efforts are needed to link the research, policy and political dialogues in order to reach a market-friendly, market-prudent policy package. We hope this chapter has identified areas in which research and policy need to move, and opened lines of communication between them.

Endnotes

[1] This is not to understate the economic, political and institutional complexity of generating broad-based agrarian growth. Moreover, there are undoubtedly other kinds of rural-based policies and activities that could contribute to the alleviation of poverty and destructive inequality.

[2] Some authors dispute whether there is any extraordinary total factor productivity or residual growth in East Asia, once human capital accumulation is accounted for. That interpretation is largely consistent with our argument, which emphasizes the impact of inequality on human capital accumulation.

[3] Many of the microeconomic mechanisms linking inequality and growth are actually linkages between *poverty* (i.e., low absolute income levels) and growth. While the two are related—an increase in inequality implies, under most measures, an increase in poverty—they are not the same.

[4] Birdsall, Graham and Sabot (Chapter 1) similarly suggest that either market or political failures can create destructive linkages between inequality and growth.

[5] Persson and Tabellini (1994) suggest another type of political-economic connection between inequality and growth: that a highly unequal economy will experience punitive political cycles of unproductive redistribution.

[6] The classical models in the Lewis and Fei-Ranis tradition explicitly assume that labor has a right to a subsistence living standard in a seemingly "pre-capitalist" rural economy. The full-blown neoclassical models starting with Jorgenson (1961) that fully endogenized all wages and employment levels in the economy, effectively generated the same result through technical assumptions about full employment and high elasticity of substitution in rural production.

[7] The authors thank Weiping Chen for her efficient review of a number of specialized monographs on agricultural policies in East Asian economies.

[8] This does not overlook the importance of coordination costs for agro-industrial crops. What Louis Putterman calls the "external" scale economies that reside in input, credit and output marketing channels can have a major impact on the structure of agricultural production. But these scale advantages are not dictated by the same technological considerations that advantage large-scale steel production over the backyard variety.

[9] Part of the rural economy's complexity emanates from the fact that other market failures interact and perhaps countervail the labor market imperfection created by these agency costs.

[10] See Williams (1986) for an excellent account of the socioeconomic crises that resulted from cotton and cattle booms in Central America. Lachman's (1987) study, although focused on intra-elite conflict that abrogated traditional forms of social protection of the peasantry, provides interesting evidence about how economic forces became a primary mechanism of enclosure and land concentration in 17th-century England.

[11] This formula only includes the current income value of land. Land may have other values as well, including returns based on expected appreciation and tax advantages. In addition, an individual's willingness to pay for land may deviate from the economic ability to pay for land based on risk and other portfolio considerations (see Olinto and Holt 1993). Moreover, in a dynamic programming context, land may have strategic accumulation value, as Carter and Zimmerman (1995) discuss.

[12] There would always be a distribution of individual reservation prices around the class average defined by the competitiveness regime; that is, more-skilled individuals would value land more highly than less-skilled individuals of the same size class. Such differential valuation by individuals within the same size class would create incentives for intra-class transactions. Here the analysis focuses on systematic *inter-class* differentials.

[13] Empirical literature on farm productivity and size typically refers to labor-cost advantages of small farms (rooted in labor market imperfections) to explain a negative relationship between size and productivity. While several contributions have suggested that the inverse relationship may be a misidentification of land quality factors spuriously correlated with size (e.g., Bhalla and Roy 1988, and Benjamin 1994 and Carter 1984), that literature has focused on an average output measure, as opposed to the land reservation price measure used to frame the discussion here.

[14] Risk and information loom large in capital market theory. For example, the fixed costs of information have been used to suggest that the full cost of borrowing (interest plus transaction/costs) decreases with loan size. Other theoretical traditions arrive at qualitatively similar conclusions based on characteristics of collateral markets such as information asymmetries, transaction costs and competitiveness. For more discussion, see Barham, Boucher and Carter (1996).

[15] If government subsidies or other programs artificially cheapen the price of capital for large farmers, that can create differential land valuation and overwhelm the potential competitiveness of small farms.

[16] Some crops are responsive to interactive labor, meaning that the quantity or quality of output increases significantly when laborers make constant and careful interactive choices.

[17] The smaller scale of family labor farms becomes a liability due to the costs of ascertaining product quality. Detecting pesticide residues, for example, can be costly. Where an intermediary or cooperative assembles small lots of output from multiple small producers, it may be too expensive to spot-check the production of each producer for such residues or other quality attributes. The fixed costs of information (it costs as much to spot-check a large lot as a small lot) create a bias against small farm production of export crops.

[18] Barrett and Carter (1998) discuss in some detail how price variability may blunt the putatively stimulative impact of a liberalized price regime on low-wealth producers who lack access to complete financial markets.

[19] For example, an orchard crop will require considerably more capital access and extended risk exposure, which amplifies the potential capital market bias against smaller-scale, lower wealth producers. On the other hand, a vegetable crop that requires a high level of interactive labor in its cultivation and harvest timing may advantage smaller-scale producers by giving them a labor-cost advantage. Mean-

while, the orchard crop may only require intensive labor for harvesting, where labor quality is less critical and piece rates can ensure effort. So both the individual and overall direction of farm-size biases depend on how much the specific characteristics of boom crops privilege certain market exchanges and size biases relative to others.

[20] This section draws on Carter and Barham (1996).

[21] While insecure property rights obviously truncate investment incentives, and therefore may dampen smallholder competitiveness in producing crops that require long-term investment (e.g., fruit trees), the security of a current occupant may be very different from the security of a potential future occupant. That land registries become outdated when nobody bothers to record transactions indicates that current landholders feel quite secure in their property rights as defined by their customary system. The need for tenure security to enhance the competitiveness of current smallholders should not be taken for granted; it is an empirical question to be evaluated carefully, case by case.

[22] Land without legally clear title may offer little security and have diminished economic value to potential occupants from outside the local social context. In this instance, land securely held by the current occupant may have relatively little collateral value to a formal financial system. Low collateral value may thus limit a smallholder's ability to participate in capital-intensive export production. However, formal financial institutions often show no interest in lending to smallholders even when they hold land titles, and the fixed transactions costs associated with formal loans may discourage smallholders from demanding formal credit (see Barham et al. 1996 and Carter and Olinto 1998). A 1990 review of the impact of land titling programs in Latin America and the Caribbean concluded that titling, in and of itself, had not improved credit access for smallholders (for further details, see Shearer et al. 1990).

[23] Binswanger and Deininger (1994), Carter and Zegarra (1996) and Carter and Mesbah (1993) discuss land market reform policies in greater detail.

[24] In a high-wage economy, access to cheap and well-motivated interactive family labor may indeed provide the decisive competitive advantage for a 100-hectare family labor farm versus a 1000-hectare wage labor or collective farm. Both the 100 and the 1000-hectare farms are large enough that the fixed costs of information that shape input and output markets are less relevant. However, that cannot be said of family labor farms with only a few hectares. For such farms, several orders of magnitude smaller than family farms elsewhere, the advantages afforded by family labor may not compensate for competitive weaknesses created by the size-sensitive financial, information, and product markets.

[25] A similar argument could be made about Asian small-scale farming. Although many East and Southeast Asian countries developed vital, competitive agricultures based on small-scale family labor farms, here the initial distributions and legal land ownership ceilings sheltered small farms from direct head-to-head competition with significantly larger farms.

[26] A covariate risk is one that effects many people simultaneously. If its depositors and borrowers are all subjected to the same shocks, a financial institution will have solvency problems. A bad crop year, for example, is likely to see increased loan defaults and withdrawal of savings deposits. Novel forms of financial intermediation, if based on local information and peer monitoring, are also likely to suffer from covariate risk problems.

References

Adams, Dale and Richard Vogel. 1986. Rural Financial Markets in Developing Countries. *World Development* 14 (4): 477-487.

Ahluwalia, M. 1976. Inequality, Poverty and Development. *Journal of Development Economics.* ISSUE

Aoki, M., K. Murdock and M. Okuno-Fujiwara. 1995. Beyond *The East Asian Miracle:* Introducing the Market-Enhancing View. Center for Economic Policy Research, Stanford University.

Barham, Bradford, S. Boucher and M. Carter. 1996. Credit Constraints, Credit Unions and Small-Scale Producers in Guatemala. *World Development* 22 (5): 792-805.

Barham, B., M.R. Carter and Wayne Sigelko. 1995. Agro-export Production and Peasant Land Access: Examining the Dynamics between Adoption and Accumulation. *Journal of Development Economics* 46: 85-107

Barrett, C. and M.R. Carter. 1998. Microeconomically Coherent Agricultural Policy Reform in Africa, in Joanne Paulson (ed.) *The Role of the State in Key Markets* (MacMillan Press).

Benjamin, D. 1995. Can Unobserved Land Quality Explain the Inverse Productivity Relationship? *Journal of Development Economics* 46(1): 51-84.

Bhalla, G.S., and Roy. 1988. Mis-Specification in Farm Productivity Analysis: The Role of Land Quality. *Oxford Economic Papers* 40: 55-73.

Binswanger, Hans P., and Klaus Deininger. 1993. South African Land Policy: The Legacy of History and Current Options. *World Development* 21(9): 1451-1475.

Binswanger, H., G. Feder and K. Deininger. 1996. Power, Distortions and Reform in Agricultural Land Relations, in J. Behrman and T.N. Srinivasan (eds.) *Handbook of Development Economics* 3 (North Holland).

Birdsall, N., D. Ross and R. Sabot. 1995. Inequality and Growth Reconsidered: Lessons from East Asia. *World Bank Economic Review* 9(3): 477-508.

Birdsall, N., and R. Sabot. 1996. Inequality, Savings and Growth. OCE Working Paper 327, Inter-American Development Bank.

Braverman, Avishay, and J. Guasch. 1989. Institutional Analysis of Credit Cooperatives, in Bardhan, P.K. (ed.), *The Economic Theory of Agrarian Institutions* (London: Oxford University Press).

Carter, Michael R. 1984. Identification of the Inverse Relationship between Farm Size and Productivity. *Oxford Economic Papers* 36: 131-45.

Carter, M.R., and B. Barham. 1996. Level Playing Fields and Laissez Faire: Post-Liberal Development Strategy in Inegalitarian Agrarian Economies. *World Development* 24(7): 1133-1150.

Carter, M.R., B. Barham and D. Mesbah. 1996. Agro-export Booms and the Rural Poor in Chile, Paraguay and Guatemala. *Latin American Research Review* 31(1): 33-65.

Carter, M.R., and Luis Galeano. 1995. *Campesino, Tierra y Mercado* (Asuncion, Paraguay: Centro Paraguayo de Estudios Sociológicos).

Carter, M.R., and D. Mesbah. 1993. Can Land Market Reform Mitigate the Exclusionary Aspects of Rapid Agro-Export Growth? *World Development*. July 1993.

Carter, M.R., and P. Olinto. 1996. Getting Institutions Right for Whom? The Wealth-Differentiated Impacts of Land Titling on Agricultural Investment and Productivity in Paraguay. Working Paper, University of Wisconsin-Madison.

Carter, M.R., and E. Zegarra. 1995. Reshaping Class Competitiveness and the Trajectory of Agrarian Growth with Well-Sequenced Policy Reform. University of Wisconsin-Madison, Working Paper No. 379.

———. 1996. Land Markets and the Persistence of Rural Poverty in Latin America: Post-Liberalization Policy Options, in R. López and A. Valdes (eds). *Poverty in Latin America.*

Carter, M.R., and F. Zimmerman. 1995. Reproducing Inequality: The Dynamics of Asset Distributions in an Inegalitarian Agrarian Economy. Working Paper.

Coles, Jonathan. 1995. Reforming Agriculture, in L. Goodman et al. (eds.) *Lessons of the Venezuelan Experience.* Baltimore: Johns Hopkins University Press.

de Janvry, A., and E. Sadoulet. 1993. Relinking Agrarian Growth with Poverty Reduction, in M. Lipton and J. van der Gaag (eds), *Including the Poor.* Washington, D.C.: World Bank.

———. 1996. Growth, Inequality and Poverty in Latin America: A Causal Analysis, 1970-1994. Working Paper, University of California-Berkeley.

de Janvry, A., E. Sadoulet and M. Fafchamps. 1989. Agrarian Structure, Technological Innovations and the State, in P.K. Bardhan (ed) *The Economic Theory of Agrarian Institutions.* Oxford University Press.

de Janvry, A., E. Sadoulet and L. Wilcox. 1979. Land and Labor in Latin American Agriculture from the 1950s to the 1980s. *Journal of Peasant Studies* 16(3): 396-425.

Eswaran, M., and A. Kotwal. 1986. Access to Capital and Agrarian Production Organization. *Economic Journal* 96: 482-498.

Feder, Gershon. 1985. The Relation between Farm Size and Farm Productivity: The Role of Family Labor, Supervision and Credit Constraints. *Journal of Development Economics* 18: 297-313.

Jorgenson, D. 1961. The Development of a Dual Economy. *Economic Journal* 71(2): 309-334.

Krueger, A., J. Schiff and A. Valdes (1989. Agricultural Incentives in Developing Countries: Measuring the Effects of Sectoral and Economy-wide Policies. *World Bank Economic Review* 2(3): 255-271.

Kuznets, S. 1955. Economic Growth and Income Inequality. *American Economic Review* 45(1): 1-28.

Lachmann, Richard. 1987. *From Manor to Market: Structural Change in England, 1536-1640.* Madison: University of Wisconsin Press.

Lewis, W. Arthur. 1953. Economic Development with Unlimited Supplies of Labor. *Manchester School of Economic and Social Studies* 22(1): 139-191.

Lipton, Michael. 1993. Land Reform as Commenced Business: The Evidence Against Stopping. *World Development* 21(4): 641-657.

Lunqvist, Lars. 1994. Economic Underdevelopment: The Case of a Missing Market for Human Capital. *Journal of Development Economics* 40(2): 219-239.

Mushinski, D. 1996. Empirical Measures of Rationing in Guatemalan Credit Markets. Working Paper, University of Wisconsin.

Persson, T. and G. Tabellini. 1994. Is Inequality Harmful to Growth? *American Economic Review* 84(3): 600-621.

Ravallion, M., and G. Datt. 1995. Growth and Poverty in Rural India. *World Bank Economic Review.*

Rodrik, Dani. 1994. King Kong Meets Godzilla: The World Bank and The East Asian Miracle *CEPR Discussion Paper* No.944.

Schweigert, Thomas. 1994. Penny Capitalism: Efficient but Poor, or Inefficient and (Less Than) Second Best? *World Development* 22 (5): 721-731.

Shearer, Eric B., Susanna Lastarria-Cornhiel and Dina Mesbah. 1991. The Reform of Rural Land Markets in Latin America and the Caribbean. Madison, WI: Land Tenure Center.

Tendler, Judith. 1997. *Good Government in the Tropics.* Baltimore: Johns Hopkins University Press.

Thrupp, L. 1995. Bittersweet Harvests and Global Supermarkets: Sustainability and Equity of Agroexport Diversification in Latin America. World Resources Institute.

Tomich, T., P. Kilby and B. Johnston. 1995. *Transforming Agrarian Economies: Opportunities Seized, Opportunities Missed.* Ithaca: Cornell University Press.

Von Braun, J., D. Hotchkiss and M. Immink. 1989. Nontraditional Export Crops in Guatemala: Effects on Production, Income, and Nutrition. Research Report. No. 73. Washington, D.C.: International Food Policy Research Institute (May).

Von Pischke, J.D., D.W. Adams and G. Dunlop. 1983. *Rural Financial Institutions in Developing Countries: Their Use and Abuse.* Baltimore: Johns Hopkins University Press.

Williams, Robert. 1986. *Export Agriculture and the Crisis in Central America.* University of North Carolina Press.

Zimmerman, F., and M.R. Carter. 1996. Dynamic Portfolio Management under Risk and Subsistence Constraints. Agricultural and Applied Economics Staff Paper no. 402, University of Wisconsin-Madison.

CHAPTER SEVEN

Economic Policy
and Labor Market Dynamics

René Cortázar, Nora Lustig, and Richard H. Sabot

The difference between East Asia and Latin America in economic performance over the last four decades has been striking.[1] In East Asia growth has been rapid and persistent, until recently.[2] By contrast, Latin America's growth has been slow and uneven. A few countries, like Brazil, have recorded high growth rates for short periods, but could not sustain them. From 1965 to 1990, GNP per capita in Latin America grew at less than 2 percent per annum, about one-third of East Asia's growth rate.

In East Asia, not only the wealthiest classes prospered, but also the relative incomes of the poor and middle class were maintained or even increased. Income levels of the poor rose rapidly, and income inequality, already low, declined further for some economies. In Latin America, by contrast, slow growth was associated with high levels of inequality in the distribution of income. There the absolute incomes of the poor have stagnated and poverty remains entrenched.

These differences in economic performance can be partly explained by the dynamics of labor supply and demand. In East Asia, exceptional labor market dynamics are manifested in labor market outcomes. The wage rate is perhaps the best index of both the labor productivity and the economic welfare of all but the wealthiest segment of the population. Rapid and sustained growth of labor demand in East Asia, together with slower growth of labor supply, converted labor from a superabundant to a scarce factor of production.

As demand grew faster than supply, wages were bid up by employers competing with one another in the attempt to attract and hold workers. The rate at which wages increased in East Asia is historically unprecedented. In Korea and Taiwan, the most dramatic examples, average real wages have grown at more than 8 percent per year since 1970, a pace which more than doubled real wages between 1970 and 1980, and more than doubled them again between 1980 and 1990.[3] The rise in the returns to labor contributed to more equitable income distribution.

Opportunities for wage employment in East Asia were expanding at the same time that conditions of wage employment were improving. Most dramatic was the rising employment in manufacturing, which drew workers out of agriculture and into rapidly growing enterprises where productivity and pay were higher. Year after year, for decades, employment in manufacturing increased by 5 to 9 percent. Because the labor force was growing at less than one-fifth that pace, a rising share of the labor force enjoyed the higher wages provided by the manufacturing sector.[4]

Labor market outcomes and the underlying dynamics were far less attractive in Latin America. Labor did not prosper in the region: few jobs were created, and those were at relatively high, but stagnant, wages. In the 1970s, few Latin American countries could sustain rates of wage growth at even half those of Korea or Taiwan. During the 1980s, real wages in Latin America were stagnant or declining, which contributed to high income inequality.

Wage employment opportunities also grew more slowly: in Colombia and Mexico, manufacturing employment grew at less than 2 percent per annum, less than the rate of growth of the labor force, while in Argentina it contracted at more than 2 percent per annum, for the two decades up to 1990.[5] In many Latin American countries, the share of wage employment in the total declined during the 1980s, even in urban areas, as workers compensated for the shortage of formal-sector wage employment by becoming self-employed in the informal sector.[6]

Why wages increased more rapidly in East Asia than in Latin America appears, on the surface, to be quite simple: slower growth of labor supply and more rapid growth of labor demand. But that explanation begs two hard questions: First, what explains the difference between East Asia and Latin America in the dynamics of their labor markets? Second, were there differences in economic policies that significantly influenced the determinants of labor market dynamics? In seeking answers, we will focus on interregional differences in the timing of the demographic transition, and differences in the pace of economic growth and the degree to which growth has been labor-demanding. One reason the dynamics of labor demand differ across the regions is labor market performance.

Poor labor market performance contributed heavily to poor economic performance in some Latin American economies, but not in others. What do we mean by labor market performance? Rapid growth of the demand for labor and skill is essential for a growing supply of labor to be utilized in high-return activities. But so is a labor market that ensures workers' skills are most productively utilized. A labor market that is efficient, flexible and responsive to changing conditions contributes to economic growth by creating an appropriate economic environment.

Government policy is often the difference between a well-performing and a poorly performing labor market. In this respect, labor market policy is like macroeconomic and trade policy. Unlike the accumulation of physical and human capital and technical progress, a well-performing labor market is not in itself a source of economic growth. Yet labor market pathologies induced by excessive or inappropriate government interventions, like macroeconomic mismanagement or a grossly distorted trade policy regime, can severely constrain the growth of output and the dynamism of the labor market. These conditions can result in the misallocation of labor. For example, inefficient allocation of educated manpower may result in a lower growth payoff to large investments in human capital—and, even worse, to the diversion of scarce savings from investment to the subsidization of labor.

Where the dynamics of supply and demand for skill is lacking, or the performance of the labor market is inadequate, educational expansion (for which East Asia is justifiably noted) may actually impede rather than stimulate growth. What has the potential to be a boon can become a bane if that potential is squandered. The rapid increase in the supply of educated workers, and the wrenching labor market adjustments and disappointed expectations that result, can sow the seeds of problems that erode the growth potential of the economy. Those adjustments and disappointments often give rise to political pressures on government for remedial action.

The response of government can actually make matters worse. To limit the political problems that result when the expectations of the educated are frustrated, government may choose to subsidize their employment. Consequently, educated workers may be paid well but produce little; and savings may be diverted from investment to consumption.[7]

Interregional Difference in Growth of Labor Force

For a given rate of growth of labor demand, the slower the increase in labor supply, the faster wages will increase. Slower growth of the labor force in East Asia meant that wages increased at a relatively faster pace. The slow growth of labor supply in East Asia is largely due to slower population growth. By comparison, during the nineteenth-century industrialization period, the population of the currently high-income countries grew annually at about 0.8 percent, doubling every 87 years. Today Latin America's population is growing at roughly three times that rate, doubling every 30 years. By contrast, East Asia's population growth has declined to levels approaching those that prevailed in the high-income countries. For example, the population growth rates of Korea, Hong Kong and Thailand are 1.1, 1.4 and 1.8 percent, respectively. It will take 65 years for Korea's population to double.[8]

This early demographic transition caused a lag in the numbers entering the East Asian labor force. Latin America's annual rate of labor force growth during the 1980s was 2.6 percent. In East Asia the rate was 1.8 percent, and declining. The labor force growth rate in Singapore is only 0.8 percent, lower than the 0.9 percent annual rate for high-income countries in the nineteenth century.

The difference between East Asia and Latin America in fertility rates, and thus the growth of labor supply, can be attributed in part to policy, and in particular to education policy. Educated mothers have fewer children. In both East Asia and Latin America, the fertility rate for women with over seven years of schooling is roughly half the fertility rate for uneducated women. But in East Asia, a much higher proportion of women, in particular poor women, are educated. Educational systems in Latin America have been as successful as those in East Asia in eliminating the gender gap in enrollments. Therefore the low educational attainment of women in Latin America is due to low *aggregate* rates of enrollment in primary and secondary schools.[9] And much of the gap in aggregate enrollment rates is due to the gap in enrollment rates among the poor.

Why does such a small proportion of poor children successfully complete basic education in Latin America? Public expenditure on education as a proportion of GNP is not the answer: that share has been roughly the same in Latin America as in East Asia. Rather, three factors stand out: greater constraints on public expenditure on basic education per eligible child, among them a bias toward universities in the allocation of public finance; weak demand in the labor market for educated workers; and high inequality in the distribution of income, meaning very low family incomes in the bottom quintile.

In East Asia, public expenditure on education was allocated to compensate for capital market failures (which prevent the poor from borrowing to finance investments in education), rather than to exploit externalities. In practice this meant allocating more public money to basic education and less to university education than in other regions. As an extreme example, in 1985 Venezuela allocated 43 percent of its public education budget to higher education, and Korea, only 10 percent.[10]

Low public funding of basic education in Latin America relegates poor children to low-quality public schools,[11] weakening their demand for education by reducing the payoff of basic education to the poor in the labor market and making it difficult for them to do well on tests that ration access to heavily subsidized public universities. In East Asia, adequate public funding of basic education gives the poor access to high-quality schooling, strengthening their demand for education.

An early fertility decline in East Asia began in the mid 1960s and was stimulated by the rapid growth of educational opportunities for girls. This resulted in much slower growth of the school-age population in the 1970s. Closing what Birdsall and Sabot refer to as a virtuous circle, the fertility decline contributed to increased public expenditures on basic education per eligible child in East Asia. In 1970, public expenditure per eligible child was not much higher in Korea than in Mexico; two decades later, it was nearly four times as great. Differences in the percentage of GNP devoted to education do not explain this. Instead, the much faster growth of Korea's GNP—which increased the absolute value of the share of output that goes to education—and Korea's much smaller school-age population (which grew by 60 percent in Mexico, while it declined by 2 percent in Korea) explain the widening gap.[12]

Stronger demand for educated workers elicits a greater supply, via the price mechanism. Investment in human capital by households is greater in East Asia than in Latin America, partly because of greater demand for educated workers. Just as the macroeconomic environment and public policy were conducive to substantial public investments in basic education, so too at the microlevel, at the level of the labor market and the household, the economic environment generated powerful eye-catching incentives for private investments in education. In East Asia, high expected returns to schooling were sustained from one decade to the next, whereas in Latin America they were not. In Latin America in the 1950s and 1960s, parents were confident that education was a means of enabling their children to achieve a level of material well-being substantially greater than their own, and the household demand for education grew rapidly. But the growth of demand for educated workers did not match the growth of supply. Instead of achieving through their education a near-certain route to a brighter future, a rising proportion of school graduates traveled a path marked by prolonged bouts of unemployment, self-employment and low earnings.[13]

Low inequality (and higher absolute incomes of the poor) in East Asia enables more of the poor to send their children to school, while high inequality (and lower absolute incomes of the poor) in Latin America constrains investment by the poor. Poor households often do not invest in their children's education even when the returns are high. Their pressing need for subsistence crowds out high-return investments and constrains the demand for education. Capital market imperfections preclude using expected earnings as collateral, making borrowing to finance investment in schooling almost impossible for those with few other assets. The higher the absolute incomes of the poor (a corollary of lower inequality), the less binding the constraint on their ability to invest in their children.[14]

Slower growth of labor demand has contributed to less attractive labor market outcomes in Latin America than in East Asia and we turn next to explanations for that slower growth. But slower growth of demand for labor in Latin America has also contributed to faster growth of labor supply. The slower labor force growth in East Asian countries following a labor-demanding growth path appears to have been, in part, endogenous. The growth of employment opportunities and earnings that results from the rapid growth of labor-demand raises the opportunity cost for women of having children. Also, the faster growth of labor demand raises the expected returns to investment in education, and eases the household liquidity constraints on such investments, thereby raising the demand for schooling. Likewise, public resources for schooling may be more abundant, raising the supply of educational opportunities.[15] Higher levels of investment in education slow the growth of supply of unskilled labor by raising the proportion of the labor force that is skilled and, as we have seen, by lowering fertility rates. As skill levels rise, countries can also exploit newer, skill-based manufacturing technologies, which shifts out the labor demand curve further.[16]

Interregional Difference in Growth of Labor Demand

Not only has labor supply grown more *slowly* in East Asia than in Latin America, but labor demand has increased at a faster pace. This is not because growth of employment has been unusually slow in Latin America. Until the 1980s, when output and employment stagnated because of the macroeconomic adjustments made necessary by debt-service problems, the pace of industrial sector employment growth in Latin America actually exceeded that of the currently high-income countries from 1880 to 1900 during their rapid industrialization. Rather, the interregional difference reflects the unusually rapid growth of employment in East Asia.[17]

Since the demand for labor is derived from the demand for output, the explanation for the interregional difference must be sought, in the first instance, in those factors which contributed to East Asia's rapid output growth: high rates of savings and investment and high rates of return on investment.[18] But the path of growth of output has also been more labor-demanding in East Asia than in Latin America. We focus on four reasons why the demand for labor has been so much more dynamic in East Asia than in Latin America: agricultural dynamism, export orientation, macroeconomic stability, and labor market performance.

Agricultural Dynamism

There is an important structural difference between the agricultural sectors of East Asia and Latin America. The distribution of landholding is much more equal in East Asia, reflecting the predominance of smallholders.[19] In Latin America the *latifundios* control a substantial proportion of arable land.[20] This difference may account for some of the greater dynamism of East Asian agriculture. But the difference between East Asia and Latin America in whether pricing, public investment,[21] taxation, and trade policies are biased against agriculture may have had more impact on the dynamism of the agriculture sector. East Asian countries avoided policy biases against agriculture. In this they were in a minority. In Latin America, however, pricing, public investment, taxation, and trade policies all tended to be strongly biased against agriculture. The rationale for this was to transfer resources to the potentially more dynamic urban industrial sector. In an attempt to hasten structural change, governments adopted policies that aggressively extracted surpluses from the agricultural sector and channeled them into industrial sector investments. The consequence was stagnant agriculture.[22]

As a strategy for inducing sustained increases in the rate of economic growth, the aggressive intersectoral transfer of resources in Latin America yielded disappointing results. For a time, capital for nonagricultural investment was abundant. However, the resultant stagnation or slow growth of incomes of the large labor force still employed in agriculture deprived the industrial sector of a potentially important domestic source of demand for its output. Limited demand meant low rates of return on investment, and less stimulus for growth. This constraining effect of limited demand was amplified by trade policies that biased incentives against the export of manufactured goods.

Ironically, over the past three decades, it was in those Asian countries where agriculture grew fastest that agriculture's share in output and employment declined most. If agricultural productivity is increasing while its share of the labor force is declining, how does a dynamic agricultural sector contribute to labor-demanding growth? Despite rapid output growth, employment in agriculture grew at the modest rate of 1.0 percent per annum in East Asia.[23] In East Asia, agriculture's direct contribution to employment generation was outweighed by its indirect contribution: Higher income in agriculture meant higher demand for manufactured inputs into agriculture—like pumps, plows, and fertilizer—as well as for consumer goods. This translated into faster growth of both nonagricultural output and the demand for labor.[24]

Because the relatively simple manufactured inputs and consumer goods de-manded by rural residents are more efficiently produced with labor-intensive tech-niques, the employment effects of these increases in demand are amplified. By con-trast, when the incomes of the urban elite increase, the tradables on which they spend their increased income tend to be capital-intensive goods. In East Asia strong domestic demand may have given early manufacturers a competitive advantage in international markets, by providing the opportunity to test-market labor-intensive goods and achieve economies of scale.

Export Orientation

East Asian countries avoided policy biases against exports. They are virtually unique in choosing—without the external pressure of a major structural adjustment pro-gram—to move away from industrial and trade policies promoting manufacturers of import substitutes. By not discriminating against exports, they avoided impos-ing constraints on the allocative and dynamic efficiency of their economies.[25] The growth of their output and of labor demand was faster as a consequence.

Export growth stimulated labor demand not only by faster economic growth, but also because manufactured exports tend to be more labor-intensive than im-port substitutes.[26] In the early stages of industrialization, the abundance of labor relative to capital yields a comparative advantage in labor-intensive goods; manu-facturing firms that succeed in the competition against foreign firms for their do-mestic market need every advantage they can muster, and so tend to produce goods and adopt techniques that take advantage of the relatively abundant, and hence inexpensive, production factor. By contrast, manufacturing firms that produce im-port substitutes behind government-constructed barriers to foreign competition can be profitable, though much less dynamic, even when the goods they produce or the techniques they adopt are capital intensive.

The potential for growth of output of manufactured exports was extraordi-nary. In the manufacturing sectors of East Asian economies, production capacity was small, relative to demand in high-income countries for labor-intensive manu-factured goods. Once they had achieved technological mastery and established marketing channels, low-cost labor gave East Asian manufacturers a powerful com-petitive advantage in labor-intensive goods: they could undercut world market prices. In effect East Asian exporters faced infinitely elastic demand for their out-put. The growth of manufactured exports was limited only by the ability to in-crease supply.[27]

Because of the rapid growth of labor-intensive manufactured exports, industrial employment as a share of total employment in East Asia grew rapidly between 1965 and 1984. In Korea and Malaysia, for example, it more than doubled. In Korea between 1975 and 1985, manufacturing employment increased by roughly 60 percent and accounted for 40 percent of the aggregate growth of employment opportunities. In Brazil, Mexico, Venezuela and Peru, export growth was much slower and the industrial sector was initially more capital-intensive. Over the same period, industrial employment as a share of total employment actually fell.[28]

East Asian governments did not move from the protection of import substitutes to a neutral trade and industrial policy regime. Rather they moved to a regime that aggressively favored exports—a strategy that distorted relative prices, and in particular, the price of capital.[29] And what were the results? One policy regime, by favoring import substitutes and breaking the rules of allocative efficiency, slowed the growth of manufacturing output and employment. Another policy regime, by favoring manufactured exports and violating those same rules, stimulated more rapid growth of output and labor demand. Why?

The explanation for this asymmetry lies in the dynamics of favored firms. Manufacturers of import substitutes have often exploited the monopoly power they were implicitly granted in the domestic market by becoming inefficient rent-seekers. Exporters are not monopolists and cannot afford to be inefficient. They have powerful incentives to increase their productivity: otherwise they would not be competitive in world markets. If their export performance does not improve, they risk losing the advantages provided by government: protection in the domestic market and access to subsidized credit.[30]

Even while growing rapidly, labor demand in East Asia has become increasingly skill-intensive. As a share of wage employment, white collar and technical employment increased steadily during the 1970s and the 1980s. In Korea, for example, it increased from 29 percent in 1980 to 36 percent in 1990, and in Taiwan, from 32 to 40 percent.[31] Skill intensification resulted, from a change in comparative advantage. East Asian exporters shifted into more technologically sophisticated and skill-intensive goods, as rapidly rising wages of unskilled labor eroded their international competitiveness in labor-intensive manufactured goods. Between 1970 and 1991 in Korea and Taiwan, exports of machinery and equipment grew much faster than such labor-intensive exports as textiles and apparel.[32] Cheap unskilled labor was now less important to international competitiveness than low-cost educated labor and technological capability.

Skill intensification also resulted from the increasing abundance of educated labor, and consequent declines in its relative price. The compression of the educational structure of wages provided employers with a strong incentive to substitute more for less-educated workers. Strong demand for educated labor, and consequent high returns to investment in education, provides one explanation for the extraordinary increase in supply of educated labor. Conversely, the growing abundance of educated workers stimulated skill intensification, hence the growth of demand for educated workers.

The skill intensification of labor demand proceeded at a much slower pace in Latin America than in East Asia. Because of their inward orientation, the manufacturing sectors of Latin America tend to be less sensitive to changes in comparative advantage. And comparative advantage is not shifting as much for them, because the wages of unskilled workers are not rising nearly as rapidly as in East Asia. Moreover, since the supply of educated labor is not as abundant as in East Asia, the decline in the relative wages of educated workers is not as marked and the incentive to shift to more skill-intensive production processes is not as strong. In sum, because the virtuous circle between increasing the demand for educated workers and their supply is weaker, Latin America has fewer educated workers and less demand for them, than does East Asia.

Macroeconomic Stability

East Asian development provides support for the premise that a successful development strategy will be market-based. Unless a government ensures macroeconomic stability, however, markets operating on their own are likely to yield socially undesirable outcomes. Macroeconomic stability is paramount for favorable labor market dynamics. Prolonged interruptions in the growth of labor demand, such as those triggered in Latin American countries by the debt crisis of the 1980s or, in East Asia, by the financial crisis of 1997–98, will slow or even erode progress toward improved labor market conditions.[33] East Asia did not undergo years of structural adjustment and stagnant labor demand like those that plagued Latin America during the 1980s, which made a substantial difference in the evolution of wages and other labor market outcomes. How long East Asia's adjustment process will take remains to be seen. The longer it takes, the more profound will be the impact on labor demand and the growth of wages.[34]

To ensure macroeconomic stability, and to promote savings and investment, the governments of East Asia kept fiscal deficits small. Low inflation rates helped keep interest rates stable, and low but positive. Until recently, external debt was limited to manageable proportions, and public or publicly guaranteed foreign debt was restricted.[35] Governments avoided the severe appreciation of exchange rates that beset much of Latin America. Finally, policymakers in these economies generally responded quickly and effectively to shocks, a flexibility that derived in part from the willingness of workers, who had shared the benefits of growth, to share the burden of adjustment.

Macroeconomic stability and low interest rates raised the returns and lowered the costs of investment in both physical and human capital. The results: both the enterprise demand and the household demand for human capital were stimulated, leading to higher rates of investment in schooling and training. A more educated workforce is more flexible (educated workers more easily learn new and different skills). The speed with which firms were able to adapt to external shocks and policy changes increased. This increased adaptability of firms, in turn, helped maintain macroeconomic stability. So, macroeconomic stability contributed to high rates of investment in human capital, which then contributed to macroeconomic stability.

The export orientation of trade and industry policies made it easier for East Asian economic managers to maintain macroeconomic stability. For the period 1970–81, Brazil's GDP grew at an average annual rate of roughly 7.5 percent; its growth rate declined sharply to less than 1 percent per annum for the period 1981–84. Korea's growth rate was not much higher than Brazil's in the 1970s but declined only marginally, to 7.5 percent during the 1981–84 period.[36] Brazil and Korea were indebted to a similar extent but differed markedly in their ability to service their debt. Between 1965 and 1983, exports as a percent of GDP remained at 8 percent in Brazil, while in Korea they increased dramatically from 9 to 37 percent. As a consequence Brazil's debt service grew to 132 percent of export earnings, while in Korea debt service remained much lower. Brazil was forced to adopt contractionary policies to cut imports as a means of servicing debt. Because Korea's exports generated the foreign exchange necessary to pay its debts, the government was not forced to impose macro constraints.[37] The comparison of Korea and Brazil extends generally to East Asia and Latin America. Rapid export growth in East Asia kept the debt-service ratio low, sustaining rapid output growth. Meanwhile in Latin America, slow growth of exports resulted in a debt-service ratio higher than 150 percent, debt crises, and a consequent rapid erosion of output growth.

Labor Market Performance

East Asian labor markets are characterized by a combination of nonconfrontational labor and an encompassing elite. By "nonconfrontational" we mean that wage labor was willing *not to*, or was unable to, use its collective power to extract short-term wage and employment gains.[38] Rather, wage-earners accepted wage and employment levels determined, respectively, by the interaction of labor supply and demand and by the equalization of wages and the marginal product of labor. They expected a free labor market to be a dynamic labor market—that future levels of wages and employment would be higher if workers accepted market outcomes and cooperated with management than if they did not.

By "encompassing" we mean that the elite behaved as if their future well-being were a function of the future well-being of those not in the elite. The elite adopted a development strategy that was not biased against agriculture or exports, and was in accord with factor endowments and comparative advantage, and that strategy benefited all groups by yielding rapid and labor-demanding growth. It ensured that labor's expectation regarding the payoff for nonconfrontation would be fulfilled—which, in turn, reinforced labor's cooperative attitude.

In Latin American labor markets, the combination of confrontational labor and a nonencompassing elite was more common. The pursuit of an inward-looking development strategy, oriented towards import substitution, encouraged these traits. This inward-oriented development strategy prevailed in Latin America from the 1930s up until the 1980s.[39] Firms were protected from competition from abroad. The labor market was segmented between a modern (protected) sector where labor legislation and collective agreements were enforced, and an unprotected or informal sector, representing a quarter to a third of the labor force, where labor legislation and collective agreements were either not enforced or, as for the self-employed, not applicable.[40]

In the competitive equilibrium created by the combination of nonconfrontational labor and an encompassing elite, the labor market is integrated: urban and rural wage rates are roughly equal. Since wage jobs are not strikingly more attractive than self-employment, there is no incentive for workers to prefer urban wage employment to rural self-employment, hence no incentive to queue for wage jobs (and be unemployed). And since there is no incentive for workers to lobby the government to expand wage employment opportunities beyond the level justified by the derived demand for labor, no wedge is driven between the wage and the marginal product of labor.

Relatively undistorted factor prices encouraged the adoption of appropriate technology and a structure of production in accord with comparative advantage. This in turn contributed to the international competitiveness of domestic enterprises, and hence to rapid growth of demand for their output. The combination of strong demand and low wages contributed to profitability. The encompassing elite invested a high proportion of retained earnings, which resulted in substantial increases in output, and the consequent demand for wage labor. The growth of labor demand outstripped supply. Not only did employment increase, but because of the dramatic demand shift, wages *were pulled up* and rose steeply.

In the distorted labor market of the sort yielded by the combination of *confrontational labor and a nonencompassing elite,* labor power raises the urban wage to well above rural incomes, creating a wage-earning elite. Though still abundant, wage labor is priced as if scarce, and employers thus have an incentive to economize in its use. Thereafter, the labor market becomes segmented, implying an intersectoral misallocation of labor, with low urban employment growth and the rural sector becoming the residual employer at low wages. Given the rural-urban earnings gap, urban unemployment then increases, as more workers migrate to the urban sector than there are jobs available.

Moreover, because urban wage employment is now much more attractive than rural self-employment, the unemployed and those employed in the rural sector become a lobby for the creation of more high-paying urban jobs. The public sector may respond by employing more workers at the high wage than warranted by the derived demand for labor, driving a wedge between the wage and labor's marginal product, which may even be zero. Those enterprises that take on excess labor will be loss-makers and thus will require subsidization.

The implications for labor market dynamics of a distorted labor market are not attractive. By overpricing superabundant labor, the economy is steered onto a detour from the labor-demanding growth path. Because of the distortion of factor prices, inappropriate labor-saving technologies are adopted and the structure of production is less in accord with comparative advantage. As a consequence, international competitiveness and the profitability of domestic enterprises are both reduced.[41] Moreover, the subsidies required to finance employment (when the wage exceeds labor's marginal product) divert savings from productive investment, further diminishing the rate of growth of labor demand, and employment and wages.

In sum, in Latin America "confrontational" labor used its power in negotiations with owners of protected firms to increase wages over and above the marginal product of labor. When the cost of labor in the modern sector surpassed the supply price of labor, domestic prices of the goods and services involved could increase, since there was no competitive pressure from foreign goods. This process contributed to the high inflation that was characteristic of Latin America. The net results of the distributive coalition between confrontational labor and owners of protected firms were increased wages for workers in the modern or protected sector, and higher prices of the goods and services produced by that sector, relative to the wages and prices of the other sectors (i.e., agriculture). This segmentation of the markets for labor and for goods constrained the demand for labor in the protected sector. Distorted factor prices encouraged the adoption of inappropriate technologies and a structure of production that was not in accord with factor endowments and comparative advantage. The inward-looking development strategies adopted by the nonencompassing elites were biased against agriculture and exports; they resulted in slower growth and led Latin economies away from a labor-demanding growth path.

In the eighties and nineties, Latin America gradually shifted from an inward-oriented to an outward-looking development strategy. Firms are under stronger competitive pressure from abroad. Hence, there is a new reason why wages should not grow faster than the supply price of labor. This is an argument for decentralized collective bargaining. It is also an argument for greater labor market flexibility. Competitive pressure from abroad requires a greater capacity to adapt to change in markets, adopt technical innovations, and allow structural change. Traditional labor legislation that makes it difficult for employers to adjust the optimal size and composition of their labor force reduces flexibility.

Why Labor Market Performance Was Superior in East Asia

Countries that chose the encompassing, nonconfrontational combination tended to encourage both exports and a more dynamic agricultural sector. When rural incomes grow rapidly, so too will the supply price of urban labor. Increases in the demand for urban labor will, therefore, yield increases in urban wages. In this case, rapid growth of urban wages is consistent with an integrated labor market. There is, therefore, less incentive for labor to demand better outcomes than those yielded by the interaction of labor supply and demand, less of a tendency for labor to shift from nonconfrontation to conflict, and a lower probability that the labor market will be segmented. In sum, when the agricultural sector is dynamic and the supply price of labor is rising, as it was in East Asia, it is easier to adhere to market determined outcomes in the wage labor market.

Conversely, policies that discriminate against agriculture and yield stagnant rural incomes are likely to result in nonconfrontation giving way to conflict in the urban labor market. When rural incomes are stagnant, then so too is the supply price of urban labor. In this case, even if the demand for urban labor is growing, the market wage will not increase—trying the patience of labor, and jeopardizing any inclination by them to be nonconfrontational. If, at the same time, the output and profits of urban enterprises are increasing while urban wages are not, the stage will be set for collective action by labor to push up their returns and segment the market. Arguments for higher wages will be made on the basis of "ability to pay" and "fairness" in the distribution of factor shares, and sight is likely to be lost of the inequity of large rural-urban income gaps and of the long-run costs of labor market segmentation. With a stagnant agricultural sector, the ruling elite is more likely to use nonmarket or interventionist mechanisms to "partition the pie."

In Taiwan manufacturing wages are only a fifth higher than agricultural wages and both grew rapidly. The labor market is remarkably integrated. By contrast, workers with the same skill level in Colombia and Jamaica earn 150 percent more in nonagricultural activities than in agricultural work.[42] And even larger differentials have been observed elsewhere.

Export orientation implies competitive pressure from abroad. In East Asia, this competition helped both labor and the elite to realize that in firms producing tradables, pushing levels of wages and employment beyond those determined by the market would result in their products being noncompetitive. This would jeopardize the very existence of the firms yielding returns to both groups. Moreover, the same competitive pressures helped create a lobby of exporters which demanded more efficient performance from those firms, often public enterprises, which provided the necessary nontradable inputs for production. This limited the tolerance for excess wages and employment in the public sector. Finally, those economies that adopted a policy of openness benefited from the easier access to imported capital equipment and technology, which in turn improved the productivity and wages of wage labor.

In the inward-looking economies of Latin America, on the other hand, protected markets meant that inefficiencies in the utilization of labor could be passed on to consumers in the form of higher prices. The emergence of the combination of confrontational labor and nonencompassing elite, and the distributive coalition to which it gave rise, was made more likely by inward-looking development strategies. At the same time the combination reinforced import-substitution strategies. The smaller the risk that lack of competitiveness in world markets would result in the failure of firms, the easier it was for both the elite and labor in the protected sector to concentrate on ways to increase their short-term returns.

Countries that chose the encompassing, nonconfrontational combination tended to have a pro-market *intellectual heritage*. The dominant intellectual heritage influenced labor's choice between confrontation and nonconfrontation, and the elite's choice between encompassing and nonencompassing policies. This framework of ideas, often inherited from ex-colonial rulers or post-colonial advisors, influenced the evaluation of the relative attractiveness of future options. In extreme cases, ideology seemed to preclude a strategy choice from the feasible set of options; in other cases, it affected the expected size of payoffs.[43]

For example, Fabian socialists believed that strict reliance on the market might yield rapid economic growth in the short run, but also a highly unequal distribution of income which, in addition to being unfair, would undermine the political stability necessary to sustain such growth. They recommended state control of the "commanding heights" of the economy and extensive government intervention as a means of preventing unpalatable distributional side-effects of the free operation of markets. This set of ideas had a profound influence on such leaders as Nasser, Nehru, Nkrumah, and Nyerere, who were all instrumental in designing the initial policy frameworks for their countries. Distrust of markets was a factor in their choice of inward-looking policies which, in turn, was a factor in their acquiescence to the wage and employment demands of wage labor. The result of negotiations with labor with regard to the distribution of the rents from import substitution often yielded high short-term returns to the elites in these socialist economies.

Socialist thought, with its roots in Marxism and the belief in the necessity of conflict between the interests of labor and private capital, also influenced labor's view of the world, of what was feasible and desirable. Ideologically "leftist" groups dismissed as naive the idea that everyone's welfare would be enhanced by cooperation between labor and capital. They believed that the elite (in their role as capitalists) were fundamentally incapable of sharing the fruits of growth equitably. This was coupled with a distrust of markets, which were perceived to be manipulated by the elite. Leftist labor concluded that the only way to avoid being exploited by capitalists was to organize collectively and press for the most favorable terms of employment.

In a similar way, the structuralist beliefs of Raúl Prebisch and others, and their associated export pessimism, influenced the decisions of Latin American leaders to follow an inward-looking development strategy. A commitment to structuralism implied a rejection of the labor-demanding, nondistributional strategy. World markets were seen to be so biased against low-income countries that policies encouraging development in accord with relative factor prices and comparative advantage would not yield rapid growth. Hence, external orientation was rejected as an option at the outset, i.e., excluded from the information set.

By contrast, capitalistic, market-oriented ideologies were influential in countries in East Asia and in post-1973 Chile. In Korea and Taiwan, which had been Japanese colonies, Japanese notions of appropriate development strategy appear to have been influential. It was Japan that pioneered both the export-oriented development strategy and the paradigm of cooperation between labor and corporate management. In East Asia, therefore, the ideas underlying encompassing policies were part of the information set, and the policies were perceived to be potentially effective. Pro-market American ideas and mercantilist British ideas (e.g., in Hong Kong) reinforced the market orientation of Japanese ideas. In post-Allende Chile, an influential group of economists and policymakers was schooled in the University of Chicago doctrine of free markets.

Labor Market Dynamics and Labor Market Performance

Favorable dynamics generated a bonanza for labor: in Korea, Taiwan, Indonesia, Malaysia and Singapore from 1970 to 1990, the real wage bill in manufacturing, the pool of money paid to labor, increased by a phenomenal 10–15 percent per annum, doubling every five to seven years.[44] Workers did so well that there was less incentive to use the collective power of labor to push up wages or expand employment opportunities beyond those justified by the derived demand for labor. And, closing a virtuous circle, by avoiding the costs imposed by labor market segmentation, superior labor market performance contributed to favorable labor market dynamics.

Unfavorable labor market dynamics contributed to inferior labor market performance. It was common in Latin America for the total pool of money paid to labor in manufacturing to be little more in 1990 than in 1970. In Argentina and Peru, it was actually less. Workers were doing so poorly that they found it tempting to use their collective power to push up wages above labor's supply price and expand employment opportunities beyond those justified by the derived demand for labor. In sum, by stimulating employer-led increases in wages and employment, and holding out the promise of more to come, the decision by the elite in East Asia to follow a labor-demanding growth path lessened the perceived need for a coalition between employers and employees to generate and distribute rents. The labor-demanding growth path reduced the inclination of workers to create a wage labor elite and segment the labor market by prematurely pushing up wages and employment. At the same time, in a virtuous circle, an efficient, flexible and integrated labor market, by avoiding the drag on growth and on labor demand that a poorly performing labor market can impose, contributed to favorable labor market dynamics.

Latin America's Labor Institutions: The Beginning of Reform

We have emphasized the marked contrast between the combination of nonconfrontational labor and encompassing policies in East Asia with the combination of confrontational labor and nonencompassing policies in Latin America. This contrast is an accurate historical description. But in the eighties and nineties, Latin America changed. Most notably, there has been a shift from an inward-oriented to an outward-oriented development strategy.

Institutions regulating collective bargaining, hiring and firing, training and minimum wages, put in place prior to this change, were appropriate for, and contributed to, a protected world governed by a distributive coalition which ensured that organized workers and employers would share rents extracted from the rest of the population. However, these institutions are not appropriate for the new, more open and competitive economic environment in which, as a result of macroeconomic and trade policy reform, a growing proportion of firms in Latin America now find themselves.

For example, many Latin countries (Argentina and Brazil among them) conducted collective bargaining at the level of the industry. Industry-level collective bargaining is much more likely to result in large wage increases, and distorted structures of wages and prices, than firm or plant-level bargaining. Unions organized at the level of the firm know that they cannot push up wages without the firm suffering a decline in employment, whereas unions organized at the industry or sectoral level are often powerful enough to both push up wages and protect prevailing levels of employment.[45] The results: greater segmentation of the labor market and less growth of output and employment.

With respect to regulations governing hiring and firing in the protected sector, the most notable feature is high severance payments. For example, in Argentina severance payments are roughly one month per year of work; there is a minimum of two months' wages. In Brazil, severance payments are smaller than in Argentina when a worker is dismissed with "just cause." When workers are dismissed without "just cause," they are roughly equal to those in Argentina (one month's salary for each year worked). Economic redundancies are not considered just cause. In Chile, too, severance payments are equally high.

Workers in the formal sector obtained their job security at the cost of more segmentation of the labor market, less employment creation (because of the increase in the cost of labor), an increase in informal jobs and reduced capacity of firms to adapt to change and engage in technical innovation. Adaptation and innovation require a flow of resources and an acceptance of higher risks. The resources required and the level of risk are both increased by the rigidities induced by severance payments. During the period of inward-looking development strategies, the pace of technological change was slow and the need to adapt to competitive pressures was limited, so the cost imposed by high severance payments was, perhaps, not all that high. Now that development strategies have become more outward-looking, strong competitive pressure from abroad requires adaptation and technical innovation, and structural change.[46]

These changes will require decentralizing collective bargaining and reforming the severance process and payments. A trend to decentralize collective bargaining has begun in the region. Chile's government took a radical step in this direction in the late seventies. In Brazil there is ongoing debate with respect to decentralization. In 1996 the Argentine government sent to Congress a labor reform bill to permit bargaining at the firm level. That would legally protect the inclusion of "opening clauses," which allow companies to negotiate with their workforce to pay wages below the minimum set in the branch-level collective contracts.[47]

These trends are the outcome of a difficult process. For many industrywide unions they would result in a sharp reduction in their social and economic power. Indeed, the labor reform proposals have triggered national strikes in Argentina.[48]

The difficulties are even greater in the public sector, where centralization of bargaining is greatest. Attempts to decentralize bargaining and to induce more flexibility in public sector labor markets generally provoke strong political reactions. The trend towards decentralization in collective bargaining does not imply that all social dialogue has to take place at a decentralized level. Collective bargaining at the level of the enterprise can coexist with a centralized social dialogue among national confederations of workers, the government and employers, on such labor policies as training programs, social security reform, and the minimum wage.

There is also a trend to reform severance payments and unemployment insurance. Brazil is debating the issue, and Chile's Ministry of Labor proposed reform measures in 1993 that are still being debated.[49] Argentina's government has drafted legislation for drastically reducing the amount of severance payments that resembles the Chilean proposals. Chilean law now provides one month of severance pay per year in a job; the reforms would allow a maximum of three months' severance pay up to a maximum of 11 years. In Argentina, instead of one month severance pay per year in a job, the proposed reforms would give one month for those that have worked less than five years, two months for five to ten years' employment, and three months for more than ten years. The resources saved would then be deposited (around 4 percent of wages) in a personal account belonging to the worker, who could draw from his own account not only if he is unemployed, but also in case he quits or retires. These deferred-compensation plans would substitute for traditional unemployment insurance. In Chile, if the contributions to the system do not suffice to fully finance the unemployment benefit, there is guaranteed access to a loan, which workers would repay once they are employed again.

This new form of protection would be free of the problems associated with severance payments. It should prove more valuable to workers, as it is a benefit certain to be received, and would not distort a worker's decision about whether to leave a job. Unlike the existing system of unemployment benefits, it does not obstruct the capacity of firms to adapt to change, or stimulate the creation of "atypical" contracts and informality. Transforming the traditional unemployment insurance (UI) into a savings-loan system would also avert the well-known problems of traditional UI systems. First, unemployment benefits increase unemployment equilibria, due to their high moral hazard: this type of insurance allows a longer job search, and stimulates a higher flow into unemployment. Second, traditional UI increases informality, as there is an incentive to look for informal jobs. None of these problems are associated with the savings-loans scheme.

Labor market reform is likely to reduce distortions of factor prices and reduce segmentation of both the labor market and the goods market. This, in turn, will induce the adoption of more appropriate technologies and a structure of production more in accord with comparative advantage, resulting in faster growth of output and of labor demand. It is probably no coincidence that the East Asian countries with high rates of growth of output and employment have low severance payments and very decentralized collective bargaining systems, as compared to Latin America.

The rapid pace of technological change, along with integration of a highly competitive world economy, are also inducing innovations in training policies. Whether governments can predict the skills required at each point in time, as well as provide up-to-date equipment in training institutions, is questionable. In response to these needs, reforms are taking place in several Latin American countries. These reforms are based on *decentralization and privatization* of the supply of training, and on *closer links* between training institutions and enterprises. In several countries such links have resulted in "dual" systems, with practical training being received in firms, as trainees, and not in the training institutions.

Labor institutions are social as well as economic institutions, an important point to remember. Plans for reform must take into account how various actors view the "fairness" of the rules of the game. Consider, for example, minimum wages, which have, at times, contributed to the segmentation of labor markets. Minimum wages may be justified economically when there is a monopsonistic labor market for low-wage workers (particularly because there are high costs to regional mobility). More important, in many countries they may be part of a social consensus regarding the economic system. In that case minimum wages should be fixed at a level consistent with full employment, and evolve in accordance with the rate of growth in labor productivity.[50]

Impediments to Labor Market Reform in Latin America

Since it is clear that the combination of nonconfrontational labor and encompassing policies yields outcomes superior to the alternative, why don't labor and the ruling elites in Latin American economies simply alter their stance and become nonconfrontational and encompassing? Why doesn't labor choose nonconfrontation, given that the present discounted value of returns to this choice would most likely vastly exceed the returns to the alternative?

While reform has begun in several Latin American countries, reform has been slow and in many cases proposals have been timid. The analysis above suggests three reasons for the failure to initiate labor reform.[51]

The first obstacle is labor's fear that the elite would not keep their part of the bargain. They foresee ending up with the low returns that result from cooperating in a distributional environment, and therefore prefer the slightly higher returns they can get from being confrontational. For the elite, too, a lack of trust in labor's promise to be nonconfrontational may induce caution regarding the adoption of nondistributional policies—since the combination of confrontational labor and nondistributional policies would be likely to yield lower returns to the elite than the distributional, rent-sharing regime with which they have grown comfortable.

Second, the fear of job loss is obviously another cause of labor resistance. The immediate adjustment to a more market-oriented policy regime usually involves some loss of jobs. Some "insider" workers would lose their jobs, and arguably, the most affected will be the least able—those who have their jobs due to political influence. They are the workers who are likely to have the most difficulty finding alternative employment, especially if the private sector can afford to be selective or is not dynamic with respect to job growth. Political appointees may also have the greatest ability to persuade the leadership to maintain the status quo.

Third, labor insiders are likely to fear losing their rents. Those with vested interests may be more concerned about the erosion of their wages than their perceived gains from reform. They may expect the disadvantage to be larger than the potential advantage—that is, they may have a kinked utility function or a high discount rate.[52] In this case, confrontation would still be the dominant strategy, despite the expectation that in the long run labor would benefit from reform. In the short run, the losers know who they are, and resist the erosion of their rents, while the more diffuse winners cannot explicitly promise compensation to the losers from the future gains to all.

Solutions to these problems can be found, especially if labor and the elite understand the potentially large benefits to both groups of taking a less confrontational stance in a nondistributional policy environment. The credibility of the elite's position (and that of labor) becomes important. Confrontation in the past is a source of mistrust in the present, as labor and the elite may both doubt the strength of the other group's commitment to a new strategy. The past administrative determination of labor market outcomes further complicates matters, as neither party has experience in interpreting the signals generated by the labor market and therefore would have difficulty monitoring the success of the new strategy. Creating appropriate commitment mechanisms thus becomes an important means to assure the credibility of both labor and the elite.

If the labor market dimension of policy reform is not adequately addressed, other dimensions of reform may fail. Good labor market performance enhances the credibility of both labor and the elite. Likewise, poor labor market performance can also be self-reinforcing. Attempts at labor market reform are, therefore, likely to be hampered by the lack of credibility of both labor and the elite. The payoff to reform can be high for both groups. The challenge is to find mechanisms that will bolster the credibility of both groups.

Endnotes

[1] This study concentrates on the seven East Asian economies still counted among developing economies, which does not include Japan. China has also grown rapidly, but its fastest growth (over 5 percent) began more recently, in 1982. Moreover, China's ownership structure, methods of corporate and civil governance, and reliance on markets are substantially different from those of the other successful Asian economies.

[2] When 60 countries are ranked by their rate of GDP growth for the period 1960–85, five of these seven are among the top six, and all seven are among the top 20. (The seven countries are the "four tigers"—Hong Kong, the Republic of Korea, Singapore, and Taiwan—and Southeast Asia's three new industrial economies—Indonesia, Malaysia, and Thailand.) Rapid growth was sustained for long periods: all seven grew at high rates both during the 1960s and from 1970 to 1985. The seven grew faster than the currently high-income countries during the decades of their most rapid growth.

[3] Sabot (1997), Table 1.

[4] Sabot (1997).

[5] World Bank (1992).

[6] *Ibid.*

[7] See Gelb, Knight and Sabot (1991).

[8] Birdsall and Sabot (1997).

[9] World Bank (1992).

[10] See Birdsall and Sabot (1997). By targeting subsidies on university education, governments in Latin America give high-income families an additional incentive to make the high-return investment that they would have made without it. Because of the greater focus on basic education in East Asia, public funds for education are more likely to benefit children from low-income families. The cost of providing a student with instruction is roughly 50 times larger at the university than at the primary level. In East Asia large numbers of poor children receive small but meaningful benefits from public expenditures on education. In Latin America it is more typical for small numbers of children from relatively high-income families to receive large, and less meaningful, financial benefits.

[11] In Brazil, for example, a substantial proportion of teachers in schools accessible to the poor have not completed primary school and are virtually illiterate and innumerate. They cannot teach what they do not know. These low-quality schools yield such low returns that, once children are old enough to contribute to the generation of household income, poor parents have little incentive to keep their children in school. See Birdsall and Sabot (1996).

[12] The greater abundance of resources helps explain why, in East Asia, increases in the quantity of schooling have been associated with improvements in the quality of schooling while in Latin America there was a tradeoff: the expansion of enrollments has resulted in the erosion of quality, particularly for the poor. See Birdsall and Sabot (1997).

[13] See Birdsall and Sabot (1996). In Brazil today, demand for education by poor households has weakened—dropout rates are increasing—as parents reevaluate the economic value of (low-quality) basic education. In Korea the demand for educated labor has remained strong, and so has household demand for schooling.

[14] Average per capita income was somewhat higher in Brazil (in 1983) than in Malaysia (in 1987), but the average per capita income of the bottom quintile in Malaysia was nearly twice the income of households at the bottom of the income distribution in Brazil. This was because the bottom quintile received 4.6 percent of total income in Malaysia, but only 2.4 percent in Brazil. In Malaysia far more of the poor sent their children to school than in Brazil. See Birdsall, Ross and Sabot (1995).

[15] See Birdsall and Sabot (1997) for a more detailed discussion of the feedback from more rapid output and employment growth to higher investment in education.

[16] As suggested by Wood (1994).

[17] See Squire (1981).

[18] See Edwards (1997).

[19] The average farm size and the Gini coefficient of farm size distribution are much smaller in East Asian than in Latin American countries for which data are available. See Birdsall and Sabot (1997).

[20] Labor intensity and yield tend to increase as farm size decreases: value added per hectare on small farms (three hectares or less) tends to be three to five times greater than the average for large farms (500 hectares or more). This implies that a reduction in the average farm size, and a more equal distribution among landholders, increase agricultural output and labor demand. See Berry and Cline (1976).

[21] In East Asia, substantial investments, especially in rural infrastructure and irrigation, prompted the adoption of high-yielding varieties, and the package of purchased inputs which were complements. In Malaysia, 55 percent of the rural population was served by electricity, as compared to only 5 percent in Argentina. See Birdsall, Ross and Sabot (1995).

[22] In East Asia resources were transferred to the industrial sector, but only after the dynamism of the sector was assured and not to the extent that it choked off agricultural growth. While some of the surplus was siphoned off by government, with land and other taxes, some of it was voluntarily transferred, via financial markets and direct investment by farmers, into nonagricultural activities. In East Asia today, resource flows are more commonly from the nonagricultural sector into agriculture as governments increasingly subsidize what has become a rapidly declining sector. See Birdsall and Sabot (1997).

[23] From 1965 to 1988, agricultural output grew at a rate of 3.2 percent per annum in the seven East Asian economies, while over the same period their agricultural labor force increased annually by only 2.2 percent. This indicates a rapid growth of overall agricultural productivity in East Asia. *Ibid.*

[24] For example, in Taiwan during the 1950s and early 1960s, agriculture was clearly the leading sector, not manufacturing for export; and roughly 60 percent of the increment to aggregate demand was domestic. More generally, in Asia the multiplier effects of agricultural growth on manufacturing, construction and services are large: an increase of 1 percent in agricultural growth is associated with a 1.5 percent increase in the growth rate of the nonagricultural sector. *Ibid.*

[25] Such constraints have been common in Latin America. See J. Page (1997).

[26] Birdsall and Sabot (1997).

[27] The potential for growth was realized: exports grew rapidly in all seven East Asian economies. In 1965 the seven produced only 3 percent of the world's exports; by 1990 they more than tripled their share, to 9.1 percent. Their export growth was much faster than that of other developing countries: in 1965 the seven East Asian economies produced only 12.2 percent of the total exports, and 14.2 percent of the manufactured exports, of developing countries; by 1990 they produced 56.3 percent and 73.5 percent, respectively. In East Asia manufactured exports grew as a share of rapidly growing total exports. And the stimulus of foreign demand resulted in industry growing as a share of rapidly growing GDP. Between 1965 and 1984, the contribution of industrial output to GDP increased by more than 200 percent in Indonesia, by at least 60 percent in Korea and Singapore and by roughly 50 percent in Malaysia. See Page (1997).

[28] Birdsall and Sabot (1997).

[29] Page (1997).

[30] Under an export promotion policy regime, even public sector firms producing intermediate goods are subject, indirectly, to the discipline of the world market. If their output is overpriced because, for example, they employ excessive numbers of workers or pay above market wages, then exporters who purchase those inputs are at a competitive disadvantage in international markets. By contrast, because of their monopoly power, firms producing import substitutes can simply pass on the higher costs of inputs to domestic consumers. Exporters, therefore, tend to pressure public enterprises to increase efficiency, while producers of import substitutes do not.

[31] Birdsall and Sabot (1997).

[32] Page (1997).

[33] More rapid growth of labor demand during the recovery period following adjustment may compensate for the slowdown, but only partially.

[34] The flexibility that East Asian economies have demonstrated in the past, the soundness of their fiscal policies and the increase in competitiveness that will result from the marked decline in their exchange rates all suggest that the interruption to growth of output and labor demand may be relatively brief.

[35] This does not imply limiting the ratio of debt to GNP. It does imply limiting debt service in relation to export earnings.

[36] The negative external shock to GDP that resulted from the sharp rise in oil prices, and associated deterioration of the terms of trade, in the 1970s and the rise, in the early 1980s, in rates of interest on outstanding debt was nearly as large for Korea (–3.8 percent per annum) as for Brazil (–5.0 percent per annum). See Birdsall and Sabot (1997).

[37] Sachs (1985) attributes the difference in export performance to exchange rate policy. Brazil's exchange rate was grossly overvalued while Korea's exchange rate may have been undervalued.

[38] In Korea, for example, the government suppressed the development and power of labor unions. While this may have kept wages from being pushed up prematurely, it also sowed seeds of discontent among workers. This explains why, years later, despite sustained rapid increases in wages, liberalization of policies towards unions was followed by labor action. Elsewhere in East Asia governments were more tolerant of unions. See A. Banerji and Sabot (1994).

[39] East Asian economies shifted much earlier from import substitution to export promotion policies.

[40] Olson (1982); Banerji, Campos and Sabot (1996).

[41] The net effect was a reduction in the rate of growth of output and, hence, labor demand. Using data from 31 countries in Latin America and the Caribbean, Martin Rama (1997) found that higher union membership rates, a proxy for "labor power", were associated with lower growth rates of GDP and employment. Increasing membership by one standard deviation was associated with a decline of .4 percentage points per year in the growth rate of per capita GDP with a decline of .8 percentage points in the growth rate of wage employment.

[42] See Birdsall and Sabot (1997).

[43] See Banerji, Campos and Sabot (1995).

[44] Birdsall and Sabot (1997).

[45] See Rama (1997). He also notes that in high-income countries nationwide, collective bargaining is generally thought to result in more moderate wage outcomes because unions recognize that raising nominal wages would increase consumer prices, limiting gains in real wages. In low-income countries, where the unionized workers are only a small proportion of the labor force, unorganized workers may believe, correctly, that they can pass most of the costs of higher wages onto unorganized labor. Pencavel (1995) therefore argues that only firm-level collective bargaining makes sense in developing countries.

[46] The search for greater flexibility is also characteristic of OECD countries. See Locke et al. (1995).

[47] This innovation has also been suggested for countries in the European Union. See OECD (1994).

[48] Although decentralized collective bargaining has yet to be written into law in Argentina, it was imposed by decree in 1991, and most of the contracts signed since then were signed at the branch or firm levels. See McGuire (1997).

[49] See Cortázar (1996).

[50] Lustig and McLeod (1997) indicate that in Latin America higher real minimum wages (within certain limits) are associated with lower poverty rates.

[51] This question is analyzed in greater detail in Banerji, Campos and Sabot (1994).

[52] Research by Knetsch (1989) and Kahneman and Tversky (1979, 1984) finds that individuals consider the potential loss of a given amount of income more important than the possible gain of an equivalent amount.

References

Banerji, Arup, and Richard H. Sabot. 1994. Barriers to Labor Reform in Developing Country Public Enterprises. Mimeo, Williams College, Williamstown, MA.

Banerji, A., E. Campos, and R. Sabot. 1996. The Political Economy of Formal Sector Pay and Employment in Developing Countries. Policy Research Working Paper 1435, World Bank, Washington, D.C.

Bates, Robert H., and Anne O. Krueger. 1993. *Political and Economic Interactions in Economic Policy Reform*. Cambridge: Blackwell.

Berry, A., and W. Cline. 1976. Farm Size, Factor Productivity, and Technical Change in Developing Countries. Mimeo, World Bank, Washington, D.C.

Birdsall, Nancy, David Ross, and Richard H. Sabot. 1995. Inequality and Growth Reconsidered. *World Bank Economic Review*.

Birdsall, N., and R. Sabot. 1997. Virtuous Circles: Human Capital, Growth, and Equity in East Asia. Mimeo, World Bank, Washington, D.C.

Bradford, Colin I. 1994. From Trade Driven Growth to Growth Driven Trade: Reappraising the East Asian Experience. Development Center Documents, OECD, Paris.

Campos, J. Edgardo, and Hadi Esfahani. 1994. The Political Aspects of Public Enterprise Reform in Developing Countries. Policy Research Department, The World Bank.

Campos, J. Edgardo, and Hilton Root. 1997. *Institutions, Leadership and the Asian Miracle: Making the Promise of Shared Growth Credible*. Washington, D.C.: The Brookings Institution.

Cortázar, René. 1996. Sharing Risk in Volatile Labour Markets. In Ricardo Hausmann and Helmut Reisen (eds.), *Securing Stability and Growth in Latin America* (Paris: OECD).

Edwards, Sebastian. 1997. Why Are Latin America's Savings Rates So Low? In N. Birdsall and F. Jaspersen, (eds.), *Pathways to Growth: Comparing East Asia and Latin America*. Washington, D.C.: IDB.

Evans, Peter. 1992. The State as Problem and Solution: Predation, Embedded Autonomy, and Structural Change. In Stephan Haggard and Robert F. Kaufman (eds.), *The Politics of Economic Adjustment*. Princeton University Press.

Frenkel, Stephen, ed. 1993. *Organized Labor in the Asia-Pacific Region: A Comparative Study of Trade Unionism in Nine Countries*. Ithaca, NY: ILR Press.

Gelb, Alan, John B. Knight, and Richard H. Sabot. 1991. Public Sector Employment, Rent-Seeking and Economic Growth. *Economic Journal* 101(408): 1186-99.

Gondwe, Derrick K. 1992. *Political Economy, Ideology, and the Impact of Economics on the Third World.* New York: Praeger.

Grindle, Merilee S. 1991. Positive Economics and Negative Politics, in Gerald M. Meier, ed., *Politics and Policy Making in Developing Countries: Perspectives on the New Political Economy.* San Francisco, CA: ICS Press, pp. 41-67.

Kahneman, Daniel, and Amos Tversky. 1984. Choices, Values and Frames. *American Psychologist* 4: 341-50.

————. 1979. Prospect Theory: An Analysis of Decision Under Risk. *Econometrica* 47: 263-91.

Knetsch, Jack. 1989. The Endowment Effect and Evidence of Nonreversible Indifference Curves. *American Economic Review* 79(5): 1277-84.

Krueger, Anne. 1990. Government Failures in Development. *Journal of Economic Perspectives* 4(3): 9-23.

Locke, Richard, Thomas Kohan, and Michael Piore. 1995. *Employment Relations in a Changing World Economy.* Cambridge: MIT Press.

McGuire, James. 1997. *Peronism Without Peron: Unions, Parties and Democracy in Argentina.* Stanford, CA: Stanford University Press, p. 225.

North, Douglass C. 1990. *Institutions, Institutional Change and Economic Performance.* Cambridge University Press, England.

OECD. 1994. *The OECD Jobs Study.* Paris: OECD.

Olson, Mancur. 1982. *The Rise and Decline of Nations.* New Haven: Yale University Press.

Page, John. 1997. The East Asian Miracle and the Latin American Consensus, in Birdsall and Jaspersen, *Pathways to Growth: Comparing East Asia and Latin America* (see Edwards above).

Pencavel, John. 1995. The Role of Labor Unions in Fostering Economic Development. Policy Research Working Paper 1467, The World Bank, Washington, D.C.

Rama, Martin. 1995. Trade Unions and Economic Performance: East Asia and Latin America. Paper for workshop on Rethinking Development in East Asia and Latin America, University of Southern California, Los Angeles, April, 1997.

Ranis, Gustav. 1991. Towards a Model of Development for the Natural Resource Poor. In Lawrence B. Krause and Kim Kihwan (eds.), *Liberalization in the Process of Economic Development*. Berkeley: University of California Press.

Sabot, R. 1997. Human Capital Accumulation and Development Strategy. In I. Székely and R. Sabot (eds.), *Development Strategy and Management of the Market Economy*. Oxford: Clarendon Press.

Schelling, Thomas. 1960. *The Strategy of Conflicts*. Cambridge: Harvard University Press.

Squire, Lyn. 1982. *Employment Policy in Developing Countries: A Survey of Issues and Evidence*. New York: Oxford University Press.

Turnham, David. 1993. *Employment and Development: A New Review of Evidence*. Paris: The Development Center, OECD.

Wood, Adrian. 1994. *North-South Trade, Employment and Inequality: Changing Fortunes in a Skill-Driven World*. Oxford: Clarendon Press.

World Bank. 1992, 1993, 1994. *World Development Report*. New York: Oxford University Press.

CHAPTER EIGHT

Equity Benefits from Financial Market Reforms

Liliana Rojas-Suárez and Steven R. Weisbrod

The arguments for financial markets' liberalization and reform are well known. Nonrepressed financial systems can contribute, inter alia, to deepening financial intermediation and improving the allocation of domestic savings, as well as increasing the real wealth of holders of bank liabilities. If the reforms include central bank independence, they also result in more efficient implementation of monetary policy. And if reform policies are aimed at reducing financial fragilities, they produce a more stable fiscal and monetary environment, thereby decreasing the amount of government resources needed to deal with systemic financial difficulties.

Notwithstanding these expected benefits, there remains the question of *who* benefits from the reforms; that is, what are the equity implications of efficiency-improving financial reforms? For example, recent literature on the subject questions whether financial liberalization has relaxed the financial constraints that have restricted small firms and households.[1]

Reforms have both direct and indirect effects on equity that are difficult to separate. Even if an improved allocation of credit does not result in increased credit to a large number of economic sectors, the resulting expansion in economic activity may improve levels of employment and real wages, and thus benefit a much larger segment of the population. Moreover, reform initiatives usually encompass a number of sectors simultaneously, making it very difficult to isolate the full effect of financial market reforms on equity.

This chapter looks at how Latin America's recent financial market reforms have affected services in the banking sector. Have the reforms improved the availability of banking services and the use of banks broadly across different economic groups? Or have they provided benefits to a narrow range of bank clients, especially those with the greatest wealth? The primary focus will be on services provided by commercial banks; due to data limitations, the analysis will not include financial services delivered by small finance companies, credit unions,[2] special government programs and the informal sector.

To investigate these questions, we must first consider the behavior of participants in a liberalized market for financial services. On the supply side, financial reform means that banks—the major suppliers of financial services in Latin America—make decisions on a profit-maximizing basis without direct government intervention either in the selection of bank customers or in the prices (interest rates) banks negotiate with their customers. However, banks generally operate under a safety net, including access to public funds in cases of emergency—through lender of last resort facilities provided by the central bank and/or through publicly provided deposit insurance schemes. Consequently, authorities recognize the need to set policies that discourage banks from taking excessive risk at public expense. These policies take the form of regulations on bank activities, such as liquidity requirements, capital requirements that restrict banks' ability to leverage, limits on loan concentration, and imposition of accounting and disclosure procedures. In addition, continuous scrutiny of bank operations is conducted through a supervisory system. Within these constraints, banks determine what services to provide to what customers. From the authorities' point of view, efficiency-improving reforms in the financial sector are those that allow banks to maximize profits subject to the social constraint that bank activities do not compromise the stability of public finances.

On the demand side, of course, banking service demands differ across customer groups. To determine whether a particular group has benefited from financial sector reform, one must identify what financial services that group demands, and how deregulation and policy reform affect the provision of these services. This chapter will focus on four major customer groups: large corporate customers, small and medium businesses, wealthy consumers, and low and middle-income consumers.[3]

The most important distinction between consumer and business demand for banking services is that businesses use banks primarily for payments transaction services and loans, whereas for consumers, banks are an important vehicle for accumulating financial assets. Within the business customer segment, small and medium businesses depend much more heavily on the local banking system for payments services than large corporations do. Among consumers, low- and middle-income consumers are more dependent on domestic banks for accumulation of financial assets than are wealthy consumers.

These varying demands for banking services mean that financial liberalization and reform will affect different customers in different ways. If financial liberalization improves the opportunity to earn a positive and stable real rate of return on deposits, low- and middle-income consumers, for whom real return on banking deposits is a priority, will benefit because they did not find this option elsewhere before financial liberalization. The impact of liberalization on services to small and medium businesses and moderately high-income consumers is much less direct. Of course, these customers also gain if their transaction balances no longer show the negative real rates of return common during periods of financial repression. However, the quality of overall service these customers obtain from banks depends not only on abolishing interest rate controls and credit allocation, but also on the degree to which liberalization fosters increased competition in the banking system.

It seems unlikely that liberalization alone—defined as removal of interest rate controls and reduced government intervention in the allocation of credit—could improve consumers' opportunities to earn a positive real rate of return on their financial wealth. Indeed, where reforms were limited to such narrow actions, consumers who lost substantial real wealth in the 1980s did not return to the banking system. However, where reform efforts were broader and policies such as proper accounting, competent supervision, and guarantees that encourage customer confidence were introduced, consumers have increased their use of banks.

Small and medium businesses also benefit from improved prospects for a positive real rate of return, although such prospects are less important in their decisions to hold bank accounts. These customers also benefit from the reduction in credit allocation programs that increased the availability of short-term loans, which are so important in helping them manage cash flow. In addition, because an efficient payments system at reasonable cost is so important to this customer group, they benefit from measures that promote efficiency in banking, such as increased competition, especially from foreign-owned banks.

How did Latin America's reforms and liberalization during the early 1990s affect the four major customer groups? To answer this question, the chapter compares the availability of banking services in the 1980s with those available in the 1990s, for the populations of Argentina, Chile, Peru and Mexico. The remainder of the chapter is organized as follows. The second section analyzes the use of banking services by various segments of the economy. Cross-sectional evidence from Chile, Mexico, and the United States illustrates how various customer groups' demands for service are met by banks. The third section assesses whether financial reforms in the region have enhanced equity. It considers how various customer segments were affected by the movement from a regulated to a reformed system in Argentina, Mexico, and Peru and compares their performance with that of Chilean banks, which have operated under a liberalized regime since the late 1970s. The final section advances some policy recommendations to further improve equity in the region's banking system.

Supply and Demand for Banking Products

Defining Banking Products

Customers demand two basic types of services from banks, broadly speaking: transaction services, and a means of maintaining real wealth levels by earning interest income.[4] The first type includes payments services, of which the major demand factors are convenience of access to the customer's account and speed of clearing payments. For example, bank customers hold checking accounts with their bank, for which they expect rapid availability of funds received as payments and accuracy in maintaining records. The demand for payments services also includes some loan services, especially overdraft privileges on checking accounts.

The second type of service is a demand for a positive real rate of return on savings balances. Whereas there are few substitutes for banking products for transaction purposes—because of the role of bank deposits, along with cash, as a universally accepted means of payment[5] —the demand for bank liabilities as a means of wealth accumulation is more sensitive to yields offered on alternative instruments, such as securities, real commodities, and real estate. From banks' asset side, customers demand loans. In this case, the customer's loan demand may be quite sensitive to the real interest rate.

From the supply side, in addition to interest payments, the bank must incur noninterest expenses to supply transaction services. This includes providing branching services, investing in payments technology, and gaining access to the interbank market through the payment of fees for lines of credit. Since loans are the major source of banks' gross interest revenues, to offer a competitive real rate of return on deposits, a bank must be able to manage credit risk efficiently. Therefore, the skills necessary for making loans are the same as those necessary for being able to offer positive real rates of return on deposits.

Two basic types of customers use the bank: businesses and consumers. While every type of bank customer demands a variety of bank products, the primary service demanded by businesses in Latin America is transaction services, whereas the primary service demanded by households is to earn real interest on their deposits. For example, in Peru in 1996, businesses held over 75 percent of demand deposits, which currently pay a zero real interest rate, but only about 15 percent of savings accounts, which pay about 5 percent in real interest. Similarly, by the end of 1994, businesses in Colombia held about 75 percent of demand deposits held by the private sector.

As size and wealth of the two kinds of customers increase, however, their demands become more similar. That is, as businesses become larger and more creditworthy, they become more concerned about earning interest on their liquid balances. Large businesses therefore are willing to pay fees to banks for sweep accounts, which remove funds overnight from checking accounts and invest them in money market instruments issued by banks as well as nonbanks. The sweep account increases businesses' expenses for obtaining payments services, but this is more than made up for by the increased interest revenue from holding money market instruments. In addition, since economies of scale in the provision of payment services imply that the cost of making payments becomes small relative to the size of the payment, large businesses are more willing to pay extra for additional payments services to achieve an interest rate of return on their liquid balances.

Likewise, as consumers' income increases, they too demand the sophisticated payments and money market products of the large corporation. Thus, at the highest levels of income and wealth, consumers will hold a smaller proportion of their bank deposits in the form of time and savings accounts than lower-income consumers. Instead, wealthy customers will turn to demand deposits and instruments paying money market rates of return. For example, in 1996, the average balance in consumer time deposits in Peru, which pay interest rates similar to money market instruments, was ten times the average balance in savings accounts, which lower-income households use to make cash payments as well as for financial savings.

The relative demands across customer groups define how banks provide products to their customers. Those from whom banks expect to receive large volumes of revenue obtain the best service. For example, even though the wholesale corporate customer sees a small service charge relative to the volume of his transactions, from the bank's point of view, this revenue stream looks large. Therefore, the bank is willing to come to the customer to provide payments and transaction services. The account is big enough for the bank officer to visit the business, so the large company can shop for the best interest rate on its liquid asset holdings. The largest firms are not even tied to the domestic market for their banking services. Hence, they can bid aggressively for service packages that minimize the cost of liquidity.

From the bank's point of view, the small and medium business customer is next in priority in terms of revenue stream earned from providing access to payments and transaction services. In this case, however, because the size of the customer is much smaller than large businesses, the customer must come to the bank rather than the bank coming to him. For small businesses that receive cash payments from the public, a bank location is an important place to deposit cash into formal transaction accounts used for purposes of paying suppliers. A bank location is also important for contact with the bank officer to provide loans to maintain firm liquidity. These businesses will give up interest to obtain greater convenience. Hence, banks build branch distribution systems for the benefit of small and medium businesses, and branch locations are chosen to make them convenient for this customer segment.

Why do lower-income consumers value their interest income and preservation of real wealth more than bank services? First, they are not as closely tied to the formal payments economy as are high-income consumers and businesses. Many of their routine bills can be paid in cash, albeit often through bank branches. In many Latin American countries, savings accounts are more important consumer transaction accounts than the accounts with check-writing privileges. Second, time costs for this customer group are relatively low, so they are unwilling to pay high service fees relative to their account balances.

Low-income consumers who work in areas where business activity is strong may benefit from the fact that small businesses demand extensive branching services. These consumers then have use of convenient branches, whose fixed costs are covered by business clients willing to pay for convenience.[6]

As consumers become more affluent, they are more willing to pay for convenience related to payments services and are more closely tied to the payments economy. Hence, they act like small businesses in their demand for services. As discussed above, as consumers become wealthier, they may switch from savings accounts to demand deposits for transaction purposes. Their liquid financial wealth will be held in high-yielding money market instruments, which may or may not be bank deposits.

Bank Products and Customer Type

As stated above, banks build distribution systems to provide for the needs of their customers. This basic principle holds for both industrial and developing countries. For example, the two U.S. banks that serve only large corporate and institutional customers, J.P. Morgan and Bankers Trust, have only two branches each in New York. In contrast, Chase and Citibank, which service retail customers as well as wholesale customers, have hundreds of branches in the New York metropolitan area. Large branch networks, of course, greatly increase the cost of servicing the retail customer base, and these customers pay for these expenses by earning lower interest on deposits and paying higher interest on loans than the wholesale customer. For example, in 1995, banks paid 4.01 percent on three-month time deposits with balances less than $100,000, whereas they paid 5.62 percent on three-month negotiable certificates of deposit with balances greater than $100,000.

Within the retail customer segment, there are vast differences in the demand for convenient distribution outlets and therefore for varying mixes of costs and interest rate levels. For example, consumer checking accounts in the United States, known as NOW accounts, paid interest of less than 2 percent at the end of 1995, while savings accounts, which do not provide check-writing privileges, paid slightly over 3 percent, and as indicated above, small three-month time deposits, which provide access to funds only at maturity, paid almost 100 basis points[7] more than savings accounts in 1995.[8]

In the United States, high-income consumers tend to use banks for accounts providing the greatest access to their funds, that is, for payments services, while lower-income consumers tend to demand bank accounts that yield higher interest rates. For example, in 1988, the consumer deposit mix at U.S. banks serving primarily lower middle-income customers was much more skewed toward time deposits than banks serving high-income customers. Banks whose market area had per capita incomes of less than $10,000 had almost 55 percent of their consumer deposits in time deposits, whereas banks serving areas where per capita income exceeded $16,000 had less than 40 percent of their consumer deposits in time deposits.[9]

Even though relatively high-income consumers demand more transaction services from banking institutions than do lower-income customers, U.S. banks do not necessarily branch to provide convenient locations to their high-income customers. This is because there is another customer group for which convenient access to banking services is even more crucial than for high-income customers. This group is small and medium businesses, many of which do a cash-intensive business requiring daily visits to the bank. As Figure 1 indicates, the number of businesses per capita in a county (which on a jurisdictional level are primarily small and medium businesses) is a very good predictor of bank branches per capita in that county.

Why do banks branch so intensively for small and middle-market businesses?

FIGURE 1

**Business Establishments* vs. Commercial Bank Branches,
New York and New Jersey Counties**

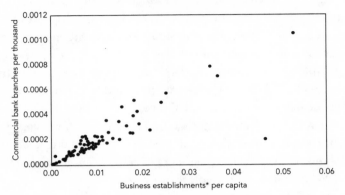

Note: Business establishments include the service, retail, and manufacturing sectors as reported by U.S. Census.
Source: New York and New Jersey county data as reported by U.S. Census, 1982 and 1986.

These businesses are heavy users of demand deposits, which, in the United States pay no interest and yield benefits only in terms of banking services. For example, in 1986, based on zip-code-level data in New York and New Jersey, bank branches with more than 125 small businesses (less than $10 million in sales) in their service area had demand deposit to total deposit ratios of about 22 percent. However, those branches with fewer than 25 small businesses in their markets had a lower demand deposit to total deposit ratio of only 17 percent.[10]

In addition, small and middle-market businesses are very likely to use the bank where they maintain a checking account to obtain short-term loans to smooth out firm liquidity. This is because it is convenient to tie the checking account product to an overdraft facility on that account. Hence, banks can partially cover branch expenses through fees and interest on these loans as well. In fact, the loan and the demand deposit are almost a joint product, since over 95 percent of small business customers with liquidity facilities hold these facilities at the same bank that provides their primary checking account.[11]

The branching decisions of Latin American banks appear to be based on similar principles. For example, in Mexico the number of bank branches per capita in a given state is highly correlated with the number of small and medium businesses per capita (see Figure 2a). Bank loans per capita and demand deposits per capita in a state are highly correlated (Figure 2b), indicating that banks make loans to customers with whom they have a demand deposit relationship.[12] This is due to two factors: first, overdraft loans are a major form of business credit and that overdraft loans are tied to demand deposits; and second, in markets where collateral repossession laws are weak, having control of payments is an important means of enforcing credit agreements. Figure 2c and 2d show a strong correlation between loans per capita and demand deposits per capita in a given state and small and medium companies per capita. This confirms that this customer base is a strong user of loan and demand deposit services.[13]

The same process appears to be at work in Chilean branching schemes across regions in that country. Although business establishment data are not available to test directly whether branching decisions are based on small and medium business customers, we have indirect evidence for this proposition. A strong correlation is seen between regional demand deposits per capita and regional short-term time deposits per capita (which are two business-oriented accounts in most Latin American markets), and short-term, unindexed loans, which are about 90 percent commercial loans (including export and import loans) (see Figure 3a).[14] Figure 3b shows the close correlation between branches per capita in a region and short-term unindexed loans per capita.[15] Moreover, there is almost no correlation between savings accounts per capita, a consumer bank product, and branches per capita (Figure 3c), suggesting that banks in Chile do not branch for the consumer business.

From Repressed to Liberalized Banking Systems: Who Benefited from Reforms?

Before banking reform and liberalization, it was quite common for Latin American governments to control interest rates paid on deposits and to direct the credit decisions of banks. This occurred whether the banking system was directly owned by the government or whether it was privately held. Because of the lack of appropriate credit evaluation procedures, directed credits frequently became nonperforming loans. Too often, authorities resolved these credit problems by engaging in inflationary policies that forced real interest rates on deposits substantially below zero and resulted in consumers losing large portions of their financial wealth. Consumers responded by disintermediating the system.

A universal aspect of liberalization in the region has been the removal of directed lending and the liberalization of interest rate ceilings. Of course, these policies in themselves do not guarantee that bank customers will gain confidence that

FIGURE 2a: Mexico

Branches vs. Small and Medium Businesses, 1994

(Per hundred persons)

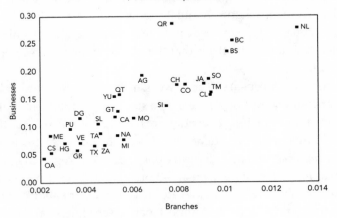

FIGURE 2b: Mexico

Demand Deposits vs. Loans, 1994

(In 10,000 nuevos pesos)

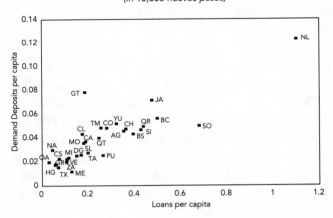

FIGURE 2c: Mexico

Small and Medium Businesses vs. Loans, 1994

(In 10,000 nuevos pesos)

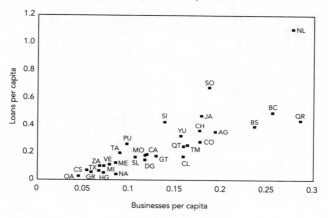

FIGURE 2d: Mexico

Demand Deposits vs. Small and Medium Businesses, 1994

(In 10,000 nuevos pesos)

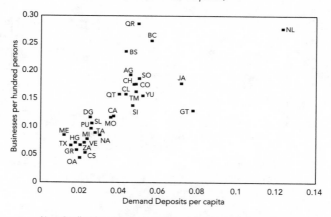

Note: Small and medium businesses are defined by both the number of employees (100–250) and net annual sales (0.9–20 million nuevo pesos). Deposit accounts are defined by the Consumer Price Index (1990=100). *Sources:* Banco de México, Indicadores Económicos; INEGI, Censo de Población y Vivienda 1990, Censos Económicos 1994; and IMF, *International Financial Statistics.*

FIGURE 3a: Chile

Demand and Short-Term Time Deposits vs. Loans, 1995

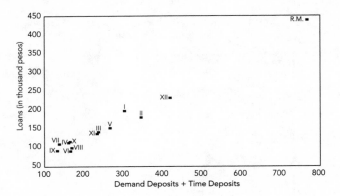

Note: Private domestic banks only.

FIGURE 3b: Chile

Branches vs. Loans, 1995

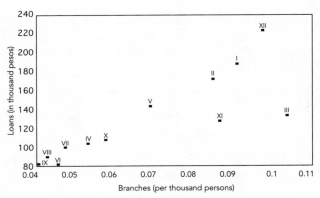

Note: Private domestic banks only.

FIGURE 3c: Chile

Branches vs. Savings Deposits, 1995

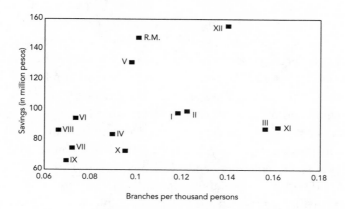

Source: Superintendencia de Banco e Instituciónes Financieras de Chile,
Información Financiera, various years.

their bank deposits will pay off in real terms; however, these policies are a necessary condition for establishing such confidence. Those who benefited most from
these reforms are the customers who expect higher rates of return on their accounts.
That means consumers as well as large businesses, the two customer groups most
interested in obtaining positive real rates of return on their liquid financial assets.
Large businesses and high-income consumers, however, have the leverage to find
these returns in domestic and foreign money markets, if the domestic banking system cannot provide them. Hence, the low- and middle-income consumers are most
likely to use domestic banks for the purpose of obtaining positive real rates of return on financial assets.

Liberalization of financial markets will encourage consumers and large businesses to return to the banking system, because it provides some assurance that
policy will not erode the real value of bank deposits. However, a framework for
monitoring bank quality is also important in providing assurance. Bank customers
need to see reforms in place that will minimize the hazard of future financial crises
and, if such a crisis does occur, ensure that real losses on deposits will be minimal.
That is, reforms need to include policies to monitor risk in the system and ensure
that safeguards are in place to prevent banks from taking excessive risks at public
expense. Regulators must also have mechanisms to deal with unanticipated banking problems, such as adequate reserve funds to support deposit insurance schemes.

Liberalization and adequate public safeguards are particularly important to the low and middle-income consumers who lack options for preserving their financial wealth outside the domestic banking system. Large businesses are less vulnerable to a nonperforming banking system, as they can go to foreign banks for interest-earning assets, transaction services and acquisition of credit.

In contrast to large corporate customers and consumers, for small and medium businesses the potential benefit from financial market reform is less associated with obtaining positive real earnings on bank deposits. The most important services that small and medium businesses want from banks are the provision of liquidity services and loans. The demands for domestic banking services by small and medium businesses tend to be less elastic relative to changes in real interest rates than are those of consumers and large businesses. This is for two reasons. First, because of their business relationships with a large number of small customers, small and medium firms depend heavily on banks for an efficient payments system. Second, in contrast to high-income consumers and large businesses, small and medium businesses have no alternative to the domestic banking system for their financing needs. Precisely because their demands are less elastic, small and medium businesses must absorb a large component of the real losses of an underperforming banking system, as other customers have a better option to withdraw their funds from the system. Thus, paradoxically, this customer segment has much to gain by reforms that improve the chances that bank deposits will maintain their real value, even though they do not flee the system in a crisis.

In addition, small and medium businesses can be particularly hurt by credit allocation programs, if these programs divert credit from their sector. Specifically, if credit allocation programs restrict the availability of overdraft loans, small and medium businesses will have to hold higher balances in their transaction accounts, which leaves them vulnerable to depreciating deposits in an inflationary environment.

Who will lose the most from repressed systems that enter into a crisis? The prediction is that those customers, primarily small and medium businesses, who demand services from domestic banks and have few choices to obtain these services elsewhere, will be forced to stick with the banks during a crisis and absorb real losses on their deposits. Wholesale business customers and high-income consumers will either leave the domestic banking system, or will be exempted from the burden of the repression. The middle-income consumers will disappear from the system because they do not get what they want—a positive real return on their money on a sustained basis. However, these consumers are likely to take real losses on their balances for two reasons. First, during the initial stage of a crisis, they will lose on the real value of their deposits if the crisis strikes before they can run the bank—a fact that was notoriously clear in Latin American banking crises of the 1980s. Second, since the only alternative for these consumers is to hold money balances in the form of cash, their holdings will be adversely affected by inflation. The poorest segments of the population do not lose much financial wealth in banking crises directly, as they were never in the system to start with. However, they do lose as a result of the inflation tax on currency holdings.

The next two subsections present evidence of (a) how banking crises under the repressed banking systems in Latin America affected low and middle-income consumers and small and medium business, and (b) how the reforms of the 1990s have benefited these two groups.

The Distributional Aspects of Repressed Financial Systems

In the 1980s, Argentina, Chile, Mexico, and Peru all experienced one or more banking crises. All of these countries except Chile have repressed financial systems, in the sense that they were subject to interest rate controls and credit allocation programs.[16] Thus, we can observe whether, within repressed systems, low and middle-income consumers and small and medium business customers bore the major impact of banking crises, compared to these customers in Chile.

The composition of bank deposits in US dollar terms changed dramatically in these four countries during a ten-year period, as seen in Figures 4a through 4d. The composition of each country's bank deposits relative to GDP during the same period is shown in Figures 5a through 5d. The periods of crisis are marked by a decline in total deposits both in terms of GDP and in terms of dollars, except for in Chile. For Argentina, the crisis occurred in 1989 and 1990 during a period of hyperinflation, extreme negative real interest rates, and forced conversion of domestic currency deposits into US dollars at highly unfavorable exchange rates. For Mexico, the crisis occurred in 1988 when inflation soared and real interest rates on standard bank deposits became negative. In that year, money market bank liabilities expanded at the expense of deposit liabilities (Figures 4c and 5c). These were bankers acceptances that were exempt from the rules governing standard deposits.[17] For Peru, the crisis occurred in 1990 and 1991 for similar reasons: hyperinflation drove real interest rates on deposits well below zero. For Argentina and Peru, the US dollar decline in deposits exceeded the decline relative to GDP, primarily because GDP in these countries fell substantially during the banking crisis.

In Chile, a banking crisis became evident in early 1983, but real interest rates

FIGURE 4a: Argentina

Deposit Composition
(US$ billions)

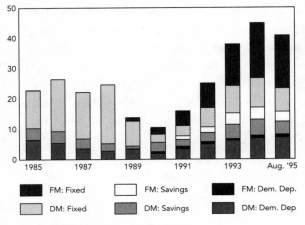

Source: ADEBA, *Memoria Anual*, various years.

FIGURE 4b: Chile

Deposit Composition
(US$ billions)

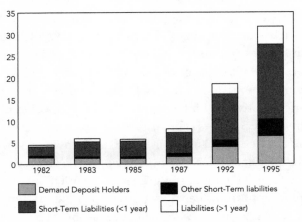

Source: Superintendencia de Banco e Instituciónes Financieras de Chile,
Información Financiera, various years.

FIGURE 4c: Mexico

Deposit Composition
(US$ billions)

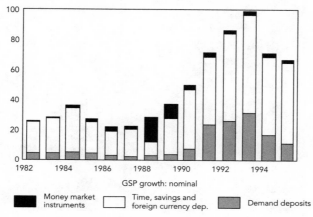

GSP growth: nominal

Money market instruments | Time, savings and foreign currency dep. | Demand deposits

Source: IMF, *International Financial Statistics.*

FIGURE 4d: Peru

Deposit Composition
(US$ billions)

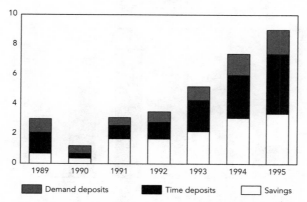

Demand deposits | Time deposits | Savings

Source: Superintendencia de Banca y Seguros, Peru. *Información Financiera Mensual,* various issues.

FIGURE 5a: Argentina

Deposit Composition
(As percent of GDP)

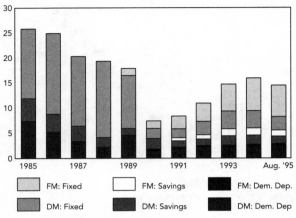

FM: Fixed   FM: Savings   FM: Dem. Dep.

DM: Fixed   DM: Savings   DM: Dem. Dep

Source: IMF, *International Financial Statistics.*

FIGURE 5b: Chile

Deposit Composition
(As percent of GDP)

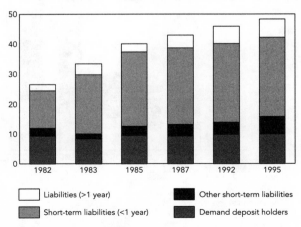

Liabilities (>1 year)   Other short-term liabilities

Short-term liabilities (<1 year)   Demand deposit holders

Source: Superintendencia de Bancos e Instituciones Financieras de Chile,
Información Financiera, various years. IMF, *International Financial Statistics.*

FIGURE 5c: Mexico

Deposit Composition
(As percent of GDP)

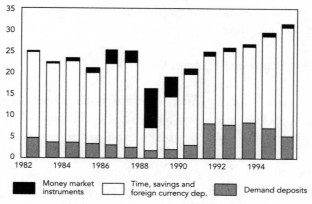

Source: IMF, *International Financial Statistics.*

FIGURE 5d: Peru

Deposit Composition
(As percent of GDP)

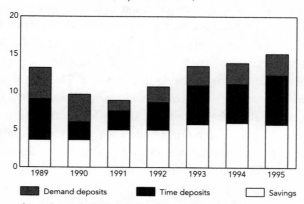

Source: Superintendencia de Banca y Seguros, Peru. *Información Financiera* Mensual, various issues.

on deposits never became negative, and deposits did not decline, either in dollar terms or as a percent of GDP. Real interest rates remained positive because the authorities did not resolve the banking crisis by imposing interest rate ceilings during an inflationary period. Instead, the central bank took steps to protect depositors from the impact of nonperforming loans.[18]

How Crisis Affects Small and Medium Business

What we know about customer demands and alternatives suggests that large businesses are least likely to be hurt from a crisis under a repressed system, whereas small businesses are not likely to be able to escape from the consequences of the crisis. An example of this is that demand deposits as a percent of GDP did not fall as much at the beginning of banking crises in Argentina, Mexico, and Peru as total deposits relative to GDP. (See Figures 5a, c and d.) Indeed, demand deposits as a percent of total deposits increased during the crisis in Argentina, Mexico, and Peru, indicating that customers who use banks for transactions purposes, primarily businesses, were the least likely customers to leave the system.

We suggested earlier that small and medium businesses are even less likely to leave the system than are relatively large business customers. To assess whether this in fact was the result, we consider what happened to demand deposits in the largest market in each of the three countries versus what happened to demand deposit holdings outside the largest market, under the assumption that large businesses are more concentrated in the major city than in other markets.

The Mexican experience is displayed in Figures 6a and b. The largest market in the country is the federal district of Mexico City. Figure 6a plots the share of demand deposits accounted for in the federal district. This share was falling between 1982, when the banking system was nationalized, and 1989, the first year of the banking crisis and before the financial reform. Moreover, for total deposits *outside* the district, the ratio of demand deposits to total deposits (including money market instruments) increased dramatically, while this ratio fell for deposits *inside* the district (Figure 6b). This suggests that, outside the federal district, the banking system lost a large number of nondemand deposit customers, but very few demand deposit customers. These observations, and the fact that demand deposits measured in terms of US dollars did not fall in 1989 (Figure 4c), show that small and medium business customers—who are more concentrated outside the capital city—stayed with Mexican banks in an absolute as well as in a relative sense.

For Argentina, we have a breakdown of demand deposit data by capital dis-

FIGURE 6a: Mexico

Demand Deposits

(Percent share of federal district in total national)

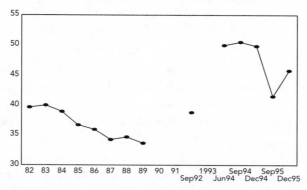

Source: Banco de México, *Indicadores Económicos,* various issues.

FIGURE 6b: Mexico

Ratio of Demand Deposits to Total Deposits

(Federal district vs. rest of country)

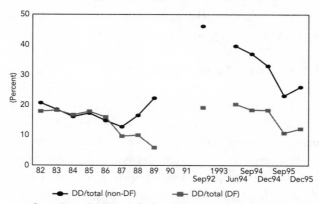

DD/total (non-DF)   DD/total (DF)

Source: Banco de México, *Indicadores Económicos,* various issues.

trict and the rest of the country only since 1990. Since 1991, the first year of reform, capital district share of demand deposits has risen substantially, from 45 percent at year-end 1990 to 54 percent in 1995 (Fig. 7). Based on other countries' experience, one can assume that 1990, the worst year of the crisis, represented the low point for demand deposits share in the capital district. Hence, we can infer that demand deposits *outside* the capital district rose more than those within the capital district during the crisis. Also, during the crisis years of 1989 and 1990, total deposits nationwide declined in dollar terms, while demand deposits rose in US dollar terms (Figure 4a). This suggests that, as in Mexico, most of the demand deposit increase in dollar terms during the crisis occurred outside the capital district. Assuming that small and medium businesses are a larger share of the economy outside of the capital district, it appears that, just as in Mexico, small and medium businesses stayed with Argentina's domestic banks during the crisis more than the country's large businesses did.

In Peru, demand deposits also increased in 1990, the year of the crisis, as a percent of total deposits to 35 percent from 30 percent the previous year (Fig. 8). However, as also indicated in Figure 8, the ratio of demand deposits to total deposits rose faster outside Lima, indicating that small businesses had fewer alternatives than large.

It is interesting that in Peru and Mexico, the share of demand deposits in total deposits declined during the second year of crisis. In Mexico, that was probably due to a decline in real economic activity during the crisis, which eventually drained liquidity from businesses. In Peru's case, however, the decline in demand deposits was too drastic to be accounted for in this manner, as we will discuss later.

How Crisis Affects Low and Middle-Income Consumers

In Argentina, during the crisis year of 1988, total deposits declined, in dollar terms, by over 50 percent (Figure 4a). Almost all of the decline depicted in Figure 4 occurred in the time and savings categories, since demand deposits in dollar terms increased slightly between 1988 and 1989. Based on the arguments advanced in Section II, we can assume that a substantial portion of these deposits, especially savings accounts, were held by the lower- and middle-income consumers; therefore, we can infer that these groups lost a substantial portion of their wealth during the crisis.[19]

In Mexico, based on Figure 4c, time and savings deposits in dollar terms nationwide fell by almost two-thirds in 1988. Since most of these accounts are usually

FIGURE 7: Argentina

Demand Deposits in National Currency
(Percent share of federal district in total national)

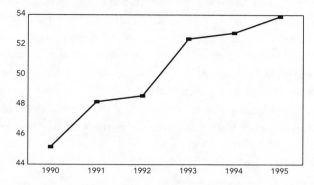

Source: Subgerencia de Estadísticas Monetarias y Financieras, Banco Central de la República Argentina, various issues.

FIGURE 8: Peru

Ratio of Demand Deposits to Total Deposits
(Percent share by regions)

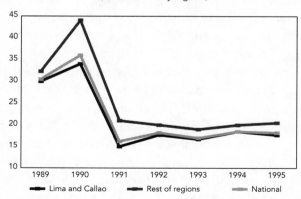

—■— Lima and Callao   —■— Rest of regions   ▬▬ National

Source: Superintendencia de Banca y Seguros, Peru.

held by consumers, the decline in the real value of time and savings deposits represents a substantial loss in wealth among lower- and middle-income consumers. This conclusion is strengthened by the fact that the dollar volume of bankers acceptances in 1988 was greater than the dollar volume of time and savings deposits (Figure 4c). Since, based on Figure 9b, most of the bankers acceptances were held in the federal district, we can infer that large corporations and wealthy individuals held almost all of these instruments. This implies that the burden of the crisis fell on the lower- and middle-income consumer.

In Peru, savings deposits fell substantially in dollar terms, indicating large losses to consumers. Time deposits also fell drastically in dollar terms (see Figure 4d).

Who Gained from Reform?

The Consumer Market

Did low- and middle-income consumers gain from reform and liberalization? The answer depends on whether they were willing to trust their domestic banking system to maintain the real value of their financial wealth after the reforms were put into place. To assess this, we reviewed whether and when consumer deposits returned to their precrisis level, both in dollar terms and relative to GDP.

In Argentina, in 1992, total deposits, as well as time and savings deposits, returned to their precrisis level in dollar terms; hence, we can conclude that by 1992, consumers had returned to their precrisis use of banks when measured in dollars.[20] However, time and savings deposits probably have not yet returned to their precrisis use of banks relative to GDP (Figure 5a).

In contrast to Argentina, time and savings deposits in Mexico did not return to their precrisis level in dollar terms after liberalization, even though total deposits in dollar terms rose from about US$40 billion in 1985 to over US$110 billion in 1994.[21] This was because most of the increase in total deposits occurred in the federal district, whose share of total deposits rose from 35 to 68 percent between 1985 and 1994 (Figure 9c). Thus, the share outside the federal district was 65 percent and 32 percent, respectively, in 1985 and 1994. According to these percentages, the dollar volume of total deposits increased from US$26 billion in 1985 to US$35 billion in 1994. However, based on Figure 6b, the proportion of *demand* deposits outside the federal district in 1985 (15 percent) had risen considerably by 1994 (about 35 percent). Hence, time and savings deposits outside the federal district actually remained about constant in dollar terms over the two periods. From Figure 5c, it is clear that these deposits actually fell relative to GDP between 1985 and 1994.

FIGURE 9a: Argentina

Federal Capital Bank Deposits
(As percent of national total)

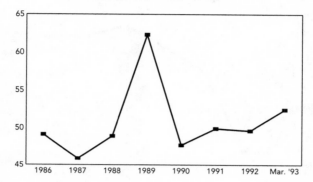

Source: IMF, *International Financial Statistics.*

FIGURE 9b: Mexico

Federal Capital Bank Deposits
(As percent of national total)

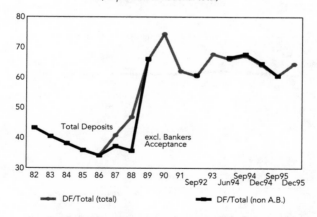

Sources: Salinas de Gortari, Carlos, *Segundo Informe de Gobierno 1990;*
Zedillo, Ernesto, *Primer Informe de Gobierno 1995;*
Banco de México, *Indicadores Económicos.*

FIGURE 9c: Peru

Lima & Callao Bank Deposits
(As percent of national total)

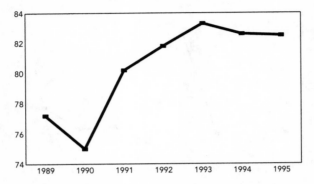

Source: Superintendencia de Banca y Seguros, Peru. *Información Financiera Mensual,* various issues.

FIGURE 9d: Chile

Santiago Bank Deposits
(As percent of national total)

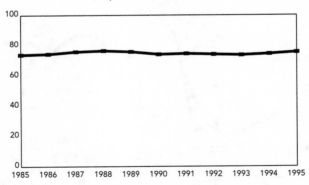

Source: Superintendencia de Bancos e Instituciones Financieras de Chile, *Información Financiera,* various years.

In Peru, as in Argentina, it seems that consumer deposits increased in dollar terms after the crisis, but most of this increase occurred in the relatively affluent consumer market in Lima and Callao. Savings deposits more than tripled in dollar terms between 1989 and 1995 (Figure 4d). Over 75 percent of these deposits are held by individuals and over 75 percent of all savings deposits are denominated in US dollars. Since the overwhelming percentage of foreign currency deposits are held in Lima, it appears that consumers outside the largest metropolitan area have not yet returned to the banking system; that is, the reforms have not yet improved the confidence of consumers outside the capital city in their local banking systems. Peru's sharp decline in demand deposits in dollar terms in 1991 (mentioned above) probably resulted from a consumer shift to savings deposits when dollar deposits became fully convertible that year.

Why were Argentina and Peru more successful at bringing consumer deposits back to the banking system after the crisis, compared to Mexico? One could argue that Argentina succeeded in encouraging consumers to use banks through its relatively large sector of provincial and municipal banks, which make up almost 40 percent of the deposits in the total banking system. However, the Peruvian numbers are only for privately held banks; they exclude the Banco de la Nación, which takes deposits from mostly nonprofit customers and has only a small retail deposit business, mostly outside Lima. An alternative explanation is that holding dollar-denominated deposits backed by a convertibility law in Argentina, and substantial foreign currency assets in both cases, improved consumer confidence that the real value of their deposits will be maintained in the event of a financial crisis.

In contrast, Mexico attempted to assure depositors of safety with an insurance scheme that guaranteed all liabilities issued by banks. That guarantee was in domestic currency, however, and foreign exchange reserves at the central bank were not enough to back up the short-term monetary assets held by the public. In this context, consumers were skeptical about this guarantee, at least in terms of a pay-off in US dollars. They were right, of course. The evidence for 1995 suggests that the nominal value of deposits did not even grow as fast as the rate of inflation.

In Chile, all deposit categories expanded significantly, both in dollar terms and relative to GDP, in the 1990s (Figure 4b). From this we can infer that consumers, like businesses, are using banks to a greater extent than they did during the crisis years.

Small and Medium Businesses

An important component of small and medium businesses' banking demands is service-driven; they have a crucial need for liquidity services. Because their demand for liquidity is relatively inelastic in response to cost, these customers had to stay with the banking system even in periods of high inflation and negative real interest rates. Thus, potentially these customers are very profitable during such periods, because banks reap the benefits of the costs they bear.

As is well known, banks will respond to the excessive profitability generated by negative real interest rates by increasing services available to customers with inelastic demands for bank services. For example, in the United States when interest rate ceilings on deposits were binding, many analysts argued that banks responded by increasing their branching systems. Because small and middle-market customers were highly profitable in inflationary economies in Latin America in the 1980s, one would expect banks to branch more intensively in the 1980s than the 1990s. Of course, that would not necessarily mean that small and medium companies obtained greater benefits under repressed systems than under liberalized systems, since they paid for these services with extreme negative real returns on their demand deposit balances. In fact, the acceptance of a reduction in service should reflect a decline in the negative real rate of return on demand deposit balances. For example, demand deposits in Peru are currently paying *ex post* negative real rates of return of about 2 percent per annum, a major improvement over returns on bank deposits in the 1980s.

To determine whether branching services to small and medium companies declined after liberalization, we investigate the relationship between branches per capita and real demand deposits per capita in the late 1980s and mid 1990s for Mexico and Peru. As indicated in Figures 10a and b, for a given ratio of branches per capita in a given state in Mexico, demand deposits per capita in dollar terms expanded rapidly between 1989 and 1994. Although real balances in demand accounts increased, banks did not respond by expanding branches to increase the level of convenience available to their customers. Thus, the cost of providing convenience per dollar of demand deposit declined during reform—an improvement in bank efficiency in providing payment systems that resulted from a decline in inflation. Small and medium business demand accounts, which are relatively inelastically supplied to the banking system, become less profitable per dollar of account because the real rate of return becomes less negative. As a result, banks reduce the number of branches, but small and medium businesses obtain services

FIGURE 10a: Mexico

Demand Deposits vs. Branches, 1988

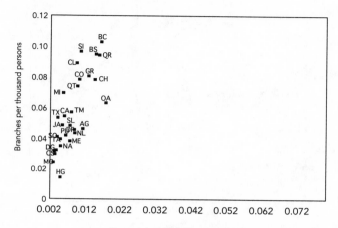

Demand deposits (million nuevos pesos)

Sources: Banco de México, *Indicadores Económicos*; INEGI, *Sistemas de Cuentas Nacionales de México; Producto Interno por Entidad Federativa,* 1993.

FIGURE 10b: Mexico

Demand Deposits vs. Branches, 1994

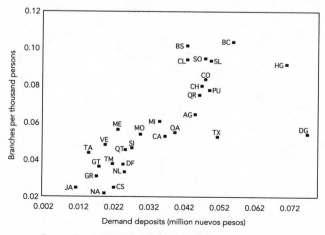

Demand deposits (million nuevos pesos)

Sources: Banco de México, *Indicadores Económicos*; INEGI, *Sistemas de Cuentas Nacionales de México; Producto Interno por Entidad Federativa,* 1993.

FIGURE 10c: Peru

Demand Deposits vs. Branches, 1989

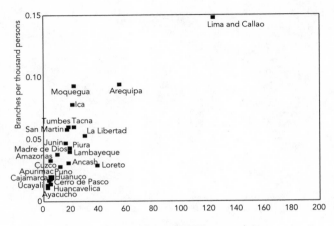

Sources: Superintendencia de Banca y Seguros, Peru. *Información Financiera Mensual*, various issues.

FIGURE 10d: Peru

Demand Deposits vs. Branches, 1994

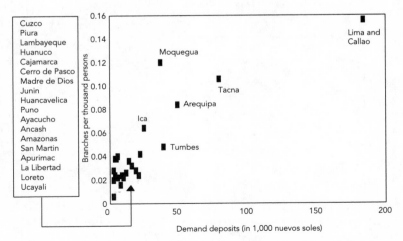

Sources: Superintendencia de Banca y Seguros, Peru. *Información Financiera Mensual*, various issues.

at a lower cost (i.e., they obtain higher real rates of return on their balances). Figures 10c and d show similar results for Peru.

Did small and medium companies gain in net from liberalization? That is, did they get anything else other than reduction in service, presumably accompanied by lower negative real rates of return on demand deposits? To find an empirical answer for this, we turn to the loan market. There has been a dispersion of loans from the largest market to smaller markets in Argentina, Chile and Peru since the banking crises in the 1980s and early 1990s (Figures 11a, b and c). The Chilean market, which entered the crises of the 1980s as a liberalized system, behaved similarly to the more repressed systems (Figure 11b); thus we cannot assume that the decentralization of loans was entirely due to reform and deregulation. However, other evidence below suggests that reforms help to increase the availability of credit to small and medium businesses.

The Argentine data (Figure 11a) provide some interesting clues about this. Loan centralization increased sharply in 1989, the first year of the Argentine banking crisis of the late 1980s. Argentina undertook to reduce the loan burden on borrowers through inflation and negative real interest rates. These losses, as indicated earlier, were absorbed by depositors. During the crisis, banks would have been hard-pressed to provide new loans to customers, because the deposit base was shrinking very quickly. Presumably, only banks' most important customers were able to access new credit under these circumstances. In markets where liquidity crises are severe and frequent, banks and their customers will form implicit contracts whereby the best customers hold their liquid deposits with banks at below open-market interest rates and, in return, banks provide guaranteed access to credit during liquidity crises.[22] These bargains are offered mostly to wholesale customers, because they have the greatest incentive to choose a bank on the basis of competitive interest rates, as indicated above.

The Mexican experience also provides some interesting insights into the behavior of government-owned versus privately owned banking systems (Figure 11d). Even though the Argentine and Peruvian banking systems were severely repressed in the 1980s, most of the major banks remained in private hands. In contrast, Mexico nationalized its banking system in 1982. From that point on, the percentage of loans made in the federal district increased continuously, while deposits in the federal district *declined* as a percent of the total. The trend in loan concentration did not reverse until the banking system was privatized in late 1991.

Further evidence that state-owned systems tend to concentrate loans in the hands of large enterprises is provided by the Chilean data. In this market, one large

FIGURE 11a: Argentina

Bank Loans in Federal Capital

(As percent of national total)

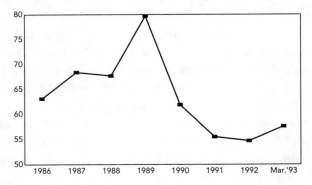

Source: ADEBA, *Memoria Anual,* various years.

FIGURE 11b: Chile

Bank Loans in Santiago

(As percent of national total)

Source: Superintendencia de Bancos e Instituciones Financieras de Chile, *Información Financiera,* various years.

FIGURE 11c: Peru

Bank Loans in Lima and Callao
(As percent of national total)

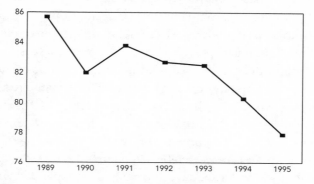

Source: Superintendencia de Banca y Seguros, Peru. *Información Financiera Mensual*, various issues.

FIGURE 11d: Mexico

Bank Loans in the Federal District
(As percent of national total)

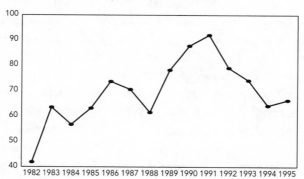

Sources: Banco de México, *Indicadores Económicos.*

state-owned bank has about 16 percent of the deposit share. It collects 44 percent of its deposits outside the largest market, compared with only 22 percent for the aggregate of privately owned domestic banks. Yet the state bank makes 84 percent of its loans in the largest market, compared to 77 percent for private domestic banks.

The beneficiaries of the relative decrease in loans to large enterprises have been small and medium businesses. As indicated earlier, there is a strong correlation between demand deposits per capita (in Latin America, primarily business deposits), and loans per capita, suggesting that most bank loans are associated with commercial purposes and tied to the demand deposit. By 1994, the amount of loans per capita made in states in Mexico and Peru, excluding the largest states, was much higher relative to demand account balances than was the case in 1988 and 1989 (for Mexico and Peru, respectively; see Figures 12 a-d). Thus, we conclude that credit availability to small and medium companies expanded with reform and deregulation.

Advancing the Reform Process

The foregoing evidence indicates that low- and middle-income consumers and small and medium businesses were the biggest losers when repressed banking systems, subject to interest rate controls and credit allocation programs, suffered crises in the 1980s. Consumers lost because they suffered substantial losses in the real value of their deposits. As a result, they became skeptical about the safety of the domestic banking system, causing severe disintermediation of the financial system. Small and medium businesses also lost the real value of their deposits, but, unlike consumers, could not afford to leave the banking system; these customers need domestic banks for the transaction and payments services they provide.

Removal of interest rate controls and credit allocation programs has improved the probability that bank deposits will pay off in real terms, which should increase the expected real wealth of low- and middle-income consumers and small and medium business owners. However, the evidence indicates that consumers have not yet regained confidence in the banking systems of some Latin American countries. If the consumer segment still is uncertain about whether bank deposits will pay off in real terms, small business owners probably have the same fears. They, however, cannot react to this fear by withholding deposits from the system: their demand for banking services is much less elastic relative to expected real interest rates than the consumer customer segment.

FIGURE 12a: Mexico

Demand Deposits vs. Loans, 1988

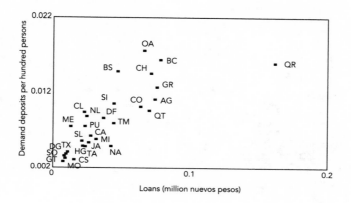

FIGURE 12b: Mexico

Demand Deposits vs. Loans, 1994

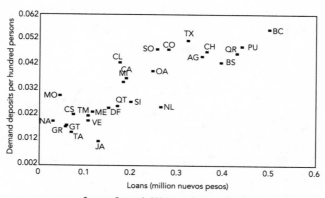

Sources: Banco de México, *Indicadores Económicos.*

FIGURE 12c: Peru

Demand plus Time Deposits vs. Loans, 1989

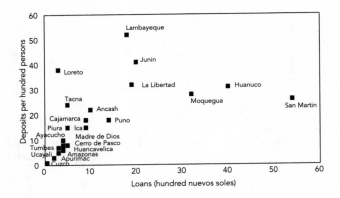

FIGURE 12d: Peru

Demand plus Time Deposits vs. Loans, 1994

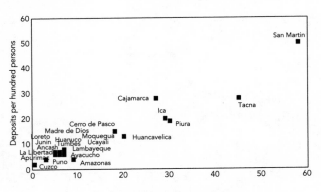

Note: Excludes Lima and Callao and Arequipa.
Sources: Superintendencia de Banca y Seguros, Peru. *Información Financiera Mensual*, various issues.

The lingering lack of confidence in banking systems can only be addressed by programs designed to increase the financial strength of banks. That of course means improved accounting methods, greater disclosure, and professional supervision. But it also requires encouraging diversity of ownership of financial institutions operating in domestic markets. Many Latin American markets need additional outside capital to ensure that bank owners maintain arm's length relationships with both their loan and deposit customers. Consumer and small business customers must be assured that major bank borrowers are not financially connected with major bank shareholders to prevent banks from making risky loans at favorable rates to insiders. Also, deposit insurance schemes ought to be limited to the retail deposit market to improve market supervision of bank asset quality.

Increased competition is also important to assure that the transaction and payment service needs of small and medium business customers are provided efficiently. There is clear evidence that branch services provided to these customers have declined since liberalization. This decline in service has been partly compensated by the increased real rate of return that small and medium enterprises obtain on their transaction balances. However, greater competition in a sound banking system would give them the opportunity to have both higher returns and better service.

Endnotes

[1] In this connection, see Jaramillo, Schiantarelli, and Weiss (1996) who analyze the issue for the case of Ecuador. Also, see the analysis in Michael R. Carter and Stephen Boucher, "Goodbye Financial Repression, Hello Financial Exclusion: The Economic Space for Financial Market Innovation." Mimeo, September 1995.

[2] Credit unions are an increasing source of finance for small enterprises in Latin America. For a discussion of their recent progress in Latin America, see Westley and Shaffer (1996). Barham, Boucher and Carter (1996) assess the role of credit unions in financing small-scale producers in Guatemala.

[3] Financial reforms affect the poorest consumers only indirectly, because they have neither sufficient wealth to use deposit-related services from banks, nor sufficient collateral to obtain bank loans. This chapter does not address those cases in which the market would provide financial services to the poor if a subsidy or government transfer were available.

[4] This corresponds to the well-known reasons for holding money, both narrowly and broadly defined, as widely discussed in the literature. For example, see Laidler (1993).

[5] Specifically, the delivery of funds from a bank's account at the central bank is a universally accepted means of payment within an economy. The customer accesses this form of payment by holding a bank account.

[6] These results follow from the economics of joint distribution where the client with the highest demand pays the largest share of the costs. See Weisbrod and Lee (1992).

[7] One hundred basis points equal one percentage point.

[8] The short maturity of these accounts ensures that the difference in rates compared to savings accounts is not due to an upward-sloping yield curve.

[9] It is interesting to compare this deposit configuration with those of Peru and Colombia, discussed above. In the United States, many middle-income consumers use transaction accounts and hold their financial wealth in time deposits, which is a description of the behavior of relatively high-income consumers in Peru. In contrast, high-income consumers in the United States hold their liquid wealth in nonbank instruments, such as money market mutual funds. The sources of the U.S. data are FDIC bank call reports and the U.S. Statistical Abstract.

[10] These data are from the FDIC Summary of Deposits for New Jersey.

[11] Banking Markets and the Use of Financial Services by Small and Medium-size Businesses. *Federal Reserve Bulletin*, Oct. 1990, pp. 801-817.

[12] The relationship between total deposits per capita and loans per capita is much weaker because total deposits include marketable time deposits, raised primarily in the larger cities. Hence, such points as Nuevo León, where Monterey is located, become large outliers. If the relationship between total deposits and total loans is charted, there is a high correlation, merely because of the market scale effect. Dividing deposits and loans by population eliminates the scale effect because it highlights any differences in per capita holdings of each item that are not systematic.

[13] The Mexican data indicate that this relationship does not hold for microenterprises per capita or for large businesses per capita.

[14] Indexed loans, which are primarily made to large business customers, are mostly booked in Santiago, the largest business market. Because unindexed loans are more dispersed throughout the country, we assume they are also made to small and medium companies. At any rate, most of the large business loans, whatever their maturity, are concentrated in Santiago. High-income consumers probably hold some of the short-term time deposits. But, because these consumers have similar demands to small businesses for transaction services, we expect their demand for branches to be high.

[15] This chart excludes the Santiago market, where loans per capita are substantially higher because many large businesses are located there.

[16] Chile liberalized financial markets in the late 1970s. Although financial liberalization also took place in Argentina at that time, controls were reimposed following a banking crisis in 1982.

[17] Usually bankers, acceptances are two-name papers—liabilities of a bank and liabilities of specific borrowers—that circulate as money market instruments. They arise in letter of credit transactions. In Mexico during the 1980s, bankers, acceptances were indistinguishable from wholesale bank deposits that were exempt from reserve requirements and interest rate ceilings.

[18] For a full analysis of banking crises in Latin America and their resolution, see Rojas-Suárez and Weisbrod (1995).

[19] This conclusion is supported by the fact that the capital district's share of total deposits increased dramatically in 1989 (Figure 9a). Because time and savings deposits represented over 75 percent of total deposits in 1989, we can be fairly certain that a large drop in noncapital district deposit share had to have been accompanied by a drop in noncapital district time and savings account share. We presume that the latter deposits were held primarily by lower- and middle-income consumers.

[20] This conclusion is reinforced by considering the postcrisis growth of deposits outside the federal capital. In 1992, deposits outside the federal capital equaled about 50 percent of total deposits, slightly above the ratio prior to the crisis (Figure 9a). This suggests that the dollar value of time and savings deposits outside the capital in 1992 exceeded the dollar level of these deposits prior to the crisis.

[21] By the end of 1994, another banking crisis hit consumers.

[22] See Rojas-Suárez and Weisbrod (1996).

References

Barham, Bradford, Stephen Boucher, and Michael Carter. 1996. Credit Constraints, Credit Unions, and Small-Scale Producers in Guatemala. *World Development* 24:5.

Jaramillo, Fidel, Fabio Schiantarelli, and Andrew Weiss. 1996. Access to Long-term Debt and Effect on Firm's Performance. *Journal of Development Economics* 51.

Laidler, David. 1993. *The Demand for Money: Theory, Evidence and Problems* (4th ed.) New York: Harper-Collins.

Rojas-Suárez, Liliana, and Steven R. Weisbrod. 1995. Financial Fragilities in Latin America: The 1980s and the 1990s. IMF Occasional Paper no. 132 (October), Washington, D.C.

————. 1996. Building Stability in Latin American Financial Markets. IDB Working Paper Series 320 (February).

Weisbrod, Steven R., and Howard Lee. 1992. Who Pays for Branches? *Journal of Retail Banking* (Fall).

Westley, Glenn, and Sherrill Shaffer. 1996. Credit Union Policies and Performance in Latin America. IDB, Mimeograph (October). OCE Policy Seminar Series.

CHAPTER NINE

Pension Reform:
An Efficiency-Equity Tradeoff?

Estelle James

During the past decade, Latin America has been in the forefront of pension reform. The experiment that started with Chile in 1980 has been carried on by Argentina, Colombia, Peru, Mexico and Uruguay. The reforms have usually been sold on grounds of their impact on efficiency and growth. What do we know about their impact on equity and equality? Traditional social security systems have frequently been justified on grounds that they are equitable and redistribute to low-income groups—this has been cited as a tradeoff for the inefficiencies that they entail. As social security systems undergo reform, are we in danger of exchanging equity for efficiency?

This paper argues that traditional systems—that is, pay-as-you-go defined benefit systems—in fact produce many inequities, both within cohorts and across cohorts. These inequities have been found in every country where these systems exist, with some of the most egregious examples in Latin America. In fact, from the vantage point of the average citizen, the inequities may be a more potent rationale for reform than the inefficiencies.

The reforms typically replace a publicly managed pay-as-you-go defined-benefit (PAYG DB) system with a system of privately managed, fully funded, defined-contribution (FF DC) accounts, supplemented by a social safety net. Such reforms reduce the preexisting equity problems. Moreover, by raising national saving, deepening the financial markets through which these savings are funneled, and reducing labor market distortions, they also enhance growth. In this sense, the recent wave of pension reforms have the potential to improve both equity and efficiency. Have they done so?

Recent research has attempted to quantify the efficiency gains in Chile and elsewhere. The distributional effects have not yet been quantified, however. While reforms removed the preexisting inequities, especially the intergenerational inequities, in some cases they seemed to create new equity problems. Some problems could be solved by changing design features of the reform, which underscores the importance of planning and implementing reform policies with great care. Other problems were due to the advantages that people with more income, assets and education have over those with less, and those are not so easily solved. At the same time, the concept of equity means different things in different societies, so one can expect to find varying distributional outcomes across reforming countries. Here the term "equity" is used to mean redistributing from high to low earners, or other redistributions explicitly agreed upon in a collective manner.

This chapter briefly outlines the inefficiencies introduced by traditional PAYG DB pension schemes, and then summarizes the inequities they created. The third part shows how reformed systems have improved efficiency and growth, and the fourth part discusses their equity effects, both positive and negative.

Inefficiencies in PAYG DB Systems

The inefficiencies introduced by PAYG DB systems are well known and will be only briefly summarized here.

High payroll taxes with negative effects on employment. Most traditional systems are financed through payroll taxes, which rise dramatically as populations age and engender labor market distortions—less employment and labor effort—unless the supply of labor is totally inelastic. In Brazil, Ecuador, Paraguay and Uruguay, payroll taxes for pensions exceed 20 percent, placing them among the highest in the world—on a par with European countries where populations are much older. While empirical evidence suggests that take-home pay rather than employment declines in industrialized countries, this is less likely to be the case in developing countries where workers can easily escape to the informal sector.

Allocation of labor to the informal sector. High payroll tax rates that are not linked to benefits lead to evasion and escape to the informal sector. Since firms in the informal sector have less access to capital and product markets, labor is likely to be less productive there. In many Latin American countries, over 40 percent of the labor force works in the informal sector, partly in order to avoid high payroll taxes. The informal sector is also growing rapidly in other regions such as Eastern Europe (World Bank 1994, p. 123).

Early retirement. Most DB plans provide for early retirement with little or no reduction in pension amount. Early retirement promises are tempting to policymakers, because they hide unemployment or constitute a giveaway to special groups. The initial cost is low, but if many workers retire early, the long-run cost is high, both in terms of its deleterious impact on the system's finances and its negative impact on the supply of experienced labor in the economy.

National saving. While many economists believe that PAYG systems have decreased national saving and therefore growth, other economists disagree; the case is still being debated. But it seems clear that funded systems can be used to increase national saving, and thereby correct suboptimal saving that may result from other causes (myopia, high private-discount rates, taxation of investment returns or corporate profits). Traditional systems do not make this efficiency-improving correction.

Low returns on publicly managed reserves. Occasionally PAYG systems accumulate reserves, as revenues may temporarily exceed expenditures. In traditional systems these reserves have been publicly managed. It is difficult to secure data on the returns to these reserves, but data gathered for the 1980s indicate that publicly managed pension reserves fared poorly and in many cases lost money—largely because public managers were required to invest in government securities or loans to failing state enterprises, at low nominal interest rates that became negative real rates during inflationary periods. At the same time, privately managed pension funds were earning high returns, in countries where they play a large role—because they were able to invest in diversified portfolios on a competitive basis (World Bank 1994, p. 95).

Clearly this poses a problem for the financial sustainability of the publicly managed funds. It also indicates that their capital may have been inefficiently allocated—making it easier for governments or state enterprises to run large deficits or spend more wastefully than if they had to rely on a more accountable source of funds—and making it more difficult for the private sector to get access to these funds for productive investment. More generally, political rather than economic objectives are likely to determine the allocation of publicly managed pension reserves, and therefore the impact on productivity is not maximized.

Misallocation of public resources. As expenditures mount, these reserves disappear, and traditional systems in many countries have run large deficits, which then become the government's responsibility. In 1990, Austria, Italy and Uruguay spent more than one-third of their public budgets on pensions. Since the government's ability to tax is limited by economic and political considerations, high public-pension spending can squeeze out government spending on growth-promoting investments such as infrastructure, education and health services, or it can lead to inflation—a long-term problem in many Latin American countries—if the government tries to maintain this spending through deficit finance.

Inequities in Traditional PAYG DB Systems

Less well known are the inequities in traditional PAYG DB systems. These inequities fall into two major categories: better treatment for high than for low-income groups within cohorts (stemming from deferred benefits), and transfers from younger to older generations (stemming from pay-as-you-go financing). Many of these inequities cannot be corrected by simple design changes—to eliminate them requires a basic structural reform.

Better treatment of high-income groups. At first glance, the benefit formulas of most public DB systems look progressive (that is, redistributive from rich to poor) or, at least, distributionally neutral. However, empirical studies of lifetime transfers (i.e., the present value of lifetime benefits received minus lifetime contributions paid), in countries as diverse as the United States, the United Kingdom, the Netherlands and Sweden, show little if any redistribution from rich to poor (see World Bank 1994, pp. 133-34). In fact, in prereform Latin America it is likely that the redistribution went the other way. How can this be?

Several factors are at work, making traditional systems inequitable while they create the appearance of equity. First of all, it is now well known that high-income people live longer than low-income people. High-income people have access to better medical technology, nutrition and information about healthier lifestyles. As a result, even if the annual benefit formula looks progressive, this is partially counteracted by the fact that high-income people live longer and collect benefits for more years. Many low-income people die before they even begin to collect pensions. This source of regressivity appears inevitably in defined-benefit schemes, as well as any other scheme where high and low-income people are mandatorily put into the same annuity pool. It can be avoided only if different annuity terms are applied according to socioeconomic status (recognizing that this signals different risk categories), or if the purchase of an annuity is not obligatory.

Second, high-income people enter the labor force later than low-income people, but often get pension credits while attending university, even though they don't contribute. This inequity could be corrected by granting credit only for years of actual contributions, but politically this has been difficult to achieve in unfunded DB plans. Third, higher-income groups frequently are eligible for superior benefit formulas. For example, in Brazil they have an easier time documenting their years of covered employment and qualifying for early retirement. In Ecuador they can borrow from the pension fund at negative real rates of return. In Costa Rica some privileged occupations have, until recently, received a replacement rate of 100 percent or more of their final wage.

Also favoring high-income people are their steeper age-earning profiles. Often DB schemes base their benefits on wages earned during the last 3 or 5 or 10 years of employment. Then, workers with steep age-earnings profiles have contributed for many years according to their lower wages when young, but receive a pension that is based on their higher wages shortly before retirement. Even if the averaging period for the reference wage base is extended to 30 or 40 years, workers with steep age-earnings profiles have a lifetime distributional advantage relative to those with flat profiles, because the present value of their lifetime contributions will be smaller even if they have the same average reference wage. This problem could be avoided by giving accrual rates that vary according to the age at which each contribution was made—but this becomes very complicated and, in the limit, very much like a defined-contribution plan.

Furthermore, given that poor people probably have a higher discount rate than rich people, the utility cost of the required contribution for the poor is probably greater than that for the rich. Adding to this is the likelihood that when a retirement plan is introduced, rich people can maintain their previous consumption levels by reducing voluntary saving, while the poor often have no voluntary saving to reduce. In other words, the shift in lifetime consumption from youth to old age is more binding for low-income groups and is more easily offset by high-income groups—an observation which is related to the higher initial discount rate of the former. These problems, incidentally, are retained for all schemes that tax people now in return for retirement income later, including the reformed schemes that put these contributions into mandatory saving plans.

Financing methods also lead to regressivity. Typically, only labor earnings are taxed—and almost invariably with a ceiling on taxable wages. This means that the full income of poor people is taxed, while only a portion of the income of rich people is taxed. Since a flat tax (the same rate for rich and poor) is generally used, it follows that poor people pay a higher proportion of their income in social security taxes than do rich people, another factor that leads to a higher discount rate and utility loss for them. This could be changed—by taxing all income, by exempting income that falls below a specified threshold, by charging progressive tax rates, and/or by removing the ceiling on taxable wages. The fact that this has practically never been done under traditional systems, however, suggests that strong political economy forces prevent those systems from redistributing income to the poor.

General revenue finance might be more progressive than the payroll tax in industrial countries, because it imposes a lower relative burden on low wage earners. However, it adds a new equity problem in developing countries where only a portion of the labor force—generally the better-off portion—is covered by social security. For example, in Brazil in the 1980s 75 percent of the top income quintile but less than 15 percent of the bottom quintile was covered by social security. If general tax revenues from the broad population are used to cover pension costs, this means that outsiders, who are less well off, are subsidizing insiders. This happens in Guatemala, where general revenues are used to finance one-third of the costs of the public pension program which covers only a small minority of its labor force, those who are relatively high earners in the formal sector (World Bank 1994, pp. 132-3).

Finally, "capricious" redistributions also occur in DB systems, e.g., from dual to single-wage-earning families, from women who work in the labor market to those who work at home, from nonevaders to evaders, and from workers who postpone retirement to those who retire early. The nontransparency of the benefit formulas enables these redistributions to occur without an open public evaluation—and enables groups with power and expertise to manipulate the system to their advantage. Besides their perverse impact on equity, these redistributions create incentives for workers (women, evaders, early retirees) to withdraw from the formal labor market and they thereby impede economic growth.

Redistributions to early cohorts from later cohorts. Generally payroll tax rates in PAYG plans are low initially, because they must cover only a small number of retirees, but they rise through time, as the system matures and the dependency rate increases. The forthcoming demographic transition exacerbates this transfer. As a result, covered workers who retire in the first 20 to 30 years of a PAYG scheme contribute for only part of their working lives, and at a low rate. Hence they receive in benefits much more than they have contributed, while their children and grandchildren get back less than they paid in and lower rates of return than they could have earned elsewhere.

For example, real rates of return were 15 percent for U.S. workers who retired in the 1950s or 1960s, and 8 percent for those retiring in the 1970s—signifying large positive transfers to these cohorts. But the rate of return is expected to fall to 2 percent for workers who retire in the future, less than they could get elsewhere—signifying a negative transfer (World Bank 1994, pp. 133-36). That is, there is a permanent transfer of income from later to earlier cohorts. If the income transfer is consumed by the old and the promise of future benefits reduces the retirement savings of the young, it accounts for the possibly negative impact of PAYG on national saving and growth. Does this transfer increase or decrease equity?

Sometimes we may want to redistribute across generations, to allow older cohorts to enjoy some of the fruits of future growth. However, a problem with using PAYG systems for this purpose is that intergenerational redistribution takes place automatically, without a full discussion, or even without a full public understanding, of what is going to happen. In most cases, the people who are being redistributed away from weren't old enough to participate in the discussion; only the gainers participated—raising questions about equity from the procedural point of view. Moreover, many of the gainers in the older generation, including those who get the largest transfers, are lifetime high earners, while losers from the younger generations include low earners.

For example, suppose the annual rate of real wage growth is 2 percent, so the average wage doubles in 36 years. Compare the income and transfers received by a high earner (who gets twice the average wage) when the pension program starts, with those of a low earner (who gets half the average wage), 36 years younger. Even taking into account real wage growth, the older worker has a lifetime income that is double that of the younger worker, yet he receives a positive redistribution from the pension plan, while the younger worker receives a low or negative redistribution (that is, he loses money), because contribution rates have risen and benefit rates fallen in the interim.

This kind of redistribution from young low earners to old high earners is especially likely to occur given that the first cohorts to be covered are usually well-off groups while later additions to the plan include poorer groups. Ironically, even within the older cohorts, the above-market rate of return they receive translates into a much larger lifetime income transfer for their wealthier than for their poorer members, since the former receive this generous return on a much larger reference wage and contribution base. In Colombia, for this reason, the absolute value of the transfer under the old PAYG system was eight times larger for a high-income worker than for a minimum wage worker (World Bank 1994, p. 135).

Finally, the younger generation as a whole loses because of the inefficiencies and growth-inhibiting features of traditional social security programs.

These intergenerational redistributions, that often favor wealthier members of the older cohorts, are unavoidable in PAYG schemes. While equity inevitably involves value judgments, most people would agree that these intra- and intergenerational redistributions are not equitable in terms of procedure or outcome. Moreover, some of the inequities imply incentives or transfers that simultaneously reduce efficiency, and some of the inefficiencies seem likely to particularly hurt low-income groups. Thus, there is ample room to improve both equity and efficiency in traditional DB PAYG systems.

Efficiency Improvements in Reformed Systems

Starting with Chile in 1980, followed by Colombia, Peru, Mexico, Uruguay and possibly Bolivia in the 1990s, many Latin American countries have been reforming their pension systems, in an effort to get greater efficiency while improving equity at the same time. These countries have instituted multipillar systems that are partially funded (instead of being largely PAYG), that utilize private management of these funds (instead of pure public management), that tie benefits directly to workers' contributions plus investment earnings (in a defined-contribution rather than a defined-benefit plan) and that, in most cases, have a separate public tax-financed mechanism for redistributing retirement income to low earners. Such systems generally contain three components, or pillars: (1) a mandatory, publicly managed, tax-financed pillar for redistribution; (2) a mandatory, privately managed, fully funded pillar for saving; and (3) a voluntary pillar for people who want more protection in old age.

The second pillar, which is FF DC, is the core of most of these plans, and is the most innovative part of the pension reforms. Essentially, people would be required to save for their old age, and this pillar would handle their savings. We will briefly explain why it is supposed to eliminate the distortionary effects described in the first part of the chapter.

Why should an FF DC plan raise efficiency? The close linkage between benefits and contributions, in a defined-contribution plan, is designed to reduce labor market distortions, such as evasion by escape to the informal sector, since people are less likely to regard their contribution as a tax. And those who do evade bear the cost in the form of lower benefits rather than passing the costs on to others. That contrasts with DB plans, where evasion requires a contribution rate increase to cover total costs, thereby setting off a vicious cycle that increases the distortionary effects.

Moreover, in a DC plan the accumulated contributions and investment earnings are eventually converted into the worker's retirement income, via an annuity or gradual withdrawals. This means that people are less likely to retire early—since if they do, they will bear the cost in the form of lower annual benefits. It also means that as longevity increases, many workers will choose to work longer instead of retiring at the previous age with a lower annual pension. Thus retirement age is automatically increased by the individual without a difficult political decision.

The principle of full funding means that countries won't make promises, in the early stage of a plan, that will result in fiscal deficits and high tax rates later on.

It also helps to build long-term national savings that will increase productivity and growth, hence raise both wages and pensions in the future. If a developing country institutes a multipillar system without a prior PAYG system, private saving will increase if the mandatory saving rate exceeds the voluntary rate and crowd-out effects are small. If an industrialized country with an existing PAYG system replaces it with a multipillar system, national saving increases if benefits are cut or taxes are increased, usually to cover transition costs. If a country with partial coverage shifts to a partially funded system, as in Latin America, we would expect a mixture of these two effects. The funds are privately managed to ensure that economic rather than political objectives dominate and that the rate of return—both to the fund and to the economy as a whole—is maximized. Private pension funds are more likely to enjoy the benefits of investment diversification, including international diversification, that enable them to increase their yield and reduce their risk— thereby enhancing efficiency. Moreover, they are likely to spur financial market development, by creating a demand for new financial instruments and institutions— especially important in middle-income countries such as those in Latin America.

For all these reasons, the reforming countries expected economic efficiency to improve with the establishment of their new pension systems. What has actually happened?

Empirical evidence of growth effects. Growth effects are notoriously difficult to quantify and prove, in part because relatively little experience and data are available. Even if we had the data, it would be difficult to build models that capture all the complex dynamic interactions; that is, it is hard to specify the counterfactual. Nevertheless, the available evidence indicates that the observed growth effects are positive and possibly large. They come mainly from increased national saving and financial market development, since the effects on retirement age and evasion are even more difficult to measure at this point. (For a summary, see James 1996).

Two types of evidence are available—simulations that estimate future changes, and econometric or descriptive analysis of actual changes. For example, in planning its mandatory occupational scheme, to which contributions will eventually reach 12 percent of payroll, Australia estimated that national saving would increase by 1.5 percent of GDP in the long run, thereby augmenting by 70 percent its current net national saving rate (which is 2.2 percent of GDP) (Bateman and Piggott 1997). In simulations for Mexico, total saving was found to rise between .4 percent and 2.1 percent of GDP, if the transition is tax-financed (or if it is debt-financed and Ricardian equivalence holds, so that private saving goes up to offset public dissaving)(Ayala 1996).

The only two countries that have had a pension reform long enough for saving effects to be estimated are Switzerland and Chile. In Switzerland the national saving rate rose from 6 to 8.5 percent of GDP in the decade after the funded second pillar became mandatory, and the entire increase occurred in pension funds and related institutions such as insurance companies (Hepp 1997).

According to regression analyses (Haindl Rondonelli 1996; also see Morande 1996), pension reform played a major role in increasing the national saving rate in Chile from 16.7 percent of GDP prereform (1976–80) to 26.6 percent postreform (1990–94). Specifically, pension saving accounts for two-thirds of the increase. A more modest positive effect on private saving, 4 percent of GNP by 1994, was found by Agosin, Crespi and Letelier (1996). All these analyses are very preliminary, given the short time period involved and ambiguities concerning the correct specification and counterfactual variables that would apply.

The fiscal costs of the transition, if financed by borrowing, may have canceled out the positive effect on private saving (see Agosin et al. 1996). However, to the degree that the transition was financed by increased taxes or reduced public consumption, the positive effect on national saving was reinforced. While we do not know what would have happened without pension reform, the Chilean government accumulated a fiscal surplus while planning for reform in the late 1970s. Shortly after reforms began in the early 1980s, the budget ran a fiscal deficit; then by the late 1980s and 1990s the government's budget was in surplus again.

Even more important is the financial market deepening induced by the reformed pension system. While insurance and annuities markets have been stimulated to grow and develop new products even in countries such as Switzerland and Australia, the biggest effect here is observed in Chile. Chilean financial markets have become more liquid as the pension funds have increasingly invested in a diversified portfolio of stocks as well as bonds; the number of traded shares and their turnover increased; demand was created for the equities of newly privatized state enterprises; information disclosure and credit-rating institutions have developed; the variety of financial instruments has grown, including indexed annuities, mortgage and corporate bonds; and asset pricing has improved. Preliminary econometric analysis indicates that financial market deepening induced by the reformed pension system increased total factor productivity by one percent per year, or half of the increase in total factor productivity in Chile (Holzmann 1996). So we have both a priori and ex post reasons to be optimistic about the efficiency and growth effects of pension reform in Latin America.

Equity under the Reformed Systems

What about equity? While a careful quantitative analysis of the distributional effects of the reforms has yet to be carried out, it appears that the worst inequities of the old system have been avoided, but some remain, and some new problems have been introduced. Moreover, an evaluation of equity effects depends closely on value judgments about what is equitable. Which is more equitable—a reduction in inequality while the average pension is unchanged or an improvement in the pension received by all income groups while inequality increases? Which is preferred— redistribution to all the poor, to the poor who have contributed for most of their working lives, or to lower-middle-class workers as well? In other words, who should get a boost in the name of equity and do we care more about absolute or relative positions? Different reform plans have different answers to these questions.

Elimination of Old Equity Problems

All of these reform plans include an FF DC pillar which should improve equity in the broad sense that they are designed to stimulate economic growth; in the long run, this is the best way to raise the income of low- and middle-class earners (see Valdes-Prieto 1994 for simulations that demonstrate this effect). Moreover, they give these low earners access to capital market investments, which previously were available only to high earners, and which have the potential to yield high returns (see *Report of the Advisory Committee on the U.S. Social Security System 1997*, which projects a higher expected return to reform options that include a large funded pillar). The replacement of DB by DC removes special benefits to privileged groups, including early retirement benefits, advantages to workers who have steep age-earnings profiles, and the subsidy of insiders by those outside the system. Funding a large part of the pension system reduces intergenerational redistribution as well as the disparate return between early groups to be covered and late entrants that occurs in pure PAYG systems. Beyond that, practically all of the reformed systems include a publicly managed component, or pillar, that is targeted to low-income groups and is therefore likely to be more equalizing than traditional systems that provided a higher pension to high wage earners. However, this public pillar takes very different forms in different countries, with different distributional effects.

Comparison of Equity Effects of Different Public Pillars

Chile provides a minimum pension guarantee to all workers who have contributed for at least 20 years, supplemented by social assistance for others. Both of these are financed not by payroll tax, but rather out of general revenue, which is a more broad-based, efficient, and probably more progressive revenue source. Partial reliance on general revenue finance reduces the disproportionate utility loss to low earners that is implied by a flat payroll tax (as discussed earlier). The danger that low-income outsiders will be subsidizing insiders is offset by the means-tested social assistance program.

The minimum guarantee, now pegged at about 28 percent of the average wage, is enough to keep pensioners out of poverty. If the annual benefit that can be financed by a worker's own accumulation is less than the minimum guarantee, the pension is topped up by the government to bring it up to the threshold. If a low-income worker (say, one earning half the average wage) contributes for only 20 years, he is likely to need some topping up, but if he contributes for 40 years, his own accumulation will probably suffice. Thus low-income workers who have lifetime formal labor market participation will not get a redistribution, and the converse is also true. No benefit at all is provided to lower-middle-class workers whose own accumulation will push them just above the threshold. If your concept of equity is to bring all people to the poverty line, the Chilean scheme is just right, but if your concept includes a redistribution to low-wage and lower-middle-class workers who have contributed for many years (as would be accomplished by a guarantee that increases with years of service), the Chilean scheme is not optimal from an equity point of view. Its cost should be very low—but we do not yet know how low, since few workers have retired under the new system.

In contrast, Argentina provides a flat benefit, also 28 to 30 percent of the average wage, to all retirees who have contributed for 30 years—a much costlier arrangement than that in Chile. Unlike Chile, Argentina's middle and upper-income workers receive the public benefit—in fact, they receive larger-than-average lifetime benefits, because of their greater longevity. But low-income workers continue to receive the largest share of the total, because they constitute the largest group. The benefit is financed by a payroll tax, up to a taxable ceiling. This financing source means that low-income groups pay a larger share of the total cost and a larger share of their total income than in Chile, and some intergenerational transfers remain.

The flat benefit in Argentina goes only to workers who have contributed for most of their lifetimes, in sharp contrast to Chile, where long-term contributors are unlikely to receive anything. This benefit and tax structure means that low wage earners with less than 30 years of participation are big losers in Argentina; women, for example, are disproportionately losers. On the other hand, middle-class workers with more than 30 years' service fare better in Argentina than in Chile; their retirement income is increased and diversified, thereby reducing risk. Thus Chile scores higher on keeping people out of poverty at the lowest possible cost, but Argentina scores higher on rewarding the average worker who has contributed to the system rather than evading, throughout his life (see Figure 1).

Australia, far away from Latin America, has also reformed its pension system but retains a means- and asset-tested benefit in its public pillar, financed out of general revenues. The Australian guarantee is more generous than that in Chile, is received by many more people (currently two-thirds of all pensioners, a proportion that should decrease as the mandatory saving plan is phased in), and therefore costs much more. The fact that it takes other income and assets into account makes it more equalizing, but may also discourage saving from other sources. While less targeted than Chile's system, it is probably more redistributive to low-income groups than Argentina's plan, because Australia's pension system is financed out of general revenues, is not tied to years of contributions, and excludes the top earners from benefits.

In all three cases, perverse intra- and intergenerational redistributions are reduced by the partial reliance on a DC plan and a public pillar more targeted toward low earners than were traditional PAYG DB plans. Other countries have chosen still other forms for their social safety nets. For example, in Mexico the government deposits one peso per day into every contributing worker's account (which will eventually yield a small benefit per year of contributing service) and workers are guaranteed a minimum pension as well. These cases provide us with an idea of the wide range of benefit and financing options available in the public pillar, and their diverse equity effects.

Remaining Problems and New Problems

New equity problems arise, however, from the design of the private-funded pillar. Some of these problems might be termed capricious distributional effects, and some of them involve systematic biases in favor of high-income groups.

Capricious distributions. Random fluctuations in the interest rate across time have unpredictable distributional effects on the pensions of different cohorts in an FF DC plan. Some cohorts will be exposed to high interest rates, while others will

FIGURE 1

Own Pension, Public Transfer and Years of Service, Argentina versus Chile

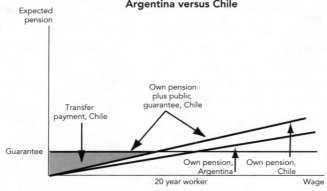

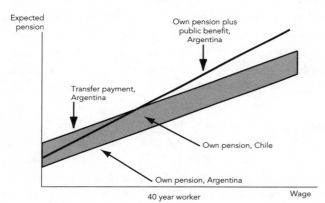

Note: Author's own schematic representation. "Own pension" is lower in Argentina because their contribution rate to the funded pillar, net of disability and survivors' insurance and administrative costs, is about 7 percent, versus 10 percent in Chile. For simplicity, rates of return and average wage are assumed to be the same in Argentina and Chile. Total public transfers depend on number of workers in each wage and year category.

face low rates during the years in which they work and accumulate. In a DC plan, the former group could receive a much higher pension than the latter—a capricious effect that is due to accidental market forces rather than individual behavior or government policy. While this does not represent "redistribution," it might be considered "inequitable." The chance that this will happen is mitigated by international diversification of investments and by the long-term nature of retirement investments; and it can be partially offset by the public pillar, which diversifies sources of retirement income. Nevertheless, different cohorts will fare differently in a DC plan, through no fault or credit of their own, for this reason.

A different type of equity problem is created in the annuities market by the interest rate at the point of retirement. If the interest rate is low at that time, this will reduce the size of the annuity that can be purchased by retiring cohorts with a given accumulation. They can avoid "locking in" to this low interest rate by purchasing variable annuities, whose value varies with the interest rate and the price of financial assets. Nevertheless, this choice between a low fixed annuity versus an uncertain variable annuity will be considered a choice between two evils by workers who are risk-averse; one might consider it inequitable that some cohorts, but not others, will face this problem. Thus, certain types of capricious distributional effects are eliminated by the shift from a DB to a DC plan, but others are created.

Systematic biases in favor of high earners. More troublesome are systematic biases that advantage high-wage earners. These biases stem from the way annuities markets and privately managed FF DC plans operate. In situations where these biases are large, the new and old pension systems may end up having very similar distributional consequences.

First, if high and low earners are put into the same annuity pool, at the point when they convert their retirement accumulation into a pension, low earners will end up paying more than their expected benefits while the opposite is true for high earners, who are likely to live longer—just as was the case under traditional DB plans. Most of the reformed systems allow low earners to avoid this loss of real income by choosing a gradual withdrawal of their retirement accumulation, instead of requiring the purchase of an annuity—but those who choose this option do so at the expense of foregoing longevity insurance. It is possible that competition in the annuities markets will eventually produce better rates for low earners, who belong in a lower risk category, but as yet this has not happened.

Second, low-wage workers are likely to have a higher discount rate and therefore to suffer a greater utility loss from the mandated saving for all the reasons that were mentioned earlier in connection with PAYG plans—their income is lower, the required contribution is a higher proportion of their total income, and they are less able to dissave part of their voluntary saving to maintain their current consumption levels, because they have little or no voluntary savings to dissave. The last point may be even more relevant to FF DC plans than to PAYG DB plans. But basically, the current cost of any mandatory retirement plan is likely to be more binding on and more painful to the young poor than the young rich. This is one reason for including a large compensating component in the system that targets future benefits to the poor, as in the public pillar of a multipillar system.

Other problems such as low coverage and high evasion may remain—the former because of compliance difficulties in developing countries with many small or self-employed enterprises and the latter because of the high discount rate of many workers and the high payroll taxes imposed for other services. However, the equity implications of low coverage and high evasion are different in DC and DC plans; in DC plans they are less likely to result in subsidies from outsiders to insiders and from nonevaders to evaders.

Third, the privately managed FF DC plans have been criticized for their higher administrative costs, compared to well-run centralized systems that enjoy economies of scale and do not incur marketing costs. If the pension investment companies cover these costs by charging a flat fee per account for their services, those with low contributions and assets will suffer a larger deterioration in their net returns. The flat fee may be nondiscriminatory, in the sense that it reflects the real cost of maintaining (keeping records, sending statements for) each account, but it nevertheless hurts low earners more than high earners. Put another way, different investment strategies and pension systems may be appropriate for high and low wage earners. If one system offers higher gross returns but also higher administrative costs that are uniform per account, while another system offers lower gross returns but lower administrative expenses per account, low earners might fare better under the latter, on a net return basis. Forcing them to choose the former may leave them with lower net returns than they could get elsewhere.

This line of thought leads to the possibility that flat fees should not be permitted in mandatory programs (implying cross-subsidies between high and low earners), or that fees charged to low earners should be subsidized by the government, or that each pension fund should be required to offer at least one investment option where the costs are small for small accounts. In the case of Chile, the spread between gross to net returns was indeed high, and it was highest for low earners, especially during the early years of the program (Shah 1996). As time passed, this spread declined and competition (or adverse publicity) forced most pension funds to phase out their flat fees, without government intervention—but the same problem remains in other Latin American countries. This may be one reason why low-wage workers have not shifted to the new system in Peru, while high-wage workers have shifted.

A fourth problem for low earners arises if they are less informed than their wealthier counterparts about financial alternatives. They may make poor financial decisions, and be misled by unscrupulous salesmen, about investment choices. In England, when workers were permitted to opt out of their employers' plans, many workers were induced to buy insurance policies that were not in their best interest. Low wage earners may be more prone to this sort of mistake, although we have no evidence that this is the case. We do have evidence from the choices made in 401(k) plans in the U.S. that low earners are more likely to be overly conservative, to choose a "safe" portfolio of government bonds, that in fact is unsafe in the sense that it is bound to yield a relatively low rate of return.

To avoid this problem it is essential to have a public education campaign informing workers about how to make good investment decisions and tight regulation of the funded pillar. The regulation should exclude unqualified pension fund managers, require diversified investments, and set forth clear information disclosure standards, thereby limiting the risk and the possibility of making very bad investment choices. So far every reforming Latin American country has imposed such regulations. Another possibility is to structure the program so that the investment choice is delegated to those with greater financial expertise, such as employers and union representatives, who act for an entire occupational or companywide group of workers, both rich and poor. This course has been followed in OECD countries such as Australia and Switzerland. While it may reduce informational problems and administrative costs, it may also create principal-agent problems, to the detriment of workers.

Nevertheless, even in a well-regulated system, the fact remains that where there is choice, inequality is likely to increase. Moreover, investment returns and labor returns may be correlated, making income distribution more unequal overall. At the same time, the expected return to all participants, both high and low earners, is greater than that expected from a continuation of the old PAYG system. This is due to the higher expected growth rate it generates and the higher return to funded plans, given the unfavorable demographics that lie ahead.

Which is better—a regimen where almost everyone gets a higher pension, but the variance among individuals has increased, or one where participants get a lower but more uniform pension? As with the choice between targeting low-income groups (Chile and Australia) versus rewarding all long-term contributors (Argentina), the answers will differ, for every society and citizen must make decisions on these issues.

Finally, opponents of multipillar pension systems have argued that once the redistributive objective becomes more transparent, as it does in all the reformed systems, high-income groups will become less willing to make transfers to low-income groups. This argument rests on the assumption that redistribution occurs in nontransparent PAYG DB systems because high earners have been fooled, but once they learn the truth, they pull back on the transfers. This is a curious line of thought, especially in view of empirical evidence indicating that traditional systems did not in fact redistribute much from rich to poor—perhaps because the rich quickly learned how the system operated and how they could manipulate it to their advantage. While the willingness of the "haves" to redistribute to the "have nots" is probably very limited, it may indeed be greater for systems that accomplish this redistribution in the cheapest and most efficient way—and the reformed systems have the edge on these grounds.

Conclusion

As Latin American countries have reformed their pension systems, they have not faced a tradeoff between equity and efficiency. In fact, this is one of many instances where countries were initially operating well within the efficiency-equity frontier; it was possible to have more of both.

The new systems show both promise and evidence of being more efficient than the old. They have also eliminated or greatly reduced some of the preexisting equity problems, stemming from poorly designed defined-benefit formulas and pay-as-you-go finance methods. At the same time, they have introduced new equity problems, stemming from annuity pricing, savings offsets, administrative costs, imperfect information and inequality under choice. Thus, perverse redistributions within cohorts are still possible, although intergenerational redistributions are less likely. While we are beginning to have empirical estimations of the growth effects of the reformed systems—and they are optimistic—as of yet we do not have empirical analyses of their distributional effects. This is, in part, because these calculations should be done on a lifetime basis and the new systems have not been in place for anyone's lifetime. It is also, in part, because we cannot calculate the changes in distribution brought about by the reforms unless we know the counterfactual, and this is quite different from the status quo, which is nonsustainable in every existing PAYG system. Finally, we may get different answers depending on whether we define equity as reducing inequality, eliminating poverty, or in some other way.

As we have seen, distributional effects depend on many detailed aspects of the system; pension reform can accommodate a variety of value judgments about equity. And diverse pension systems, both reformed and unreformed, can end up having similar distributional effects, albeit by different routes. While efficiency improvements from pension reform have the potential to improve everyone's welfare, in reality the gains are unevenly distributed and some people lose. Who wins and who loses depends in part on how different groups use the opportunities presented to them—and this is likely to be positively correlated with prior income, assets and education. But it also depends on many detailed features of the reform, in particular the design of the public pillar and the treatment of administrative costs in the private pillar, which must therefore be specified with great care and with calculations about the distributional effects of alternative options.

Those who believe that a particular country's configuration of political power shapes the distributional consequences of its policies, would argue that both the new and old pension systems are endogenous and will bring about very similar distributions. On the other hand, if the adoption of a new pension system can reflect and reinforce a changing pattern of political power, then it may be designed to have different and more equitable distributional consequences than the old. We can aim for that goal and strive to bring it about, but only future empirical analysis can tell us whether it has been achieved.

References

Agosin, M. R., G. Crespi T., and L. Letelier S. 1996. Explicaciones del Aumento del Ahorro en Chile. Centros de Investigación Económica. Inter-American Development Bank.

Ayala, U. 1996. The Savings Impact of the Mexican Pension Reform. World Bank Discussion Paper.

Bateman, H., and J. Piggott. 1998. Mandatory Occupational Pension in Australia. *Annals of Public and Cooperative Economics*, forthcoming.

Haindl Rondonelli, E. 1996. Chilean Pension Fund Reform and Its Impact on Saving. Universidad Gabriela Mistral, Discussion Paper.

Hepp, S. 1998. The Swiss Multi-Pillar System. *Annals of Public and Cooperative Economics*, forthcoming.

Holzmann, R. 1996. On Economic Usefulness and Fiscal Requirements of Moving from Unfunded to Funded Pensions. University of Saarland Working Paper.

James, E. 1998. New Models for Old Age Security—Experiments, Evidence and Unanswered Questions. *World Bank Research Observer* (August).

Morande, F. 1996. Savings in Chile: What Went Right? Inter-American Development Bank Working Paper Series 322.

Report of the Advisory Committee on the U.S. Social Security System. 1997.

Shah, H. 1997. Towards Better Regulation of Private Pension Funds. World Bank Policy Research Paper no. 1791 (June), Washington, D.C.

Valdes-Prieto, S. 1994. Distributive concerns in substituting a pay-as-you-go by a fully funded pension system. *Revista de Análisis Económico* 9(1): 77-104.

World Bank. 1994. *Averting the Old Age Crisis: Policies to Protect the Old and Promote Growth.* Washington, D.C.: World Bank and Oxford University Press.

CHAPTER TEN

Reforming Former Public Monopolies: Water Supply

Raquel Alfaro, Ralph Bradburd, and John Briscoe

Until very recently, urban water supply and sanitation were considered services both necessary and appropriate for governments to provide. The rationale was that water is a basic human need, that potable water is essential for life; its value in other uses is high as well, so that lack of adequate access to water is a defining characteristic of severe poverty (World Bank 1994, p. 20). Water and sewerage distribution services[1] also meet the most stringent definitions of a natural monopoly, including an almost complete lack of contestability. Natural monopoly, combined with the inelastic demand for water at low levels of consumption, imply that private monopoly in water and sewerage provision could lead to significant social welfare losses. These factors, combined with significant potential externalities, fostered the view that the public interest required the supply of water to be assured by government and provided by a public-owned utility, with government planning and coordination at the highest level even in very large countries.

The identification of access to water as a "basic human right" promoted the conviction that water tariffs should be set at levels "affordable" to the poor, with water expenditures "ideally" accounting for no more than five percent of a poor family's budget.[2]

These views, which may be termed "the public service delivery model," led to government policies whose effects were mixed, at best. On the one hand, most countries have experienced remarkable increases in access and service quality, despite rapid increases in urban population. In Brazil, for example, the proportion of the total population with access to safe drinking water increased from 55 percent in 1970 to 87 percent in 1990; other Latin American countries achieved impressive gains in water services coverage as well (World Bank 1994, Table A.2). In addition there were significant increases in the human resources and institutional capacity for water and sanitation services and regulation.

Unfortunately, the public service delivery model brought with it serious problems as well. The view that water is a basic human need or, in public finance terminology, a "merit good," created strong pressures for government-owned utilities to subsidize water tariffs so that poor and low-income families would not be priced out of the market. Indeed, the "social tariff" became a mainstay of the water sector in Latin America, practiced in virtually every country. The intent was benign, but in practice the social tariff yielded little benefit to the poor, and may actually have reduced their welfare.

In too many cases, even though the public enterprise suppliers' water tariff was low, piped service was inadequate and, in many cases, unavailable to poor and low-income families. This combination of low price and short supply was no bargain for the poor; it forced them to purchase water from vendors, to collect and carry water from distant sources, or to utilize unsanitary water available nearby. Water from vendors is vastly more expensive than piped water—ten to twenty-fold is a common ratio (World Bank 1994). Consumption of nonpiped water that does not meet standards of potability is also costly. If it is boiled before use, the considerable costs of boiling must be taken into account. Those costs can be very high; with the outbreak of cholera in Peru, the Ministry of Health urged all residents of Lima to boil their drinking water for ten minutes. But the expense of this would amount to 29 percent of the average household income in *pueblos jóvenes* (squatter settlements) according to Gilman and Skillicorn (1985). If water is not boiled and is contaminated, there can be devastating consequences associated with morbidity and mortality.

Despite good intentions, the real price of water under the social tariff regime was very high for many poor and low-income families, and probably higher than it would have been without a social tariff. The social tariff has usually operated in a manner that left the water utilities without financial resources to properly maintain existing delivery systems, much less to expand and upgrade coverage.[3] Inevitably, services to the poor were the most seriously affected.[4] The steep prices that poor and low-income families have paid for water because they lacked access to sanitary piped water, and the consequent high proportion of their income for water expenditures, suggests that real income inequality in Latin American countries has been greater than standard measures would indicate.[5]

In many cases, water tariffs were set below costs of production, often below short-run operating costs. Operating revenues were thus far below the level necessary to sustain an investment program. This meant that when government subsidies dried up, it was impossible to extend services to cover all. The outcome re-

Table 1. Income Level and Water Subsidies

Consumption quintile	Percent of total subsidy
0–20 percent	0
20–40 percent	12
40–60 percent	22
60–80 percent	27
80–100 percent	39

Source: World Bank calculations, based on Bazzanella 1995.

flected the "hydraulic law of subsidies"—those who get no services get no subsidy, and when there is rationing, the poor are always at the end of the line.[6]

The problem was exacerbated by the fact that the social tariff was not well targeted: in most cases, subsidized tariffs were extended to all consumers, not restricted to the poor.[7] The financial burden of subsidized tariffs was thus greatly increased, whether the burden fell on the water utility or the government at some level. With all consumers receiving the subsidized price, those who used the most water (invariably the middle class, rather than the poor) received the highest level of subsidy.

The de facto inequality of the social tariff is well illustrated by the city of Belém in Brazil. As shown in the table above, those who benefit most from the social tariff are high-consumption, well-to-do families, while the poor, unserved families get nothing.

The service delivery model relied on huge resource transfers to the water utilities. In Brazil, they amounted to about US$1 billion a year from the mid-1970s to the mid-1980s. For Mexico City alone, subsidies for water and sewerage amounted to US$1 billion a year, or about 0.6 percent of Mexico's GDP (World Bank 1992). Such outlays placed a great burden on countries' efforts to balance government budgets and in many cases were simply unsustainable.[8]

The discussion to this point has focused on how the public service delivery model and associated social tariff have failed to address the problem of poor and low-income families' access to safe and affordable water. Similar problems occurred in the area of sewerage services, but here there was far less "success" in extending coverage. A study of Costa Rica, Uruguay and the Dominican Republic showed that because rationing of sewerage was more severe than for water, the inequity was greater (Petrie 1989). Inadequate sewerage coverage contributed to the deterioration of the poor's access to safe water, leading to increased morbidity and mortality, as became evident when cholera returned to Peru and then to Latin America more generally. Even where sewerage systems exist, wastewater has rarely been treated, both due to management failures and because of inadequate investment in wastewater treatment and disposal facilities. In Latin America, only about 5 percent of household and industrial discharges are treated at all (Rivera 1996), and most sewage treatment plants constructed in Latin America perform very poorly. In Mexico, more than 90 percent of the municipal wastewater treatment plants are not functional (Briscoe 1993). The result is predictable—a sharp deterioration in the quality of surface and groundwater quality throughout the region.

The problem of inadequate sewage services under the public service delivery model has compounded Latin America's difficulties addressing the challenge of sustainable water resources management. Below-cost water tariffs and the associated heavy burden of providing subsidized water services have reduced the government funds available for investments in sewage treatment. This creates a vicious circle, in which inadequate sewerage facilities exacerbate the need for investments to provide potable water—both for those who are currently connected to the network and for those who are not. At the same time, water subsidies reduce the funds available for doing so. The situation on the Paraíba do Sul river in Brazil—both a sewer for São Paulo and the water supply for Rio de Janeiro—is a striking example of a widespread phenomenon.

Forces for Change

Over the past decade, several simultaneous and interconnected "revolutions" have taken place in Latin America. The state-driven development model ended, and a "market-friendly" model replaced it. There is greater concern about the effects of budget deficits. Other major changes include the democratization of political institutions, decentralization, and increasing attention to environmental issues. These changes have led to new thinking about ways that water and sanitation services can and should be provided. Although the process of transition from old to new is far from complete, some broad directions are clear, and some lessons have been derived from experience.

The new internationally accepted principles for sound water management have been widely adopted in the region.[9] There are two central principles, one instrumental and one institutional. One is that water should be managed not just as a social, but also as an economic, good. The other is that water should be managed by the government at the lowest appropriate level (the subsidiarity principle), with much greater involvement of the private sector and communities themselves.[10] The first does not advocate a "pure market" approach, because the externalities involved in water use suggest the need for government involvement in some form. Rather, the new thinking supports the use of policies that recognize and benefit from economic incentives.

Different countries are taking various approaches to turn these principles into practice. This chapter presents a selective review of those approaches and derives some lessons from experience. The discussion centers on five key issues: 1) the water and sewerage needs of the poor; 2) "decentralized" provision of water and sewerage services provision; 3) how to regulate commercially oriented providers; 4) how the transition to commercially viable practices affects labor; and 5) sustainable water use and development.

Issue 1: The Needs of the Poor

The "social tariff" has not been an effective instrument for delivering water and sanitation services to poor and low-income families. Although high tariffs clearly impose a burden on these families, the social tariff approach often dooms the poor to no access to services at all—a far greater burden. Nevertheless, there are several promising approaches to meeting poor and low-income families' needs for water and sewerage services without abandoning considerations of affordability. Most of these approaches involve greater low-income community involvement in water and sewerage service provision.

"Marketing" is an important part of successful efforts to provide service to poor communities. Although largely ignored under the service delivery model, marketing has great potential for transforming poor communities from revenue sinks to revenue sources, simultaneously serving the needs of the communities and increasing funds available for infrastructure expansion and improvement.

Marketing encompasses a wide variety of activities. One of these is consultation with poor communities[11] to have them choose the price/service level combination they feel is optimal. Residents of poor and low-income communities may be unable to afford the full cost, or even a reasonable share of the full cost, of the water services that would be demanded by higher-income groups.[12] But the value they place on a less expensive and therefore affordable level of service may be far above the cost of providing it, and they can enjoy significant gains in welfare from having a choice beyond all-or-nothing service. The Brazilian condominial sewerage system is an excellent example of how such choice mechanisms can operate in practice. Households are presented with a range of sanitation options, ranging from no improvement, to low-cost backyard sewers, to medium-cost sidewalk sewers, to high-cost conventional sewers. The choices made by households vary systematically and logically in accordance with income (de Melo 1985).

Marketing can also take the form of extending innovative financing arrangements to poor and low-income families. Financing connection costs has been a major impediment in less developed areas (World Bank Water Demand Research Team 1993); many utilities in Latin America have, sensibly, financed connection costs and recovered these via a surcharge. In Chile, the Santiago water utility (EMOS) realized that many potential customers were unable to pay for connection to a piped-water system on a lump-sum basis or on a short-term installment basis. In response, the company offered a variety of extended payment plans, some of which stretched repayment of connection costs over a period of years. In this way, the customers gained access to safe piped water at an affordable price, greatly reducing their overall costs for water, and the company increased its revenues in two ways—directly, by increased monthly revenues from customers, and indirectly, by reducing the amount of water diverted through illegal connections.

Marketing also involves community outreach programs. The experience of EMOS in Santiago, where the utility provided its poor and low-income customers with instruction on how to properly use water and sanitation services, demonstrates the benefits to both customers and utilities from such efforts. The instruction included matters such as estimating total monthly water use, how to pay bills, and what items can and cannot be disposed of in sewerage systems. The customers gained by avoiding large water bills due to immoderate use and the utility gained by reducing maintenance costs on water and sewerage systems and by reducing bills-in-arrears difficulties. In Santiago, Chile, where (as discussed later) poor families receive a water subsidy from the central government channeled through the municipal government, EMOS discovered that significant community outreach programs were necessary even to ensure that poor families registered to receive subsidies to which they were entitled.

"Marketing" activities directed at the poor may appear to suggest manipulation or exploitation of the vulnerable. Water utilities' marketing activities, however, should be viewed rather as a way of improving understanding of customers' concerns and of meeting their needs more effectively. Indeed, Chile's EMOS refers to its service users as "clients" rather than "customers," to emphasize that in spite of the monopolistic nature of its business, the service users should be treated as if they had the option to abandon the company for a better one. In effect, EMOS views its marketing activities as part of the process of fulfilling the *commercial* potential of serving the needs of poor and low-income families.[13] Clearly, when service users—including poor and low-income families—are paying for water service, and tariffs are such that the utility profits when providing it, the relationship between the utility and the customer assumes an entirely different character from the typical situation under the service delivery model in which each customer is just an additional drain on revenues.[14]

While it is "community outreach" or "marketing" of a different sort, the experiences of many Latin American utilities have demonstrated the benefits of forging close ties of communication and cooperation with local governments in planning and implementing the expansion of water and sanitation services infrastructure. This cooperation is particularly important for extending services to families that live in extralegal communities in periurban areas.

For some very poor families, monthly fees for piped water may create a financial burden that society regards as unacceptably high; in these cases, assistance must be provided. The critical problem is to find ways to provide that assistance in a very targeted fashion. If instead the subsidy becomes extended to all or to a large subset of customers,[15] this will not only threaten the utility's financial viability, but also forfeit the efficiency benefits of properly pricing water.

Chile's response to this dilemma is instructive. Santiago's water tariff system, in which water service charges are set to cover full costs, is politically and socially viable because of water subsidies. They are granted within the framework of the Chilean central government's "overcoming poverty" program, which provides subsidies to poor families for water and sewerage services.[16] Municipalities carry out surveys to determine the social condition of the families requesting the subsidy and classify them in order of priority, with poorest families receiving first priority. Once the central government transfers the amount for subsidies to the municipalities, the municipalities use them to pay their correspondent share of the water bill of the families that have qualified for the subsidy. The share ranges from 15 percent to 75 percent, with the poorest families receiving the highest subsidy shares. This payment is made directly by the municipality to the water utility. Annual subsidies for all water and sewerage services in the country are about US$25 million and are given to approximately 450,000 families to cover, on average, about 50 percent of their water bill. In the case of EMOS, Santiago's water utility, subsidies represent about US$4 million per year, equivalent to 2.3 percent of its total billing.

An important advantage of the subsidy voucher approach is its flexibility. In particular, increasing or decreasing the number of people receiving subsidized water, or the size of the subsidy, does not have a direct impact on the revenues of the utility.[17] Therefore, such a change need not require extensive negotiations, contractual adjustments or compensatory payments to the utility.

In countries where a Chilean-type subsidy approach is not feasible due to insufficient administrative or financial capacity, it becomes harder to find ways to meet poor and low-income families' water and sanitation needs. If we assume that the service-delivery approach is not only financially unsustainable but actually makes the poor worse off, then the poor could benefit from marketization of water and sanitation services, even if unaccompanied by targeted assistance to the poor.

But this may be viewed as too naive. And if the Chilean subsidy approach is considered impracticable, policymakers may look for some other method to reduce poor families' costs for water and sanitation services. One alternative method is a cross-subsidy scheme based on some form of nonlinear pricing; here, a minimal family consumption level is subsidized by above-cost charges to business customers or customers who have supra-average consumption or enjoy "special" service. But even if cross-subsidy schemes were feasible in some circumstances and could be sustained over long periods, they generally result in inefficient pricing from a resource allocation perspective. Efforts to reduce the cost of "minimal service" through cross-subsidization were a fixture of utility regulation in many countries, including the United States, and the role they played in the electricity, telephone, airline, and railroad sectors has been well-documented. Further, cross-subsidy approaches may encourage socially costly efforts to avoid the price discrimination upon which such schemes depend. Such efforts include both illicit behavior, such as corrupting meter-readers or diverting water before it is metered, and legal, but costly, behavior such as developing private wells and other independent sources of water supply.[18]

In addition to these problems, cross-subsidy schemes are not easily sustainable in nonmonopoly situations. Where competition is introduced, cross-subsidy schemes are extremely vulnerable to "cherry-picking" predation, in which competitors, by minimizing the extent to which they serve the subsidized market, are able to profitably undercut the prices to the subsidy-financing high-price consumers.

As a result of these inherent problems, cross-subsidy schemes often require heavy monitoring of customers and a heavy-handed regulatory approach. The former adds to direct costs; so does the latter, but more seriously, it tends to foster precisely the kinds of undesirable incentives and inefficiencies that have accompanied the service delivery approach. Further research into ways of improving cross-subsidy schemes would be worthwhile, but in the meantime, this approach should be viewed with caution. The policy of offering customers a choice of several service/price offerings, discussed above, appears to be a superior method of meeting the needs of low-income consumers. It addresses both the need to provide affordable yet adequate service to low-income communities and the need to maintain incentives for utilities to serve them.

Another approach to serving the needs of poor and very low-income families is "coproduction" of services. Here, the residents of poor communities provide labor for installing and maintaining the "feeder" infrastructure, while the formal utility retains responsibility for production of the "trunk" infrastructure. This approach is controversial, and it is useful to consider its advantages and disadvantages.

The costs to families of *not* having any on-plot water service or sewerage infrastructure[19] are high; therefore, coproduction can clearly be beneficial when families' and governments' financial and managerial constraints make it the only available option for providing water and sewerage services to the poor. In addition, coproduction activities can serve as a catalyst for development of political institutions in poor communities.

There have been some notable successes in community coproduction of water and sewer services, including the condominial approach first adopted in northeast Brazil and now elsewhere in that country, and a similar program that has brought low-cost sewerage services to hundreds of thousands in Karachi, Pakistan. When coproduction approaches are well-designed, the community members themselves have strong incentives to ensure that water and sewerage feeder lines are properly constructed and maintained, reducing water losses from accidents and illegitimate diversion of water (Briscoe 1995). "Low-tech" and labor-intensive techniques that generally characterize coproduction approaches can also serve as a means of providing employment opportunities for community residents. Finally, because improvements in water and sanitation services increase the attractiveness of residing in a neighborhood, such improvements can contribute significantly to the stability of communities. To the extent that community residents have some property rights to their homes, water and sewerage improvements can even increase families' real wealth.

The idea of giving users a range of price-quality options from which to choose, fits well with the social funds approach (Graham 1994). In the social fund model, communities essentially have block grants, and it is up to them to choose how much they wish to spend on different types and qualities of services. Even when these grants are fully subsidized, communities face an opportunity cost and an associated incentive to make sensible choices.

There are potential disadvantages of the coproduction approach as well. In particular, it may create difficulties for utilities that must integrate "nonstandard" infrastructure into their own systems. For obvious reasons, this may complicate efforts to use incentive mechanisms to encourage efficiency, including privatization efforts.

The political response to promotion of coproduction approaches may also present a problem. The presumptive argument for community coproduction approaches involving nonstandard techniques is that the alternative is markedly inferior service, or, indeed, no service at all. If, however, the barrier to extending to poor communities the same level of service enjoyed by wealthy communities is not scarce resources, but rather a lack of political will or innovative management, then coproduction approaches utilizing nonstandard techniques may simply reduce the total expenditures on water and sewerage infrastructure in poor and low-income communities. The latter is clearly more of a possibility in wealthier middle-income countries such as Chile than in most developing countries, which are severely pressed for financial resources. In the poorer countries, insistence on a choice between top-of-the-line service or none at all will almost certainly harm the interests of poor and low-income families. This is even more true in light of the wider benefits of improved water and sanitation, including the new opportunities for microenterprise and small-scale business employment when good water and sanitation services are available in poor communities at a reasonable price.

Last but not least, in considering ways to meet the needs of poor and low-income families, we should note the potential contribution of democratic political institutions (Sen 1995; Ahsah, Laplante and Wheeler 1996). When the poor have a political voice, government agencies have a far greater incentive to find innovative solutions to meet their needs. The pressure to extend water and sanitation services to poor communities in São Paulo, Brazil, once democracy was introduced there, and the response to that pressure, is a testimony to what can be accomplished when the necessary political will is mobilized (Watson 1992). The democratization of Latin America is serving as a powerful catalyst for improvements in coverage and operational efficiency of water and sewerage services, and as incomes grow, for water-related environmental improvements as well.

Issue 2: Who Should Provide Services?

Government ownership and operation of monopolistic water and sewerage providers does not have to result in inefficient operation and suboptimal service, but it often has in the past (for examples, see Rivera 1996). And when there is inefficiency in the provision of water services, it is almost always the poor "at the end of the pipe" who suffer disproportionately. There are several reasons for the generally poor performance of public water utilities.

- Water and sewerage service is a natural monopoly, even more so than electricity generation or telecommunications services. As a result, customers cannot easily impose discipline on a utility that offers an inferior price/service combination by abandoning it for another provider who offers a superior one. For the same reason, relative performance comparisons for the purpose of encouraging efficient operation are difficult. Thus, both market and bureaucratic constraints on management inefficiency are weak.
- Government, as "owner" and operator of water utilities, has multiple objectives and no explicit approaches for making the appropriate tradeoffs between them. Even in the best of circumstances, this greatly complicates the tasks of managers and, a fortiori, the task of evaluating managerial performance.
- In public-owned firms, there is no person or group who gets the profits, no "residual claimant" whose overriding goal, subject to socially determined constraints, is maximizing the difference between revenues and costs. Therefore, absent a significant performance-based incentive system, there is no manager or officer(s) of the water utility whose income, or wealth more broadly defined, will be significantly increased through superior performance of the utility. The consequence of this under the old model was operational inefficiency. Many utilities were overstaffed, often with unqualified personnel, with between 10 and 20 employees per 1,000 water connections in 1991 in most Latin American utilities, compared to about 3 in Santiago[20] and between 2 and 3 in Europe (see Briscoe 1993). Levels of unaccounted-for water were also high, in some cases extraordinarily so—close to half the total water throughput. The latter was in part a consequence of leaks due to inadequate maintenance of infrastructure and in part due to "commercial losses" resulting from illegal connections, underregistering meters and inadequate billing and collection practices.

- The lack of a residual claimant, or senior managers whose income is strongly performance-determined, also means there is often no one with a strong incentive to vigorously resist political plunder of the utility, which can take place through patronage employment, appeasement pricing,[21] or through corrupt procurement and billing practices.

The problems described above were frequently compounded by government's dual role as producer and regulator. The lack of private owners or powerfully motivated managers reduced utilities' resistance to regulators' or politicians' pressures to reduce tariffs. An IDB study (Foster 1996) shows that in Latin American countries for which data are available, tariffs in the early 1990s were only about 27 percent of operating costs.[22] The revenue consequences of this situation contributed to utilities' failure to make adequate investment in infrastructure expansion and maintenance. Though the government, as regulator, may have kept prices low, it failed to provide the means, the incentive, or the regulatory pressures to achieve high levels of service in terms of coverage and reliability of service. But even here the matter is not uncomplicated. As long as the utilities were objects of political plunder, any increase in revenues that might have resulted from higher tariffs would probably have been dissipated rather than used productively. In this circumstance, even a well-intentioned regulator (or the public) may see little benefit in raising tariffs to more fully cover costs.

This is yet another example of a vicious circle; at the same time, it suggests a way out. The Buenos Aires concession (Idelovitch and Ringskog) is relevant here. In the first two years of operation, this private operator has increased water production by 27 percent, increased the population served by water and sewerage by 9 percent and 6 percent, respectively, and reduced response time for repairs by 73 percent. The company has also undertaken a tenfold increase in investment and managed to reduce the tariff by one-quarter. The keys to this impressive performance are greatly improved operational efficiency (the number of employees per thousand connections has fallen by 43 percent, and the number of meters in service increased by 460 percent). More generally, if utilities do begin to operate efficiently, and revenues are used to improve service, resistance to tariff increases may be much less than previous experience might suggest.

One clear lesson from Latin American experience is that lack of separation between the regulating and regulated entities made it extremely difficult for either to function effectively and contributed to the failure of the service delivery model. Outlined below are some positive changes taking place in the provision of water and sewerage services.

New approaches. Separating responsibilities for production and regulation (separating "poachers from gamekeepers") is a necessary, but not sufficient, change in policy. Experience to date shows the significant benefits from transforming water utilities into commercially oriented entities that embody strong incentives for technically efficient and economically viable operation. In some cases, this can occur within the context of public water authorities; indeed, the Latin American experience, with EMOS and SANEPAR (of Paraná in Brazil) prime examples, shows that under the right circumstances it is possible to successfully commercialize water utilities that remain government-owned. In these cases, subcontracting to the private sector is used extensively. There are numerous options for private sector participation, many of which can be used in combination.

Private sector participation. Private sector participation is perhaps the most widely discussed element of the "new thinking" with regard to provision of water and sewerage services. There is a broad range of experimentation taking place in Latin American countries, with varying degrees of private sector participation. Here we provide a few examples that will give a sense of what is being attempted and with what results.

Service contracts. Service contracts refer to contracting with private firms to carry out all or part of the activities involved in providing water and sewerage services. The "contractors" bid for the service contract, which, depending upon the nature of the activity being contracted out, might specify price, quality parameters, operational objectives and other terms.

The purpose of service contracting is to increase efficiency in provision of some activity or set of activities. It is the least difficult form of private sector participation to implement, because the public-owned utility retains overall operational responsibility and responsibility for financing fixed assets (Idelovitch and Ringskog 1995).

Service contracts with relatively short duration (frequent rebidding) can be an effective instrument for introducing competition and its derivative efficiencies into some aspects of water and sanitation services. In order to ensure appropriate incentives, contract renewal should depend on both price and performance, and efforts should be made to attract new bidders whenever contracts come up for renewal. If the technical characteristics of the activity permit it, there is probably some benefit to starting out with two or more firms receiving service contracts at the outset, rather than allowing one to have the contract and then in theory leaving the door open for competition later. This allows for performance comparisons and also, by expanding the number of experienced firms, increases the likelihood that any given service contract will change hands when it comes up for renewal. This helps prevent any particular contractor from developing an entrenched position.

(Absent this, the door to new competition may be left closed long enough for the hinges to rust.)

EMOS, in Santiago, Chile, has successfully contracted with the private sector to provide a wide variety of activities related to its status as provider of water and sanitation services.[23] These include planning and economic studies, research studies, construction and rehabilitation, repair and maintenance of infrastructure, computer services, billing, payroll, cleaning and maintenance of buildings, transport, meter reading, meter repair and maintenance, cutting and reinstallation of services, public relations, industrial relations services (including training and collective bargaining assistance), and some legal and audit services. Putting all these services out for contract has led to lower costs and greater efficiency and has allowed management to focus on management per se and on core activities. EMOS does not contract out activities that it can perform internally at lower cost, nor does it contract out services that might put at risk service delivery or confidential information.

Putting services out for contract is not, by itself, a sure route to efficiency. Utilities that are not well-managed themselves are unlikely to effectively administer either the awarding of contracts or the monitoring function necessary to ensure contractual compliance. One implication of this is that reform of public-owned utilities may have to precede efforts to improve efficiency through service contracts.[24]

Management contracts. This is a form of service contract in which a private firm assumes responsibility for the whole range of day-to-day management and operations for part or all of the geographic area served by the utility. Management contracts typically tie compensation to performance, including both quality of service and success in collecting payments from customers. In principle, this can lead to improved service and operating efficiency; however, if the contract itself, the means by which it is awarded, or general institutional conditions in the country are such as to undercut the private management's incentives for efficiency, the actual benefits will be far below potential. If management lacks real autonomy or if contract continuity is heavily dependent upon political factors, management is unlikely to succeed in resisting politicians' pressures for patronage employment, concessional rates for particular customers, and other impediments to efficient operation (World Bank 1994). On the other hand, if properly designed and implemented, management contracts can substantially improve the functioning of public-owned utilities and set the stage for greater levels of private sector participation.

Mexico City has experimented with a limited form of private sector participation, dividing the city into four quadrants with a limited management contract for each. The results have been disappointing, demonstrating that even relatively simple forms of private participation depend upon government political will for their success.

Lease contracts (affermage). In a lease, or *affermage* contract, the public-owned firm retains ownership of the firm, is responsible for all existing debts, all new capital investments not maintenance-related, and generally is responsible as well for setting tariffs. The lessee is responsible for operation, maintenance, and management.

Lease arrangements typically have an extended duration, usually of 10-15 years. This has the advantage of encouraging expenditures on maintenance of infrastructure, provided of course that the lessee feels that government contractual obligations will be honored and that any periodic tariff revision procedures will not operate in a manner that effectively appropriates all profits. Because the profits of the lessee depend upon the difference between tariff revenues and costs, incentives for efficient operation of the utility are strong. The primary disadvantage of lease arrangements is the lack of fully compatible incentives with respect to investment and operating expenditures.

Lease arrangements do not require the operator to acquire the assets of the utility, and therefore lease arrangements can be attractive in situations where private financing would be a problem or in situations where past insecurity of property rights makes investors reluctant to invest large amounts in immovable assets. If all goes well, a lease operation can pave the way for deeper forms of private sector participation (PSP) such as concession contracts or even full privatization in the future (Idelovitch and Ringskog 1995). This form of PSP is widely used in France and in a number of African countries, including Cote d'Ivoire, Guinea and Senegal.

Concessions. A concession is similar to a lease arrangement, except that here the concessionaire, the holder of the concession, is responsible not only for operations and management but also for capital investments for infrastructure expansion. The public water authority's fixed assets remain in public hands and provisions are made for compensated transfer of the concessionaire's unamortized new investments to the public authority at the end of the concession period, which are typically 30 years long.

Concession arrangements have all the advantages of lease arrangements but can yield greater efficiencies because the concessionaire has responsibility for both investment and operations, thus avoiding the incentive incompatibility problems that arise when these tasks are the responsibility of separate entities.[25] Concession arrangements require more complex contracts than lease arrangements because the concessionaire puts more at risk; as a result, more time and resources are required to lay the groundwork for bidding on concessions.

Argentina's experience with the water utility concession in Buenos Aires provides clear lessons for others considering concession arrangements for water and sanitation services.[26] The impetus for private sector participation was the dismal performance of the public water utility, Obras Sanitarias de la Nación (OSN), which suffered from excess personnel, an unaccounted-for water rate of 45 percent, unreliable service, poorly maintained facilities and high levels of political interference in its operations. In addition, there were insufficient public funds available for necessary investments in infrastructure expansion, improvement and maintenance.

After some false starts during which progress was impeded by OSN management's lack of enthusiasm for real reform, in 1991 the decision was made to privatize OSN. The private concession did not begin to operate the system until roughly mid 1993, and the length of time required for the process gives a good picture of the complexity of the task. A full description of the process is outside the scope of this document, but some aspects require at least a brief mention.

First is the role of legal and other institutional prerequisites to private sector participation. In Argentina, the legal code prohibited cutting off a customer's water for nonpayment.[27] Without a change in this law, potential concessionaires would probably have found the project too risky. Similarly, financial risks were reduced by permitting free convertibility of currency.

Next, substantial effort was necessary to lay the basis for the bidding process. An important activity was hiring a trusted, independent consulting firm to gather and organize the kinds of information necessary for preparation and evaluation of bids. This included detailed assessments of the condition of OSN's physical plant, financial analysis, determination of technical and operational objectives for the concession, and a thorough review of the legal and tax environment within which the concession would operate. This was a lengthy process and not an inexpensive one—World Bank technical and financial support played an important role here. Subsequent events proved the value of thorough prebidding preparation.

Preparation of the bidding documents was also a complex and time-consuming task. The bidding documents, which specified the criteria for awarding the concession, also provided information on the physical and human capital assets of OSN as well as OSN's financial liabilities, specified concession service standards, and defined the regulatory framework, including details of dispute resolution mechanisms. The bidding and bidding evaluation themselves involved processes that required significant time and expertise.

The private water and sewerage concession created for Buenos Aires is the largest such concession in the world. It specifies ambitious performance targets rather than investment targets, covering such factors as water and sewerage coverage, water and water service quality, percentage of wastewater receiving primary and secondary treatment, and unaccounted-for water, including a target-attainment timetable that extends over the 30-year life of the concession. By contract, water tariffs are to be reassessed periodically.

The performance targets imply high levels of investment, in the range of US$4 billion ($4,000,000,000) over the 30-year life of the concession, with about $1.2 billion in the first five years alone. Potential concessionaires, including the winning bidder, apparently were reluctant to commit to investing this heavily with their own resources in the early phases of operation; much of this investment is expected to be financed from operating revenues and loans from multilateral agencies and commercial banks. This has two important implications.

First, multilateral agencies can play an important role in getting concession (or full privatization) initiatives off the ground. In particular, if agreements are structured so that any government contract violations that significantly harm the concessionaire must necessarily jeopardize the multilaterals' investments, such violations become unattractive from the government's perspective. Thus, the multilateral's involvement serves to reduce concessionaires' perceived (and actual) "political" risk even beyond the direct impact of reducing the concessionaire's at-risk capital. In effect, in Oliver Williamson's terms, the government's concern with maintaining good relations with the multilateral agency provides a "hostage" (Williamson 1983) that alleviates concessionaires' concerns regarding opportunistic behavior on the part of the sovereign government.[28]

Second, the concession process was complicated because of having to overcome mutual concerns regarding good faith. To the extent that countries and companies have more (positive) experience with concessions and other forms of private sector participation, and as political and institutional stability become more the norm in Latin America, the difficulties of constructing mutually acceptable contracts should decline.[29]

Early indications of the "success" of the transfer of OSN's operations to the concessionaire are encouraging. There have been major improvements in both reliability and quality of water service; sewage treatment has improved as well; and water tariffs are substantially lower than they were prior to award of the concession. There was a significant increase in efficiency accompanied by a very substantial reduction in workforce from 7,600 to 4,000, the latter involving implementation of two voluntary retirement programs, one financed by the central government at a cost of US$40 million prior to the concessionaire assuming responsibility for operations, and the other, financed by the concessionaire at a cost of US$50 million, occurring after the concessionaire took over operations.

The experience of the Buenos Aires water and sewerage concession in its first year of operation also provides a good lesson in the problems and potentials of incomplete contracts, which are inevitable because of the need for contractual flexibility or because of contractual ambiguity, both intentional or unintentional. In the beginning of the second year of the concession, ETOSS, the regulating entity, granted the concession an extraordinary rate increase of 13.5 percent, because of the concession's demonstrated need for funds to speed the investment program to solve some urgent water quality and sewerage problems, and because of high-than-anticipated labor costs. At present, this flexibility appears to have permitted an outcome superior to all stakeholders, although clearly ETOSS cannot permit a situation to develop in which the concessionaire is unable to credibly resist excessive labor demands for higher wages.

Contractual flexibility or ambiguity can also lead to unnecessary disagreements between regulatory authorities and concessionaires. Apparently, differences in ETOSS' and the concessionaire's interpretation of the contract and disagreements over whether ETOSS should regulate performance-related outcomes or the means to achieving them have led to tensions between the two. One lesson that may be drawn from this is that, because it is impossible to write complete contracts in an uncertain and changing environment, and because, as we have seen, flexibility can be beneficial, effective dispute resolution mechanisms must be an integral part of the initial contract let out for bid.

It is evident that the Buenos Aires concession was an important icebreaker in Latin America. Recently a major concession contract was concluded for the city of Limeira in São Paulo State in Brazil (Financial Times 1996), with the concessionaire being a joint venture of a major Brazilian construction company with an international water operator, a combination that is likely to become the norm in Latin America.

BOTs and BOOTs. Build-operate-transfer (BOT) or build-own-operate-transfer (BOOT) agreements offer an attractive method for securing private investment for construction of bulk water and sewerage services infrastructure. Private construction may also be less expensive than public construction in situations where public-financed construction will be encumbered with political interference or union wage or work-rule requirements that elevate costs well above competitive levels. Assuming that the relevant contracts have appropriate incentive structures, private operation of the plants constructed under BOT or BOOT agreements may yield efficiency improvements relative to public operation as well.

BOT or BOOT-built plants in most cases must interface with the public authority's system. Where the utility is run efficiently, BOTs can play a useful role. For example, most of the massive upcoming investment in wastewater treatment in Santiago will be by BOTs. Where the public water authority is not well managed, however, the outcome can be catastrophic because it can result in ever greater losses of water and revenue. A second concern is with the assignment of risk; if the operator does not assume contractually a fair share of the commercial risk, consumers can end up paying for the operator's poor performance. This was the case in Mexico's disastrous experience with toll roads, where the government "guaranteed" traffic that did not materialize.

Full privatization. The United Kingdom is the only country in the world with significant experience with full privatization of water and sewerage services. After thorough consideration of global experience with various forms of PSP in delivering water and other forms of infrastructure, Chile is now moving ahead with full privatization of some regional utilities. General issues regarding regulation of private entities will be discussed in the next section.

In summary, the various approaches to involving private sector participation offer great promise for improving delivery of water and sanitation services in Latin America. Obtaining the benefits of private sector participation will not be an easy process, however; it will take time, money, and political will. Where public water authorities retain an important role in water services provision, commercialization and reform of those entities should be considered a prerequisite for successful private sector participation.

One very promising implication of the Latin American experience with water utility reform to date is that the potential efficiency improvements are enormous. In some cases, it may be possible to have water tariffs that cover full costs without having to raise water tariffs that much above current levels—or even to reduce them, as in Buenos Aires. In other cases, the efficiency gains will not be large enough to offset reductions in subsidies and the need for additional funds to finance essential maintenance and expansion of infrastructure. In these latter cases, particular care must be taken to ensure that tariff increases do not engender a political backlash against water utility reform, as occurred, for example, in Aguascalientes, Mexico, in 1995 (Rivera 1996), the United Kingdom, and elsewhere.

Issue 3: What Are the Regulatory Options?

Some have argued that the greatest benefit from the insertion of the private sector into the water sector is that it brings the provision/regulation issue to the surface.[30] But major questions remain on how to regulate, and indeed, how to introduce effective regulation when the institutional history in many Latin American countries is such that business and government entities are to some degree mutually suspicious—business entities, because property rights and legal institutions have been fragile in the past, and government entities, because business practices have not been perceived as sufficiently sensitive to the public interest.[31]

When "commercialization" occurs through management and performance contracts, leases, concessions, or BOTs and BOOTs, contracts rather than regulatory entities provide the mechanism for setting the parameters of providers' behavior. This is one great advantage of these approaches. If contracts are well-crafted, each party's obligations and expectations are clearly articulated and understood, and the opportunities or disputes are reduced (though not eliminated). And when both parties find their interactions under contractual situations to be satisfactory, it can help to create conditions that will make other regulatory approaches feasible. This is important, because regulation generally operates in a manner that is not fully defined by the enabling legislation, creating uncertainties for both regulators and regulated entities that can lead to dysfunctional outcomes in situations of mutual distrust.

Interesting policy issues arise when a municipality has a very poorly functioning public water authority with poor prospects for reform, but also no effective regulatory body currently operating or able to operate in the short term. Water and sewer services are natural monopolies and are likely to remain so. This is in contrast to other sectors, such as electricity generation and telecommunication services, where the underlying technologies are changing and making the market more "contestable," and where, as a consequence, permitting a (temporary) monopoly to function unregulated might well produce an outcome superior to that of an inefficient public provider (see Bradburd 1995). The natural monopoly characteristic of water and sewer services, in combination with issues of public safety and environmental externalities, make them poor candidates for unregulated operation.

The above factors might seem to suggest that some regulation, even if imperfect, is better than none. But caution is necessary here. In the absence of institutional safeguards, the power to regulate is the power to expropriate, and if regulatory power is wielded in this manner early on in the process of involving the private sector, future private sector participation, with all the advantages it may offer for efficiency and nongovernmental sources of funding, may be jeopardized. In this situation, regulation by contract may be the best option until regulatory capabilities, both in terms of personnel and appropriate social institutions, are in place.

If the decision is made to regulate by means of a regulatory agency rather than by means of contracts, the regulating entity's powers must be carefully delimited. The purpose of commercializing water and sewerage service is to take advantage of market-based incentives for efficiency in operations and investment, while not abandoning water quality and quality of service objectives. If regulators attempt to recapture all the profits that accrue from superior performance, the incentive to participate and perform well is undercut. Similarly, attempts to implement regulatory micromanagement of water utilities are likely to prove counterproductive both in the short and long run. The regulatory approaches of Argentina and Chile are instructive here. The Argentinean regulatory perspective has been characterized as being fundamentally suspicious of business motives. There, access to private funding rather than the advantages of market-based incentives seems to have been the rationale for permitting private sector involvement in water and sanitation services. The Argentinean regulatory approach, which significantly circumscribes managerial autonomy, reflects the underlying lack of trust in business behavior. This approach is not likely to be effective in the long run. In contrast to this, Chilean regulators have adopted the view that firms, given appropriate incentives to guide their behavior, will function in a manner consistent with the public interest. Decisionmaking is left in the hands of management. To date, the Chilean model seems to be functioning quite well; nevertheless, possible adjustments to the legal framework are being studied as a prerequisite to full privatization.

Regulatory regimes, once established, tend to become resistant to change. This regulatory rigidity derives from several sources, including government reluctance to change the rules, for fear that doing so might harm its reputation for making credible commitments to the private sector. Private entities may be reluctant to see change in systems under which they receive economic rents, and regulatory personnel may resist changes that would reduce the value of their experience-based human capital.[32]

Given the forces that promote regulatory rigidity, and given that the optimal form of regulation at any moment depends upon parameters whose values are likely to change with economic growth, it would appear wise to avoid creating regulatory systems that are elaborate and complex. The lighter the regulatory touch, and the more transparent the system, the easier it will be to change when it is necessary to do so. Similarly, policies that have built-in mechanisms that encourage growth of regulatory agencies are likely to create regulatory inefficiency and inflexibility in the long run. In Buenos Aires, for example, the regulatory agency is funded in effect by a surtax on consumers' bills that is set at 2.7 percent of total water billings (Idelovitch and Ringskog 1995). Not only does this represent an extremely high financial burden, but it also sets the stage for development of a bloated regulatory bureaucracy.

Clearly, one of the great policy challenges is to find ways to adapt the Buenos Aires-type concession model so that the administrative complexity and burden of that model is reduced. This may involve permitting greater managerial autonomy as well as making use, at least during the short run, of external administrative and technical auditing expertise.

Issue 4: Will PSP Reduce Demand for Labor?

In many countries, organized labor is a potent force opposing greater involvement of the private sector in public utilities, with the argument being that "privatization will mean fewer jobs." The Buenos Aires case provides some interesting insights into the dynamics of labor in a reforming utility.

As discussed earlier, OSN's workforce of about 7,500 in the preconcession period was trimmed to 4,000 by the combined efforts of the public water authority and the concessionaire. This was accomplished by two retirement buyout programs, one prior to, and one following, the concessionaire's taking over operations. Both programs were voluntary, which clearly reduced opposition to, and frictions associated with, reductions in staffing. Although use of the retirement buyout option was facilitated in the Buenos Aires case by the high proportion of workers over the age of 50 (roughly 30 percent),[33] the Argentinean example suggests that labor buyout programs can be usefully applied elsewhere.

Another instructive aspect of the Buenos Aires transition from a public water authority to a concession is that the reduction in the within-company workforce has been more than offset by the large number of jobs created by the increase (from US$10 million a year to US$125 million a year!) in the water utility's investment program. The concessionaire estimates that over 8,000 jobs have been created via contracts in the process, far more than were lost through staff reductions. Those public-owned water authorities that are most inefficient will require the largest staff reductions to reach acceptable norms of operating efficiency; however, these are likely to be the very companies who will need the greatest expansion of investment for expansion, improvement, and maintenance of infrastructure in the postreform period, with the attendant need for labor.

Workers losing positions due to operating staff reductions may not have the skills to benefit from increases in new employment opportunities. Worker retraining programs may be a useful option here. In any event, provided that financing can be found, buyout programs that lead to a significant decrease in the present value of personnel expenses, or that overcome political resistance to reform, may be a sound investment. (For this reason, the World Bank, which previously would not finance labor-reducing programs, will now consider doing so.)

Issue 5: How to Secure Reliable Bulk Water Supplies and Improve Environmental Quality

Securing reliable bulk water supplies and reducing degradation of surface water and underground aquifers is a critical task for Latin American countries. As indicated earlier, the "water and sanitation agenda" is not just an agenda of the provision of household services, but also one of management of water resources in an environmentally and financially sustainable way. This is a task that few industrialized countries have successfully met, even with the comparatively great financial resources at their disposal.[34]

Treating water as an economic good, and taking advantage of the policy options that this suggests, can reduce the financial burden of sustainably meeting water needs. In recent years a number of arid countries and regions have made major advances in the use of water markets to facilitate the voluntary transfer of water from low-valued uses (typically agricultural) to higher-valued uses (mostly urban and industrial water supply, but also high-value agriculture and environmental purposes). A wide variety of types of markets has emerged, ranging from the successful single-season water bank of California (Howitt et al. 1992) to the permanent transfer of rights, as in Australia. In Latin America, the longest and most interesting experience with formal water markets is in Chile, where, since 1981, water rights have been separated from land rights and can be traded. Major issues still need to be addressed in the Chilean water rights system (particularly the interactions between consumptive and nonconsumptive rights, and the need for a market-friendly river basin management system). From the perspective of urban utilities in Chile, however, the water markets have been a great success. They enable cities to both lease and purchase water rights from nearby farmers (who make a handsome profit), rather than having to incur the (much higher) costs of developing new sources (Briscoe 1995 and Pena 1996).

Along with efficiency effects, water-market policies have a distributional equity impact to which policymakers must be attentive. We have argued above that
the "social tariff" approach failed to deliver adequate services to the poor, and that
commercialization of water and sanitization services may not exacerbate, and may
actually reduce, inequality.[35] Nevertheless, as Carter and Coles argue in Chapter 6,
establishing property rights and market-friendly institutions, and allowing laissez-
faire functioning of those markets may work to the disadvantage of the poor in
markets where significant information and capital market imperfections remain.
Three comments on the Chilean experience are in order. First, water rights were
relatively well-distributed because of an earlier land reform in Chile. Second, tradable water rights have contributed to the growth of agricultural production and
thus of employment. Third, there was insufficient effort to ensure that indigenous
people registered their traditional water rights, a problem that is now being re-
dressed. Thus it may be important to search for inequality-reducing policies within
the context of market-oriented approaches. One approach might be to undertake
institutional reforms that would improve poor and low-income families' ability to
benefit from marketization of water. For example, establishing poor families' titles
to their homes, as suggested by Hernando de Soto (1997), would improve their
access to credit markets and reduce the capital-market-access advantage of large
landowners when water rights are marketed.

A second potential strategy is "water reform," which in the context of
marketized water could affect income inequality in much the same way as land
reform. The effect of this could be significant: water is already a scarce commodity
in some areas and is likely to become increasingly so over a wider geographic area
in the future. At this point, before clear property rights have been established and
water fully marketized, there is a unique opportunity to engage in water rights
redistribution. First, water reform can be presented as part of a package from which
upper-income families will gain; and second, resistance to redistribution will only
increase over time, as growing water scarcity elevates the scarcity rents associated
with that resource.

Establishing water markets is only one of many policies that can be pursued
to improve water resource allocation. The size and complexity of the challenge
suggests that the full range of options be explored. One example of the promising
developments is the implementation of French-type river basin management in
southeast Brazil (Rio Doce, Paraíba do Sul). The core of this approach is to have all
stakeholders participate in setting policies, and to ensure that they weigh costs and
quality simultaneously.

Conclusion

Marketization of water and private sector participation are important, but are not a panacea. Ensuring a safe, secure and sustainable water supply in Latin America—where currently only a very small proportion of the sewage is collected and treated—will ultimately require a huge financial investment, and market-oriented policies alone will not alter that fact. For example, in Santiago, Chile at present, only 2 percent of sewage is treated. To achieve total (100 percent) coverage, EMOS has estimated that an investment of about US$600 million will be required in the next 10 to 15 years. And Brazil's Tietê clean-up project has an estimated bill of $1,500 million. Clearly, many countries will be hard-pressed to find the resources required to achieve this very important part of the policy agenda.

Private sector participation and commercialization of public water authorities can certainly help to address Latin America's need for safe and reliable water. Also required will be institutional changes that encourage the development of water markets; better-targeted water subsidy schemes; and community involvement and outreach/educational programs. There are still other mechanisms to promote efficient development and use of water resources, such as development of BOTs and other innovative initiatives. But none of these initiatives will provide a free lunch, or, more to the point, a free drink. Whatever approach is ultimately adopted, the costs will be very large. Unfortunately, the costs of *not* meeting sustainable water use objectives are even greater.

Endnotes

[1] The natural monopoly condition is strongest in distribution of water and collection of household wastes, rather than collection of water (either from surface sources or underground aquifers) or water treatment. However, legal, administrative and contracting costs render even the latter activities substantially less than fully competitive. If legal institutions can be developed to reduce the contracting costs associated with multiple participants in water supply and waste removal and treatment, these markets may become open to competition "in the market" as opposed to just "for the market."

[2] World Bank Water Demand Research Team 1993, p. 48.

[3] In Cartagena, Colombia, for example, the public utility providing water and sewerage had made no investments in the 11 years prior to its turning operations over to the private sector (Rivera 1996, p. 23).

[4] In addition, the inadequate sanitation infrastructure, due in part to utilities' financial pressures resulting from the social tariff approach, has had environmental impacts that were particularly harmful for the poor. This is because untreated wastewater (from both residential and industrial sources) frequently is shunted away from higher-priced land around high-income areas and directed to low-value land, where the poor are likely to reside.

[5] See Chapter 2 for a discussion of income inequality in Latin America.

[6] This is another example of the costs of income inequality. Absent such inequality, pressures to provide subsidized services—the benefits of which often go largely to the nonpoor—would be easier for governments to resist.

[7] This outcome is not surprising. Once any group is designated by the government as "deserving" some preferential treatment, another group may claim that its presubsidy circumstances were not materially different from the designated "deserving" group (a horizontal equity argument), or that the postsubsidy welfare rankings differ unfairly from the presubsidy rankings, leading to pressures to extend the subsidies (Owen and Braeutigam 1978). The political connections and strategic political importance of the middle-and upper-income groups can lead to subsidies being extended eventually to all consumers. In the absence of metering, possibilities for arbitrage may also complicate efforts to price-discriminate in favor of the poor in providing water services.

[8] See Chapter 4 for evidence on the extent of macroeconomic volatility in Latin American countries. This volatility, and the pressures it put on government budgets, made it impractical to rely on large government general-revenue subsidies to operate and expand water and sewerage systems.

[9] See the International Conference on Water and the Environment 1992: The Dublin Statement and Report of the Conference, World Meteorological Organization, Geneva.

[10] The "subsidiarity" principle also implies that the government and public enterprise utilities should reserve for themselves only the functions that are not of private sector interest.

[11] A recent World Bank multicountry study (World Bank Water Demand Research Team 1993) has developed an effective method for assessing the demand for improved water services. The study included three sites in Latin America: Haiti (Whittington et al. 1990) and northeast and southeast Brazil (Briscoe et al. 1990). This study confirmed some broad hypotheses: willingness to pay was systematically related to the socioeconomic situation of the family, and to the relative attractiveness—distance, quality and reliability—of the new and existing supplies. In performing this marketing task, it is essential that women be adequately represented in the community liaison group, both in numbers and in opportunities to freely express their views. Because of traditional household labor division, the costs of inadequate or inconvenient water supplies often fall on female household members. See Rathberger (1995) and Zwarteveen (1995) for a discussion of this issue in the African context.

[12] Underestimating the limits of affordability and the price elasticity of demand can wreak havoc with commercialization efforts. In Conakry, Guinea, a lease contract for water supply resulted in greatly expanded (public) investment in water supply infrastructure. That increased the quality of water available and the number of connections, as well as raising the proportion of *metered* household connections from 5 percent to 95 percent. To cover costs, the price of piped water was raised from 24 cents per cubic meter in 1989 to 90 cents in 1995. This proved too high for such a low-income area: almost a third of all connections are now inactive because of nonpayment, and financial losses are large (Rivera 1996).

[13] See Alfaro (1996a).

[14] Note the similarities here to the Birdsall and Londoño "horizontal model" of social service provision (Chapter 5). In particular, they emphasize the impact of transforming social service recipients into consumers, whose consumption decisions provide producers the incentives and information that are the basis of efficient allocation in market-based systems.

[15] Here is another area where sensitivity to affordability, service level, and price may have a payoff. In low-income countries, where targeted subsidies to the poor may not be an option, an alternative may be to offer a menu of service/price packages. The offered packages can be structured so that consumers with different income levels "self-select" into the option intended for them, with little leakage due to well-off consumers choosing the package intended for the poor. See Srinagesh and Bradburd (1989).

[16] Subsidies are also provided for health, housing and education services.

[17] It could have an *indirect* impact, because total household expenditures on water are influenced by the level of the water subsidy. The impact would presumably be smaller if subsidies are reduced as a result of reductions in poverty. Studies indicate income elasticities of demand for water consumption of between .1 and .5 and price elasticities for residential consumers in the range of -.3 to -.6 (Rivera 1996, citing Cestti, Yepes and Dianderas 1996).

[18] In Cancún, Mexico, water tariffs become very high at consumption levels above 15,000 cubic meters per month, and some hotels are investigating the possibility of disconnecting from the system and obtaining water from desalinization plants (Rivera 1996).

[19] Externalities loom large here. The costs of nonprovision of sewerage services to an individual family, depending on topography and hydrology, may not be that large; the costs to families, as a community, of inadequate sewerage are high.

[20] EMOS in 1993 had about two employees per 1,000 water connections. Taking into account contractors' personnel, the figure is still below three.

[21] By appeasement pricing, we mean extending subsidized prices to middle-and upper-income groups.

[22] The social tariff is not the only causal factor here: inefficiency has played a large role as well. If water utilities in Latin America were operating on the efficiency frontier, current tariffs would cover a much higher percentage of operating costs. We discuss this issue further below.

[23] See Alfaro (1996b).

[24] See *World Development Report 1994: Infrastructure for Development* (Washington, D.C.: World Bank, 1994, p. 37) for a more detailed discussion of this issue.

[25] See Idelovitch and Ringskog (1995) for a more complete discussion of concession arrangements, as well as other forms of private sector participation such as BOT, BOOT, reverse BOOT, and joint owner-ship arrangements.

[26] This section draws heavily on Idelovitch and Ringskog (1995).

[27] This is an example of how the "social good" characteristic of water may have led to well-intentioned policies that thwarted efficient functioning of a market for water, ultimately working to the detriment of the poor whom the policies were presumably intended to protect.

[28] Rodrik and Zeckhauser (1988) discuss sovereign government's difficulty in making credible commit-ments not to "change the rules of the game." Multilaterals' involvement in the project facilitates the government making such a credible commitment.

[29] By the same token, if political shifts cause frequent abrogation of contracts, the viability of private-financed investment in water and sewerage sanitation is likely to be threatened. Problems of this sort have arisen in Tucuman Province, Argentina and Puerto Vallarta, Mexico. Indeed, in Caracas, Venezu-ela, private investors have been discouraged from bidding for concessions because they lacked faith in the political commitment to the process of private participation (Rivera 1996).

[30] Only in rare cases—Santiago is one—has there been an explicit regulatory framework for public sec-tor utilities in a developing country context.

[31] It should be noted in this context that "hit-and-run" behavior on the part of firms is encouraged when property rights are not secure. Presumably the institutional changes occurring in Latin America will serve to discourage opportunistic behavior on the part of private business entities.

[32] See Bradburd (1996) for a more detailed discussion of the roots and consequences of regulatory rigidity.

[33] See de Yeregui (1996) for greater detail on this issue.

[34] The approach in industrialized countries has generally been to "set the standards and then think about raising the money." The shortcomings are apparent in Europe (where it will take Germany, at current investment levels, over 40 years to meet current EU wastewater standards) and in the United States, where the "unfunded mandates" debate has become a major one.

[35] A similar argument is articulated in Chapter 9 by Estelle James. James argues that reforms of traditional social security systems do not necessarily entail a sacrifice in equity in pursuit of efficiency, largely because the traditional systems were less equity-oriented than the public perceived them to be.

References

Afsah, Shakebm, Benoit Laplante, and David Wheeler. 1996. Controlling Industrial Pollution: A New Paradigm. Policy Research Working Paper 1672, The World Bank, Washington, D.C.

Alfaro, Raquel. 1996a. Linkages between Municipalities and Utilities: An Experience in Overcoming Urban Poverty. Paper presented to the Round Table: The Provision of Services for the Urban Poor in LAC. World Bank, Washington, D.C.

———. 1996b. Introducción de la Competencia en un Monopolio Natural y del Elemento Social en un Gestión Empresarial. *Privatización y Responsabilidad Social, Programa de Gestión Urbana PGU Oficina Regional para América Latina y el Caribe.* Serie Gestión Urbana, Volumen 5.

———. 1996c. The Metropolitan Sanitary Company, Santiago, Chile: Results of a Shared Effort. *Report of Beijing Water Conference,* UNCHS, 1996.

Bazzanella, Vera L. 1995. Tarifas Sociais no Brasil. Prosanear Project, Brasilia.

Bradburd, Ralph. 1995. Privatization of Natural Monopoly Enterprises: The Regulation Issue. *Review of Industrial Organization,* June.

———. 1996. Regulatory Rigidity: Causes, Consequences and Policy Implications for LDCs. Williams College Research Memorandum Series # 152, February.

Briscoe, John. 1993. When the Cup Is Half Full: Improving Water and Sanitation Services in the Developing World. *Environment* 35(4): 7-37.

———. 1995. Financing Water and Sanitation Services: The Old and New Challenges. Keynote address to The World Congress of the International Water Supply Association, Durban.

Briscoe, John, P.F. de Castro, C. Griffin, J. North and O. Olsen. 1990. Towards Equitable and Sustainable Rural Water Supplies: A Contingent Valuation Study in Brazil. *World Bank Economic Review.*

Cestti, Rita, Guillermo Yepes, and Augusta Dianderas. 1996. Managing Demand for Urban Water Utilities. Mimeo. Transport, Water and Urban Development Department, World Bank, Washington, D.C.

de Melo, José Carlos. 1985. Sistemas Condominiais de Esgotos. *Engenharia Sanitária* 24(2).

de Soto, Hernando. 1997. Converting Assets to Capital. Presentation at Conference on Inequality-Reducing Growth in Latin America's Market Economies, January 28th, Inter-American Development Bank, Washington, D.C.

de Yeregui, C. 1996. Concession des services d'eau et d'assainissement de Buenos Aires. EDI/UADE Seminar on Private Sector Participation in the Water Sector, Johannesburg, July.

Financial Times. 1996. Brazil's Pioneer Limeira Project Attracts State and Federal Interest. *Financial Times World Briefing* 54 (February).

Foster, Vivien. 1996. Policy Issues for the Water and Sanitation Sectors. Infrastructure and Financial Markets Division, Social Programs and Sustainable Development Dept., Inter-American Development Bank, Washington, D.C.

Gilman, R.H., and P. Skillicorn. 1985. Boiling of Drinking Water: Can a Fuel-Scarce Community Afford It? *Bulletin of the World Health Organization* 63(1): 157-63.

Graham, Carol. 1994. *Safety Nets, Politics, and the Poor: Transitions to Market Economies*. Washington, D.C.: The Brookings Institution.

Howitt, R., N. Moore and R.T. Smith. 1992. A Retrospective on California's 1991 Emergency Drought Water Bank. California Department of Water Resources, Sacramento.

Idelovitch, Emanuel, and Klas Ringskog. 1995. *Private Sector Participation in Water Supply and Sanitation in Latin America*. Washington, D.C.: The World Bank.

Owen, Bruce M., and R. Braeutigam. 1978. *The Regulation Game: Strategic Use of the Administrative Process*. Cambridge, MA: Ballinger.

Pena, Humberto T. 1996. Water Markets in Chile: What They Are, How They Have Worked and What Needs to be Done to Strengthen Them. Fourth Annual World Bank Conference on Environmentally Sustainable Development, Washington D.C., September.

Petrie, A.H. 1989. *El Gasto Público Social y Sus Efectos Distributivos*. Santiago: ECIEL.

Rathberger, Eva. 1995. Women, Men and Water Resource Management in Africa. Mimeo.

Rivera, Daniel. 1996. *Private Sector Participation in the Water Supply and Wastewater Sector: Lessons from Six Developing Countries*. The World Bank: Washington, D.C.

Rodrik, Dani, and Richard Zeckhauser. 1988. The Dilemma of Government Responsiveness. *Journal of Policy Analysis and Management* 7(4): 601-620.

Sen, Amartya. 1995. *Inequality Re-examined*. Harvard University Press.

Srinagesh, Padmanabhan, and Ralph Bradburd. 1989. Quality Distortion by a Discriminating Monopolist. *American Economic Review* (March).

Watson, Gabrielle. 1992. Water and Sanitation in São Paulo, Brazil: Successful Strategies for Service Provision in Low-Income Communities. Masters Thesis in City Planning. Cambridge: MIT Press.

Williamson, Oliver. 1983. Credible Commitments: Using Hostages to Support Exchange. *American Economic Review* 73(4) (September):519-540.

World Bank. 1992. Development and the Environment. *World Development Report, 1992.* Washington, D.C.: Oxford University Press for IBRD.

————. 1994. Infrastructure for Development. *World Development Report, 1994.* Washington, D.C.: Oxford University Press for IBRD.

World Bank Water Demand Research Team. 1993. The Demand for Water in Rural Areas: Determinants and Policy Implications. *The World Bank Research Observer* 8:1.

Zwarteveen, Margreet. 1995. Linking Women to the Main Canal: Gender and Irrigation Management. International Institute for Environment and Development, Gatekeeper Series.

CHAPTER ELEVEN

Inequality and Growth: Implications for Public Finance and Lessons from Experience in the United States

Joseph Stiglitz

Economists once spoke about tradeoffs between equity and efficiency as if one were separate from the other. That thinking was based on the first and second fundamental theorems of welfare economics, in particular the assumption that efficient redistribution could be carried out through lump-sum taxes and transfers.[1] Now developments in the real world, together with advances in the theory of public finance, have fundamentally altered this premise. One striking example is the East Asian miracle, which has demonstrated that more egalitarian distributions may be growth-enhancing. More recently, some Latin American countries have found that if reforms promote efficiency in several economic sectors, they can also have positive effects on equity.

There is much room for optimism regarding this. Our recent experience in the United States lends some insights into the possibilities of reforms, as well as the tradeoffs. Although we explicitly seek policies that promote both equality and growth, often those objectives cannot be simultaneously achieved. In these cases, additional policy measures are necessary to ensure that those at the bottom are not too disadvantaged by the inevitable tradeoffs many policies entail.

The lessons from the United States are relevant to Latin America for several reasons. First, countries throughout Latin America have been adopting the market-oriented economic model that has long characterized the United States. At the same time, virtually every country in the region, except Cuba, now has a democratic government. Thirdly, Latin America's approach to social welfare policies resembles the United States' "liberal market" approach more than the universal welfare systems common in Europe. Finally, the region's income distribution patterns are closer to those in the United States than to those in Europe.

Yet Latin America differs substantially from the United States in institutional development, an area that is critical to effective public investments. The institutional framework necessary to effectively represent public preferences, and then to channel the investments that result from public choices, is far less developed in Latin America than in the United States. Institutional underdevelopment does not preclude the possibility of public investments that can simultaneously enhance efficiency and equity. Yet by reducing the effectiveness of those investments, it may exacerbate tradeoffs in the areas and sectors where they exist.

The first section of this chapter sets out the theoretical framework of the "new public finance." The second explains the importance of public investments in education, an area where growth can be promoted at the same time that inequality is reduced. While this is a win-win situation, other situations can be double losses, where growth may be impaired and inequality increased. The third section of the chapter discusses how certain kinds of tax cuts fall into that category. The fourth section explains how trade liberalization is a policy area with real possibilities for an equity-efficiency tradeoff.

The final section concludes with a warning about excessive focus on win-win situations. Although there is considerable scope for these, the hardest questions involve hard choices. These choices have often been submerged in the political discourse. The United States may be embarking on a path of lower growth—and less inequality—than would have been chosen in a more open policy debate. Choices about public investments in Latin America, and the tradeoffs that result, are similarly affected by the nature of public debate.

Distortionary Taxation and Enhancing Economic Growth

While it has long been recognized that income and other commonly used taxes are distortionary, recent theory has attempted to explain why taxation is essentially *always* distortionary.[2] We don't have lump-sum taxes that vary according to the ability and other immutable conditions of individuals. Taxes are distortionary because *real* governments have distributive objectives, and thus wish to impose different taxes on different individuals. However, the variables they can use for differentiating taxes are changeable. The instruments of tax policy that are required to implement distributive objectives are endogenous—that is, they entail *basing taxes on variables that are affected by tax policy.*

Tax policy cannot be implemented without impacts on individual behavior that go beyond the pure income effects. That is, lump-sum taxes, which individuals can do nothing to avoid, affect behavior—because individuals have less to spend, must reduce their spending on some goods, and typically respond by reducing their expenditures on most, if not all, goods. Thus, all taxation has distortionary effects. The same can be said for all means-tested expenditure programs, including welfare and Medicaid. So long as benefits depend on variables that are affected by individual behavior, they will be distortionary; and since there is no way to assess eligibility other than by looking at such variables, distortions are unavoidable.

Because taxes are distortionary, it is important to consider how individuals will change their behavior *after* taxes. There always is a reaction to the tax system, whether it is to avoid or to exploit the tax regime. (And note that a symmetric argument applies for the effect of public expenditure on individual consumption). In the past we considered the before-tax earnings (or at least wage) distribution as given, or roughly given. Analyses of optimal taxation assessed the tradeoff between the after-tax distribution and the level of national income. But, in fact, tax policy affects the *before-tax* distribution of income in a variety of ways. For instance, tax policy affects savings, thus capital accumulation. A more circuitous but potentially equally powerful effect is the impact of taxes on wage distribution. Taxes on capital (or profits), for instance, can affect the distribution of earnings: If we assume that skilled and unskilled labor have different degrees of complementarity with capital, then any tax that influences investment decisions will also alter the relative demand for skilled and unskilled labor, and thus the distribution of earnings as well. Not only are taxes distortionary, but changes in the tax system may affect the distribution of income in unexpected and complicated ways. (Again, the same can be said for direct government expenditures.)

The key question is: Given that taxes are distortionary, what measures would affect the *before-tax* distribution of income in ways that improve equity? For if there are such measures, we don't have to use distortionary redistributive taxes to the same extent to achieve a given income distribution. In general, it would be desirable to engage in policies that change the *ex ante* distribution—even if such policies are somewhat distortionary—to reduce the distortionary burden of the *ex post* redistributive policies.

Efficiency with Equity: Policies to Increase Spending for Preschool Programs and College Education

The importance of education as a public investment priority in the United States is reflected in budgetary trends in recent years. The logic behind assigning such a high priority to education is that improved access to education can lead to lower inequality together with faster growth.

The growth effects of education are well documented.[3] A large body of evidence demonstrates that more educated workers are generally more productive, learn new things faster, and thus are better able to absorb new and changing technologies. All of this is reflected in a wage premium of 5 to 15 percent for each additional year of schooling.[4] For methodological reasons, the macroeconomic consequences of improving education are harder to identify. Correlations that emerge in cross-country regressions, however, support the claim that education increases a country's steady-state level of output.[5]

There are two sources of inequality in wages in a perfectly functioning labor market: differences in human capital and differences in ability. Among individuals of similar abilities, if some have more access to education than others, those with greater access will enjoy a higher income. Poor individuals may either lack the resources to invest in higher education, or may find their implicit cost of capital is so high that education is not a desirable investment. Moreover, elementary and secondary schools in poor neighborhoods may be less effective than schools in richer neighborhoods, and thus children in poorer neighborhoods get less "human capital" during those critical years. If elementary and secondary education complement tertiary education, then disadvantaged children will also derive a lower return to investments in tertiary education.[6] In addition, some children receive less human capital at home than do others, so that if home and school-based human capital are complementary, the returns to publicly provided schooling will be lowered.

There is evidence that all three sources of inequality are present in the United States: poorer children start school with educational disadvantages; the quality of education that they are provided in public schools is poorer; and they have less access to higher education.

Lack of access, in turn, means that the United States is not investing efficiently in its human resources. Consider the following evidence. In the United States the overall returns to education have increased substantially in the last 15 years.[7] For example, the income differential between a high school graduate and a college graduate has almost doubled.[8] Yet in spite of the fact that there are such high returns to college education, not everybody in our society has been responding in the same way. For children of upper- and middle-income individuals, enrollment rates in universities have been increasing substantially. This is not the case with children of lower-income families: for them, the response has been relatively small. The result has been an increasing disparity in enrollment rates in college of children of upper- and lower-income families.[9] Why is it that some groups—such as the children of poor families or minorities—continue to invest so much less than others? Why, in particular, did some groups respond so differently to the huge changes in the returns to education? The answer to this question lies in three rather obvious factors.

First, there are no perfect capital markets, and over the last 20 years the mean income of families in the bottom income quintile has decreased in real terms.[10] Parents with low incomes cannot afford to send their children to college and, since people cannot borrow against their future income, neither they nor their children can borrow for it.

Second, the cost of going to college has increased. Over the last decade, tuition payments in public universities and colleges have increased by 50 percent in real terms.[11] It is not that the cost of education has increased that much. State subsidies have not kept pace with the increase in costs. As a result, the tuition charged in public two- and four-year colleges has increased at a much faster pace than the increase in the cost of education (i.e., than the increase in wages and salaries of educational workers).

Finally, between 1980 and 1994 the real value of the maximum Pell grant, the main federal program for low-income students, decreased by more than 25 percent.[12] The roughly 10 percent increase in real terms in the last three years has only partially reversed the erosion of this crucial program.[13]

The net result is underinvestment in higher education, particularly by children of poor families. The implication for policy is clear: a policy that supports investment in college education, particularly by the poor, would both promote economic growth and increase equality (by affecting the pretax distribution of income). This was the rationale for increases in federal support for college education during the Clinton administration, even in a period when there were cuts in overall fiscal expenditure. Two major programs provided support for college education: a new direct lending program[14] and a significant expansion of the Pell grant program. In addition, a program of tax deductions and tax credits for going to college for lower- and middle-income individuals was proposed.[15]

This was coupled with efforts to improve the overall equality of educational opportunity at each point in the production process. The program of Goals 2000 sought to improve standards in all schools; and since there was particular concern about standards in the poorer schools, the students in these schools stood to benefit most.[16] It tried to redesign federal assistance to poor schools to target more of the money to the most needy through, for example, the school construction initiative, although those efforts were blunted by Congress.

Another area that was accorded considerable effort to improve educational equity is preschool education. Funding for Head Start (a program for disadvantaged preschool children to prepare them for going to regular school) by 1997 had increased 43 percent over its 1993 level.[17] The rationale was simple: students who are better prepared when they enter school will do better in school and are less likely to drop out. There is evidence that those enrolled in headstart programs do have lower drop-out rates.

The concern about dropouts was motivated not just by economics. Evidence shows that in the United States, there are large social costs to children not completing high school. The data available do not distinguish causal mechanisms, but there is a clear association between criminality and lack of high school education.[18] On any particular day, something like 25 percent of males between the ages of 18 and 35 who are not high school graduates are in the ambits of the criminal justice system. One out of four is either in prison or on parole or probation, whereas the corresponding number for high school graduates is 4 percent. A state like California spends more on the construction of prisons than on higher education, and it spends more per year to send a kid to prison than to college.

A number of studies have found a clear link between childhood poverty and failure in school; in fact, knowledge of this link was behind the idea of headstart programs.[19] By the time they are ready for elementary school, children have accumulated a considerable amount of human capital—some more than others. And there is a threshold; a minimum level of private human capital is the necessary complement to the public capital provided by the elementary school. Middle-class children get that capital from their parents, but children that have grown up in poverty do not, and so they end up disadvantaged. The program, in providing that quantum of capital, increases the efficiency of learning and, ultimately, the quantity of learning. It has high returns and it also increases equity.

In sum, I have argued that educational policy may be used to reach both the efficiency and equity objectives of fiscal policy. Interestingly, in this case, both effects are produced through the labor market. In particular, the equity effect flows from an investment that increases the capacity to earn income; it does not flow from a post-tax income transfer.[20]

Inefficiency with Inequity, or Vice-Versa: Undesirable Tax Reforms

While educational reforms represented a win-win situation, where growth and equity could be increased, there was also considerable political pressure to enact lose-lose policies, which could lower growth and increase inequity. To be sure, the debate was not framed that way. Tax reform is also justified in terms of its benefits to growth and equity. But much of the impetus for tax reform came from upper-income individuals who pay a significant fraction of their income in taxes.

The "argument" for tax reform often begins with a legitimate source of concern: the low U.S. saving rate and its consequences for investment. A number of people have argued that we ought to encourage savings through a change in the tax structure. The argument for it is simple: A lower tax on income from savings is equivalent to an increase in the effective interest rate, and higher interest rates lead to higher saving.

The argument, however, is disingenuous. The interest elasticity of savings is low. It would take a very large increase in the expected post-tax effective real interest rate to induce most Americans to save significantly more. Moreover, the American middle class already has much of its savings exempt from taxation (through Individual Retirement Accounts and, more importantly, through pensions).

The effect on aggregate savings may well be negative, as the lower tax revenue leads to an increase in the fiscal deficit (negative government savings) that is greater than the induced private savings. (This is the case for most reasonable estimates of the elasticity of supply of savings.) And as savings is decreased, growth will be decreased. At the same time, the primary beneficiaries will be upper-income individuals—those with significant savings.

In sum, the whole debate on tax relief on savings, while it was presented as in the "national interest of raising the American savings rate," was really one for tax breaks for the very rich. This is an example of a lose-lose reform: lose on growth, lose on equity.

Efficiency-Equity Tradeoffs: Trade Policy

The previous sections tackled a fairly easy target: find the win-win solutions and apply them, and avoid lose-lose reforms. What happens when there *are* tradeoffs? How do we deal with them in a world without neutral lump-sum taxes, where we no longer believe that government can satisfy everyone? The issue then is how to compensate losers.

This problem is exemplified through the concurrent debate over another important policy issue in the United States: trade liberalization. As is well known, the push for open trade (e.g., the Uruguay Round, NAFTA) has been opposed by strong, well-organized groups. There is no question that many of these groups have lost or will lose with lower trade barriers; for example, imports have driven parts of the American textile industry into decline. (Interestingly, the United States has become a major *net exporter* of textiles. But this is due entirely to the high-tech and capital-intensive branches of the industry. The bottom end of the market has lost out to cheaper and better imports and, of course, consumers have gained.)

In fact, for the United States as a whole, exports have increased enormously over the last four years, rising 37 percent in real terms.[21] Indeed, exports account for almost one-third of the overall growth in the economy.[22] Trade has been one of the real engines of recent economic growth in the United States.[23] The problem is that the net gain has been realized along with concern about a negative distribution effect concentrated at the bottom end of income distribution—precisely where people have seen their real incomes fall. From this association it has been easy to argue that trade has *caused* the fall in income. A more comprehensive analysis shows that trade is just one of several factors that may have contributed to increasing inequality; and according to some, it accounts for almost none.[24] Other factors like technology play a far more dominant role.

There are two clear implications for those of us concerned about equity: first, it is important to recognize that some may be adversely affected by trade—or by technological change. There is a market failure: individuals cannot buy insurance against these risks, and they often cannot borrow to buy the training required to move into a new job. But the rationale for government action goes beyond the market failures. The government has a responsibility for assisting individuals in the transition (through training or loans). The second implication is that the assistance should not be limited to those adversely affected by trade (indeed, ascertaining the cause of a job loss is often a hopeless exercise).

The public investment in the transition safety net could have high returns: by facilitating the transition, it reduces the time individuals spend being unproductive between jobs. But even if there were limited direct efficiency gains, the transition safety net would be desirable, and not just on arguments for "fairness"—that a few should not bear the costs of a reform that benefits society as a whole.

In addition to the efficiency and equity arguments, another rationale for building the transition safety net is based on political economy: Because we are convinced that the overall returns to trade are large, it is important to have this kind of assistance to build stronger constituencies *for trade reform*. This is an example where there can be a positive indirect interplay between efficiency and equity, if you have the right programs in place. Without those programs, political resistance will be greater, and it will be harder to effect an efficiency-enhancing move.

Conclusion

There are many opportunities for simultaneously improving equity and efficiency (growth). We should be actively engaged in looking for these opportunities. However, not all social and economic problems can be approached with win-win policies: there are hard tradeoffs that any society must face. Decisions are made all too often in a piecemeal way, without a hard look at their full implications.

Two obvious examples come to mind: Under current projections, by the middle of the next century, the United States will be spending about 20 percent of its GDP on entitlement programs for the elderly.[25] Many of these elderly are not poor. In fact, the poverty rate among the elderly today is lower than in the population as a whole, and this trend may well continue.[26] Indeed, under Medicare, elderly millionaires are subsidized by poor workers—hardly an improvement in equity.[27] Moreover, the progressivity of these programs may be seriously mitigated by the fact that wealthier individuals tend to live longer.

The entitlement programs can be reformed in ways that reduce the drain on the federal government while providing additional funds for growth-enhancing investments. These are examples of win-win policies. But in the course of reform, we face some fundamental choices: Should we cut back somewhat on expenditures for the elderly in order to provide more resources for investment in the future? In the long run, our society may be defined by how those choices are made.

The second example concerns expenditures on science and technology. Under current budget proposals, these will be cut (in real terms) by about 20 percent over the next five years.[28] There is overwhelming evidence that investments in science and technology yield high returns, and that public and private expenditures are complementary. Over the years, investments in science and technology have contributed significantly to U.S. economic growth. Unlike expenditures on education, however, the distributional consequences of investment in technology are not clear. Improved technology has probably contributed to inequality by increasing the relative demand for skilled workers. Also, in a world with balanced budgets and roughly constant taxes as a share of GDP, spending more in one area requires the government to spend less in other areas. Our decision *not* to cut back expendi-

tures more on entitlement programs was an implicit growth-versus-equity decision, but it was not openly made. Would Americans have been willing to accept a
small cutback in these programs, in order to ensure America's technological leadership in the next century?

Similarly in Latin America, there are many opportunities for win-win strategies. More efficient and equitable investments can be made at current public expenditure levels in many sectors, such as health, education, and social security. At
the same time, Latin American countries also face the constraints of balanced budgets, and with a smaller tax base than the United States has. Thus the expenditure
tradeoffs among sectors may be even higher. For instance, the equity benefits of
government investments in small-scale agriculture—to benefit the rural poor, in
countries where small farms are neither competitive nor efficient—must be weighed
in light of the potential growth payoffs of investments in other economic sectors, or
in secondary education. Meanwhile, the fiscal burden of providing a minimum
pension for low-income workers in the social security system, in countries with
large informal sectors, must be considered in light of public expenditures that would
be more broadly shared by poorer workers, such as in public health. Finally, the
underdeveloped institutional framework in Latin America often limits the potential of investments in a number of sectors, where regulatory or delivery systems are
skewed in favor of privileged groups. Many countries simply lack the institutional
framework required to ensure that public investments are broadly shared.

Broad and well-informed democratic debate about the implications of these
investments in Latin America would probably favor investments that contribute to
future growth, rather than current transfers for particular sectors of the population. Just as in the United States, however, the piecemeal nature of the debate, and
the political weight of organized sectors that protect their shares of current expenditures, make it difficult to reallocate such expenditures to investments without
immediately visible benefits. Yet the current reform context in Latin America, and
the institutional changes already achieved under democratic auspices, allow cautious optimism about the prospects for improving efficiency and equity in public
finance in the region.[29]

Endnotes

[1] The fact that people thought the two could be separate, already suggests that certain elements of the theory were always remote from the *realpolitik* of policymaking.

[2] For a general discussion, see Stiglitz (1988).

[3] See Chapter 5 of this volume.

[4] For a general survey, see Willis (1986). More recently, see Kane and Rouse (1995) and Ashenfelter and Krueger (1994).

[5] See Barro (1991) and Mankiw, Romer, and Weil (1992).

[6] For present purposes, it matters little why these schools provide less human capital—whether it is lower expenditures, or, for instance, externalities arising from the mix of students in the classroom, or from less effective monitoring from parents.

[7] Psacharopoulos (1993).

[8] CEA (1997a), p. 167.

[9] Choy and Premo (1996).

[10] U.S. Census. *Historical Income and Poverty Tables.* The dispute over the appropriate measure of inflation casts some doubt on the comparison of real income levels across time. (http://www.census.gov/hhes/income/histinc/f03.html).

[11] U.S. Bureau of the Census, *Statistical Abstract of the United States: 1996.* Government Printing Office, Washington, D.C. Table no. 290.

[12] CEA (1996).

[13] Unpublished Office of Management and Budget data.

[14] One may ask, why choose to do directed credit instead of lending through the banking system? Why not use the private sector? These are good questions. But the problem is that, as it is implemented in the United States, the privately administered educational loan program leads to an inefficient use of resources. Under the program, the federal government maintains the residual risk and gives a large fee to the banks to administer the program. They bear no risk and get a high return. At the Council of Economic Advisors, we tried to suggest that if the private sector were to be engaged in this, it ought at least to face competition: to accept a competitive bidding process for the determination of the administrative fee. This idea was not well received. The banks in the program were only enthusiastic about private markets without competition. With competition, there would be no super-normal profits—and what would be the point of the whole exercise if profits were eroded!

Because we could not get a competitive private lending program, the Administration introduced a direct lending program with a lower cost of lending. More important than that, we also introduced a new lending instrument, one which it would have been hard for the private sector to administer. Among the options given students was one in which the amount that the student repays is related to his/her income. The design is a bit like the variable-rate mortgages that they have in England, where payments are fixed but the maturity of the debt is variable, and could be extended through capitalization of interest due. In the program, after 20 or 25 years, the loan is forgiven. If the student goes into a low-paying job like teaching, the amount paid back would essentially be subsidized. The view is that most children do not think about a 25-year horizon in their lives, so they won't choose to go into a low-paying profession just to avoid repaying the loan in full. In other words, our view was that the moral hazard created by the possible subsidy would not lead to a serious distortion in the labor market. (It will take 25 years, unfortunately, to find out whether there is a significant moral hazard effect.)

[15] These tax deductions and credits should, however, be viewed more as part of a program of tax reductions than a program of education expenditures. There is considerable doubt over the efficacy of these tax deductions and credits in increasing enrollments, and a general consensus that if increasing enrollment were the objective, it would have been better to spend the money in enhanced Pell grants, or in some other expenditure program. For political reasons, the Administration wanted to reduce taxes; given that taxes were to be reduced, the challenge was to find ways of doing so that might have some educational benefits, or more broadly improve the pretax distribution of income.

[16] There was some concern that the program could have adverse effects: if the poorest schools were not able to bring their students up to those standards, then the gap between them and the rest of the country could actually increase. Employers would have a legitimate reason not to hire students who failed to meet the standards, and thus children from these schools would face even more dismal employment opportunities. Advocates of Goals 2000 believed that increasing public attention—and support—would be provided to these schools, as the disparity in performance became increasingly visible.

[17] OMB (1997b).

[18] Freeman (1991).

[19] For a review of the literature, see Barnett (1992). See also Currie and Thomas (1995).

[20] Of course, not all decisions about educational policy favor equity and efficiency. Consider the case of subsidies for R&D and for science and technology more broadly. There is considerable evidence that the rates of return on some of these investments are higher than on investments in college education. Yet, it is clearly going to another group in the population. These funds support the elite research institutions that are typically related to the upper-income groups. It may be, therefore, that by focusing on areas where there is a complementarity between efficiency and equity we are giving up things where the growth returns might be higher.

[21] CEA (1997b).

[22] Author's calculations using the above.

[23] Trade's contribution to growth is, admittedly, small when estimated by the standard static analysis of the gains to trade. In fact, as the economy moves to full employment, the link between trade and growth is not at all obvious. But the point is that, induced by external demand, trade directs resources from sectors where they are less productive to sectors where they are more productive. This is comparative advantage at work — and it may generate significant gains in efficiency (productivity). Back in the 19th century, manufacturing was the frontier. Resources moved from agriculture to manufacturing and that shift was one of the major identifiable sources of growth (see, for example, Edward Denison, *Accounting for United States Economic Growth, 1929-1969*, Washington, D.C.: Brookings, 1974). Today, the frontier is the external market, and moving resources into the export sector enables us to move from less productive to more productive sectors. The main effect on growth appears in the so-called "residual." By definition it does not appear in the standard models that are based on an accounting framework designed to exclude the residual, or most of it.

[24] Jagdish Bhagwati, "Play It Again Sam: Yet Another Look at Trade and Wages" (unpublished manuscript, 1997). The reasoning is simple: Trade is supposed to hurt low-wage workers by lowering the relative price of unskilled-labor-intensive products, thereby decreasing the U.S. domestic demand for unskilled labor, and thereby decreasing their equilibrium relative wage. But while trade has expanded enormously, there has not been a large decrease in the relative price of unskilled labor-intensive products. These results are not inconsistent with the observation that particular workers in particular industries lose their jobs, as the factories in which they work shut down. The effect on wages depends on the overall demand for unskilled and skilled labor; and trade creates new jobs as it destroys others.

[25] CEA (1997a), p. 97.

[26] Defined-benefit social security systems are regressive to the extent that the wealthy tend to live longer than the poor. See Chapter 9 by Estelle James.

[27] Premiums pay only one-quarter of the cost of seeing doctors (Part B), with the remaining cost picked up by the Treasury, and thus subsidized by taxpayers more broadly.

[28] OMB (1997a).

[29] The institutional changes that are still required, the political obstacles to making them, and the prospects for success, are the subject of this volume's final chapter.

References

Ashenfelter, Orley, and Alan Krueger. 1994. Estimates of Economic Returns to Schooling from a New Sample of Twins. *American Economic Review* (December).

Barnett, W. Stephen. 1992. Benefits of Compensatory Preschool Education. *Journal of Human Resources* 27(2): 279-312.

Barro, Robert. 1991. Economic Growth in a Cross Section of Countries. *Quarterly Journal of Economics* 106 (May).

CEA (Council of Economic Advisers). 1996. Economic Report of the President 1996. Washington, D.C.: Government Printing Office, p. 216.

———. 1997a. *Economic Report of the President 1997*. Washington, D.C.: Government Printing Office, pp. 97, 167.

———. 1997b. *Economic Indicators, June 1997.* Washington, D.C.: Government Printing Office.

Choy, Susan, and Mark Premo. 1996. *How Low-Income Undergraduates Financed Postsecondary Education: 1992-93.* Washington D.C.: National Center for Education Statistics.

Currie, Janet, and Duncan Thomas. 1995. Does Head Start Make a Difference? *American Economic Review* 85:3 (June).

Freeman, Richard. 1991. Crime and the Employment of Disadvantaged Youths. NBER Working Paper No 3875.

Kane, Thomas, and Cecilia Rouse. 1995. Labor Market Returns to Two and Four-Year College: Is a Credit a Credit and Do Degrees Matter? *American Economic Review* 85(3): 600-614.

Mankiw, N. Gregory, David Romer, and David Weil. 1992. A Contribution to the Empirics of Economic Growth. *Quarterly Journal of Economics* 107 (May).

OMB (Office of Management and Budget). 1997a. *Analytical Perspectives FY 1998.* Washington, D.C.: Government Printing Office.

———. 1997b. *Budget of the United States Government, Fiscal Year 1998.* Washington, D.C.: Government Printing Office.

Psacharopoulos, George. 1993. Returns to Investment in Education–A Global Update. World Bank Policy Research Working Paper No. 1067, Washington, D.C.

Stiglitz, Joseph. 1988. Pareto Efficient and Optimal Taxation and the *New* New Welfare Economics. *Handbook of Public Economics Volume II*, Alan Auerbach and Martin Feldstein (eds). Elsevier Science Publishers/North-Holland, Amsterdam, pp. 991-1042.

Willis, Robert. 1986. Wage Determinants: A Survey and Reinterpretation of Human Capital Earnings Functions. In *Handbook of Labor Economics Volume I*, Orley Ashenfelter and Richard Layard, eds., Elsevier Science Publishers/North-Holland, Amsterdam.

CHAPTER TWELVE

The Political Economy of Institutional Reform in Latin America

Carol Graham and Moisés Naím[1]

Public management is not the arena in which to find Big Answers; it is a world of settled institutions designed to allow imperfect people to use flawed procedures to cope with insoluble problems.

James Q. Wilson[2]

For most of the 1980s and well into the 1990s, macroeconomic stabilization dominated the policy debate in Latin America. The need to tame high inflation, restore growth, and stabilize economies became the obsession of policymakers and scholars alike. This obsession paid off. Latin America's macroeconomic turnaround of the early 1990s has been widely successful.[3] By the mid 1990s, the obsession changed. The goal that now dominates the attention of policymakers, multilateral institutions, and researchers is "institution building." This goal is at the core of many of the win-win, efficiency and equity-enhancing reforms that have been identified throughout this volume.

Unfortunately, institution building in the public sector is less amenable to the kinds of blunt and very visible solutions that tamed macroeconomic instability. The preoccupation with institution building will yield more disappointments and fewer results in the short term than the previous focus on macroeconomic reforms. The diagnosis is correct: In order to reduce poverty and inequality and become more competitive, Latin American countries must significantly increase the number of public institutions with the capacity to achieve their objectives. The problem is not the diagnosis but the prescription, or rather the lack thereof. In fact, "institution building" is a catch-all concept that encompasses a wide variety of goals that have always been at the core of overcoming underdevelopment.

Policymakers are again asking age-old questions: how to improve basic health and education systems, how regulatory systems can function better, who should provide basic services and infrastructure, and how they should be paid for. There has been a "rediscovery" of underdevelopment, and a realization that something is missing in the policy framework. Macrostability, which seemed a major goal in the 1980s, is now seen as only a precondition.

Building the institutions necessary for sustainable growth is a crucial and yet more difficult part of the equation.[4] Institutions are necessary to stimulate growth, and to make it sustainable and broadly shared.[5] The East Asian tigers had much higher growth rates and more equitable patterns of distribution during their take-off years than does Latin America. They also had higher savings and investment rates.[6] Effective institutions, in addition to good macropolicies, were critical to this record.[7] Failure to make progress on this front in Latin America could lead to an electoral backlash against reform, a phenomenon that some observers warn has already begun.[8] Proceeding with institutional reforms across sectors, meanwhile, has tremendous potential to enhance efficiency and equity in the region's growth process.

While macroeconomic and institutional reforms comprise two very distinct stages in the reform process, the shift from one to the next is not always clearly delineated. In most countries there is a *continuing* need for some elements of the first stage—in particular fiscal adjustment and exchange rate management—even after most macroeconomic reforms are in place. Macroeconomic reforms are diverse, yet all of them have three characteristics in common: reform decisions center on changing the rules guiding macroeconomic behavior; reforms are adopted by the executive branch in relative isolation from the rest of the political system; and new policies imply the dismantling of many existing agencies, rather than the building of new organizations.[9] Institutional reforms are quite different, and entail changing organizations and establishing whole new sets of rules: the creation and development of the institutions needed to support the new economic policies (such as regulatory and export promotion agencies, and social safety nets), as well as the upgrading of existing public agencies devastated by decades of neglect, under investment, and capture by special interests.

The motivation for macroeconomic reforms is usually clear: the fear of imminent economic collapse and external pressures from financial markets and international lending agencies. Institutional reforms, however, require a more elusive motivation of a broad national consensus about the direction of economic and social policies. The government must solicit the cooperation and participation of numerous agencies and organizations involved in the provision or regulation of public services. These groups tend to be politically powerful and highly organized, and often have a strong stake in the status quo. Potential beneficiaries of reform—the users of public services—are numerous, but diffuse and poorly organized. Reform of public institutions takes time, and the results (such as improvements in education or judicial services) are not easily measurable. Yet these are precisely the results that are critical to Latin America's achieving an inclusive and equitable growth path.[10]

Despite these difficulties, many countries in the region have implemented reforms across a range of institutions, with varying degrees of progress among the countries, as well as differences in results of similar reforms. We identify three such stages: a stable and open economy; a competent economy; and a competitive economy[11] (see Table 1). These stages are characterized by the mix and extent of reforms undertaken. A stable and open economy is capable of regaining stability in the face of various kinds of shocks; a competent economy is capable of sustaining macroeconomic equilibrium; and a competitive economy can both sustain stability and support export sectors that are competitive on the world market and have value added beyond primary products such as minerals and petroleum.

While there is increasing consensus on the need for institution building and reform, and governments and multilateral banks are beginning to designate substantial amounts of resources towards these objectives, there is little intellectual clarity about how to achieve them. There is confusion about the definition of institutions and about the different kinds of institutions. Without a clear diagnosis of the diverse sorts of institutional failure and underperformance, there can be little agreement on strategies for reform. There is even less clarity about the wide range of political dynamics that underlie institutional failure or underperformance. The scope of sectors is extremely broad, ranging from education to telecommunications to the judiciary.

These issues are very complex, and far too numerous to be addressed here. Instead, this chapter will suggest a framework to organize the thinking about institutional reform. First, we review some of the approaches to defining institutions; a more detailed review appears in the appendix to this chapter. Next, we attempt to clarify the general concept of institutions, and then provide a taxonomy of the typical failures and causes of underperformance among various institutions. We identify the costs that these failures have for both efficiency and equity. We then review the general political conditions that, while not sufficient, are necessary to ensure a minimal probability of success for institutional reform, and then suggest some strategies for implementation. In the final section, we discuss the prospects for institutional reform in Latin America.

Table 1. Stages of Economic Reforms

LEVEL OF ECONOMY	Financial reform	Macroeconomic stabilization	Pension reform	Privatization	Trade	Effective social services	Judicial reform	Tax reform	Labor reform
Stable, open	Advanced	Advanced	Advanced	Advanced	Advanced	Almost none	Almost none	Almost none	Almost none
Competent	Advanced	Advanced	Advanced	Advanced	Advanced	Partial	Almost none	Partial	Almost none
Internationally competitive	Advanced	Advanced	Advanced	Advanced	Advanced	Advanced	Advanced	Partial	Partial

Progress of reforms

Advanced
Partial
Almost none

Source: Authors' categories and IDB (1996).

Towards a Definition of Institutions

The term *institution* has wide-ranging connotations, and has been studied from the perspective of many academic disciplines (see Appendix to this chapter). Institutions have been defined as equilibria, as norms, as rules, and as organizations. Several authors, using different methodologies, have arrived at a definition that encompasses these approaches: institutions are the regulations that stem from repeated human interaction, and that generate credible commitments affecting specific behavior.[12] The institutional framework is structured by rules, norms, and shared strategies, as well as by how those evolve from and interact with the physical environment. Similarly, Douglass North defines institutions as the formal and informal rules governing economic and social behavior, rules that reflect individual countries' histories and cultures.[13]

These definitions suggest that institutions have two rather distinct traits. On the one hand, to be credible and effective, and serve their regulatory functions, institutions have to maintain independence and neutrality. On the other, institutions are to some extent endogenous to the social, economic, and cultural contexts in which they operate. In theory institutions should offer continuity and certainty, providing economic actors a degree of certainty when governments or regimes change. Yet institutions can only have this effect if they are widely known and understood (i.e., have credibility). A certain amount of legitimacy or credibility is necessary to get compliance with rules, and at the same time a certain amount of compliance is necessary to maintain legitimacy. In Latin America, the unpredictability of government intervention and lack of consistent enforcement of private contracts and property rights have had devastating effects on investment and growth.[14] The restrictions that institutions impose must offer incentives for cooperative behavior, so that compliance with rules and norms is not a zero-sum game, but one in which the majority of actors benefit.[15]

Institutions and organizations share many features, and there is an overlap between their functions and definitions. Like institutions, organizations are a collection or bundle of rules and routines, as well as of individual actors. Some institutions have a distinct trait, however, in that they also represent rules (formal and informal) that are *not* expressed in an organizational hierarchy, and that mediate exchanges among and within economic sectors, cities, villages, cultures, and societies. These institutions, which can be thought of as "meta" institutions, are distinguished by their broad mandates, such as the making of laws or the provision of education services. Other institutions, whose mandates are more operational, such as building roads or distributing milk to schoolchildren, are virtually indistinguishable from organizations.

Institutions are ultimately political in nature, as they have authority over the allocation of resources and power. Thus they are not totally independent of the political context in which they operate. While institutions can and at times do assign resources and power in a just and unbiased manner, they are still products of the political balance and bargains that originally gave them respect and authority.[16] In Latin America, even traditionally strong institutions, such as independent Central Banks, have been undermined by determined politicians at times.[17]

Institutions also reflect societal values and differ across societies. In some societies they reflect underlying agreements on more equity, while in others they reflect tolerance for higher levels of inequality, patterns which are then perpetuated by the institutional framework. Alberto Alesina and Roberto Perotti use formal econometric methods to demonstrate that in societies where there are no institutional mechanisms to correct extreme inequality, the poor have greater incentives to engage in rent-seeking activities and/or to vote for populist politicians, both of which hinder investments and growth.[18] And in some countries, as in many in East Asia, institutions reflect an uncompromising commitment to education, while in others, as in many Latin American countries, the importance accorded to basic education is often more theoretical than practical.

A Taxonomy of Institutions

The term *institution* covers a wide range of rules, norms, and sets of actors, which have very different functions, objectives, clients, and geographic scope, have different degrees of discretion in decisionmaking, and are accountable to different kinds and levels of authority. Nevertheless, it is possible to classify different kinds of institutions, both by their function and by the specific traits that characterize their operations.

Broadly speaking, there are four kinds of institutional functions (see Table 2). The first of these is the making of rules and laws. The institutions that fall into this category are legislatures, ministries, municipal councils, and other related bodies. A second category of institutional function is the enforcement and adjudication of rules and laws. The institutions involved here are courts, control boards (in areas such as banking or the environment), and regulatory bodies. The third institutional function is the provision of public services. These are the institutions that guarantee the provision of different types of public services, ranging from transportation

Table 2. Institutional Functions

	Practical examples	Geographic scope and clientele served	Mandate	Degree of autonomy*
Making of rules/laws	Legislatures, ministries, municipal councils, executive, supreme courts	Nationwide—affecting entire populations, wholesale clientele	Broad—output difficult to measure	High—constrained only by constitution and/or executive veto. Ministries constrained by legislature.
Enforcement of rules and laws	Court systems, control boards, regulatory agencies, central banks	Tend to be municipal—a specific clientele, "quasi" public in nature, wholesale clientele	Specific—output is measurable**	Mixed—often subject to public scrutiny, authority handed down by rule-making institutions
Provision of public services	Water and sewage, roadway maintenance, agriculture	Usually a large, measurable population, wholesale/retail clientele	Defined, measurable objectives	Minimal—embedded in bureaucracy and constrained by regulations
Provision of public goods	Defense	"Super/quasi" public, retail clientele	Broad—output difficult to measure	Minimal—"inside" the bureaucracy, relies on public sector
	Education, health and human services	"Quasi" public—operations may vary from region to region, retail clientele		

* Closely related to this category are two others: degree of discretionary decisionmaking and level of accountability required for effective function.

** While specific outputs are measurable, such as numbers of arrests, the measurable outputs do not provide a complete picture of the efficiency and equity of judicial systems.

infrastructure, such as highways, to agricultural extension services. The final category is the provision of public *goods*. These include "super" public goods, such as defense, and "quasi" public goods, such as health and education.[19]

Among these distinct institutional functions, there are major differences in the nature of their objectives. Meta institutions have very broad mandates with outputs that are difficult to measure precisely. Those with more operational mandates have much more specific objectives. There are also differences in the nature of the clients that these institutions serve. Rulemaking bodies may have entire nations as "clients," as do health systems. In contrast, transport agencies can target their clients: the users of transportation services in a particular region. Regulatory agencies can tailor their services to the participants in a particular economic sector, such as banking or telecommunications.

There are also differences in institutions' degree of discretionary decision-making. Lawmaking institutions are usually constrained only by constitutions and/or executive veto. In contrast, law enforcement institutions must adhere to a set code of rules. Ministries are often constrained by both executive objectives and by lawmaking institutions. The organizational locus—where institutions are positioned within the state apparatus—also makes a major difference in how much institutional autonomy they have. Institutions placed outside the "normal" public bureaucracy, such as some regulatory agencies and independent central banks, have far more autonomy than those institutions that are firmly imbedded in the bureaucracy, such as education and health ministries. In addition, the latter must rely on large numbers of personnel within the public sector bureaucracy in order to operate, which makes it more difficult to give them greater autonomy.

Different institutional functions also require different levels of accountability. While the provision of subsidized fertilizers or school lunches does not have to be closely monitored and can be subcontracted out to the private sector, that of defense or justice requires far more public accountability. There are also differences in the products. Some public goods and services are delivered "wholesale," such as defense, laws, or regulatory services. Others must be delivered "retail" and tailored to specific population groups and locations, such as education, health, and social welfare services.

Finally, there are major differences in the geographic scope of institutional functions, which range from locally provided public services, such as the building of roads or schools or the collection of local property taxes, to those that have a broader, national character, such as the making of laws and the provision of defense. There are also differences among countries: some countries treat health and education as "super" public goods that are delivered nationwide from the central government, while others allow a host of local and private providers to participate in the provision of these services, treating them as "quasi" public goods that can be differentiated according to local and individual preferences, and in some cases even privatized.

A Taxonomy of Institutional Malfunction

There are a host of explanations for institutional failure. We have identified three categories into which the most common institutional failures fit, and which apply to most countries (see Table 3). These are resource-related failures, politically driven failures, and systemic or organizational failures. The first of the *resource-related* failures is **chronic congestion:** overdemand for and underfunding of key public services. In most countries in Latin America (and most other developing regions), expectations and demands have far outpaced public sectors' capacities to respond. A combination of growing populations and increased levels of education has raised expectations and public capacities to utilize and demand more public services. Because public services tend to be underfunded, this results in a vicious circle. As overdemand and underfunding reduce the quality of services, those who are able to pay for private services "exit" the system, and then are less willing to pay taxes to finance public ones. This has major implications for equity, particularly in the case of public services that are key to poverty reduction, such as basic health and education. The level of funding for particular services tends to reflect the political power of users more than it does the level of demand for services. Budgets for the military or for universities tend to be more immune to public budget cuts than budgets for prisons or for primary education, for example. A second resource-related failure is **poor or inadequate inputs.** Thus universities receive poorly trained high school students, and regulatory bodies have to manage with inadequate legal frameworks.

A third resource-related malfunction, which is also politically driven, is **concentration of funding on personnel costs.** This leaves insufficient resources and staff attention for the resolution of key organizational issues, and precludes the flexibility that is necessary for institutions to adapt to contextual changes. Another politically driven malfunction is the capture of institutions by special interests. These interests may be public sector unions in some institutions, such as those that provide public services. In others, such as regulatory agencies, they may be powerful agents in the private sector, as in banking or industry.

Table 3. Sources of Institutional Malfunction

Type of malfunction	Source of malfunction	Characteristics	Institutions most at risk
Resource-related	Chronic congestion (overdemand and underfunding)	Typical for new initiatives. Erodes quality, equity, tax/resource base. May limit access to those who wield sufficient influence. Private alternatives flourish.	□ ▲ ❖
	Inadequate input	Insufficiently educated workforce. Lack of thorough, competent legal and regulatory standards, outdated hardware resources.	❖
	Concentration of funding on personnel costs	Insufficient resources for resolving key organizational issues/objectives. Precludes flexibility and innovation.	❖
Politically driven	Capture by special interests	An external, related group exercises influence over directives and ideology.	□ (regulatory agencies) ❖
	Corruption	Distorts objectives of the institution. Affects all levels of functions, from personnel to executive decisionmaking.	○ □ ▲ ❖
	Politicization	Recruitment, appointments and remunerations heavily influenced by political patronage.	○ □ ▲ ❖
	Volatility	Institutional priorities fluctuate due to shift in internalized priorities or political turnover.	○ □ ▲ ❖
Organizational	Goal ambiguity	Lack of clarity manifested in overambitious objectives (e.g. overregulation).	□ ❖
	Monopoly/monopsony control	Only one body provides service and only one body supplies workers.	❖
	Degree of government involvement	A "hands-on approach" by government (especially in terms of the economy or monetary policy).	□ (too much) ❖ (too little)

Key: ○ Rule/lawmaking □ Enforcement ▲ Providers of public services ❖ Providers of public goods

A related source of failure is **politicization** of the personnel function. Recruitment, appointments, and remunerations are heavily influenced by political patronage and not by merit. **Corruption** is another politically driven malfunction that leads to a distortion of a host of key functions: contracts for supplies; allocation among beneficiaries or clients (users of subsidized services such as urban hospitals often monopolize benefits at the expense of less privileged users in more remote regions); and decisions (for example certain areas, and therefore real estate developers, can be privileged by zoning classification, or certain firms can be privileged when privatization decisions are made).

A final politically driven source of failure, which often becomes systemic, is **volatility**. Exogenous shocks or political turnovers create volatility in the political priority that is accorded certain sectors, which affects their goals, level of funding, and organizational structures over time. It is virtually impossible to plan when budget levels swing year to year, or when there are repeated changes in the top management. **Goal multiplicity** within the same agency is an organizational or systemic failure. Institutions such as education ministries, which aim to provide universal higher-level education free of charge, often perform poorly at providing the most basic levels of services to needy groups. Regulatory frameworks that attempt to predetermine market outcomes often fail to provide the basic rules necessary for markets to function.

Monopoly/monopsony control over public institutions is another organizational source of malfunction. In many sectors, the government is the sole employer and the unions the sole provider of labor. This tends to politicize labor-management relations. This relationship becomes even more polarized when there are clear partisan distinctions. A related organizational or systemic failure is **asymmetry** between the degree of government involvement required for efficient institutional function and the degree of involvement chosen by particular governments. While independence is good for central banks, for example, there are many cases where governments interfere extensively in their operations. In contrast, education ministries need a fair amount of executive commitment and resources to continue to adapt to demographic and technological changes. Yet they are often very low on the list of government priorities, and receive little executive attention.

The Epidemiology of Institutional Illnesses

In the same manner that individuals in certain trades are prone to certain occupational hazards and diseases, some institutions are more prone to particular kinds of failures than to others. Agencies in charge of regulating telecommunications are unlikely to be paralyzed by congestive overdemand. Public hospitals, on the other hand, are often crippled by chronic congestion and demand from users. In some countries an excess of rules and laws impedes the normal functioning of markets and civil society. In contrast, shortages of key public services tend to erode quality of life as well as economic competitiveness in many countries.

In the case of congestive overdemand for public services, such as roads or water, it is difficult for dissatisfied users to exit. Therefore, access problems can develop in addition to quality effects. As shortages give power to those in control of access, those with the means to influence them (money, political power) tend to have an advantage in gaining access. Lower-income groups fare the worst, as they have the least means to exercise influence, and often have to rely on alternative and more expensive sources for public services, such as purchasing water from trucks.[20]

Judicial and law enforcement services are a critical set of public goods that suffer from overdemand and insufficient access. Here too it is difficult to exit, and overloaded legal institutions tend to give more access to those who wield sufficient influence.[21] Inefficient legal institutions have three kinds of costs to economic growth. The most important is the loss to property-right value, due to lack of predictable enforcement of rules. The second is the transaction costs of operating in an environment with dysfunctional third-party adjudication and corruption. These are costs the poor can least afford, and they tend to resort to informal sources of justice and protection from crime.[22] Third are the invisible costs of economic opportunities foregone, due to the high risks entailed in conducting business without adequate legal protection.[23]

Not surprisingly, the same institutions that suffer most from congestive overdemand also suffer from chronic underfunding, which makes it even harder to satisfy excess demand. Lack of funding leads to a deterioration in the quality of public goods and services, which increases the rate of exit in those areas where there are private alternatives. Wealthier groups giving up their stakes in public systems can further exacerbate resource problems, often leading to major differences in the quality of services received by the poor.[24] For public services such as roads and telecommunications, underfunding, differential access, and poor quality can have detrimental effects on the growth performance and competitiveness of the economy in general. Underfunding is also an issue for law enforcement and judicial services. Poorly paid police and judges are far more likely to accept bribes and other forms of corruption. Again this has equity implications, as the poor are the least likely to have the resources necessary to influence rulings in their favor.

Poor or inadequate inputs are a problem for most institutions, although to varying degrees. If universities receive poorly trained students over time, economic performance and competitiveness will eventually suffer. In the regulatory arena, even well-funded agencies with the best-trained regulators will have difficulty operating in an inadequate legal and regulatory framework. There are distinct equity as well as efficiency implications to this type of public sector failure, which is self-perpetuating. The private sector will increasingly attract better inputs, such as lawyers, doctors, and teachers, while the public sector must rely on inferior inputs and will then produce inferior outputs, which will be utilized disproportionately by the poor.

Because of both resource limitations and the politics of bilateral labor monopoly, many public sector institutions, and particularly those in the services that require large numbers of personnel, such as health and education ministries, suffer from a concentration of expenditures on personnel. This leaves little funding for maintenance, investment, policy innovation, and training.

"Capturing" afflicts institutions in several different ways. The first is the capturing of institutional function or policies by powerful clients. This can interfere with the proper function of regulatory agencies in contexts where powerful firms also exercise political influence. This applies across a range of sectors, from finance to public infrastructure, and can tilt the regulatory framework in favor of large-scale actors at the expense of individual providers and users. It can also occur where providers of social services dominate institutional functions because they have a monopoly on service provision.[25] This typically occurs in ministries that rely on large numbers of personnel in order to operate, such as health and education. Public sector unions often dominate all personnel decisions, and thus have enormous influence. Capturing affects the policies of key institutions; discrete decisions, such as those pertaining to zoning rules, pharmaceutical licenses, and import permits; and public procurement and resource allocations to private corporations.

All public institutions are vulnerable to two variant subcategories of capturing: politicization and corruption. Those that control the distribution of benefits (such as contracts for public infrastructure, access to land titles, permits, and subsidized credits) or personnel appointments (as in the case of teachers, public health workers, and civil servants) are magnets for corruption.[26] Such institutions become even more vulnerable when salary scales are low and accountability mechanisms are very weak. In these instances, there is a reverse causality of sorts: those who can, will bribe their way out of enforcement mechanisms by paying off poorly paid officials, whose incentives to enforce rules are inversely related to their level of pay.

Volatility, in the form of external shocks and political turnover, is a source of failure that affects all institutions. Political turnover usually shifts priorities *among* sectors, as well as economic policymaking more generally. Some politicians will place more emphasis on education and others on infrastructure. Political turnover also affects operational rules, organizational structure, and personnel issues, particularly if partisan issues are guiding personnel turnover during the transition. In many countries, a change in the governing party can affect the composition of the civil service well beyond the top managerial positions, creating a major turnover in high-level personnel. In some, major changes in personnel occur even without a change of government, merely due to the replacement of a minister in the same administration. Such turnover will also affect economic policymaking institutions, such as finance ministries and central banks, unless there is a clear commitment to continuity in macroeconomic management. Most new governments in Latin America still replace key top-level economic policymakers unless there is a certain amount of built-in institutional autonomy, as is the case with some central banks.[27]

Two types of institutions suffer most from goal ambiguity and overly ambitious objectives. The first of these are regulatory agencies. When such agencies lack clearly defined regulatory frameworks, their tendency is to overregulate, usually introducing a host of disincentives to compliance. In contrast, specialized agencies with very clear purposes, such as the enforcement of simplified tax laws or clearly defined property rights legislation, tend to be far more effective at meeting their objectives.[28]

The second set of institutions that suffer from this type of failure are ministries that deliver "quasi" public goods. Their outputs, such as health and education services, are difficult to measure and monitor. Quality is as important as quantity in determining performance outcomes and take-up by beneficiaries. Thus ministries often operate with poorly defined goals and output targets. In some countries goals are so poorly defined that ministries fail to provide even the most basic of services, while spending a great deal of resources on the provision of specialized social services for particular (usually more privileged) groups (such as high-technology health care for urban areas).[29]

The phenomenon of bilateral labor monopoly/monopsony is also most pervasive in the institutions that provide public goods and need large numbers of personnel to operate. As the services provided by schools and hospitals are critical to most citizens' daily lives, and institutional functions are labor-intensive, labor relations have much more political weight than in the case of other institutions. Service provision is usually determined by a national-level contract between a single employer (the state) and a single provider (the union). While most presidents could easily survive a strike of tax collection inspectors, the potential political damage resulting, from a prolonged public health workers' or teachers' strike is much greater. Teachers and public health workers' unions have traditionally been more organized and politically active than have unions in other professions involved in providing public services, such as accountants or engineers.[30]

A final failure, that of different levels of executive interference in different sectors, is rather paradoxical. Some sectors, such as central banks and finance ministries, are better off with less executive interference. Yet they are usually accorded high priority and executive involvement, as many governments are tempted to tailor monetary and fiscal policy to meet short-term political objectives. Others, such as education and health ministries, suffer from inadequate executive-level attention (as is suggested by lower average salary levels and higher levels of ministerial turnover). Governments tend to pay more attention to agencies that provide public infrastructure, such as roads, schools, and hospitals, than they do to the line ministries that provide health and education services. This is particularly evident when these agencies have a high level of discretion, and can produce rapid and visible results, increasing the short-term political rewards. The regionwide trend to social funds is a good example.[31] The political costs of interfering in ministries, meanwhile, such as challenging public sector unions, are usually high; and the benefits of reform, such as improving the quality of education, are long-term goals.[32]

The Politics of Institutional Reform

In the same way that different institutions suffer from different forms of organizational malfunction, the politics of institutional reform vary according to the institution. Obviously the politics underlying institutional improvements in the health sector are different from those shaping the reform of tax collection agencies. Political dynamics vary according to the number of actors, the organizational potential of actors, the respective roles of users and providers, and whether the institution's functions are dispersed geographically or under centralized control. The level of "social capital" (such as organizational capacity and information networks) is likely to affect the response of both consumers and providers to new choices and incentives, and the results will have different effects on equity and efficiency.

Not surprisingly, there is no one recipe for making institutional reform politically viable. Yet some general conditions, while not sufficient, are necessary to ensure a minimal probability of success. First of all, stable macroeconomies are indispensable, and the government's record in implementing economic reforms can be a determining factor in the implementation of institutional reforms. Countries that proceed rapidly and extensively on the macroeconomic reform front in response to extreme crisis are often able to take advantage of the ensuing political momentum to proceed with institutional reforms. Rapid and far-reaching reform tends to undermine the position of entrenched interest groups in the public sector, allowing governments political opportunities to implement a second set of reforms. In contrast, stalled or gradual reform allows the opposing forces more opportunities to coalesce, and to protect positions of privileged access to public sector expenditures.[33] In addition, rapid reformers obtain positive economic results more quickly, which often gives them the political momentum to proceed further and implement the kinds of institutional reforms that lock in prudent macroeconomic management over time, such as autonomous central banks.[34] In recent years, Argentina, Bolivia, and Peru all implemented rapid economic reforms in a crisis situation, and in each case the government was able to push ahead with some institutional reforms, which ranged from the setting up of new economic "watchdog" organizations, to tax and social security reform.

Rapid economic reform is indispensable in creating the political space for further reforms in the institutional arena. Yet some types of institutional reform, such as that of rulemaking and other "meta" institutions, must be implemented more slowly and cautiously than reforms of operational institutions, such as tax collection agencies, for which we have more clearly prescribed reform strategies. In general, "meta" institutions are more likely to have traits that reflect their particular societies than are operational ones.

Secondly, once a reform strategy exists, effective government communication is important to institutional reform, as large numbers of actors have to be convinced to cooperate for an extended period of time, not just to acquiesce to a short-term loss. Even more critical is coalition-building, which includes but transcends effective communication, and is aimed at engaging influential actors—with more staying power than technocrats—and giving them a stake in the reform.[35] In many instances of failed reform, lack of public understanding of the nature of the crisis, and of the reform measures required, underlie political failure. Successful reformers are often able to "sell" difficult measures to the public through extensive public relations campaigns.[36] Communication and coalition-building strategies are more appropriate and effective in reforms that introduce choice in sectors such as education, health, and social security, where success often hinges on the active participation of parents, patients, and workers, than in others such as tax reform, where popular acquiescence is required, rather than increased voice or choice. Adequate communication is particularly important to facilitating the poor's participation in new incentive structures, as the poor tend to be disadvantaged in terms of their access to information as well as to income.

Thirdly, some reforms, such as tax reform, have almost symbolic political implications, and serve to facilitate progress in other arenas. Other reforms, such as the setting up of currency boards or autonomous central banks, can be utilized as a means to lock in macroeconomic policy reforms and to avoid repeating mistakes of the past. Tax reform, for example, symbolizes the institutionalization of a societal consensus to abide by the fiscal constraints necessary for growth, and suggests at least a minimum public understanding of the dangers of deficit finance. The setting up of autonomous central banks, meanwhile, locks in a long-term public commitment to preventing inflation.[37] The implementation of these reforms by no means guarantees success in other kinds of institutional reform, but does signal a political commitment and an underlying consensus on the need for reforms in the institutional arena.

Another important set of reforms, which alters the political balance and provides a new institutionality for changes in the way public goods are delivered, is the elimination of public monopolies over the distribution of key services, ranging from health and education to public utilities. Once new (usually local level) actors are allowed to participate and gain a stake in new systems, it is difficult if not impossible to reverse reforms, as several examples of education and health reforms demonstrate (discussed below). Institutional arrangements that broaden access and encourage the participation and contribution of new actors in the delivery and management of public goods can be effective means to attain and preserve more progressive allocations of public social expenditure. Transfer programs, which distribute public resources to passive recipients, are less likely to create a broad base of stakeholders, and therefore are more easily reversible. A related strategy to create support for reform among the *providers* as well as the *users* of public services is to seek or create pockets of good performance *within* the public sector, even among very inefficient institutions, which can then serve as examples or provide impetus for further reforms.[38]

Finally, decentralization is widely used as a catch-all solution, and, while effective in some contexts, can divert public attention from resolving institutional problems at the central level. More than any other reform, decentralization has become a catch-all term that has in some contexts diverted attention from the need to reform central-level public institutions. In part, this is because decentralization fits nicely with the current philosophy of reducing the size of the state. Rather than resolve inefficiencies at the government level, responsibility for key services is devolved to local governments that are presumed to be more accountable to end-users.[39] Yet decentralization is not a panacea. Devolving control of various functions, such as personnel management, administration, and some aspects of finance, to the local level may provide services that are more responsive to local demands, as well as new incentives for local actors to participate and contribute. However, it cannot substitute for the resolution of fundamental organizational and incentives issues at the center. And local governments and bureaucracies are often even weaker and more inefficient than the institutions of the central state. In some contexts, interest groups or rent-seeking agents have more power over local governments than they do at the central level. In others, there are major disparities in the distribution of skilled personnel or resources among municipalities, raising equity concerns.

Strategies for Reform

It is no surprise that the politics of reforming institutions is complex and skewed towards maintaining the status quo. Providers of public services tend to be highly organized and have the political power that stems from controlling a monopoly. The potential beneficiaries of reforms—users—are numerous, but poorly organized, and often not well-informed. Given these political asymmetries, there is an important role for strategies that change performance incentives within public sector institutions, as well as those that alter the political balance in favor of consumers. There are several sets of strategies that can contribute to these objectives, although they range in applicability depending on the nature of the institutions.

The first set of strategies are those that increase the stakes for users through increased *choice* in public services, primarily by providing exit options (such as voucher education schemes, private social security schemes, and introducing competition among providers of utilities), and/or increasing the *voice* of users in the management and delivery of services (such as local management boards for health and education, some decentralization strategies, and group insurance schemes for health services).[40] A second type of strategy aims to build support for the reform process by spreading the wealth that it generates, such as through popular capitalism and voucher privatization schemes, thereby creating new stakeholders in the reform process.[41]

A third set of strategies attempts to change the incentives for providers, and to increase the *loyalty* or commitment of their workforce. The change most often recommended in this area is to reduce the overall size of the civil service while introducing more generous and competitive salary scales for those workers that remain.[42] Not surprisingly, this is one of the most politically difficult strategies to implement. However, recent studies suggest that financial remuneration is not the only incentive that civil servants respond to, and that introducing more opportunities for upward mobility and for merit-based promotion, increasing the responsibility of lower-level or local public servants in policy formulation, as well as incorporating their inputs, can have substantial effects on performance.[43]

Strategies that increase the stakes of users through increased choice can take many forms. New education policies in Chile gave the option to choose private instead of public schools through a system of government-subsidized vouchers, which were accepted by the private schools. A significant proportion of the population opted for private schools. Chile's private education system is of high, although not universal, quality, and has created a significant number of new stakeholders, both among users (parents) and providers (the state-subsidized private schools).[44] In Colombia, a health reform based on financing through individual capitation and the provision of services through organized competition, increased the access of 8 million Colombians to health insurance and mobilized the equivalent of 1 percent of GDP in new resources in a period of little over a year, as well as fundamentally changing the organizational structure of the public health system.[45] In Chile, the introduction of a private social security scheme attracted the majority of workers previously in the public scheme; some observers also credit it with raising national savings.[46] The Chilean social security reform has been copied or adapted by many countries in Latin America, including Peru and Argentina.

Another strategy for altering the political balance in favor of reform is to increase the voice of users by allowing them to participate in the administration and financing of services at the local level. In Peru, community-based health boards, CLAS (Centros Locales de Administración de Salud), have been introduced on a pilot basis, and are responsible for administering services, generating resources, and hiring and firing additional personnel. The CLAS now manage the resources that are collected as fees for services, rather than sending them back to the regional health organizations, as under the previous system. In the past, up to 80 percent of the resources generated at the local level did not return from the regional organizations. Not surprisingly, the primary opponents of the reform have been the regional-level representatives of the health ministry.[47] The CLAS have expanded coverage and hours of service in many poor rural areas, and indicators such as infant mortality have improved in some areas. And despite initial opposition, the CLAS now have the support of local-level public health workers. In Bolivia, the *participación* program, which entailed a major reallocation of resources and responsibility for basic service delivery to local governments, allocates resources according to the priorities set by locally elected committees. The program has revitalized local government and created a new set of local-level actors with a stake in reform.[48]

Strategies designed to "spread the wealth" by broadening the base of participation in reform can also alter the political balance in favor of institutional reform. In the Czech Republic, a mass voucher privatization scheme is credited with building widespread support for the privatization process and making it irreversible. In Chile, "popular capitalism," which gave public enterprise workers the option to buy shares in their companies when they were privatized, distinguished the second and more successful wave of privatizations in the mid 1980s from the first wave in the 1970s, which was characterized by concentrated ownership in both the newly privatized state-owned enterprises and the financial system.[49] In Peru, a program to encourage low-income individuals to invest in newly privatized enterprises offers small share sizes, payable in installment plans and at low interest rates. In 1996, approximately 250,000 low- and middle-income investors bought shares in auctions for public telephone and cement companies.[50]

The central government has a critical role to play in the implementation of all of the above strategies, in three key areas. These are the provision of adequate regulation, the provision of adequate information and training, and addressing major imbalances in equity. The latter role is particularly important when the services that are affected are the most basic of public goods, such as education. While these reform strategies can alter the political balance and improve the way that public institutions operate, they can also have very negative effects on those individuals or communities that face severe poverty constraints, and are therefore not able to respond to the new incentives or structures through which public goods are being delivered.[51]

While this is hardly a comprehensive review of these kinds of strategies, it does suggest that there are ways in which governments can alter the political balance in favor of institutional reforms. Strategies that change performance incentives within institutions apply across a range of institutional sectors. Strategies based on voice and choice, meanwhile, apply to the institutions that provide public goods and services rather than to those that make or enforce rules. It is also extremely important to recognize that there are no "silver bullets." The success of particular reform strategies will hinge on the overall political context and leadership, on sectoral characteristics, and on the extent and nature of the problems to be resolved.[52]

Prospects for Institutional Reform in Latin America

The obstacles to achieving the wide range of goals of institutional reform in Latin America are many. There will also be differences among outcomes that reflect the endogenous nature of countries' institutions. And reformers in the region will have to overcome longstanding perceptions about the lack of credibility and effectiveness of institutions, especially among small-scale economic actors and low-income groups.[53] Despite the obstacles, a number of regionwide trends make it a propitious time for implementing institutional reforms.

Unlike in East Asia, where credible institutions and a relatively equal distribution of assets encouraged public support for continuity in economic policies and strengthened the existing institutional structure early on, in Latin America the incentives were structured so as to encourage redistributive demands and policy swings on the one hand, and the conducting of most economic transactions outside the system of formal rules on the other. In Latin America, redistribution has been limited to intermittent short-term income transfers, and asset ownership remains highly unequal. This unequal distribution of assets, coupled with weak public sector institutions, has resulted in weak confidence in government policy, and encouraged rent-seeking or tax evasion by key economic actors, and populist economic promises by politicians.[54] Over time this eroded the capacity of institutions to deliver public goods and services effectively, and therefore public faith in them. The severe economic crisis of the 1980s exacerbated this trend. This resulted in increasing reliance on what North refers to as "informal" rules: cultural and societal norms of behavior, and an increasing disregard for the "formal" rules established by the judicial and political systems.[55]

Part of the story of reforming institutions in Latin America will lie in building a new faith in the formal institutions of the state, such as political and judicial systems. Such faith is necessary for critical actors to contribute the resources necessary to building a state that operates effectively, "resources" that range from paying tax revenues to providing political support for change. It is also necessary to encourage potential beneficiaries (individual citizens) to contribute through their active participation and support for reforms, such as through participation in new private social security schemes or on local management boards for health and education services. In this light it is no surprise that Chile, with its traditionally strong public institutions, leads the region in implementing institutional reform, and that other countries, which must establish new confidence in state institutions as well as rebuild them, lag further behind.[56]

Progress in certain reforms that have symbolic effects, such as a tax reform that is perceived to be equitable and efficient, may be a good starting point for restoring faith in institutions.[57] Progress may be more difficult to achieve in the short term in other critical areas, such as judicial systems, where we do not have established blueprints for reform. Judicial reform is particularly important in establishing a level playing field for new (and smaller) economic actors, and should be the focus of particular attention.[58] Still, the extent and scope of current reforms in a number of countries, particularly in the tax and social security areas, provide a good starting point. As other chapters note, these reforms have had positive effects on equity as well as efficiency.

The prospects for reform are also affected by Latin America's changing political context. Most countries in the region are now democracies, at least in terms of competitive elections, broad participation, and civil and political liberties. The number of countries that have implemented reform under democratic auspices has increased, and empirical studies reveal no significant difference between the records of democratic or authoritarian regimes in implementing macroeconomic reforms.[59] Yet the greater complexity of institutional reforms will test the capacity and legitimacy of the region's diverse democratic regimes even further. The progress of institutional reforms will depend on achieving growth with equity, and on a host of other variables including leadership, political cultures, civil society, ethnic/cultural divisions, and the military.[60] This diversity will result in different levels of implementation capacity.[61]

Years of economic crisis, insufficient funds, and political volatility have eroded the capacity of public sectors to perform their designated functions, much less to introduce innovative policy changes. Yet precisely because states are seen as weaker than in the past and there is greater acceptance of a more determining market role, and because states have performed poorly in delivering basic services, public *expectations* of the state are far lower than in previous decades. This makes adamant opposition to change far less likely. Political parties have also seen their public support erode along with declining faith in the state, and now parties are much less critical to the political backing of most governments in the region than before.[62] The severe economic crisis of the 1980s and early 1990s, meanwhile, weakened the power of traditional opposition or interest groups such as public sector unions. Thus democratic governments often have more autonomy than their predecessors did, whether authoritarian or democratic.

The long-term implications of the erosion of dominant party systems and interest groups throughout the region are not yet clear. In the short term, it has had some benefits beyond giving governments more room to maneuver. The decline of partisan influence makes it more likely that voters will vote retrospectively (i.e., by judging government performance). This will make governments more conscious of their performance on the economic and social policy fronts, which may create additional pressure to strengthen institutions.[63] And, as in macroeconomic reforms, a certain momentum will come from external influence and the demonstration effects of progress in neighboring countries.[64] The decline in support for the traditional, often clientelistic political parties may eventually result in their undertaking internal reforms to broaden their base of representation, as recently occurred in some parties in Bolivia.

In sum, despite substantial obstacles, there are clear opportunities to implement institutional reforms in the region. These reforms are essential for most countries to establish competitive economies capable of generating the sustained levels of growth necessary to reduce poverty and inequality. Yet because of the endogenous nature of certain institutions, as well as their diversity and complexity, progress is likely to be uneven, both across countries and across sectors. Better understanding of the distinctions among institutions and of the diverse elements that their reform entails is an important starting point. Progress in some areas, such as judicial reform, which helps level the playing field for smaller- sized economic actors, and in the education arena, which provides critical investments in the human capital of the poor, will be particularly important to simultaneously enhancing equity and efficiency. Finally, strategies for reform which incorporate beneficiary participation in the process—at least in the arena of public goods and services—are more likely to contribute to the necessary renewal of public confidence in state institutions than are top-down strategies implemented from the center.

Appendix: Approaches to the Study of Institutions

Institutions as Formal and Informal Rules

Rather than attempt an exhaustive review of the literature, we provide a taxonomy of approaches to the study of institutions. Its categories are defined by the institutional function or roles that authors emphasize and the different methodologies they employ (see Table 4).

Several writers have focused on the regulatory role that institutions play in determining economic performance and societal consensus more generally. Douglass North defines institutions as "the rules of the game in a society or, more formally,

Table 4. A Taxonomy of Approaches to the Study of Institutions

PERSPECTIVES	INSTITUTIONAL FUNCTIONS ANALYZED					
	Growth / economic performance	Governance	Equity	Effect on policy outcomes	Public administration	Public goods/ services
Regulatory (new institutional economics; multidisciplinary)	Borner et al. Fukuyama Kornell and Kalt North Putnam	Bates Borner et al. Fukuyama Levi Putnam Shepsle Thelen and Steinmo	North Putnam			Putnam Ostrom
Economic	Alesina et al. Barro Birdsall and Sabot	Alesina	Alesina Benabou Birdsall and Sabot			Birdsall and Sabot
Political economy (political science; new institutional economics)	Haggard et al. Grindle Geddes Naím	Haggard et al. Nelson Weaver and Rochman	Nelson Graham	Naím Cox and McCubbins	Geddes Grindle Naím McCubbins	Graham
Industrial organization			Hommes Londoño		Hausmann Hommes Londoño	Hausmann Hommes Londoño
Public administration					Wilson McCubbins	Wilson

...the humanly devised constraints that shape human interaction. In consequence they structure incentives in human exchange, whether political, social, or economic."[65] These rules are both formal (such as political and judicial), and informal (such as culture and social norms). Both types have an important impact on governance and economic performance. One aspect of informal rules is captured by Robert Putnam's concept of social capital. After studying the differences in social organization and social cohesion among communities, Putnam concluded that they are key to explaining differential outcomes in governance and in economic development. "Citizens in civic communities expect better government, and (in part through their own efforts), they get it. They demand more effective public service and they are prepared to act collectively to achieve their shared goals."[66] North and Putnam have both contributed greatly to our understanding of differences in performance outcomes across countries and regions.[67]

Their work suggests that improving the performance of institutions at the least entails developing a certain degree of societal consensus on how institutions should perform and what they should and should not deliver. Francis Fukuyama explores how different cultures and societal values shape economic performance.[68] In the same manner, cultures and values shape institutions, and thus the formal and informal rules governing social interaction. Yet if there is little consensus within societies, institutions will also reflect this lack of coherence, as will the respect, or lack thereof, that society accords them. They will neither have legitimacy nor attain compliance.

Other authors have analyzed the manner in which institutions regulate, and approach institutions as rules. In quite different ways, Elinor Ostrom and Mancur Olson have examined how institutions affect collective behavior. Olson argues that the proliferation of actors and interest groups erodes institutions, and thus decreases incentives for compliance with formal rules and for rational individuals to act in the common interest. Ostrom, on the other hand, examines the role of institutions in overcoming this so-called "tragedy of the commons," and argues that stable institutions of self-government can be created if problems of supply, credibility, and monitoring are resolved credibly.[69] In more recent work, Olson and colleagues have explained divergences in economic performance in various countries by the existence or absence of "market-augmenting" institutions. They distinguish between spontaneous market interactions, such as barter, which take place in all societies, and those in which trade is not self-enforcing, necessitating third-party enforcement. In the latter, institutions are the necessary rules or contracts. Countries where they are lacking will not fulfill their economic potential.[70]

Other writers, including Robert Bates, Margaret Levi, and Kenneth Shepsle, have taken a "rules" perspective to institutions, and have contributed a great deal to our ability to make some general assumptions about institutions.[71] In order to do so, most of these models take interests as given and assume all actors are rational and have full information. An interesting counterperspective, which is less theoretical but nonetheless useful, is that of the "historical institutionalists," such as Kathleen Thelen and Sven Steinmo.[72] They see institutions as shaping broader interests as well as strategies. Institutions form a dense matrix that includes the market, the bureaucracy, the political context, families, and religions, and creates a complex mix of sometimes conflicting preferences. New or reformed institutions, meanwhile, are always built with pieces of preexisting ones, implying a high degree of path dependence. This makes it more difficult to generalize about outcomes, yet helps explain cross-country differences.

Silvio Borner, Aymo Brunetti, and Beatrice Weder apply the rules perspective to the Latin American context.[73] They describe the devastating effects that uncertainty about the rules of the game have on private investment and specialization. Institutional uncertainty shows up in two forms: unpredictability of government intervention and the lack of consistent enforcement of private contracts. The main cause of this uncertainty is the highly discretionary power of the executive, which changes laws at will and enforces existing ones inconsistently, which creates "the ideal breeding-ground for rent-seeking by powerful interest groups..."[74] Their approach applies to most developing economies.

Institutions, Growth, and Equity

In recent years, a number of authors have utilized formal economic methods to study the role of institutions in the political economy of growth and distribution. Alberto Alesina and Roberto Perotti, for example, explore the role that democratic institutions have in determining growth performance, focusing on political instability—in this case defined as executive turnover. They find that there is no evidence, on average, of a democracy with civil liberties having costs for economic development. If anything, it may be the other way around: that democracies with civil liberties promote economic development. "But establishing democratic institutions is not the 'deus ex machina' that resolves all problems of development. A sound and stable political-economic climate is essential."[75] Here Alesina and Perotti's work, like that of North, Putnam, and Fukuyama, suggests that rather vague concepts such as social capital, societal consensus, and informal rules have determining effects on institutional and economic performance. And, like Borner and his colleagues, Alesina and Perotti highlight the negative effects that institutional uncertainty have for growth.

Alesina also examines institutional structures and distributional outcomes, and their effects on growth. In societies where there are no institutional mechanisms to correct extreme inequality, the poor have greater incentives to engage in rent-seeking activities, and/or to vote for more taxation, which can discourage investment and growth.[76] Redistributive policies are more likely to have negative effects on growth in contexts where institutions are inefficient.[77] Nancy Birdsall and Richard Sabot have examined how the distributional and institutional frameworks can provide incentives for more "efficient" redistributive strategies, which have effects such as increased savings and investments in basic education by the poor.[78]

Institutions and Policy Reforms

Another body of literature focuses on the role of institutions in influencing reform outcomes. Stephan Haggard and several coauthors analyze how institutions—such as political party systems, bureaucratic structures, and the institutional structures surrounding government–interest group relations—play a central role in determining reform outcomes, as well as in sustaining them.[79] There is general agreement that the quality of the state bureaucracy affects economic policymaking and performance, but far less agreement about which administrative capacities matter, and how they relate to and are affected by the institutions that govern them. Another issue for debate is why some institutional structures develop more efficiently than others.[80]

To address these questions, Merilee Grindle has focused on how the incentives guiding the behavior of bureaucrats within institutions determine policy outcomes, and how changing these incentives is often critical to the success of economic reform, and to institutional performance more generally.[81] Matthew McCubbins has also written about the incentives guiding the behavior of bureaucrats in the public administration. Using a principal agent approach, he develops two alternative scenarios which affect the behavior of bureaucrats. The first is that of "police patrols," or the effectiveness of the means of oversight or monitoring of the performance of bureaucrats. The second or "fire alarms" approach focuses on the capacity of the consumers of public goods and services to demand accountability from the public administration.[82]

Barbara Geddes provides a different perspective, challenging the emphasis on the role of the bureaucracy. Geddes argues that institutions, including competent bureaucracies, are created by political leaders for their own purposes. Once created, they can acquire some independent political weight and thus influence future policy choices. Yet while professionalized and more or less independent agencies tend to survive and become lobbies for a particular policy orientation, such as market reforms, they can also be destroyed by determined politicians.[83] The weight of political leaders vis-à-vis institutions, meanwhile, varies according to the longevity, credibility, and capacity of bureaucratic structures (as distinct from but related to institutions).

Numerous authors have focused on how political institutions can affect economic growth by establishing a credible commitment to policy, and therefore a good investment climate.[84] McCubbins and Cox have explored the role of political institutions in determining policy outcomes, and argue that political actors' incentives are significantly influenced by the rules governing electoral competition, while their capabilities are determined jointly by their electoral success and the constitutionally stipulated powers of the various posts at stake. Different combinations of incentives and capabilities determine the extent to which the state can act decisively and the degree to which it is responsive to broad public interests as opposed to narrow special interests.[85]

Kent Weaver and Bert A. Rockman define institutions in terms of government capabilities. They posit that political institutions shape the decisionmaking process, which in turn influences government capabilities, and, ultimately, policy outcomes. They identify three tiers of institutional traits that affect government capabilities. The first is whether the system is presidential or parliamentary. The second is regime type and government type. And the third and broadest tier is the character of broad framework institutions, secondary institutional characteristics, political conditions and policymakers' goals, socioeconomic and demographic conditions, and past policy choices. They find that institutional effects are often bidirectional and contingent on the particular context, and that in order to enhance government capacity, the right set of institutions needs to be matched to the "right" set of problems.[86]

Moisés Naím focuses on the broader policy context necessary for economic and institutional reforms.[87] He notes that, in contrast to macroeconomic reform, there is no urgency driving institutional reform. Its implementation requires the formation of a broad societal consensus. The importance of such a consensus for economic and institutional performance is also noted by North, Putnam, and Fukuyama. Naím highlights how little we know about building such a consensus in countries where it is lacking, and the absence of a concrete set of policy guidelines for institutionalizing it once it exists. He also notes a paradox that exists in many countries: Typically, and rather tragically, the agencies that deal more directly with the poor—such as ministries of education and health—tend to be black holes of corruption and inefficiency, while "islands of excellence" are more often found among central banks and agencies related to the main export commodity of the country—such as coffee, oil, and copper.

Joan Nelson examines the interactions between political and economic reforms. She points to the increasing tensions between rapid, technocratic, topdown macroeconomic reforms and the strengthening of democratic procedures and institutions, which, as Naím also notes, require far more consultation and consensus-building. Nelson also points to the important role that distributive issues and conflicts play in this process, and how institutional reforms pose more permanent distributive threats than do stabilization policies: privatization and government reorganization threaten jobs; labor market reforms and liberalization tend to reduce the power of unions; and targeting social welfare policies to the most needy tends to reduce subsidies to workers and middle-class groups.[88]

More recently, Nelson has examined institutional reforms in the social sectors. She emphasizes the strong element of path dependency underlying the structure and performance of institutions, and questions the feasibility of the engineered gradual reforms recommended by the traditional "institutionalist" perspective. She posits that there is a high probability that incremental changes will be defeated by the broader context. Thus gambling on rapid and far-reaching reform, which changes all of the rules and some of the context at the same time, may be more effective.[89]

Carol Graham has explored the role of distributive issues during macroeconomic reform.[90] She maintains that innovations in short-term safety net policies, such as incorporating the participation and contribution of beneficiaries, can serve as a basis for more permanent institutional reforms in the social sectors. Yet the policy framework is critical. Rapid and extensive economic reform provides political opportunities for governments to implement institutional reforms at a time when the overall policy framework is in flux. Slow or stalled reform, in contrast, allows organized interest groups with strong stakes in the status quo more opportunities to protect their positions.

An Industrial Organization Perspective

Another body of literature, best exemplified by the works of Rudolf Hommes and Juan Luis Londoño, describes how highly centralized institutional arrangements affect policy outcomes in the critical area of social services. In particular, they study the effects of monopsony and monopoly structures on the performance of social sector institutions.[91] They highlight resulting problems of efficiency in expenditure allocation; low input quality, such as poorly trained personnel and poor infrastructure; inequity in the distribution of services; lack of community participation; concentration of decisionmaking at the central level; and inadequate incentives structures. Overcoming these problems entails changing the manner in which systems are regulated, clarifying both rules and roles; separating the financing and provision of services and relying on outcome-based rather than input-based allocation mechanisms; and increasing accountability among providers of services. These changes also entail empowering the consumers of public services so that they can both contribute to better service provision and demand accountability.[92]

Public Administration

A potential challenge to the industrial organization approach that recognizes its limitations is James Q. Wilson's work on reforming public bureaucracies. Wilson evaluates the extent to which private sector incentives and management models can be used to reform the operations of the public sector bureaucracy. He concludes that some private sector techniques—such as increased choice for users, increased autonomy for bureaucrats, a greater role for decentralized actors, and a looser regulatory framework—can have a positive impact on certain operations of the public sector, such as schools and postal services. However, those techniques do not apply to defense and law enforcement institutions. Ultimately public sector institutions face different constraints and incentives than private firms do, and must provide certain goods regardless of whether the market finds them desirable. Thus while incorporating private sector incentives into public sector management may solve a specific set of problems in some public institutions, it is not a panacea for all the issues that institutional reform needs to address. Wilson's work highlights the importance of unbundling the different kinds of institutions and their respective roles and challenges.[93]

This is not intended to be an exhaustive review, but rather to demonstrate that we are in a "pre-paradigmatic" stage in the study of institutions. We have several different levels and units of analysis, and the different strands rarely "speak" to each other. In addition, most approaches still treat institutions as a generalized set of rules and/or organizations, and little has as yet been done to unbundle them. Prior to developing a concrete set of reform policies, we need to clarify the conceptual framework surrounding the wide range of public sector institutions, their diverse roles and relationship to macroeconomic reforms, and the distinctive administrative and political features that characterize their operations.

Endnotes

[1] The authors would like to thank Alan Angell, Ajay Chibber, Jorge Domínguez, Merilee Grindle, George Graham, Peter Hakim, Joan Nelson, John Sheahan, Judith Tendler, Joseph Tulchin, Nancy Truitt, John Williamson, and the participants at the IDB/MacArthur Foundation conference for helpful comments, and Kris McDevitt and Gualberto Rodríguez for valuable research assistance.

[2] Wilson cited in, "Can the Bureaucracy be Deregulated?" in John J. DiIulio, Jr., ed., *Deregulating the Public Service: Can Government Be Improved?* (Washington, D.C.: The Brookings Institution, 1994), p. 59.

[3] See, for example, Sebastian Edwards, "The Disturbing Underperformance of the Latin American Economies," paper prepared for the InterAmerican Dialogue Plenary Meeting, May 1996. A more optimistic interpretation is found in Easterly et al., which finds that the region responded positively to changes in policies and did well to return to its historic growth rate of 2 percent in 1990-93, given ongoing policy changes and global growth slowdown. See William Easterly, Norman Loayza, and Peter Montiel, "Has Latin America's Post-Reform Growth Been Disappointing?" Mimeo, The World Bank, 1995.

[4] This theme has been constant in papers about reform in recent years; for a summary, see Moisés Naím, entitled "Latin America's Journey to the Market: From Macroeconomic Shocks to Institutional Therapy," *International Center for Economic Growth Discussion Papers* 62 (1995).

[5] Sebastian Edwards argues that in order to reduce poverty in the region, growth must be much higher than the 2.8 percent regional average for 1991-1995. The World Bank estimates that the minimum rate of growth necessary for poverty reduction is 3.4 percent. Higher growth is also necessary to provide a politically sustainable allocation of the benefits of reform. See Edwards (1996).

[6] Aggregate investment in Latin America was 20 percent of GDP in 1993, versus 36 percent in the fast-growing economies of East Asia. Savings in 1994 in Latin America were 19 percent of GDP, while they were 35 percent in East Asia. See Edwards (1996). For the effects of equity on savings, see Nancy Birdsall, Thomas Pinckney, and Richard Sabot, "Inequality, Savings, and Growth," Mimeo, Inter-American Development Bank, Washington, D.C., November 1995.

[7] José Edgardo Campos and Hilton Root, *The Key to the Asian Miracle: Making Shared Growth Credible* (Washington, D.C.: The Brookings Institution, 1996).

[8] See, for example, "The Backlash in Latin America: Gestures Against Reform," *The Economist*, 30 November 1996.

[9] For detail, see Naím (1995).

[10] See Alan Angell and Carol Graham, "Can Social Sector Reform Make Adjustment Sustainable and Equitable?" *Journal of Latin American Studies* 27:1 (February 1995).

[11] These categories were originally suggested by Jean-François Richard.

[12] See Sue E.S. Crawford and Elinor Ostrom, "A Grammar of Institutions," *American Political Science Review* 89:3 (September 1995); and Alberto Díaz-Cayeros, "Un Análisis Institucional del Papel del Estado," paper presented to Tinker Foundation Forum on the Role of the State in Latin America and the Caribbean, Cancún, Mexico, 24-26 October 1996.

[13] Douglass North, *Institutions, Institutional Change, and Economic Performance* (Cambridge: Cambridge University Press, 1990).

[14] See Silvio Borner, Aymo Brunetti, and Beatrice Weder, *Institutional Obstacles to Latin American Growth* (San Francisco: International Center for Economic Growth, 1992). See also, by the same authors, *Political Credibility and Economic Development* (New York: St. Martin's Press, 1995).

[15] See Crawford and Ostrom (1995); and Díaz-Cayeros (1996).

[16] See Díaz-Cayeros (1996).

[17] It is probably easier for a president to undermine the Central Bank in Peru, for example, where most government institutions have generally low public esteem, than the Bundesbank in Germany or the Federal Reserve Board in the U.S., both of which have well established track records and a high degree of public confidence. Peru had one of the most independent central banks in Latin America, but was completely undermined by President Alan García in the late 1980s. See Barbara Geddes, "The Politics of Economic Liberalization," *Latin American Research Review* 30:2 (1995). In Venezuela the Central Bank, which had been historically controlled by the executive, was given almost complete autonomy by Congressional law in the early 1990s, only to be "recaptured" by the executive a few years later in the aftermath of a severe banking crisis.

[18] Alberto Alesina and Roberto Perotti, "The Political Economy of Growth Literature: A Critical Survey of the Literature," *World Bank Economic Review* 8:3 (1994).

[19] "Super" public goods are those whose provision is very difficult to transfer to the private sector, while quasi public goods are those that can be provided by private suppliers with the indirect support of the public sector.

[20] For an analysis of how much more the poor pay for services such as water and electricity, see Blanca Adrianzen and George G. Graham, "The High Costs of Being Poor," *Archives of Environmental Health* 28 (June 1974).

[21] The very wealthy are often able to resort to private sources of security.

[22] For detail, see Hernando de Soto, *El Otro Sendero* (Lima: Editorial El Barranco, 1986). A telling example is found in a study of court performance in Argentina and Ecuador: the plaintiff's income has a powerful effect on the times to disposition observed in alimony cases, with wealthier plaintiff's having much quicker dispositions. See Edgardo Buscaglia and Maria Dakolis, *Judicial Reform in Latin American Courts: Experiences from Argentina and Ecuador,* World Bank Technical Paper no. 350, Washington, D.C., 1996.

[23] See Buscaglia and Dakolis (1996).

[24] Much of the literature on U.S. and European welfare systems notes that in "particularistic" welfare systems (i.e. those aimed at the deserving poor), the rich have a tendency to exit, a problem that does not exist in systems where benefits are universally available. See Gosta Esping-Andersen, *Three Worlds of Welfare Capitalism* (Princeton: Princeton University Press, 1990); and Theda Skocpol, "Universal Appeal," *The Brookings Review* (Summer 1991).

[25] Robert Coase's work on the nature of the firm provides a theoretical framework for analyzing the capturing phenomenon. See his chapter in Oliver Williamson and Stony Winter, ed., *The Nature of the Firm: Origins, Evolution, and Development* (New York: Oxford University Press, 1991).

[26] See Moisés Naím, "The Corruption Eruption," *Brown Journal of International Affairs* (Summer 1995).

[27] For a discussion of the benefits of independent central banks, see Alex Cukierman, Steven B. Webb, and Bilin Neyapti, "Measuring the Independence of Central Banks and Its Effects on Policy Outcomes," *World Bank Economic Review* (September 1995).

[28] For detail on Peru's experience with specialized and autonomous tax collection and property rights registration agencies, see Philip Keefer, "Reforming the State: The Sustainability and Replicability of Peruvian Public Administration Reforms," Mimeo, The World Bank, Washington, D.C., September 1995.

[29] In Brazil in 1982, for example, 78 percent of public health funds was spent on high technology procedures for relatively small groups of urban patients, at least some of which could afford to finance these services out of private medical insurance. See Nancy Birdsall and Estelle James, "Efficiency and Equity in Social Spending: How and Why Governments Misbehave," The World Bank, Working Papers WPS 274, May 1990.

[30] See Hausmann in Bradford, ed. (1994).

[31] For detail on these institutions, see Graham (1994).

[32] For a detailed example of this dynamic in Peru, see Carol Graham and Cheikh Kane, "Opportunistic Government or Sustaining Reform: Electoral Trends and Public Expenditure Patterns in Peru, 1990-1995," *Latin American Research Review* (forthcoming).

[33] See Graham (1994).

[34] See Michael Bruno and William Easterly, "Inflation's Children: Tales of Crises That Beget Reform," paper presented to the American Economics Association Annual Meetings, January 1996. For the role of central bank independence, see Alex Cukierman, Steven Webb, and Bilin Neyapti, "Measuring the Independence of Central Banks and Its Effects on Policy Outcomes," *World Bank Economic Review* 6:3 (1992). For a discussion of the fate of rapid versus gradual reformers, see Anders Aslund, Peter Boone, and Simon Johnson, " How To Stabilize: Lessons from Post-Communist Countries," *Brookings Papers on Economic Activity* 1 (1996).

[35] For an overview study on the importance of communication in building consensus for reform, see Leila Frischtak and Izak Atiyas, eds., *Governance, Leadership, and Communication: Building Constituencies for Economic Reform* (Washington, D.C.: The World Bank, 1996).

[36] For examples in Peru, Zambia, and Senegal, see Graham (1994). For the case of Venezuela, see Moisés Naím, *Paper Tigers and Minotaurs: The Politics of Venezuela's Economic Reforms* (Washington, D.C.: The Carnegie Endowment, 1993), as well as Juan Carlos Navarro, "Reversal of Fortune: The Ephemeral Success of Adjustment in Venezuela, 1989-93" in Frischtak and Atiyas (1996).

[37] For tax reform, see Navarro in Frischtak and Atiyas (1996), and for central banks, see Cukierman and Webb (1995).

[38] This is discussed in detail by Judith Tendler in *Good Governments in the Tropics* (Baltimore: Johns Hopkins University Press, 1997).

[39] Naím (1995), p. 33.

[40] The importance of these concepts was first noted by Albert Hirschman in *Exit, Voice, and Loyalty: Responses to Decline in Firms, Organizations, and States* (Cambridge: Harvard University Press, 1970).

[41] These strategies are discussed in detail in Carol Graham, *Private Markets for Public Goods: Raising the Stakes in Economic Reforms* (The Brookings Institution, work in progress).

[42] The lack of differentiation of salary scales is particularly notable at the managerial level. Latin America has a higher rate of ministerial turnover than most countries in East Asia, and ministers are paid much less on average. See the box titled, "If you pay peanuts, you will get monkeys for your ministers" in Naím (1995).

[43] See Grindle (forthcoming); and Tendler (1997).

[44] The reform was implemented under military regime, which obviously made it easier to override public opposition, particularly from the teachers' union. Yet since the transition to democracy in 1990, the new voucher system remains intact, with minor modifications. The proportion of primary pupils enrolled at private schools rose from 20 percent to 35 percent during the period the reforms were implemented (1980-1987). See Tarsicio Castañeda, *Para Combatir la Pobreza* (Santiago: Instituto de Estudios Públicos, 1990). Harsher critics of the reform focus more on the variability in student performance among the new private schools rather than the aggregate numbers, which do suggest some overall performance improvements. See Ernesto Schiefelbein, "Restructuring Education Through Economic Competition: The Case of Chile," *Journal of Educational Administration* 29:4 (1991), pp. 17- 29.

[45] Juan Luis Londoño, "Managed Competition in the Tropics," Paper presented to the International Health Economics Association Conference, Vancouver, May 1996; and Juan Luis Londoño and Julio Frenk, "Structured Pluralism: Towards a New Model for Health System Reform in Latin America," Paper presented at Special Meeting of Ministers of Health of Latin America and the Caribbean, Washington, September 29-30, 1995.

[46] See Giancarlo Corsetti and Klaus Schmidt-Hebbel, "Pension Reform and Growth," Policy Research Working Paper no. 1471, The World Bank, Washington, D.C., June 1995.

[47] See Carl E. Taylor, "Report to the Honorable Minister of Health of Peru: An Evaluation of CLAS– A New Component of Health Care Reform in Peru," Mimeo, Johns Hopkins University School of Public

and International Health, January, 1996; and Patricia Paredes, "Shared Administration in Primary Health Care Facilities: The Case of Peru," Mimeo, Johns Hopkins University, 1995.

[48] The municipal share of total public investment has risen from 11 percent to 39 percent, and the number of municipalities has increased from 61 to 311 since the implementation of the law. See George Gray Molina, "Social Investments under Popular Participation in Bolivia: Explaining Municipal Investment Choices," Mimeo, Harvard Institute for International Development and Unidad de Análisis de Políticas Sociales, La Paz, November 1996.

[49] This concentration was in part responsible for a major financial sector crisis. Bank bailouts cost up to 3 percent of GDP in 1983. For detail see Rolf Luders, "Massive Divestiture and Privatization: Lessons from Chile," *Contemporary Policy Issues 9* (October 1991).

[50] See Carol Graham, "Popular Capitalism Makes Headway in Peru," *The Wall Street Journal,* 19 April 1996.

[51] An example is the Chilean voucher education scheme, where poor rural populations fared the worst, in part due to their inability to pay transaction costs involved in switching to private schools and their inadequate access to information. See Varun Gauri, Unpublished Ph.D. dissertation, Princeton University, 1996.

[52] For a good example of how different strategies have varied results according to the country setting, see "World Education League: Who's Top?" *The Economist,* 29 March 1997.

[53] Edgardo Buscaglia, for example, notes that one of the obstacles to effective judicial function in Latin America is the perception of corruption and lack of confidence in the administration of justice, a phenomenon which is more pronounced among small economic units and low-income families. See Buscaglia, "Judicial Reform in Latin America," *Policy Studies* (forthcoming).

[54] A slightly oversimplified way of thinking of this is as the classic prisoner's dilemma posed in game theory. With reiterated games (i.e., experience), prisoners will be much less likely to cooperate in a context where the government's redistributive policies squander resources or concentrate them in the hands of a few, and therefore the chances of benefiting are very slight. For an empirical exploration of the effects of inequality on rent-seeking behavior, see Alesina (1994). Bowles and Gintis, meanwhile, argue that inequality impedes economic performance by discouraging the evolution of "productivity-enhancing" government structures. Cited in Karla Hoff, "Market Failures and the Distribution of Wealth: A Perspective from the Economics of Information," *Politics and Society* 24:4 (December 1996).

[55] See North (1990).

[56] Case in point is social security reform in Peru, where a "Chile-style" pension reform has been implemented. Low-income workers remain reluctant to make the extra contribution required to join the new scheme, as their faith in any public or publicly guaranteed savings scheme is extremely low. See Carol Graham, "Raising the Stakes in the Social Services, Social Security, and Privatization in Peru," in *Private Markets for Public Goods.* For a review of the role of Chile's public institutions in its economic reform program, see Genaro Arriagada and Carol Graham, "Chile: Sustaining Adjustment During Democratic Transition" in Haggard and Webb (1994).

[57] In Peru, for example, the reformed tax collection agency Sunat received wide public acclaim, not only because it was able to generate much increased tax revenues, but because it punished large and powerful businesses who violated the rules as regularly as it punished small ones. See C. Graham, "Raising the Stakes in Social Services: Peru" in *Private Markets for Public Goods.*

[58] In the absence of an impartial and effective judiciary, the performance of mutually beneficial transactions depends on the presence of pre-existing reputations and repeated transactions among parties. The requirement excludes many potentially beneficial transactions involving previously unfamiliar parties from occurring, forfeiting potential economic benefits. See Buscaglia, "Judicial Reform in Latin America."

[59] See Stephan Haggard and Robert Kaufmann, *The Political Economy of Democratic Transitions* (Princeton: Princeton University Press, 1993); and Stephan Haggard and Steven B. Webb, *Voting for Reform: Democracy, Political Liberalization, and Economic Adjustment* (New York: Oxford University Press/World Bank, 1994); and Karen Remmer, "The Political Economy of Elections in Latin America," *American Political Science Review* 87 (July 1993), pp. 393-407.

[60] For a review of the literature about the current state of democracy in the region, see Janet Kelly, "Democracy Redux: How Real is Democracy in Latin America?," *Latin American Research Review,* forthcoming.

[61] For an excellent discussion of how different political contexts affect policy outcomes, see Thomas Carothers, "Democracy Without Illusions," *Foreign Affairs* 76:1 (January/February 1997).

[62] Party opposition from within regimes tends to be more effective in undermining reform efforts than that which is outside the regime. See Barbara Geddes, "The Politics of Economic Liberalization," *Latin American Research Review* 30:2 (1995).

[63] See M. Coppedge, "District Magnitude, Economic Performance, and Party System Fragmentation in Five Latin American Countries," *Comparative Political Studies,* forthcoming. For a detailed analysis of how the decline of parties resulted in more "retrospective" voter behavior in Peru, see Graham and Kane (forthcoming).

[64] See Kurt Weyland, "The Political Economy of Market-Oriented Reform in Latin America, Africa, and Eastern Europe," Mimeo, Vanderbilt University, November 1996.

[65] See North (1990).

[66] Robert Putnam, *Making Democracy Work: Civic Traditions in Modern Italy* (Princeton: Princeton University Press, 1993), p. 182. For example, a recent political economy study of U.S. Indian reservations explains differences in development performance by focusing on the interaction *between* institutional structures and social capital.

[67] Stephen Cornell and Joseph Kalt, "Successful Economic Development and Heterogeneity of Governmental Form on American Indian Reservations" in Merilee Grindle, ed., *Getting Good Government: Capacity Building in the Public Sectors of Developing Countries* (Cambridge: Harvard University Press, forthcoming).

[68] Francis Fukuyama, *Trust: The Social Virtues and the Creation of Property* (New York: The Free Press, 1995).

[69] See Elinor Ostrom, *Governing the Commons: The Evolution of Institutions for Collective Action* (New York: Cambridge University Press, 1990); and Mancur Olson, *The Logic of Collective Action: Public Goods and the Theory of Groups* (Cambridge: Harvard University Press, 1965).

[71] See Christopher Clague, Philip Keefer, Stephen Knack, and Mancur Olson, "Contract-Intensive Money: Contract Enforcement, Property Rights, and Economic Performance," Center for Institutional Reform and the Informal Sector (IRIS), Working Paper no. 151, February 1995.

[72] See Robert Bates, *Beyond the Miracle of the Market: The Political Economy of Agrarian Development in Rural Kenya* (Cambridge: Cambridge University Press, 1989); Margaret Levi, *Of Rule and Revenue* (Berkeley: University of California Press, 1988); and Kenneth Shepsle, "Studying Institutions: Some Lessons from the Rational Choice Approach," *Journal of Theoretical Politics* 1:2 (April 1989), pp. 131- 49.

[73] Sven Steinmo, Kathleen Thelen, and Frank Longstreth, *Structuring Politics: Historical Institutionalism in Comparative Analysis* (Cambridge University Press, 1990).

[74] See Borner et al. (1992).

[75] Borner et al. (1992), p.40.

[76] See Alesina and Perotti (1994). Adam Przeworski, meanwhile, finds no credible correlation between type of regime and growth, although he does point to many characteristics of democracy that are good for growth. See Adam Przeworski and Fernando Limongi, "Political Regimes and Economic Growth," *Journal of Economic Perspectives* 7:3 (Summer 1993), pp. 51-69. See also various works by Robert Barro on democratic institutions and growth.

[77] Alesina and Perotti (1994).

[78] For another innovative approach to institutional structures and the efficiency of redistributions, see Roland Benabou, "Unequal Societies," *NBER Working Papers*, no. 5583, May 1996.

[79] Nancy Birdsall, David Ross, and Richard Sabot, "Inequality and Growth Reconsidered: Lessons From East Asia," *World Bank Economic Review* 9:3 (1995).

[80] See Stephan Haggard and Steven B. Webb, *Voting for Reform: Democracy, Political Liberalization, and Economic Adjustment* (New York: Oxford University Press/World Bank, 1994); and Stephan Haggard and Robert Kaufmann, *The Political Economy of Democratic Transitions* (Princeton: Princeton University Press, 1995).

[81] See Robert Bates and Anne O. Krueger, *Political and Economic Interactions in Economic Reform* (Cambridge: Basil Blackwell, 1993); Peter Evans, *Embedded Autonomy: States and Industrial Transformation* (Princeton: Princeton University Press, 1995); Haggard and Kaufmann (1995); and Geddes (1995).

[82] See, for example, Merilee Grindle, ed., *Getting Good Governance: Capacity Building in the Public Sectors of Developing Countries* (Cambridge: Harvard University Press, forthcoming).

[83] See McCubbins, Matthew, D., and Matthew F. Thies, "Congressional Oversight Overlooked: Police Patrol versus Fire Alarms," *American Journal of Political Science* 28 (1984), pp. 165-179.

[84] See Geddes (1995).

[85] See North (1990). See also World Bank, *Bureaucrats in Business: The Economics and Politics of Government Ownership* (Washington, D.C.: The World Bank, 1995).

[86] Gary Cox and Matthew McCubbins, "Structure and Policy: The Institutional Determinants of Policy Outcomes," paper prepared for the World Bank, Policy Research Department, October 1996.

[87] R. Kent Weaver and Bert A. Rockman, *Do Institutions Matter? Government Capabilities in the United States and Abroad* (Washington, D.C.: The Brookings Institution, 1993).

[88] See Naím (1995). Joan M. Nelson, ed., *A Precarious Balance: An Overview of Democracy and Economic Reforms in Eastern Europe and Latin America* (San Francisco: International Center for Economic Growth and Overseas Development Council, 1994).

[89] See Joan Nelson, Introduction to Report of the National Academy of Sciences Task Force on Economic Transformation: Institutional Change and Social Sector Reforms, September 19-20, 1996.

[90] See Carol Graham, *Safety Nets, Politics, and the Poor: Transitions to Market Economies* (Washington, D.C.: The Brookings Institution, 1994).

[91] See also "Making Social Services Work," *Economic and Social Progress in Latin America, 1996 Report* (Washington, D.C.: IDB, 1996), and Ricardo Hausmann, "Sustaining Reform: What Role for Social Policy?" in Colin Bradford, ed., *Redefining the State in Latin America* (Paris: OECD, 1994).

[92] "Making Social Services Work."

[93] See Wilson in DiIulio (1994).

References

Alesina, Alberto, and Roberto Perotti. 1994. The Political Economy of Growth Literature: A Critical Survey of the Literature. *World Bank Economic Review* 8(3).

Bates, Robert H. 1989. *Beyond the Miracle of the Market: The Political Economy of Agrarian Development in Kenya.* Cambridge: Cambridge University Press.

Bates, Robert H., and Anne O. Krueger. 1993. *Political and Economic Interactions in Economic Policy Reform: Evidence from Eight Countries.* Cambridge: Basil Blackwell.

Birdsall, Nancy, David Ross, and Richard Sabot. 1995. Inequality and Growth Reconsidered: Lessons From East Asia. *World Bank Economic Review* 9(3).

Borner, Silvio, Aymo Brunetti, and Beatrice Weder. 1992. *Institutional Obstacles to Latin American Growth.* San Francisco, CA: International Center for Economic Growth.

———. 1995. *Political Credibility and Economic Development.* New York: St. Martin's Press.

Bradford, Colin, ed. 1994. *Redefining the State in Latin America.* Paris: OECD.

Buscaglia, Edgardo, and Maria Dakolis. 1996. Judicial Reform in Latin American Courts: Experiences from Argentina and Ecuador. World Bank Technical Paper no. 350. Washington, D.C.

Campos, José Edgardo, and Hilton Root. 1996. *The Key to the Asian Miracle: Making Shared Growth Credible.* Washington, D.C.: The Brookings Institution.

Carothers, Thomas. 1997. Democracy Without Illusions. *Foreign Affairs* 76(1).

Castañeda, Tarsicio. 1992. *Combating Poverty: Innovative Social Reforms in Chile during the 1980s.* Santiago: Instituto de Estudios Públicos.

Cukierman, Alex, Steven B. Webb, and Bilin Neyapti. 1994. Measuring Central Bank Independence and Its Effect on Policy Outcomes. *World Bank Economic Review* 6(3).

de Soto, Hernando. 1986. *El Otro Sendero.* Lima: Editorial El Barranco.

Díaz-Cayeros, Alberto. 1996. Un Análisis Institucional del Papel del Estado. Paper presented to Tinker Foundation Forum on the Role of the State in Latin America and the Caribbean. Cancún, Mexico.

DiIulio, Jr., John J., ed. 1994. *Deregulating the Public Service: Can Government Be Improved?* Washington, D.C.: The Brookings Institution.

Easterly, William, Norman Loayza, and Peter Montiel. 1995. Has Latin America's Post-Reform Growth Been Disappointing? Mimeo. Washington, D.C.: The World Bank.

Edwards, Sebastian. 1996. The Disturbing Underperformance of the Latin American Economies. Paper prepared for the InterAmerican Dialogue Plenary Meeting.

Esping-Andersen, Gosta. 1990. *The Three Worlds of Welfare Capitalism.* Princeton: Princeton University Press.

Evans, Peter. 1995. *Embedded Autonomy: States and Industrial Transformation.* Princeton: Princeton University Press.

Fukuyama, Francis. 1995. *Trust: The Social Virtues and the Creation of Prosperity.* New York: The Free Press.

Geddes, Barbara. 1995. The Politics of Economic Liberalization. *Latin American Research Review* 30(2).

Graham, Carol. 1994. *Safety Nets, Politics, and the Poor: Transitions to Market Economies.* Washington, D.C.: The Brookings Institution.

————. Raising the Stakes in the Social Services, Social Security, and Privatization in Peru. In *Private Markets for Public Goods.* The Brookings Institution (work in progress).

Graham, C., and Cheikh Kane. 1998. Opportunistic Government or Sustaining Reform: Electoral Trends and Public Expenditure Patterns in Peru, 1990-1995. *Latin American Research Review* 33:1.

Grindle, Merilee S., ed. 1997. *Getting Good Government: Capacity Building in the Public Sectors of Developing Countries.* Cambridge, MA: Harvard University Press.

Haggard, Stephan, and Robert R. Kaufman. 1995. *The Political Economy of Democratic Transitions.* Princeton: Princeton University Press.

Haggard, S., and Steven B. Webb. 1996. *Voting for Reform: Democracy, Political Liberalization, and Economic Adjustment.* New York: Oxford University Press and Washington, D.C.: World Bank.

Hirschman, Albert O. 1972. *Exit Voice and Loyalty: Responses to Decline in Firms, Organizations, and States.* Cambridge, MA: Harvard University Press.

Hoff, Karla. 1996. Market Failures and the Distribution of Wealth: A Perspective from the Economics of Information. *Politics and Society* 24(4).

IDB (Inter-American Development Bank). 1996. Making Social Services Work. *Economic and Social Progress in Latin America, 1996 Report.* Washington, D.C.: IDB.

Levi, Margaret. 1989. *Of Rule and Revenue*. Berkeley: University of California Press.

Londoño, Juan Luis, and Julio Frenk. 1995. Structured Pluralism: Towards a New Model for Health System Reform in Latin America. Paper presented at Special Meeting of Ministers of Health of Latin America and the Caribbean. Washington, D.C.

Naím, Moisés. 1995. The Corruption Eruption. *Brown Journal of International Affairs*.

———. 1995. Latin America's Journey to the Market: From Macroeconomic Shocks to Institutional Therapy. *International Center for Economic Growth Discussion Papers*, no. 62.

———. 1993. *Paper Tigers and Minotaurs: The Politics of Venezuela's Economic Reforms*. Washington, D.C.: The Carnegie Endowment.

Nelson, Joan M., ed. 1994. *A Precarious Balance: An Overview of Democracy and Economic Reforms in Eastern Europe and Latin America*. San Francisco, CA: International Center for Economic Growth and Overseas Development Council.

North, Douglass. 1990. *Institutions, Institutional Change and Economic Performance*. Cambridge: Cambridge University Press.

Olson, Mancur. 1971. *The Logic of Collective Action: Public Goods and the Theory of Groups*. Cambridge: Harvard University Press.

Ostrom, Elinor. 1991. *Governing the Commons: The Evolution of Institutions for Collective Action*. New York: Cambridge University Press.

Putnam, Robert, Robert Leonardi and Raffaella Y. Nanetti. 1994. *Making Democracy Work: Civic Traditions in Modern Italy*. Princeton: Princeton University Press.

Skocpol, Theda. 1991. Universal Appeal. *The Brookings Review*.

Steinmo, Sven, Kathleen Thelen, and Frank Longstreth. 1992. *Structuring Politics: Historical Institutionalism in Comparative Analysis*. Cambridge: Cambridge University Press.

Tendler, Judith. 1997. *Good Government in the Tropics*. Baltimore, MD: Johns Hopkins University Press.

Weaver, R. Kent, and Bert A. Rockman, ed. 1992. *Do Institutions Matter?: Government Capabilities in the United States and Abroad*. Washington, D.C.: The Brookings Institution.

Williamson, Oliver, and Sidney Winter. 1993. *The Nature of the Firm: Origins, Evolution, and Development*. New York: Oxford University Press.

World Bank. 1995. *Bureaucrats in Business: The Economics and Politics of Government Ownership*. Washington, D.C.: The World Bank.

List of Authors _____

Raquel Alfaro is Director of the Water and Sanitation Division of Senior Engineering Consultants, in Santiago, Chile. From 1980 to 1996, she held various positions with the Metropolitan Water and Sanitation Company of Chile, becoming its general manager in 1990. Trained as a civil engineer, Ms. Alfaro is a leading advocate for universal access to water and sanitation, with emphasis on water conservation and protection of the environment.

Nancy Birdsall is Executive Vice President of the Inter-American Development Bank. She previously held various policy and management positions at the World Bank, most recently as director of the Policy Research Department. Between 1987 and 1991, she was chief of the World Bank's Environment Division for the Latin American region. Dr. Birdsall has been a senior adviser to the Rockefeller Foundation and a member of various study committees of the National Academy of Sciences. She has written extensively about development issues, most recently on income distribution and growth in Latin America and East Asia.

Ralph M. Bradburd is the David A. Wells Professor of Political Economy at Williams College in Massachusetts, where he teaches in the Department of Economics and the Center for Development Economics. Dr. Bradburd specializes in industrial organization and economic development, and his research often focuses on the ways in which those two fields intersect. In recent years, he has analyzed issues involving antitrust regulation in developing countries and public enterprise monopoly privatization.

John Briscoe is currently Senior Water Advisor at the World Bank, where he has been working for 11 years. He holds a B.Sc. in Civil Engineering from the University of Cape Town and a Ph.D. in environmental engineering from Harvard University. Dr. Briscoe has carried out projects throughout the developing world, with long-term work in South Africa, Bangladesh, Mozambique and Brazil.

Michael R. Carter is Professor of Agricultural and Applied Economics at the University of Wisconsin-Madison. His research focuses on the nature of agrarian growth and transformation in low-income economies, giving particular attention to how the distribution of land and other assets shapes, and is shaped by, economic growth.

Dr. Carter's recent projects include a three-country study of the impact of agro-export booms on low-income households in Latin America.

Jonathan Coles is Chair of Mavesa, a leading food manufacturer in Venezuela and the Andean Region. From 1990 to 1993, a time when the first stage of reforms in Venezuela were taking place, he was Venezuela's Minister of Agriculture and Livestock. As minister, he launched many institutional changes in food policy. He has written about his experience in government (*Reforming Agriculture in The Venezuelan Experience*, Woodrow Wilson Center Press, 1995) and teaches a seminar on Agricultural Policy at the Instituto de Estudios Superiores de Administración (IESA).

René Cortázar is the Executive Director of National Television of Chile. He has been a senior research economist for CIEPLAN (Corporación de Investigaciones Económicas para Latinoamérica), and served as Minister of Labor and Social Security in Chile from 1990 to 1994.

Michael Gavin is Lead Research Economist in the Office of the Chief Economist at the Inter-American Development Bank, where he carries out research on macroeconomic and financial issues. Prior to joining the Bank, he was associate professor of economics at Columbia University. He has also worked or consulted for the Federal Reserve Board, the World Bank, and the IMF.

Carol Graham is Senior Fellow in Foreign Policy Studies and co-director of the Center on Social and Economic Dynamics at the Brookings Institution. She is the author of numerous books and articles, including *Safety Nets, Politics, and the Poor: Transitions to Market Economies* (Brookings, 1994), and *Private Markets for Public Goods: Raising the Stakes in Economic Reform* (Brookings, 1998). Dr. Graham has advised several governments and international institutions on the design of safety net programs and on social policy reform.

Ricardo Hausmann is Chief Economist of the Inter-American Development Bank. He was formerly Venezuela's Minister of Coordination and Planning and has served as a member of the Board of Directors of the Central Bank of Venezuela. After receiving a Ph.D. in economics from Cornell University, he was a visiting fellow at Oxford and at CEPREMAP (Paris), and later became professor of economics at Instituto de Estudios Superiores de Administración (IESA) in Venezuela, where he founded the Center of Public Policy. Dr. Hausmann serves on the standing committee for the Econometric Society's Latin American chapter and on the Board of the Latin American and Caribbean Economic Association.

Enrique V. Iglesias is President of the Inter-American Development Bank, having been elected for a third five-year term in April, 1998. A native of Spain, Mr. Iglesias graduated from the University of the Republic of Uruguay in Economics and Business Administration and thereafter pursued specialized study in the United States and France. He was president of the Uruguayan Central Bank from 1966 to 1968, and later served as executive secretary of the UN Economic Commission for Latin America and the Caribbean (1972–85), and as Uruguay's foreign minister (1985–88). During his tenure, President Iglesias has successfully negotiated two substantial capital increases for the IDB, which have greatly strengthened the Bank's assistance to borrowing member countries in their programs for reform, liberalization and integration.

Estelle James is Lead Economist for the Policy Research Department at the World Bank. She received her Ph.D. in Economics from MIT, and formerly served as professor of economics, chair of the Economics Department and dean of Social and Behavioral Sciences at the State University of New York at Stony Brook. She has authored books and numerous articles on various aspects of public finance and human resources, including the economics of education, non-profit organizations, and old age security.

Juan Luis Londoño, a social policy entrepreneur, is President of *Poder & Dinero,* Colombia's leading business magazine. He previously served as Lead Economist at the Inter-American Development Bank, and as Minister of Health in Colombia. Among his recent publications is *Poverty, Inequality, and Human Capital Development in Latin America, 1950-2025* (World Bank, 1996).

Eduardo Lora is Senior Research Economist at the Inter-American Development Bank. He holds a M.Sc. in Economics from the London School of Economics and has been executive director of FEDESARROLLO, a Colombian think tank. Mr. Lora's main areas of expertise are labor economics and applied general equilibrium models.

Nora Lustig is currently Senior Advisor and Chief of the Poverty and Inequality Advisory Unit at the Inter-American Development Bank. A native of Buenos Aires, Argentina, she received her B.A. and Ph.D. in economics from the University of

California at Berkeley. From 1993 to 1997, she was a senior fellow in the Foreign Policy Studies Program at the Brookings Institution. Dr. Lustig's research has focused on the economics of Latin American development, with emphasis on topics such as the determinants of poverty and inequality, labor markets and living standards, and economic crises.

Moisés Naím is the Editor of *Foreign Policy* magazine. He was formerly Venezuela's Minister of Trade and Industry, and has served at the World Bank as a executive director and senior adviser to its president. He holds a doctorate from MIT and has been both a professor and dean of the faculty at IESA, in Caracas. Dr. Naím has written extensively about economic reforms, the political and economic aspects of international trade and investment, and the causes and effects of globalization.

Richard H. Sabot is the John J. Gibson Professor of Economics at Williams College in Massachusetts. Dr. Sabot has been a senior research fellow in the World Bank's Policy Research Department and has worked in Brazil, Colombia, Egypt, Kenya, Korea, Pakistan, Portugal, Romania, Tanzania, and Thailand. Among his recent publications is *Opportunity Foregone: Education in Brazil* (co-editor, with N. Birdsall; IDB, 1996). His primary areas of research are development economics, education and labor.

Liliana Rojas-Suárez is presently Chief Economist for Latin America at Deutsche Morgan Grenfell, New York. She was formerly Principal Advisor, Office of the Chief Economist, Inter-American Development Bank. She has written and edited many books and articles, most recently *Safe and Sound Financial Systems: What Works for Latin America* (IDB, 1997).

John B. Sheahan is the William Brough Professor of Economics, Emeritus, at Williams College in Massachusetts. He has taught at El Colegio de México, worked as an advisor in the Departamento Nacional de Planeación in Colombia, and done extensive research in Peru. Among his publications are *Patterns of Development in Latin America: Poverty, Repression, and Economic Strategy* (Princeton, 1987).

Joseph E. Stiglitz is currently Senior Vice President for Development Economics and Chief Economist at the World Bank. He previously served as chair of the U.S. Council of Economic Advisers starting in June 1995, and was a member of the council and an active member of President Clinton's economic team starting in 1993. He has been a professor of economics at Princeton, Yale, and All Souls College in Oxford, England, and is presently on leave from Stanford University, where he is the Joan Kenney Professor of Economics.

Steven R. Weisbrod is presently a private consultant on banking and financial issues in emerging markets. From 1981 through 1989, Dr. Weisbrod worked in the Corporate Planning Department of Chemical Bank, becoming head of the department in 1986. From 1976 to 1981, he was an economist in the Banking Studies Department at the Federal Reserve Bank of New York, becoming chief of the department in 1979. He earned a Ph.D. in economics from the University of Chicago.